13TH EDITION
PART TWO

College Accounting

JAMES A. HEINTZ, DBA, CPA
Professor of Accounting
Indiana University
Bloomington, Indiana

ARTHUR E. CARLSON, PhD
Professor of Accounting
School of Business Administration
Washington University, St. Louis

ROBERT W. PARRY JR., PhD
Associate Professor of Accounting
Indiana University
Bloomington, Indiana

AV80MA2
PUBLISHED BY
SOUTH-WESTERN PUBLISHING CO.
CINCINNATI, OH   WEST CHICAGO, IL   DALLAS, TX   LIVERMORE, CA

AV80MA2   ISBN: 0-538-80402-5

1 2 3 4 5 6 7 8 9 Ki 7 6 5 4 3 2 1 0 9

Printed in the United States of America

Developmental Editor: Dave Robinson
Associate Editors: Jean Privett
                   Mark Sears
Editorial Associates: Nancy Watson
                      Laurie Merz
                      Mary Mullins
Senior Staff Designer: Barb Libby
Internal Design: Designworks
Production Artist: Darren Wright
Marketing Manager: G. M. "Skip" Wenstrup
Cover quilt artwork: © Carol Keller 1988

Library of Congress Cataloging-in-Publication Data

Heintz, James A.
    College accounting.   Part 2 / James A. Heintz, Arthur E. Carlson,
Robert W. Parry, Jr. — 13th ed.
        p.   cm.
    Carlson's name appears first on the earlier edition.
    ISBN 0-538-80402-5   ISBN 0-538-80409-2 (soft)
    1. Accounting.   I. Carlson, Arthur E.   II. Parry, Robert W.,
        III. Title.
HF5635.C227   1990c
657'.044—dc20
                                                    89-21954
                                                    CIP

PREFACE

This textbook is designed for career oriented students of accounting, business administration, computer science, and office technology. An understanding of accounting is essential for anyone who desires a successful career in business, in many of the professions, and in many branches of government. This book provides a thorough and efficient introduction to fundamental accounting concepts and principles. The emphasis throughout the text is on student understanding. Toward this end, the use of professional jargon and references to official accounting pronouncements are minimized, while the content is kept totally consistent with current accounting standards.

Important Features of the Thirteenth Edition	The basic foundation that made this text continually successful for many years has been retained in the thirteenth edition. However, in response to user feedback and independent reviews by accounting educators, there have been numerous improvements to the last edition. The text material has been reorganized both as a whole and within specific chapters, and new materials have been added.

Chapter Objectives. As in the twelfth edition, each chapter begins with the chapter objectives. These objectives have been refined and are keyed to text material throughout each chapter by the use of marginal captions. This aids the learning process by keeping the student focused on the relevant objectives at each point in the chapter.

Illustrations. Accounting documents and records, diagrams, and flowcharts are used throughout the text to help students visualize important concepts. There is increased use of illustrations in the thirteenth edition, particularly when any new accounting principles or procedures are introduced.

NEW

Demonstration Problem and Solution. A complete demonstration problem and solution are provided at the end of the last module in each chapter. The problem is a comprehensive application of key concepts and principles introduced in the chapter. It is designed to give the students guidance and confidence in their ability to solve the exercises and problems based on the chapter material.

▨▨▨ **Key Terms—Expanding Your Business Vocabulary.** Each key term in a chapter appears in boldfaced color type to help students recognize its importance. An Expanding Your Business Vocabulary section is then provided at the end of each chapter, listing all key terms in the chapter and the pages on which definitions can be found. In this way, the student can see the terms used in context rather than defined in isolation.

▨▨▨ **Building Your Accounting Knowledge.** Building Your Accounting Knowledge review questions are provided at the end of each chapter module. The questions provide students with an opportunity to immediately test their recall of important chapter concepts.

NEW

▨▨▨ **Exercises and Problems.** Two complete sets of exercises and problems (Series A and B) have been prepared to facilitate instructor usage and student learning. At the end of each chapter module, an assignment box directs students to the related section of the study guide and to the appropriate exercises and problems provided at the end of the chapter.

NEW

▨▨▨ **Mastery Problem.** A comprehensive mastery problem follows the exercises and problems at the end of each chapter. This problem is usually similar to the demonstration problem in content and purpose, except that no solution is provided. This problem can be used either to test or to further strengthen the students' overall grasp of the chapter materials.

Important Changes and Additions in the Thirteenth Edition

In addition to the features noted above, numerous changes have been made in the organization and content of the thirteenth edition. These changes were made to facilitate student learning of the fundamental accounting process, to give increased emphasis to material that is important to first-year accounting students, to address new financial reporting requirements, and to improve the efficiency of the presentation. Some of the more important changes are as follows.

▨▨▨ **Reorganization.** While the entire thirteenth edition has been reorganized, the restructuring of the first ten chapters is of particular importance in two respects. First, the chapters provide a clear progression from cash to modified cash to accrual basis accounting. This approach facilitates learning of the accounting process by focusing first on the simplest setting—accounting for cash movements. Basic accounting concepts are more readily grasped because the student can identify with the cash basis setting. The modified cash basis is then presented with limited "exceptions" to the cash basis. Once again, the student can readily understand such a system. The presentation gradually builds to a complete accrual accounting system. This provides a realistic yet pedagogically sound progression from a simple to a relatively complex accounting environment.

The second important aspect of the reorganization is that the complete accounting cycle is presented before addressing the details of accounting for such items as cash and payroll. Accounting for cash is now covered in Chapter 5, after the modified cash basis system has been explained and the illustration of the accounting cycle has been completed. Payroll has been moved to Chapter 8, after the accrual accounting system has been presented. This sequencing enables the teacher and student to focus on the fundamental accounting process first and then to build on the fundamentals with related details.

NEW **Receivables.** A new chapter (11) has been added on accounting for accounts receivable. The coverage is more thorough than in the twelfth edition. Material that was addressed piecemeal in the twelfth edition is now contained in a single, more complete chapter.

NEW **Departmental Accounting.** A new module on departmental accounting has been added as part of Chapter 18, effectively replacing the consolidated operations topic covered in the twelfth edition. The consolidations materials are appropriate for a more advanced course, while departmental accounting is likely to be more useful to an introductory accounting student. The usefulness of departmental reports for management decision making is emphasized. Key issues covered include the difference between direct and indirect expenses, assignment and allocation of expenses, and measurement and interpretation of departmental operating income and direct operating margin.

Accounting for Investments and Intangible Assets. Chapter 25 has been expanded and reorganized to include coverage of short- and long-term investments in stocks and bonds. Major topics include application of the lower of cost or market method of accounting for short-term debt and equity securities and passive, long-term investments, and the use of the equity method of accounting for active, long-term investments. As noted above, accounting for a controlling interest in the securities of another firm through the preparation of consolidated financial statements has been eliminated.

NEW **Statement of Cash Flows.** A new chapter (26) on the statement of cash flows has been added. This chapter illustrates the direct method of preparing the statement of cash flows for a merchandising company. In addition, a new section has been added to Chapter 29 illustrating the indirect method of preparing the statement of cash flows for a manufacturing company. These chapters expand the coverage provided in the twelfth edition and are consistent with new reporting requirements.

Cost Accounting and Manufacturing Companies. The three-chapters (27-29) covering cost accounting for a manufacturing business have been reorganized and rewritten. Job order cost accounting and process cost accounting are covered more thoroughly than in the twelfth edition, and the distinction between the two accounting systems is clarified. Presentation of both the job order and process cost systems emphasizes the underlying documentation, the flow of charts through the system (using flowcharts, journal entries, and T accounts), and the accounting reports generated. The functioning of a job order cost accounting system in a small manufacturing company is illustrated.

Financial Statement Analysis. The financial statement analysis chapter (30) has been repositioned as the final, capstone chapter in the text. This chapter has also been rewritten to provide more thorough coverage of the interpretation, rather than just the computation, of key financial statement data. In addition, a brief introduction to the analysis and interpretation of financial statement variables is provided in both Chapter 10 and Chapter 20.

Practice Sets. The dependency of the practice sets on the text has been greatly reduced. Chapters 3-4, 9-10, 19-20, and 28-29 offer background material that can be used to introduce a practice set. However, the coverage of practice set related material in the chapters is only sufficient to demonstrate the use of accounting in a particular type of business. Additional details needed for using the practice sets are provided with the sets themselves. This greatly increases the user's flexibility in using the text and any of the following practice sets: Andrea Marree, Computer Consultant; Northern Micro, a wholesale/retail microcomputer supplier; Mitchell & Jenkins a retail/wholesale sporting goods store and WeMake Toys Inc., a toy manufacturer using a job order cost system.

NEW

Study Guide. A completely new study guide has been prepared for the thirteenth edition. For each chapter module,, the study guide begins with a brief discussion of the important learning objectives. This helps students recall the key points from the chapter. The written assignments consist of a series of questions, exercises, and problems tailored to facilitate achieving the related learning objectives. The exercises are designed to focus on specific learning objectives and the problems pull together related concepts within the chapter module. Upon completion of the study guide material, the Mastery Problem at the end of each chapter may be used to draw together concepts from the entire chapter. By completing the study guide assignments, students should master the important materials from the chapter.

NEW

Software. Two new educational software programs are available. The Electronic Problem Solver is a general ledger program designed to solve selected end-of-chapter problems. It is also designed to allow an instructor to add additional problems. The second software program is a spreadsheet application template diskette of selected end-of-chapter problems using Lotus™ 1-2-3™.[1]

NEW

▒▒▒ Working Papers. A bound set of forms for end-of-chapter exercises, problems, and mastery problems is available for the student.

▒▒▒ Check Figures. There are two sets of check figures—an abbreviated form for end-of-chapter materials and a more comprehensive set for study guide activities.

**Resources
Available to
the Instructor**

▒▒▒ Instructor's Resource Guide. This manual contains a variety of teaching resources. Each chapter contains a condensed overview of the subject matter followed by a brief chapter outline and then specific teaching suggestions relating to the content of the chapter. Also included is a lesson plan with lecture notes for each chapter. Teaching transparency masters are provided to support major chapter concepts.

▒▒▒ Solutions Manual—Text. This manual contains solutions to all end-of-chapter materials including the questions, exercises, problems, and mastery problem. The solutions have been developed to parallel the student working papers.

▒▒▒ Solutions Manual—Study Guide. This manual contains solutions to the questions, exercises, and problems in the study guide. The format parallels the student edition of the study guide with solutions inserted.

▒▒▒ Transparencies. Solution transparencies are available for all exercises, problems, and mastery problems in the text.

▒▒▒ Test Bank. This book contains true or false questions, multiple choice questions, and problems with solutions. A microcomputer version (MicroSWAT III) of this printed material is also available.

▒▒▒ Achievement Tests. Two sets (A and B) of preprinted tests are available for each chapter. In addition, two preprinted placement tests are available.

NEW

▒▒▒ HyperGraphics. HyperGraphics is an instructional delivery system employing software. The delivery system is achieved through the use of a

---

[1]Lotus™ 1-2-3™ are registered trademarks of the Lotus Development Corporation. Any references to Lotus or 1-2-3 refers to this footnote.

personal computer, a liquid crystal display, and an overhead projector. Student response pads are optional items. The resulting computer-based teaching and learning environment can enhance both classroom instruction and self study. A student study guide called Accounting Notes is used in conjunction with this system.

Acknowledgments

We thank the following reviewers of our manuscript for their valuable contributions:

Mary Dianne Bridges
South Plains College

Robert Campbell
Montcalm Community College

Ted A. Duzenski
Augusta Technical College

Michael A. Evans
MTI Business School

Richard A. Fornicola
South Hills Business School

Jo Ann Frazell
Southeast Community College

Stephen S. Hamilton
Lane Community College

Mildred A. Lanser
Santa Barbara Business College

Shirley W. Leung
Los Medanos College

Joan Ryan
Lane Community College

Albert J. Walczak
Linn-Benton Community College

We also thank all faculty whose suggestions contributed in a substantive way to the development of this textbook and Jane Parry for her verification and proofreading of the end-of-chapter and study guide materials.

James A. Heintz, DBA, CPA
Indiana University

Arthur E. Carlson, PhD
Washington University, St. Louis

Robert W. Parry, Jr., PhD
Indiana University

Contents

CHAPTER 11

Accounting for Accounts Receivable

Chapter
Objectives

Careful study of this chapter should enable you to:

- Explain why businesses extend credit and consider uncollectible accounts an acceptable part of doing business.

- Apply the direct write-off method of accounting for uncollectible accounts.

- Apply the allowance method of accounting for uncollectible accounts.

- Estimate uncollectible accounts using the percentage of sales method.

- Estimate uncollectible accounts using the percentage of receivables method.

- Explain the effects of the entries made under the allowance method on a firm's financial statements.

Explain why businesses extend credit and consider uncollectible accounts an acceptable part of doing business.

Most firms are able to increase sales by extending credit to customers or by making it easier for customers to qualify for credit. It is generally the responsibility of the credit department to decide whether a customer should receive credit approval. For business customers, this decision may be based on a review of the firm's financial statements or a credit rating from a local or national credit organization. For individual customers, information on salary, other debts, savings accounts and debt-paying history may be requested. Based on this information, the credit department generally authorizes a line of credit up to a specified amount.

Whenever a company elects to make sales on account, it is inevitable that some receivables will become uncollectible. This may be due to mistakes on the part of the credit department or due to changing economic circumstances for the customer. Whatever the cause, these losses are considered a normal consequence of extending credit. In fact, in terms of maximizing profits, a moderate amount of uncollectible accounts is a sign of a well-balanced credit policy. To avoid incurring any uncollectible accounts, the credit department would need to perform an extensive review of each application and apply strict credit standards. This type of policy would be costly to administer and would deny credit to many customers who probably would pay their bills even though they were unable to meet the very strict credit standards. Customers denied credit are likely to take their business elsewhere, sales will be lost, and profits will be reduced. On the other hand, a credit policy that is too liberal will result in excessive uncollectible accounts which also will reduce profits.

There are two methods of accounting for uncollectible accounts: (1) the direct write-off method, and (2) the allowance method. The purpose of this chapter is to explain these methods and the impact of uncollectible accounts on the financial statements.

Direct Write-Off Method

Apply the direct write-off method of accounting for uncollectible accounts.

Under the **direct write-off method** the expense associated with an uncollectible account is recognized when it has been determined that a customer will not pay the amount owed. For example, if it has been decided that the account receivable of John Lafollette for $500 has become uncollectible, the following entry would be made:

Uncollectible Accounts Expense	500	
Accounts Receivable (J. Lafollette)		500
To write off account found to be uncollectible.		

The direct write-off method has one advantage. It is very simple to apply. However, there are three disadvantages of using this method. First, since efforts to collect the account often extend over many months, the revenue associated with the sale might be recognized in one period and the expense resulting from the uncollectible account recognized in another. This is a violation of the **matching concept** which states that expenses incurred to produce particular revenues should be matched with those revenues. In this case, the expense of extending credit to make a sale should be recognized in the same period as the revenue from the sale.

Second, the amount of uncollectible accounts expense recognized in a given period is subject to manipulation by management. This manipulation occurs because there is no general rule for deciding when an account becomes uncollectible. Thus management can use its subjective judgment in deciding when to recognize uncollectible accounts expense.

Third, the amount of accounts receivable reported on the balance sheet does not represent the amount of cash actually expected to be collected. Thus the assets are overstated by the amount of uncollectible accounts reported in accounts receivable. For these reasons, the direct write-off method is not acceptable for financial reporting purposes unless the uncollectible accounts are expected to be so small that they would have no effect on the reported financial condition of the firm. This method is permitted, however, for income tax purposes.

Recovery of Accounts Previously Written Off

Occasionally an account that was written off will be collected. The proper entries for the recovery depend on the period in which the cash is collected. When the write-off and recovery are made in the same accounting period, the entry for the write-off should be reversed and the collection entered in the usual manner as illustrated below.

19-B		
Aug. 15 Uncollectible Accounts Expense...............	500	
Accounts Receivable (J. Lafollette)...........		500
To write off account found to be		
uncollectible.		
Dec. 20 Accounts Receivable (J. Lafollette)	500	
Uncollectible Accounts Expense............		500
To reinstate account.		
20 Cash......................................	500	
Accounts Receivable (J. Lafollette)..........		500
Collection on account.		

If Lafollette pays his account in the following accounting period, his account is reinstated by debiting Accounts Receivable and crediting Uncollectible Accounts Recovered. This account is credited instead of Uncollectible Accounts Expense because a credit to the expense account would understate uncollectible accounts expense for the current year. Uncollectible Accounts Recovered is reported on the income statement as other revenue. These entries are illustrated below.

19-B		
Aug. 15 Uncollectible Accounts Expense...............	500	
Accounts Receivable (J. Lafollette)..........		500
To write off account found to be		
uncollectible.		

```
19-C
Jan. 20  Accounts Receivable (J. Lafollette) . . . . . . . . . . .      500
             Uncollectible Accounts Recovered . . . . . . . . . .              500
           To reinstate account.


        20 Cash . . . . . . . . . . . . . . . . . . . . . . . . . . . . . . . . . . . . . .      500
             Accounts Receivable (J. Lafollette) . . . . . . . . . . .              500
           Collection on account.
```

Allowance Method

Apply the allowance method of accounting for uncollectible accounts.

When it is possible to make a reasonable estimate· of the amount of uncollectibles, the allowance method is required for financial reporting purposes. Under the allowance method, the following procedures are used:

1. At the end of each accounting period, an estimate is made of the amount of uncollectible accounts.
2. An adjusting entry is made to recognize the uncollectible accounts expense and reduce reported receivables for the amount of estimated uncollectible accounts. This is accomplished by making the following adjusting entry:

```
Dec. 31 Uncollectible Accounts Expense . . . . . . . . . . . . . .      xxx
             Allowance for Doubtful Accounts . . . . . . . . . . .              xxx
```

Note that it is not possible to credit Accounts Receivable because it is not known at this point in time which of the specific customers will fail to pay. Instead, a contra asset account, Allowance for Doubtful Accounts (also referred to as Allowance for Uncollectible Accounts or Allowance for Bad Debts) is credited. As explained in Chapter 9 and shown below, the balance of this account is deducted from Accounts Receivable on the balance sheet. The remaining amount often is referred to as the net receivables because it represents the amount the firm actually expects to collect.

Current assets:

```
Accounts receivable . . . . . . . . . . . . . . . . . . . . . . . . . . . . . . . . . . . . . . . . . . .     xxx
Less allowance for doubtful accounts . . . . . . . . . . . . . . . . . . . . . . . . . . . . . .     xx  xxx
```

3. In a subsequent period, when a specific uncollectible account is identified, the following entry is made to write off the account and reduce the balance in Allowance for Doubtful Accounts:

Jan. 16 Allowance for Doubtful Accounts   xxx
        Accounts Receivable   xxx

Estimating Uncollectibles

Two basic methods are used for estimating the amount of uncollectibles at the end of the accounting period: the percentage of sales method and the percentage of receivables method. The percentage of sales method introduced in Chapter 9 will be reviewed here, and the percentage of receivables method will be explained.

Estimate uncollectible accounts using the percentage of sales method.

Percentage of Sales Method. Based on past experience within the firm and industry, management identifies a percentage relationship between the amount of credit sales and the expected amount of uncollectible accounts. This percentage is then applied to the sales on account for the period to determine the amount of uncollectible accounts expense to be recognized. For example, if past experience indicated that 2% of credit sales are generally uncollectible and credit sales for the period are $300,000, then uncollectible accounts expense would be $6,000 ($300,000 × .02). The following adjusting entry would be made:

Dec. 31 Uncollectible Accounts Expense   6,000
        Allowance for Doubtful Accounts   6,000
        Estimated uncollectible accounts expense for
        the period.

The percentage of sales method often is referred to as an income statement approach to estimating uncollectible accounts. This method emphasizes proper estimating and reporting of uncollectible accounts expense on the income statement and the matching of expenses with revenues. Note that the Allowance for Doubtful Accounts (a balance sheet account) may have a debit or credit balance prior to adjustment. This is the result of underestimating or overestimating uncollectible accounts at the end of the prior period. This balance is not considered when estimating the expense for the period. In the above illustration, for example, the balance in Allowance for Doubtful Accounts could have been a credit of $500 or a debit of $300, but the same adjustment for $6,000 would have been made.

This does not mean that the balance in Allowance for Doubtful Accounts is totally ignored. If estimates of uncollectible accounts are reasonably accurate, the balance of the Allowance for Doubtful Accounts should be near zero just prior to making adjusting entries at year end. If actual write-offs are significantly higher or lower than estimated uncollectible accounts over a number of periods, a large debit or credit balance will accumulate in this account. In this situation, the percentage of credit sales used to estimate uncollectible accounts should be modified in future periods.

Percentage of Receivables Method. Under the percentage of receivables method, the accounts receivable are analyzed to estimate the amount that will not be collected. This is generally done by classifying each customer's account by the length of time the account has been outstanding. It is assumed that the probability that an account will not be collected increases with the length of time the account has been outstanding. Because of the emphasis on the length of time the accounts have been outstanding, this process is often referred to as aging the receivables.

An aging schedule similar to the one illustrated on page 467 is often used to analyze the receivables and estimate the uncollectible amount. First, the specific accounts receivable are categorized according to the length of time the amounts have been outstanding. Then the amount of receivables in each category is multiplied by an estimate of the percent that will be uncollectible. This percentage is based on past experience and increases as the number of days past due increases. Finally, the estimates for each category are totaled to determine the amount of receivables that are not expected to be collected. This amount should be reported in the Allowance for Doubtful Accounts on the balance sheet. Based on the aging schedule on page 467, the balance should be $5,500.

Under this method, the adjusting entry at the end of the period for uncollectible accounts expense is affected by the current balance in the Allowance for Doubtful Accounts. If the Allowance for Doubtful Accounts has a credit balance of $300, as shown below, the following adjusting entry would be made:

Estimate uncollectible accounts using the percentage of receivables method.

Uncollectible Accounts Expense	5,200	
Allowance for Doubtful Accounts		5,200

Uncollectible Accounts Expense		Allowance for Doubtful Accounts	
19--		19--	
Dec. 31 Bal. 5,200		Dec. 31 Bal. 300	
		Dec. 31 Adj. 5,200	
		Dec. 31 Bal. 5,500	

AGING SCHEDULE OF ACCOUNTS RECEIVABLE

Customer	Total	Not Yet Due	Number of Days Past Due					
			1-30	31-60	61-90	91-180	181-365	Over 365
W. Billiard	$ 3,000	$ 2,500	$ 500					
K. Campbell	950				$ 650		$ 300	
J. Farley	4,325	3,800				$ 525		
L. Gilbert	1,900	1,500			400			
E. Rome	3,950	3,200					$750	
B. Zimmerman	200						200	
Total	$101,060	$65,400	$18,200	$8,250	$6,310	$1,800	$750	$350
Estimated percent uncollectible		2%	5%	10%	20%	30%	50%	80%
Total estimated uncollectible accounts	$ 5,500	$ 1,308	$ 910	$ 825	$1,262	$ 540	$375	$280

After the adjusting entry is posted, the balance in Uncollectible Accounts Expense is $5,200 and the balance in Allowance for Doubtful Accounts is $5,500. The uncollectible accounts expense of $5,200 is reported on the income statement. Net receivables of $95,560 are reported on the balance sheet, as shown below.

Current assets:

Accounts receivable	$101,060	
Less allowance for doubtful accounts	5,500	$95,560

Occasionally the Allowance for Doubtful Accounts will have a debit balance. If this account had a debit balance of $400, as shown below, the following adjusting entry would be made:

Uncollectible Accounts Expense	5,900	
Allowance for Doubtful Accounts		5,900

Uncollectible Accounts Expense		Allowance for Doubtful Accounts	
19-- Dec. 31 Bal. 5,900		19-- Dec. 31 Bal. 400	19-- Dec. 31 Adj. 5,900 Dec. 31 Bal. 5,500

After the adjusting entry is posted, the balance in Uncollectible Accounts Expense is $5,900 and the balance in Allowance for Doubtful Accounts is $5,500. The uncollectible accounts expense of $5,900 is reported on the income statement. Net receivables of $95,560 are reported on the balance sheet, as shown below.

Current assets:

Accounts receivable......................................	$101,060	
Less allowance for doubtful accounts......................	5,500	$95,560

The percentage of receivables method <u>often is referred to as a balance sheet approach to estimating uncollectible accounts</u>. This is because the emphasis is on proper reporting of the net receivables on the balance sheet. To do this, the amount of the adjusting entry is determined by the difference between the current balance of the Allowance for Doubtful Accounts and the balance required based on the aging schedule.

Write-Off of Uncollectible Accounts

Explain the effects of the entries made under the allowance method on a firm's financial statements.

The entry to write off an uncollectible account is the same under either the percentage of sales or the percentage of receivables method. Allowance for Doubtful Accounts is debited and Accounts Receivable is credited for the amount of the uncollectible account. Although it would seem that writing off an account receivable would have a negative impact on the firm's reported financial condition, the fact is that this entry has essentially no effect on any of the major elements of the financial statements. Remember, the primary purpose of the allowance method is to recognize the uncollectible accounts expense and the related reduction in net receivables in the same period in which the sales were made. This is accomplished at the end of each period by making the adjusting entry:

Uncollectible Accounts Expense	xxx	
Allowance for Doubtful Accounts...................		xxx

Note that this entry effectively reduces net income and net receivables.

Once an uncollectible account is identified, there should be no substantive effect on the financial statements because the firm has anticipated the fact that there will be uncollectible accounts and has already reported the probable effects by making the above adjusting entry. To illustrate, assume that on December 31, 19-A, the balance sheet reported the following information concerning Accounts Receivable:

Current assets:

Accounts receivable......................................	$101,060	
Less allowance for doubtful accounts......................	5,500	$95,560

On January 15, 19-B, it is decided to write off Bill McDonald's account for $500 by making the following entry:

Allowance for Doubtful Accounts	500	
Accounts Receivable (B. McDonald)		500

If the balance sheet was prepared immediately after posting the above transaction, the following information would be reported for Accounts Receivable:

Current assets:

Accounts receivable......................................	$100,560	
Less allowance for doubtful accounts.....................	5,000	$95,560

Note that both Accounts Receivable and the Allowance for Doubtful Accounts have been reduced by $500. Thus there is no change in the reported net receivables. The firm expected to collect $95,560 before writing off McDonald's account and still expects to collect $95,560 after writing off his account. Management knew that there would be uncollectible accounts. Now they know that McDonald is one of them.

Recovery of Accounts Previously Written Off

Occasionally an account that was written off will be collected. When this happens, two entries are required. First, the account must be reinstated. Second, the receipt of the remittance must be entered. Reinstating an account simply requires reversing the entry made to write off the account. If a check for $500 was received on February 1 from Bill McDonald, whose account was written off on January 15, the following entries would be made:

Feb. 1 Accounts Receivable (B. McDonald).............	500	
Allowance for Doubtful Accounts.............		500

1 Cash	500	
Accounts Receivable (B. McDonald)..........		500

It might be simpler to debit Cash and credit Allowance for Doubtful Accounts. However, this shortcut should not be taken. By reinstating McDonald's account, the accounts receivable subsidiary ledger will reflect the fact that McDonald has paid his account. Without the reinstatement the subsidiary ledger will only report that McDonald's account was written off as uncollectible. This information will be important to McDonald and the firm should he desire credit in the future.

BUILDING YOUR ACCOUNTING KNOWLEDGE

1. Why do businesses extend credit and consider uncollectible accounts an acceptable part of doing business?
2. What factors should be considered when extending credit to a customer?
3. What problems are created by a very strict credit policy that attempts to avoid incurring any uncollectible accounts?
4. Describe the accounting procedures when using the direct write-off method to account for uncollectible accounts.
5. What three basic disadvantages are associated with applying the direct write-off method?
6. Under what condition is the direct write-off method acceptable for financial reporting purposes?
7. Under the direct write-off method, what impact does the write off of a customer's account have on the financial statements?
8. Under the direct write-off method, what impact does the recovery of an uncollectible account have on the financial statements?
9. Under what conditions should the allowance method be used for financial reporting purposes?
10. Describe the accounting procedures when using the allowance method to account for uncollectible accounts.
11. Explain how to compute net receivables.
12. Describe the process followed when estimating uncollectible accounts under the percentage of sales method.
13. Describe the process followed when estimating uncollectible accounts under the percentage of receivables method.
14. What impact does the adjusting entry for uncollectible accounts have on the financial statements?
15. Under the allowance method, what impact does the write off of a customer's account have on the financial statements?
16. Under the allowance method, what impact does the recovery of uncollectible accounts have on the financial statements?

Assignment Box

To reinforce your understanding of the preceding text material, you may complete the following:

Study Guide
Textbook: Exercises 11A1 through 11A4 or 11B1 through 11B4
Problems 11A1 through 11A3 or 11B1 through 11B3

EXPANDING YOUR BUSINESS VOCABULARY

What is the meaning of the following terms:

Demonstration Problem

Budke and Budke, a landscaping service, uses the allowance method to record the following transactions related to accounts receivable. Adjusting and closing entries also completed during the most recent year ended December 31, 19-- are described below.

Mar. 6 Received 50% of the $12,000 balance owed by Columbia Gardens, a bankrupt business, and wrote off the remainder as uncollectible.

June 12 Reinstated the account of Ronald Stillman, which had been written off in the previous year as uncollectible. Entered the receipt of $2,250 cash in full settlement of Stillman's account.

Sept. 19 Wrote off the $13,800 balance owed by Kelly Richeson, who has no assets.

Nov. 9 Reinstated the account of Jackie Kwas, which had been written off in the preceding year as uncollectible. Entered the receipt of $2,175 cash in full settlement of Kwas's account.

Dec. 27 Wrote off the following accounts as uncollectible, in compound entry form:

Blair and Smith............	$10,480
Landscapes Unlimited......	8,570
Beekman Brothers..........	22,500
B.J. McKay...............	9,300

Dec. 31 Based on an aging analysis of $1,460,000 of accounts receivable, it was estimated that $73,500 will be uncollectible. Made the adjusting entry.

31 Made the entry to close the appropriate account to Expense and Revenue Summary.

Required:

1. Open the following selected accounts, entering the credit balance indicated as of January 1 of the most recent year:

131.1	Allowance for Doubtful Accounts......	$95,000
331	Expense and Revenue Summary.......	—
554	Uncollectible Accounts Expense	—

2. Enter the transactions and the adjusting and closing entries described above in general journal form. After each entry, post to the three accounts named, and determine the new balances.

3. Determine the net receivables as of December 31.

Solution

1. and 2.

Account Allowance for Doubtful Accounts — Account No. 131.1

Date		Item	Post Ref.	Debit	Credit	Balance Debit	Balance Credit
19--							
Jan.	1	Balance	✓				95,000.00
Mar.	6		12	6,000.00			89,000.00
Jun.	12		13		2,250.00		91,250.00
Sept.	19		13	13,800.00			77,450.00
Nov.	9		13		2,175.00		79,625.00
Dec.	27		13	50,850.00			28,775.00
	31		13		44,725.00		73,500.00

Account Expense and Revenue Summary — Account No. 331

Date	Item	Post Ref.	Debit	Credit	Balance Debit	Balance Credit
19--						
Dec. 31		13	44,725.00		44,725.00	

Account Uncollectible Accounts Expense — Account No. 554

Date	Item	Post Ref.	Debit	Credit	Balance Debit	Balance Credit
19--						
Dec. 31		13	44,725.00		44,725.00	
31		13		44,725.00	-0-	

2.

	Journal			Page 12	
Date	Description	Post Ref.	Debit	Credit	
19--					
Mar. 6	Cash		6,000.00		
	Accounts Receivable (Columbia Gardens)			6,000.00	
6	Allowance for Doubtful Accounts	131.1	6,000.00		
	Accounts Receivable (Columbia Gardens)			6,000.00	

	Journal			Page 13	
Date	Description	Post Ref.	Debit	Credit	
19--					
June 12	Accounts Receivable (R. Stillman)		2,250.00		
	Allowance for Doubtful Accounts	131.1		2,250.00	
12	Cash		2,250.00		
	Accounts Receivable (R. Stillman)			2,250.00	
Sept. 19	Allowance for Doubtful Accounts	131.1	13,800.00		
	Accounts Receivable (K. Richeson)			13,800.00	
Nov. 9	Accounts Receivable (J. Kwas)		2,175.00		
	Allowance for Doubtful Accounts	131.1		2,175.00	
9	Cash		2,175.00		
	Accounts Receivable (J. Kwas)			2,175.00	

Dec.	27	Allowance for Doubtful Accounts	131.1	50,850.00	
		Accounts Receivable (Blair & Smith)			10,480.00
		Accounts Receivable (Landscapes Unlimited)			8,570.00
		Accounts Receivable (Beekman Bros.)			22,500.00
		Accounts Receivable (B.J. McKay)			9,300.00
	31	Uncollectible Accounts Expense	554	44,725.00	
		Allowance for Doubtful Accounts	131.1		44,725.00
	31	Expense & Revenue Summary	331	44,725.00	
		Uncollectible Accounts Expense	554		44,725.00

3. Accounts receivable (12/31/--) $1,460,000
Less allow. for doubtful accts............................... 73,500
Net receivables $1,386,500

*NOTE: Now that you have reviewed the Demonstration Problem and Solution you may complete the **Mastery Problem** at the end of the chapter activities.

Applying Accounting Concepts

Series A

Exercise 11A1—Entries for Uncollectible Accounts Receivable Using the Direct Write-Off Method. In general journal form, record the following transactions in the accounts of Hansen and Robson, who use the direct write-off method of accounting for uncollectible accounts receivable:

Feb. 5 Sold merchandise on account to J.A. Zionts, $2,000.

June 12 Received $1,200 from J.A. Zionts and wrote off the remainder owed on the sale of February 5 as uncollectible.

Nov. 30 Reinstated the account of J.A. Zionts that had been written off on June 12 and received $800 cash in full settlement.

Exercise 11A2—Entries for Uncollectible Accounts Receivable Using the Allowance Method. In general journal form, enter the following transactions in the accounts of Baker and Wilson who use the allowance method of accounting for uncollectible accounts receivable:

May 10 Sold merchandise on account to J.T. Gannon, $5,000.

Sept. 30 Received $2,500 from J.T. Gannon and wrote off the remainder owed on the sale of May 10 as uncollectible.

Dec. 15 Reinstated the account of J.T. Gannon that had been written off on Sept. 30 and received $2,500 cash in full settlement.

Exercise 11A3—Provision for Doubtful Accounts, Percentage of Sales and Percentage of Receivables. At the end of the current year, the accounts receivable account of Wonder Color Printers has a debit balance of $190,000, and credit sales for the year total $1,800,000. Give the end-of-period adjusting entry in general journal form to enter the estimate for uncollectible accounts expense under each of the following independent assumptions.

(a) The Allowance for Doubtful Accounts has a credit balance of $1,000.
   (1) The percentage of sales method is used and uncollectible accounts expense is estimated to be 1% of credit sales.
   (2) The percentage of receivables method is used and an analysis of the accounts produces an estimate of $19,900 in uncollectible accounts.
(b) The Allowance for Doubtful Accounts has a debit balance of $500.
   (1) The percentage of sales method is used and uncollectible accounts expense is estimated to be 3/4 of 1% of credit sales.
   (2) The percentage of receivables method is used and an analysis of the accounts produces an estimate of $11,800 in uncollectible accounts.

Exercise 11A4—Provision for Doubtful Accounts Based on Percentage of Receivables. Leonard's TV Sales and Service estimates the amount of uncollectible accounts using the percentage of receivables method. After aging the accounts, it is estimated that $5,000 will not be collected. Give the end-of-period adjusting entry in general journal form to enter the estimate for uncollectible accounts assuming the following independent conditions exist prior to the adjustment:

(a) The Allowance for Doubtful Accounts has a credit balance of $400.
(b) The Allowance for Doubtful Accounts has a debit balance of $200.
(c) The Allowance for Doubtful Accounts has no balance.

Series B

Exercise 11B1—Entries for Uncollectible Accounts Receivable Using the Direct Write-Off Method. In general journal form, record the following transactions in the accounts of Norton and Suiter, who use the direct write-off method of accounting for uncollectible accounts receivable.

Mar. 5 Sold merchandise on account to K.D. Silas, $1,500.
Jul. 14 Received $900 from K.D. Silas and wrote off the remainder owed on the sale of March 5 as uncollectible.
Dec. 30 Reinstated the account of K.D. Silas that had been written off on July 14 and received $600 cash in full settlement.

Exercise 11B2—Entries for Uncollectible Accounts Receivable Using the Allowance Method. In general journal form, record the following transactions in the accounts of Kunes and Kwas, who use the allowance method of accounting for uncollectible accounts receivable:

June 10 Sold merchandise on account to D.H. Javer, $3,750.
Oct. 31 Received $1,875 from D.H. Javer and wrote off the remainder owed on the sale of June 10 as uncollectible.
Dec. 20 Reinstated the account of D.H. Javer that had been written off on Oct. 31 and received $1,875 cash in full settlement.

Exercise 11B3—Provision for Doubtful Accounts; Percentage of Sales and Percentage of Receivables. At the end of the current year, the accounts receivable account of Bi-Rite Products has a debit balance of $142,500, and credit sales for the year total $1,350,000. Give the end-of-period adjusting entry in general journal form to enter the estimate for uncollectible accounts expense under each of the following independent assumptions:

(a) The Allowance for Doubtful Accounts has a credit balance of $750.
   (1) The percentage of sales method is used and uncollectible accounts expense is estimated to be 1½% of credit sales.
   (2) The percentage of receivables method is used and an analysis of the accounts produces an estimate of $19,925 in uncollectible accounts.
(b) The Allowance for Doubtful Accounts has a debit balance of $375.
   (1) The percentage of sales method is used and uncollectible accounts expense is estimated to be 1.25% of credit sales.
   (2) The percentage of receivables method is used and an analysis of the accounts produces an estimate of $15,850 in uncollectible accounts.

Exercise 11B4—Provison for Doubtful Accounts Based on Percentage of Receivables. Perkins Pontiac Sales and Service estimates the amount of uncollectible accounts using the percentage of receivables method. After aging the accounts, it is estimated that $3,750 will not be collected. Give the end-of-period adjusting entry in general journal form to enter the estimate for uncollectible accounts assuming the following independent conditions exist prior to the adjustment:

(a) The Allowance for Doubtful Accounts has a credit balance of $300.
(b) The Allowance for Doubtful Accounts has a debit balance of $150.
(c) The Allowance for Doubtful Accounts has no balance.

Series A

Problem 11A1   Entries Related to Uncollectible Accounts

Hartke Nurseries uses the allowance method to record the following current transactions, adjusting entries, and closing entries during the year ended December 31, 19--.

Feb. 9 Received 60% of the $10,000 balance owed by Fragrant Flowers, a bankrupt business, and wrote off the remainder as uncollectible.

May 28 Reinstated the account of David Connally, which had been written off in the preceding year as uncollectible. Entered the receipt of $1,980 cash in full settlement of Connally's account.

Aug. 17 Wrote off the $10,600 balance owed by Kim Sertl, as uncollectible.

Oct. 5 Reinstated the account of Kathi Long, which had been written off in the preceding year as uncollectible. Entered the receipt of $5,900 cash in full settlement of Kathi Long's account.

Dec. 28 Wrote off the following accounts as uncollectible (make a compound entry): Traynor and Tuckman, $9,840; Creative Landscapers, $7,950; Greenway & Sons, $19,400; K.E. Cade, $8,400.

31 Based on an aging analysis of the $1,220,000 of accounts receivable, it was estimated that $62,500 will be uncollectible. Made the adjusting entry.

31 Made the entry to close the appropriate account to Expense and Revenue Summary.

Required:

   1. Open the following selected accounts, entering the credit balance indicated as of January 1, 19--.

131.1   Allowance for Doubtful Accounts $59,000
331   Expense and Revenue Summary ....   —
554   Uncollectible Accounts Expense ....   —

2. In general journal form, enter the current transactions and the adjusting and closing entries described above. After each entry, post to the three named accounts and determine the new balances.
3. Determine net receivables as of December 31.

Problem 11A2   Provision for Doubtful Accounts; Percentage of Sales and Percentage of Receivables

At the completion of the current fiscal year, the balance of the accounts receivable account for Naylor's Novelties was $56,000. Credit sales for the year were $620,400.

Required:

Make the necessary adjusting entry in general journal form under each of the following assumptions. Show calculations for the amount of each adjustment and the resulting net receivables.

(1) The Allowance for Doubtful Accounts has a credit balance of $600.
  (a) The percentage of sales method is used and uncollectible accounts expense is estimated to be 1.5% of credit sales.
  (b). The percentage of receivables method is used and an analysis of the accounts produces an estimate of $6,800 in uncollectible accounts.
(2) The Allowance for Doubtful Accounts has a debit balance of $900.
  (a) The percentage of sales method is used and uncollectible accounts expense is estimated to be 1% of credit sales.
  (b) The percentage of receivables method is used and an analysis of the accounts produces an estimate of $7,800 in uncollectible accounts.

Problem 11A3   Aging Accounts Receivable (Percentage of Receivables)

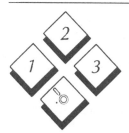

An analysis of the accounts receivable of Cane Company as of December 31, 19--, reveals the following:

Age Interval	Balance	Estimated Percent Uncollectible
Not due	$150,000	2%
1-30 days past due	8,000	5
31-60 days past due	6,200	10
61-90 days past due	3,800	25
91-180 days past due	2,400	35
181-365 days past due	1,600	55
Over 365 days past due	600	85
Total	$172,600	

Required:

1. Prepare an aging schedule as of December 31, 19--, using the following columns:

Age Interval	Balance	Estimated Percent Uncollectible	Estimated Amount Uncollectible

2. Assuming that the allowance account had a credit balance of $1,020 before adjustment, give the end-of-period adjusting entry in general journal form to enter the estimate for the uncollectible accounts expense.

Series B

Problem 11B1   Entries Related to Uncollectible Accounts

Linen Warehouse uses the allowance method to record the following current transactions, adjusting entries, and closing entries during the year ended December 31, 19--.

Jan.   8   Received 70% of the $7,500 balance owed by Apex Asbestos, a bankrupt business, and wrote off the remainder as uncollectible.

Apr. 27   Reinstated the account of Aaron Hauser, which had been written off in the preceding year as uncollectible. Entered the receipt of $1,485 cash in full settlement of Hauser's account.

July 16   Wrote off the $7,950 balance owed by Danielle Goodman as uncollectible.

Sept. 3   Reinstated the account of Jannette Wilber, which had been written off in the preceding year as uncollectible. Entered the receipt of $4,425 cash in full settlement of Jannette Wilber's account.

Dec. 27   Wrote off the following accounts as uncollectible (make a compound entry): Mora and Ney, $7,380; Mayer Homes, $5,960; Slyman & Sons, $14,550; P.C. Ferguson, $6,300.

31   Based on an aging analysis of the $915,000 of accounts receivable, it was estimated that $46,875 will be uncollectible. Made the adjusting entry.

31   Made the entry to close the appropriate account to Expense and Revenue Summary.

Required:

1. Open the following selected T-accounts, entering the credit balance indicated as of January 1, 19--.

131.1	Allowance for Doubtful Accounts	$44,250
331	Expense & Revenue Summary	—
554	Uncollectible Accounts Expense	—

2. In general journal form enter the current transactions and the adjusting and closing entries described above. After each entry, post to the three named accounts and determine the new balances.

3. Determine net receivables as of December 31.

Problem 11B2   Provision for Doubtful Accounts; Percentage of Sales and Percentage of Receivables

At the completion of the current fiscal year, the balance of the accounts receivable account for Crawford's Greeting Cards was $112,000. Credit sales for the year were $1,240,800.

Required:

Make the necessary adjusting entry in general journal form under each of the following assumptions. Show calculations for the amount of each adjustment and the resulting net receivables.

(1) The Allowance for Doubtful Accounts has a credit balance of $1,200.
    (a) The percentage of sales method is used and uncollectible accounts expense is estimated to be 1.5% of credit sales.
    (b) The percentage of receivables method is used and an analysis of the accounts produces an estimate of $13,600 in uncollectible accounts.

(2) The Allowance for Doubtful Accounts has a debit balance of $1,800.
    (a) The percentage of sales method is used and uncollectible accounts expense is estimated to be 1% of credit sales.
    (b) The percentage of receivables method is used and an analysis of the accounts produces an estimate of $15,600 in uncollectible accounts.

Problem 11B3   Aging Accounts Receivable (Percentage of Receivables)

An analysis of the accounts receivable of Foster Company as of December 31, 19--, reveals the following:

Age Interval	Balance	Estimated Percent Uncollectible
Not due	$112,500	1.5%
1-30 days past due	6,000	4
31-60 days past due	4,650	8
61-90 days past due	2,850	20
91-180 days past due	1,800	30
181-365 days past due	1,200	45
Over 365 days past due	450	75
Total	$129,450	

Required:

1. Prepare an aging schedule as of December 31, 19--, using the following columns:

Age Interval	Balance	Estimated Percent Uncollectible	Estimated Amount Uncollectible

2. Assuming that the allowance account had a credit balance of $765 before adjustment, give the end-of-period adjusting entry in general journal form to enter the estimate for the uncollectible accounts expense.

Mastery Problem

Sam and Robert are identical twins. They opened identical businesses and experienced identical transactions. However, they decided to estimate uncollectible accounts in different ways. Sam elected to use the percentage of sales method, and Robert elected to use the percentage of receivables method. Listed below are the summary transactions and other relevant information for both businesses for 19-B. Remember, both businesses experienced the same events: credit sales, collections of receivables and write-offs. The only difference between the businesses is the method of estimating uncollectible accounts.

		Sam	Robert
(a)	Balance of Accounts Receivable (1/1/19-B)	$ 50,000	$50,000
(b)	Balance of Allowance for Doubtful Accounts (1/1/19-B)	5,000	5,000
(c)	Sales on account during 19-B	550,000	550,000
(d)	Collections on account during 19-B	530,000	530,000
(e)	Uncollectible accounts written off during 19-B	4,500	4,500
(f)	Collections made on accounts written off during 19-B	500	500

Required:
1. Enter the above information in the general ledger accounts for Sam. Be sure to debit *and* credit appropriate accounts for items (c) through (f).
2. Sam estimates that 1% of all sales on account will be uncollectible. Compute the estimated uncollectible accounts expense and enter the appropriate adjusting entry in the ledger accounts on December 31, 19-B.
3. Compute net receivables for Sam on December 31, 19-B.
4. Enter the above information in the general ledger accounts for Robert. Be sure to debit *and* credit appropriate accounts for items (c) through (f).
5. Robert prefers to base the estimate of uncollectible accounts on an aging schedule of accounts receivable. Using the information provided below, compute the estimated uncollectible amounts and enter the appropriate adjusting entry in the ledger accounts.

Customers	Unpaid Invoices: Invoice Dates and Amounts		
Beets, D.	10/7, $2,300	11/15, $1,200	12/18, $8,500
Cook, L.	6/1, $1,200	8/15, $2,500	
Hylton, D.	9/23, $4,300	10/22, $2,500	12/23, $2,800
Martin, D.	10/15, $5,400	11/12, $3,200	12/15, $1,500
Stokes, D.	9/9, $ 200	12/15, $9,500	
Taylor, T.	11/20, $ 400	12/10, $1,400	
Thomas, O.	12/2, $5,500		
Tower, R.	12/15, $2,300		
Williams, G.	11/18, $2,800	12/8, $8,000	

All sales are billed n/30. The aging chart below is used to estimate the uncollectibles using the percentage of receivables method.

Days Past Due	Percent Uncollectible
Not yet due	2%
1-30 days	5%
31-60 days	10%
61-90 days	25%
91-120 days	50%
over 120 days	80%

6. Compute net receivables for Robert on 12/31/19-B.

Accounting for Notes and Interest

A major characteristic of modern business is the extensive use of credit. Each day hundreds of millions of transactions involve the sale of goods or services in return for promises to pay at a later date. Sales of this type are said to be "on account," and are often described as charge sales. As mentioned in Chapter 7, credit cards are often used to facilitate such transactions. When a credit card account is opened, a form or document is signed by the customer. This form obligates the customer to pay for all purchases within a specific number of days after a bill for the purchases is received from the business. When a purchase is made "on account," the buyer needs only to sign a sales slip or sales ticket that acknowledges the receipt of the merchandise or service.

Credit card sales represent only a portion of all credit transactions for businesses. Because of this a more formal type of credit transaction is discussed in this chapter. Specifically, the use of and accounting for promissory notes are explained.

The Promissory Note

Describe and explain the nature and use of promissory notes.

A **promissory note** (usually referred to as a note) is a written promise to repay a borrowed sum of money. Notes are often used for the extension of credit for periods of more than 60 days, or for transactions involving large amounts of money. Such notes are considered **negotiable commercial paper** if they are:

1. In writing and signed by the person or persons agreeing to make payment.
2. An unconditional promise to pay a certain amount of money.
3. Payable either on demand or at a definite future time.
4. Payable to the order of a specified person or firm, or to the bearer.

The following is a promissory note which has all the characteristics of a negotiable commercial paper. Paul DeBruke is known as the **maker of the note** because he promises to pay a certain amount of money ($1,542.50) at a definite future time (90 days after June 9). Sarah Morney is called the **payee of the note** because she is the one who is to receive the specified amount of money. Notice that to Paul DeBruke it is a note payable while to Sarah Morney it is a note receivable.

$ 1,542.50	June 9	19-A

Ninety days *after date* I *promise to pay to*

the order of Sarah Morney

One thousand five hundred forty-two 50/100 *Dollars*

Payable at Brentwood Bank

With interest at 9% per annum from date

No. 6 *Due* Sept. 7, 19-A Paul De Bruke

Promissory Note

Notes may be interest-bearing or non-interest-bearing. The note illustrated is interest-bearing with interest at 9% per year. Sometimes no rate of interest is specified on the note although the transaction will involve some interest.

For example, a borrower might give a $1,000 non-interest-bearing note, payable in 60 days to a bank in return for a loan of $985. The $15 difference between the amount received ($985) and the amount that must be repaid ($1,000) when the note matures (is due) will become interest expense that will be paid at maturity. Interest accrues gradually over time. Accounting for this type of transaction is explained on page 492.

Calculating Interest

In calculating interest on notes, it is necessary to take the following factors into consideration:

1. The principal of the note
2. The rate of interest
3. The period of time involved

The principal of the note is the face amount of the note that the maker promises to pay at maturity. This amount is separate from any specified interest. The principal is the base on which the interest is calculated.

The rate of interest usually is expressed in the form of a percentage, such as 8% or 10%. Ordinarily the rate is an annual percentage rate, but in some cases the rate is quoted on a monthly basis, such as 1 1/2% a month. A rate of 1 1/2% a month is equivalent to a rate of 18% a year payable monthly (1 1/2% × 12 = 18%).

The time of the note consists of the days or months from the date of issue of a note to the date of its maturity (or the interest payment date if it comes earlier). When the time is specified in months, the interest is calculated on the basis of months rather than days. For example, a 3-month note issued on June 1 is payable on September 1, and the interest should be calculated on the basis of 3 months or 1/4 of a year (3 mos. / 12 mos. = 1/4 yr.). However, when the time of a note is specified in days or when the due date is specified in a note, the interest should be computed using the exact number of days that will elapse from the date of the note to the date of its maturity. In making this computation, the day of maturity is counted but the day on which the note is issued is not. For example, if a $1,000, 9% note is dated March 1, and the due date is specified as June 1, the time should be computed as shown:

Days in March	31
Deduct date of note, March 1	1
Days remaining in March	30
Add: Days in April	30
Days in May	31
Note matures on June	1
Total time in days	92

In computing interest, it is customary to consider 360 days as a year. Most banks and business firms follow this practice, though some banks and all federal government agencies use 365 days as the base in computing daily interest. In any case, the formula for computing interest is:

$$I = PRT, \text{ where:}$$
$$I = \text{amount of interest}$$
$$P = \text{amount of principal}$$
$$R = \text{rate of interest}$$
$$T = \text{time (usually a fraction of a 360-day year)}$$

Thus, for the $1,000, 9% note described above, interest on the due date would be $23 ($1,000 × 9% × 92/360). The gradual accumulation of interest on the note to a **maturity value** (the total of the principal plus interest) of $1,023 is shown by the following time line:

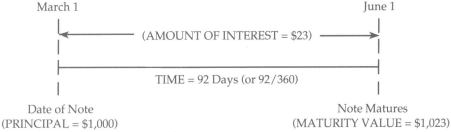

Accumulation of Interest Time Line

In the case of long-term notes, the interest may be payable periodically, such as semi-annually or annually.

The 30-Day, 12% Method

There are short cuts that can be used in computing interest on the basis of a 360-day year. The interest on any amount for 30 days at 12% can be determined simply by moving the decimal point in the amount two places to the left. The reason for this is that 30 days is 1/12 of a year, and interest on any amount at 12% for 1/12 of a year is the same as the interest at 1% for a full year. Thus, the interest on $650 for 30 days at 12% is $6.50.

The 30-day, 12% method can be used in many cases even though the actual time may be other than 30 days and the actual rate other than 12%. For example, consider the following notes:

Note No. 1	*Note No. 2*
$3,000, 8%, 30-day note	$4,000, 10%, 90-day note
Interest Calculation	*Interest Calculation*
Interest at 12% for 30 days = $30	Interest at 12% for 30 days = $40
Interest at 8% = 8/12 × $30 = $20	Interest at 12% for 90 days = $120
	Interest at 10% = 10/12 × $120 = $100

Interest can also be determined from published tables. These tables are widely used by financial institutions and by other business firms.

Determining the Due Date

As explained above, the period of time between the date of issue and the maturity date of a note may be stated in either days or months. If the time of the note is stated in days, the due date is the specified number of days after the issue date. For example, the due date of a 60-day note dated March 10 is calculated as follows:

Time of note		60 days
Days in March	31	
Date of note	10	21
Days remaining		39
Days in April		30
Days remaining = Due date: May		9

If the time of the note is stated in months, the due date is determined by counting the number of months from the date the note was issued. The note is due on the date in the month of maturity that corresponds with the date the note was issued. For example, a three-month note dated August 10 would be due November 10. If there is no date in the month of maturity corresponding to the issue date, the due date is the last day of the month. For example, a three-month note dated January 31 would be due April 30.

Accounting for Notes Receivable Transactions

Describe and process transactions involving the receipt, collection, renewal, discounting, and dishonor of notes receivable.

Businesses other than lending institutions such as commercial banks and savings and loan associations generally encounter five types of transactions involving notes receivable:

1. Note received from a customer to obtain an extension of time for payment of an obligation
2. Note collected at maturity
3. Note renewed at maturity
4. Note discounted before maturity
5. Note dishonored

Note Received from a Customer to Obtain an Extension of Time for Payment

To obtain an extension of time for the payment of an account, a customer may issue a note for all or part of the amount due. A merchant may be willing to accept the note because it is a written acknowledgment of the debt and it is likely to bear interest.

Assume that Michael Putter owes the Linesch Hardware Co. $2,000 on open account. The account is past due and Linesch insists upon a settlement. Putter offers to give a 90-day, 10% note dated June 8, and Linesch accepts Putter's offer. The transaction is entered in the books of the Linesch Hardware Co. as follows:

June 8 Notes Receivable	2,000	
Accounts Receivable (M. Putter)		2,000
Received a note from Michael Putter.		

If instead of giving a note for the full amount, Putter gives a check for $250 and a note for the $1,750 balance, the transaction would be entered in Linesch's books as follows:

June 8 Cash	250	
Notes Receivable	1,750	
Accounts Receivable (M. Putter)		2,000
Received check and note from Michael Putter.		

Note Collected at Maturity

When a note receivable matures, it may be collected by the holder or it may be left at a bank for collection. If the maker of the note resides in another locality, the note may be forwarded to a bank in that locality for collection. A few days before the maturity of a note the maker usually is reminded of the due date, the amount that must be paid, and where the amount is to be paid. When the bank makes the collection, it notifies the holder that the net amount has been credited to the holder's account. This notification is made on a form similar to the following credit advice.

ADVICE OF CREDIT

Planet Bank
Bonne Terre, Missouri

TO Linesch Hardware Co.

Account No. 315 30959   September 11 **19** —A

WE CREDIT YOUR ACCOUNT BALANCE AS FOLLOWS:

Michael Putter's note	$2,000.00	
Interest for 90 days at 10%	50.00	
	$2,050.00	
Less collection charge	10.00	$ 2,040.00

OFFSETTING DR.

APPROVED _R. Shaw_

Credit Advice

The necessary accounting procedure for a bank collection is illustrated in the following example. Assume that Linesch left Putter's 90-day, 10% note for $2,000 at Planet Bank for collection, and on September 6 received notice that the note had been collected including the accrued interest of $50. The bank fee for collecting the note amounted to $10.

The transaction is entered in Linesch's books as follows:

```
Sept. 6  Cash ......................................  2,040
             Collection Expense ..........................     10
             Notes Receivable ............................           2,000
             Interest Revenue ............................             50
             Received credit for the proceeds of Michael
             Putter's note collected by the bank.
```

Note Renewed at Maturity

If the maker of a note is unable to pay the amount due at maturity, it may be possible to renew all or part of the note. If, instead of paying the note for $2,000 at maturity, Putter is allowed to pay only the interest, $50, and give a new note for 60 days at the same rate of 10% interest, the transaction is entered in Linesch's books as follows:

```
Sept. 6  Cash ......................................     50
             Notes Receivable (new note) .................  2,000
             Notes Receivable (old note) .................           2,000
             Interest Revenue ............................             50
             Received a new note for $2,000 from Michael
             Putter in renewal of his note due today and
             $50 in cash for the interest on the old note.
```

Note Discounted

If a business needs cash before the due date of a note, it can endorse the note and transfer it to a bank. This process is called discounting a note receivable. The bank charges a fee called a bank discount (implied interest to maturity) based on the maturity value of the note for the time between the date of discounting and the due date of the note. The maturity value of the note less this discount is called the proceeds, which is the amount of cash received by the business discounting the note.

To illustrate, assume that the $2,000, 10%, 90-day note receivable from Putter dated June 8 is discounted by Linesch at the bank on July 8 at a rate of 12%. The amount of the discount and proceeds would be calculated using the following three steps:

1. Face + Interest = **Maturity Value**
    $2,000 + $50 = $2,050

2. Maturity Value × Discount Rate × Discount Period* = **Discount Amount**
    $2,050   ×   12%   ×   60/360   = $41

*Discount period = July 8 through September 6 = 60 days

3. Maturity Value − Discount Amount = Proceeds
        $2,050   − $41   = $2,009

This transaction may be illustrated in time line form as follows:

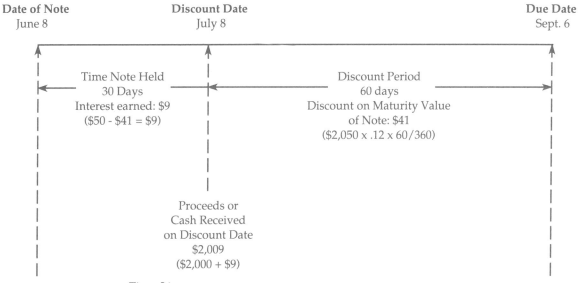

Date of Note	Discount Date	Due Date
June 8	July 8	Sept. 6

Time Note Held
30 Days
Interest earned: $9
($50 - $41 = $9)

Discount Period
60 days
Discount on Maturity Value
of Note: $41
($2,050 x .12 x 60/360)

Proceeds or
Cash Received
on Discount Date
$2,009
($2,000 + $9)

Time Line

The excess of the $2,009 proceeds over the $2,000 face value of the note represents interest revenue of $9. This transaction is entered in Linesch's books as follows:

Sept. 6 Cash	2,009	
Notes Receivable		2,000
Interest Revenue		9
Michael Putter's note discounted.		

When a note receivable is discounted, it is possible for the proceeds to be less than the face value of the note. When this happens, the difference between the proceeds and the face value of the note represents interest expense. For example, if the proceeds from discounting the $2,000 note receivable from Putter had been only $1,992, the transaction would have been entered as follows:

Sept. 6 Cash	1,992	
Interest Expense	8	
Notes Receivable		2,000
Michael Putter's note discounted.		

Note Dishonored

If the maker of a note refuses or is unable to pay or renew it at maturity, the note is said to be dishonored. A dishonored note cannot be negotiated, which means that it loses its legal status as a note receivable. Usually the amount is transferred from the notes receivable account to the accounts receivable account pending final disposition of the obligation involved. For example, if Linesch is unable to collect the interest-bearing note for $2,000 received 90 days before from Putter, the following entry is made in Linesch's books:

Sept. 6 Accounts Receivable (M.Putter)...............	2,050	
Notes Receivable		2,000
Interest Revenue		50
Michael Putter's note dishonored.		

If the claim against Putter should turn out to be completely worthless, the $2,050 will be removed from Accounts Receivable and treated as an uncollectible account. The accounting involved in this type of transaction was discussed in Chapter 11.

If the dishonored note is one that had been discounted at a bank, the bank usually notifies the endorser (the original payee of the note) and asks for payment. The endorser generally is obligated to pay the amount due. The amount paid by the endorser to the bank, including the principal, interest, and any bank fees, should be recorded by the endorser as an account receivable from the maker of the note. For example, if the $2,000 note receivable discounted on July 8 for proceeds of $2,009 was dishonored by Putter at maturity, the following entry would be made on Linesch's books:

Sept. 6 Accounts Receivable (M. Putter)...............	2,050	
Cash		2,050
Michael Putter's note dishonored.		

Notes Receivable Register

Prepare a notes receivable register.

When many notes are received in the course of business, it may be advisable to keep an auxiliary record. An auxiliary record of notes receivable that provides more detailed information than a ledger account is usually known as a notes receivable register. One form of a notes receivable register is reproduced at the top of pages 490 and 491. The information contained in the register is obtained directly from the notes received. The notes are numbered consecutively as they are entered in the register. (This number should not be confused with the maker's number in the lower left-hand corner of the note, as shown in the illustration on page 481.) The due date of each note is determined and entered in the proper When Due column. The interest to maturity is calculated and entered in the Interest Amount column. When a remittance or a new note is received in settlement of a note, the date is entered in the Date Paid column.

Notes Receivable Account

The information contained in the notes receivable account should agree with that entered in the notes receivable register. The following account contains a record of the notes that were entered in the notes receivable register on pages 490 and 491. Notice that each note is identified by the number assigned to the note. If the notes are not numbered, each note should be identified by writing the name of the maker in the Item column of the account.

ACCOUNT **Notes Receivable**   ACCOUNT NO. **121**

DATE		ITEM	POST. REF.	DEBIT	CREDIT	BALANCE DEBIT	BALANCE CREDIT
19-- Apr.	4	No. 1	J2	4 6 8 12		4 6 8 12	
	21	No. 2	J2	6 0 0 00		1 0 6 8 12	
May	2	No. 3	J3	7 5 7 20		1 8 2 5 32	
	19	No. 4	J3	8 2 0 00		2 6 4 5 32	
June	1	No. 3	CR5		7 5 7 20	1 8 8 8 12	
	3	No. 1	CR5		4 6 8 12	1 4 2 0 00	
	20	No. 2	CR5		6 0 0 00	8 2 0 00	
	20	No. 5	J4	5 0 0 00		1 3 2 0 00	

Proving The Notes Receivable Account

Periodically (usually at the end of each month) the notes receivable account is proved by comparing the balance of the account with the total of the notes owned as shown by the notes receivable register. Note that the following schedule of notes owned on June 30 has the same total as the balance in the notes receivable account illustration.

Schedule of Notes Owned

No. 4	$820
No. 5	500
	$1,320

PAGE 2   **NOTES RECEIVABLE REGISTER**

| DATE RECEIVED | | No. | BY WHOM PAYABLE | WHERE PAYABLE | | DATE MADE | | |
				BANK OR FIRM	ADDRESS	MO.	DAY	YEAR
Apr.⁹⁻ᴬ	4	1	L.A. Peters	First State Bank	Eureka	Apr.	4	'A
	21	2	J.M. Slawski	Opportunity Bank	University City	Apr.	21	'A
May	2	3	S.M. Alpart	Farmers' Bank	Kirksville	May	2	'A
	19	4	L.L. Sheinbein	Central Trust	Jefferson City	May	19	'A
June	20	5	J.M. Slawski	Opportunity Bank	University City	June	20	'A

Note Receivable Register (Left Page)

Accrued Interest Receivable

Explain and process end-of-period adjustments for interest earned but not yet collected.

While interest on a note literally accrues day by day, it is impractical to keep a daily record of such accruals. If the life of a note receivable is within the accounting period, no entry is made for the interest until the amount is received.

If, however, the business owns some interest-bearing notes receivable at the end of the accounting period, neither the net income for the period nor the assets at the end of the period will be correctly stated unless the interest accrued on notes receivable is taken into consideration. The amount of the accrued interest can be computed from the notes themselves or from the data provided by a notes receivable register. The accounts are then adjusted by debiting Accrued Interest Receivable and by crediting Interest Revenue for the amount of interest that has accrued to the end of the period. Assume that at the end of a fiscal year (ending June 30), a business owns four interest-bearing notes as shown in the following schedule:

Schedule of Accrued Interest on Notes Receivable

Principal	Date of Issue	Rate of Interest	Days From Issue Date to June 30	Accrued Interest June 30
$800.00	April 15	9%	76	$15.20
500.00	May 5	10	56	7.78
545.80	May 29	9	32	4.37
700.00	June 12	9	18	3.15
Total accrued interest on notes receivable				$30.50

The following entry would be made on June 30 for the accrued interest:

June 30	Accrued Interest Receivable	30.50	
	Interest Revenue.........................		30.50
	Interest accrued on notes receivable as of June 30.		

NOTES RECEIVABLE REGISTER PAGE 2

TIME	WHEN DUE					AMOUNT				INTEREST				DISCOUNTED			DATE PAID		REMARKS
	J	J	J	A	D					RATE		AMT.		BANK	DATE				
60 da.		3				4	6	8	12	8%		6	24				June	3	
60 da.		20				6	0	0	00	9%		9	00				June	20	Renewal for $500
30 da.		1				7	5	7	20	9%		5	68				June	1	Sent for coll. 5/30
90 da.				17		8	2	0	00	9%	1	8	45						
60 da.				19		5	0	0	00	9%		7	50						Renewal of Note No. 2

Notes Receivable Register (Right Page)

In the financial statements at the end of the year, the balance of the interest revenue account, which will include the $30.50 earned but not yet received, will be reported in the income statement. The balance of the accrued interest receivable account will be reported in the balance sheet as a current asset.

Accounting for Notes Payable Transactions

Describe and process transactions involving the issuance, payment, and renewal of notes payable.

There are generally four types of transactions involving notes payable:

1. Note issued to a supplier to obtain an extension of time for payment of an obligation
2. Note issued as security for cash loan
3. Note paid at maturity
4. Note renewed at maturity

Note Issued to a Supplier to Obtain an Extension of Time for Payment

When a firm wishes to obtain an extension of time for the payment of an account, a note for all or part of the amount due may be acceptable to the supplier. Assume that Linesch Hardware Co. owes Bella & Co. $654.70. By agreement, on June 11 Linesch issues to Bella a check for $54.70 and a 90-day, 10% interest-bearing note for $600. This transaction is entered in Linesch's books as follows:

June 11 Accounts Payable............................	654.70	
Cash....................................		54.70
Notes Payable............................		600.00
Issued check for $54.70 and note for $600 to Bella & Co.		

Note Issued as Security for Cash Loan

Many firms experience brief periods during the year in which receipts from customers are not adequate to finance their operations. During such periods, firms commonly borrow money from banks on short-term notes to help finance their business operations. Assume that on June 16, Linesch borrows $6,000 from the Planet Bank on a 60-day, 10 1/2% interest-bearing note. The transaction is entered as follows:

June 16 Cash	6,000	
Notes Payable		6,000
Borrowed $6,000 at the bank on a 60-day, 10 1/2% note.		

Commercial banks often deduct interest in advance, and this procedure is known as **discounting**. The nature of this transaction and the procedures for handling it are very similar to those presented on pages 486 and 487 for discounting notes receivable. For example, instead of the transaction described above, suppose that Linesch borrowed on a $6,000, 60-day, non-interest-bearing note which the bank discounted at 10 1/2%. The bank would calculate the implied interest on the note to maturity, known as **bank discount**, and deduct this amount from the $6,000 face of the note.

The amount of the discount and the proceeds to Linesch Hardware Co. would be calculated using the following three steps:

1. Face + Interest = **Maturity Value**
   $6,000 + 0 = $6,000
2. Maturity Value × Discount Rate × Discount Period = **Discount Amount**
   $6,000 × 10 1/2% × 60/360 = $105
3. Maturity Value − Discount Amount = **Proceeds**
   $6,000 − $105 = $5,895

This transaction may be illustrated in time-line form as follows:

Date of Note	Discount Rate	Due Date
JUNE 16	10 1/2%	AUG. 15

Discount Period
60 DAYS

Proceeds		Discount		Maturity Value
$5,895	+	$105	=	$6,000

Time Line

Thus, Linesch Hardware Co. would receive only $5,895 proceeds ($6,000 − $105), and the transaction would be entered as follows:

June 16 Cash	5,895	
Discount on Notes Payable...................	105	
Notes Payable		6,000
Discounted at 10 1/2%, a $6,000, 60-day, non-interest-bearing note.		

The $105 debit to the discount on notes payable account represents an offset to the $6,000 note payable. Linesch's liability at this time is only $5,895, which is the net amount or proceeds received from the bank. Discount on Notes Payable is a contra-liability account and is reported as a deduction from Notes Payable on the balance sheet. The $105 discount gradually becomes interest expense. It is recognized in full when the note matures on August 15, and the $6,000 principal amount of the note is repaid. Accordingly, Linesch Hardware Co. will enter the payment of the note at maturity as follows:

Aug. 15 Notes Payable	6,000	
Interest Expense	105	
Cash		6,000
Discount on Notes Payable		105
Paid 60-day, non-interest-bearing note due today, and recognized interest expense at 10 1/2%.		

Although the stated rate of interest was 10 1/2% on both the "interest bearing" and "discounted" notes, the financial effects of the two notes are not the same. With the interest bearing note, $6,000 was obtained for 60 days at a cost of $105—exactly 10 1/2% ($105 / $6,000 = 1.75% for 60 days; 10.5% for 360 days). With the discounted note, $105 was paid for the use of $5,895 for 60 days—a rate of nearly 10.7%, which is known as the effective rate of interest ($105 / $5,895 = 1.781% for 60 days; 10.687% for 360 days).

Note Paid at Maturity

A note made payable to a bank for a loan is commonly paid at that bank upon maturity. When notes made payable to other payees mature, payment may be made directly to the holder or to a bank where the note was left for collection. The maker knows who the payee is but may not know who the holder is at maturity because the payee may have transferred the note to another party. When a note is left with a bank for collection, it is customary for the bank to mail the maker a notice of

maturity. For example, assume that Bella & Co. forwards the 90-day, 10% note for $600 received from Linesch on June 11 to the Planet Bank for collection. The bank would notify Linesch before the maturity date by sending a notice similar to the following illustration:

Bonne Terre, Missouri

Your note described below will be due ──────

MAKER-COSIGNER-COLLATERAL	NUMBER	DATE DUE	PRINCIPAL	INTEREST	TOTAL
J. Linesch Linesch Hardware Co.	19360	9/9/--	$600.00	$15.00	$615.00

ENDORSER

TO J. Linesch
Linesch Hardware Co.
Box 362
Bonne Terre, MO 63628-5544

Note: Please bring this notice with you.   PAYABLE AT: **Planet Bank**

Notice of Maturity of Note

Upon receiving this notice, Linesch issues a check to the bank for $615 in payment of the note and interest. The transaction is entered in Linesch's books as follows:

Sept. 9 Notes Payable	600	
Interest Expense	15	
Cash		615
Paid note issued June 11 to Bella & Co., plus interest.		

Note Renewed at Maturity

If the maker is unable to pay a note in full at maturity, it may be possible to renew all or a part of the note. For example, on September 9, Linesch could pay the $15 interest and $100 on the principal of the $600 note issued to Bella & Co. on June 11, and give a new 60-day, 10% note for $500. This transaction would be entered as follows:

```
Sept. 9 Notes Payable (old note) ....................  600
        Interest Expense ...........................   15
            Cash .......................................       115
            Notes Payable (new note) .................       500
                Issued a check for $115 and a note for $500
                to Bella & Co. in settlement of a note for
                $600 plus interest.
```

Notes Payable Register

Prepare a notes payable register.

When many notes are issued in the usual course of business, it may be advisable to keep an auxiliary record. An auxiliary record of notes payable that provides more detailed information than a ledger account is known as a notes payable register. A notes payable register is reproduced on pages 496 and 497.

The information contained in the register may be obtained directly from the note or from a note stub. Blank notes are usually made up in pads with attached stubs. The stub is used for entering such essential information as amount, payee, where payable, date, time, rate of interest, and number. The due date of each note is determined and entered in the proper When Due column of the register. The interest at maturity is also calculated and entered in the Interest Amount column. When a note is paid, the date is entered in the Date Paid column.

Notes Payable Account

The information contained in the notes payable account should agree with the information entered in the notes payable register. The following account contains a record of the notes that were entered in the notes payable register on pages 496 and 497.

ACCOUNT **Notes Payable**   ACCOUNT NO. **216**

DATE		ITEM	POST. REF.	DEBIT	CREDIT	BALANCE DEBIT	BALANCE CREDIT
Apr.	14	No. 1	J2		2 1 4 9 61		2 1 4 9 61
May	13	No. 2	CR4		8 0 0 0 00		10 1 4 9 61
June	2	No. 3	J3		1 3 5 7 35		11 5 0 6 96
	13	No. 1	CP5	2 1 4 9 61			9 3 5 7 35

PAGE *1*		NOTES PAYABLE REGISTER					
DATE ISSUED	No.	TO WHOM PAYABLE	WHERE PAYABLE		DATE MADE		
			BANK OR FIRM	ADDRESS	MO.	DAY	YEAR
Apr. 14 19-A	1	*L.L. Knoop*	*First State Bank*	*Eureka*	*Apr.*	*14*	*19-A*
May 13	2	*Opportunity Bank*	*Opportunity Bank*	*Univ. City*	*May*	*13*	*19-A*
June 2	3	*Bloodgood Brothers*	*Opportunity Bank*	*Univ. City*	*June*	*2*	*19-A*

Notes Payable Register (Left Page)

Proving the Notes Payable Account

Periodically (usually at the end of each month), the notes payable account is proved by comparing the balance of the account with the total notes outstanding as shown by the notes payable register. Note that the following schedule of the notes outstanding on June 30 has the same total as the balance in the notes payable account illustration.

Schedule of Notes Outstanding

No. 2 .... $8,000.00
No. 3 .... 1,357.35
$9,357.35

Accrued Interest Payable

Explain and process end-of-year adjustments for interest incurred but not yet paid.

Neither the expenses for a period nor the liabilities at the end of the period will be correctly stated unless the interest accrued on notes payable is taken into consideration. The mechanics of calculating the amount of interest accrued on notes payable are the same as in the case of notes receivable. If a notes payable register is kept, it should provide the information needed for computing the amount of interest accrued on notes payable. If the total amount of the accrued interest was calculated to be $269.12, and the fiscal period ended June 30, the proper adjusting entry would be made as follows:

June 30 Interest Expense............................ 269.12
   Accrued Interest Payable................... 269.12
   Interest accrued on notes payable as of June 30.

In the income statement at the end of the year, the balance of the interest expense account will include the $269.12 incurred but not yet

	WHEN DUE												AMOUNT		INTEREST			DATE PAID	REMARKS
TIME	J	F	M	A	M	J	J	A	S	O	N	D			RATE	AMOUNT			
60 da.						13							2 1 4 9 61		9%	3 2 24		June 13	Settled 2/14 inv.
90 da.							11						8 0 0 0 00		10%	2 0 0 00			
30 da.					2								1 3 5 7 35		11%	1 2 44			Settled 4/2 inv.

NOTES PAYABLE REGISTER   PAGE *1*

Notes Payable Register (Right Page)

paid. The balance of the accrued interest payable account will include the $269.12 and will be reported in the balance sheet as a current liability.

Endorsement of Notes

Describe and illustrate the various types of endorsement on notes.

A promissory note is usually made payable to a specified person or firm, though some notes are made payable to "Bearer." If the note is payable to the order of a specified party, that party must endorse the note in order to transfer it to another party. To **endorse** means to sign one's name as payee on the back of a note.

The two major types of endorsements are (1) the blank endorsement and (2) the special endorsement. The endorsement is called a **blank endorsement** when only the payee's name is signed on the left end of the back of the note. The endorsement is called a **special endorsement** if the words "Pay to the order of" followed by the name of a specified party and the payee's signature appear on the back of the note. The legal effect of both types of endorsement is much the same. However, a blank endorsement makes a note payable to the bearer, while a special endorsement identifies the party to whose order payment is made.

Under certain circumstances, the maker of a note may arrange for an additional party to join in the promise to pay, either as a cosigner or as an endorser of the note. A **cosigner** signs below the maker's signature on the face of the note. If the other party makes a blank endorsement on the back of the note, it is called an **accommodation endorsement**. In either event, the payee of the note has an additional person responsible for payment, which is intended to add security to the note.

If a partial payment is made on a note, it is common practice to record the date of the payment and the amount paid on the back of the note. This is called **endorsing the payment**.

Illustrated on page 498 is the promissory note originally made payable to the order of Sarah Morney. (See illustration of note on page 481.) The maker of the note, Paul DeBruke, had Donna Gabar become an accommodation endorser. Later, the payee, Morney, transferred the note to T. L. Fischer by a special endorsement. On July 9, $500 was paid on the note.

Blank
Endorsement ⟶
(Accomodation)

Special ⟶
Endorsement

Endorsed ⟶
Payment

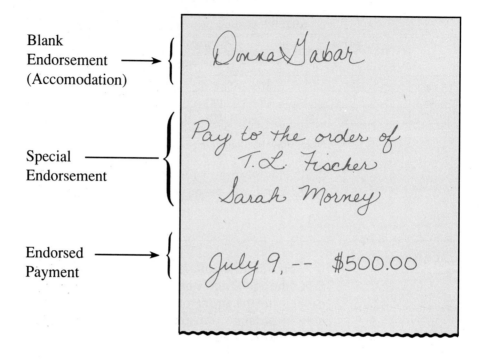

Building Your Accounting Knowledge

1. What are the four features that a promissory note must have in order to be considered negotiable commercial paper?
2. What three factors must be taken into consideration in calculating interest on notes?
3. In computing the exact number of days of interest on a note, what date is counted? What date is not counted?
4. What number of days is considered as a year by most banks and business firms in computing interest?
5. If the time of a note is stated in months, how is the due date determined?
6. What generally are the five types of transactions involving notes receivable?
7. If a note receivable is discounted at a bank, on what amount and for what time period does the bank compute the discount?
8. If a note receivable that was discounted at a bank is dishonored by its maker, what is the responsibility of the person discounting the note?
9. What generally are the four types of transactions involving notes payable?
10. How are accrued interest receivable and accrued interest payable reported on the balance sheet?

▨ **Assignment Box**

To reinforce your understanding of the preceding text material, you may complete the following:
> Study Guide
> Textbook: Exercises 12A1 through 12A7 and 12B1 through 12B7
> Problems 12A1 through 12A3 and 12B1 through 12B3.

Expanding Your Business Vocabulary

What is the meaning of each of the following terms?

accommodation endorsement (p. 497)
bank discount (p. 486)
blank endorsement (p. 497)
contra-liability (p. 493)
cosigner (p. 497)
credit advice (p. 485)
discounting (p. 486)
dishonored (p. 488)
effective rate (p. 493)
endorse (p. 497)
endorsing the payment (p. 497)
maker of the note (p. 481)

maturity value (p. 483)
negotiable commercial paper (p. 481)
notes payable register (p. 495)
notes receivable register (p. 488)
notice of maturity (p. 493)
payee of the note (p. 481)
principal of the note (p. 482)
proceeds (p. 486)
promissory note (p. 481)
rate of interest (p. 482)
special endorsement (p. 497)
time of the note (p. 482)

Demonstration Problem

Barbar Brothers, partners in a wholesale hardware business, completed the following transactions involving notes and interest during the first half of 19--:

Jan. 11 Received a $500, 60-day, 10% note from Paul Heinsius in payment of an account receivable.

Jan. 18 Borrowed $10,000 from Landmark Bank issuing a 90-day, 11% note.

Feb. 6 Received an $875, 30-day, 9% note from Deborah Douglas in payment of an account receivable.

Feb. 21 Issued a $650, 60-day, 11% note to Swanson & Johnson, a supplier, in payment of an account payable.

Mar. 1 Received a $1000, 90-day, 10% note from Steve Roberts, a customer.

Mar. 11 Received a check for $881.56 from Deborah Douglas in payment of note due Mar. 8 including interest.

Mar. 13 Received a check for $508.33 from Paul Heinsius in payment of note due Mar. 12 including interest.

Mar. 31 Discounted the $1,000 Steve Roberts note at Manchester Bank at a discount rate of 12%.

Apr. 18 Paid Landmark Bank $10,275 for note due today, including interest.

Apr. 22 Paid Swanson & Johnson $661.92 for note due today, including interest.

May 31 Steve Roberts dishonored his $1,000 note due at the Manchester Bank yesterday. Paid Manchester Bank $1,000, plus interest, plus a $10 protest fee, for the dishonored note.

June 20 Issued a $750, 90-day, 9% note to Greene Acres, a supplier, in payment of an account payable.

Required:

Record each transaction in a general journal.

Solution

Journal

Date	Description	Post Ref.	Debit	Credit
19--				
Jan. 11	Notes Receivable		500.00	
	Accounts Receivable			500.00
	60-day, 10% note—P. Heinsius			
18	Cash		10,000.00	
	Notes Payable			10,000.00
	90-day, 11% note—Landmark Bank			
Feb. 6	Notes Receivable		875.00	
	Accounts Receivable			875.00
	30-day, 9% note—D. Douglas			
21	Accounts Payable		650.00	
	Notes Payable			650.00
	60-day, 11% note—Swanson & Johnson			
Mar. 1	Notes Receivable		1,000.00	
	Accounts Receivable			1,000.00
	90-day, 10% note—S. Roberts			
11	Cash		881.56	
	Notes Receivable			875.00
	Interest Revenue			6.56
	Principal and interest—D. Douglas's note			
13	Cash		508.33	
	Notes Receivable			500.00
	Interest Revenue			8.33
	Principal and interest—P. Heinsius's note			

Journal

Date	Description	Post Ref.	Debit	Credit
19--				
Mar. 31	Cash		1,004.50	
	Notes Receivable			1,000.00
	Interest Revenue			4.50
	Discounted Steve Roberts' note at			
	Manchester Bank.			
	Principal $1,000.00			
	Interest to maturity 25.00			
	Maturity value $1,025.00			
	Less: Discount			
	($1,025 × 12% × 60/360) 20.50			
	Cash proceeds $1,004.50			
Apr. 18	Notes Payable		10,000.00	
	Interest Expense		275.00	
	Cash			10,275.00
	Paid Landmark Bank note due today.			
22	Notes Payable		650.00	
	Interest Expense		11.92	
	Cash			661.92
	Paid Swanson & Johnson note due today.			
May 31	Accounts Receivable		1,035.00	
	Cash			1,035.00
	Paid Manchester Bank for dishonored			
	Steve Roberts' note.			
	Principal $1,000.00			
	Interest 25.00			
	Protest fee 10.00			
	$1,035.00			
June 20	Accounts Payable		750.00	
	Note Payable			750.00
	90-day, 9% note—Greene Acres			

*Note: Now that you have reviewed the Demonstration Problem and Solution you may complete the **Mastery Problem** at the end of the chapter activities.

Applying Accounting Concepts

Series A

Use a 360-day year in all of the following exercises.

Exercise 12A1—Interest Computation. Compute the interest on each of the following notes:

(a) $1,000, 60-day, 10%.
(b) $800, 90-day, 12%.
(c) $1,200, 120-day, 9%.

Exercise 12A2—Journal Entries for Notes and Interest Receivable. Prepare the appropriate general journal entry for each of the following transactions:

(a) Received an $882, 90-day, 9% note from a customer in payment of an account receivable.

(b) Received $64 in cash and a $600, 60-day, 10% note from a customer in payment of an account receivable.

(c) Received proceeds of the note in Transaction (b) at maturity and paid the bank a $12 collection fee.

Exercise 12A3—Journal Entries for Notes and Interest Receivable. Prepare the appropriate general journal entry for each of the following transactions:

(a) Received $19.13 in interest plus an $850, 60-day, 10% note in settlement of an $850, 90-day, 9% note due today.

(b) Recorded a dishonored $1500, 60-day, 11% note receivable which was due today.

Exercise 12A4—Adjusting Entry for Accrued Interest Receivable. Assume that at the end of the fiscal year ending June 30, a business owns three interest-bearing notes as shown in the following schedule:

Principal	Date of Issue	Rate of Interest
$1,200	May 15	11%
$1,400	May 30	10%
$1,000	June 25	11%

Prepare the adjusting entry at June 30 to recognize the accrued interest receivable on these notes.

Exercise 12A5—Journal Entries for Notes and Interest Payable. Prepare the appropriate general journal entry for each of the following transactions:

(a) Paid a supplier $38.75 and issued a $500, 60-day, 11% note to the supplier in payment of an account.

(b) Paid the $500 note in Transaction (a) at maturity.

Exercise 12A6—Journal Entries for Notes and Interest Payable. Prepare the appropriate general journal entry for each of the following transactions:

(a) Borrowed $10,000 from the bank on a 90-day, 12% note.

(b) Borrowed $5,000 from the bank on a 90-day, non-interest-bearing note which the bank discounted at 11%. (You must compute the proceeds of this note.)

(c) Paid $300 and issued a new $10,000, 90-day, 12.5% note in settlement of the note in Transaction (a) at its maturity.

(d) Paid the $5,000 non-interest-bearing note in Transaction (b) at maturity.

Exercise 12A7—Adjusting Entry for Accrued Interest Payable. Assume that the total amount of accrued interest on notes payable at the fiscal year end, March 31, is $93.45. Prepare the adjusting entry at fiscal year end to recognize the accrued interest payable on these notes.

Series B

Use a 360-day year in all of the following exercises.

Exercise 12B1—Interest Computation. Compute the interest on each of the following notes:

(a) $1,200, 60-day, 9%.
(b) $1,000, 90-day, 10%.
(c) $1,500, 120-day, 12%.

Exercise 12B2—Journal Entries for Notes and Interest Receivable. Prepare the appropriate general journal entry for each of the following transactions:

(a) Received a $972, 60-day, 10% note from a customer in payment of an account receivable.
(b) Received $87 in cash and an $800, 90-day, 11% note from a customer in payment of an account receivable.
(c) Received proceeds of note in Transaction (b) at maturity and paid the bank a $13 collection fee.

Exercise 12B3—Journal Entries for Notes and Interest Receivable. Prepare the appropriate general journal entry for each of the following transactions:

(a) Received $16.67 in interest plus a $1000, 30-day, 11% note in settlement of a $1000, 60-day, 10% note due today.
(b) Recorded a dishonored $1500, 90-day, 9% note receivable which was due today.

Exercise 12B4—Adjusting Entry for Accrued Interest Receivable. Assume that at the end of the fiscal year ending September 30, a business owns three interest-bearing notes as shown in the following schedule:

Principal	Date of Issue	Rate of Interest
$ 900.00	July 10	10%
$1,000.00	July 20	9%
$1,500.00	Aug. 24	10%

Prepare the adjusting entry at September 30 to recognize the accrued interest receivable on these notes.

Exercise 12B5—Journal Entries for Notes and Interest Payable. Prepare the appropriate general journal entry for each of the following transactions:

(a) Paid a supplier $58.50 and issued a $600, 90-day, 9% note to the supplier in payment of an account.
(b) Paid the $600 note in Transaction (a) at maturity.

Exercise 12B6—Journal Entries for Notes and Interest Payable. Prepare the appropriate general journal entry for each of the following transactions:

(a) Borrowed $12,000 from the bank on a 60-day, 11% note.
(b) Borrowed $6,000 from the bank on a 90-day, non-interest-bearing note which the bank discounted at 10%. (You must compute the proceeds of this note.)

(c)   Paid $220 and issued a new $12,000, 60-day, 11.5% note in settlement of the note in Transaction (a) at its maturity.

(d)   Paid the $6,000 non-interest-bearing note in Transaction (b) at maturity.

Exercise 12B7—Adjusting Entry for Accrued Interest Payable. Assume that the total amount of accrued interest on notes payable at the fiscal year end, Oct. 31, is $79.35. Prepare the adjusting entry at fiscal year end to recognize the accrued interest payable on these notes.

Series A

Problem 12A1   Journal Entries for Notes and Interest Receivable; Notes Receivable Register

Ross Boone operates a merchandising business. Occasionally short-term notes are accepted from customers who are unable to pay their accounts when due and who seek extensions of time by issuing notes. Following is a narrative of transactions involving notes received during the current year.

It is recommended that the required entry in the notes receivable register be made immediately after the related transaction has been entered in the general journal.

Apr. 18   Received a $1,000, 90-day, 10% note dated April 16 from Nancy Noyes in payment of an account receivable.

May 16   Received a $750, 60-day, 11% note dated May 14 from Joseph Roman in payment of an account receivable.

May 25   Received an $800, 90-day, 9% note dated May 22 from Susan Coleman in payment of an account receivable payable at Third National Bank, Stewart, Tennessee.

July 13   Received $763.75 from Joseph Roman in payment of note due today including interest.

July 15   Received $1,025 from Nancy Noyes in payment of note due today, including interest.

Aug. 21   Received $808 from Third National Bank in payment of Susan Coleman's note due yesterday, including interest, less a $10 bank collection charge.

Oct. 29   Received a $1,200, 60-day, 11% note dated October 24 from William Hebeler in payment of an account receivable.

Dec. 23   Received $1,222 from William Hebeler for note due today, including interest.

Required:

1.   Prepare entries in general journal form for the foregoing transactions.

2.   Using a notes receivable register like the one illustrated in the text, make the required entries to provide a detailed auxiliary record of the notes received by Ross Boone. Number the notes consecutively, beginning with No. 1.

Problem 12A2   Journal Entries for Discount and Dishonor of Notes Receivable

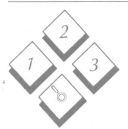

Alice Wetzel owns and operates a merchandising business. On May 1 of the current year, she received a $10,000, 60-day, 10% note from a customer, James O'Donnell, in payment of an account receivable, payable at People's Choice Bank of Kansas City, Missouri.

On May 31, Wetzel discounted the O'Donnell note at People's Choice Bank of Kansas City at a discount rate of 12%.

On June 30, O'Donnell dishonored the $10,000 note and Wetzel was obliged to pay the bank the face of the note, plus interest, plus a $15 protest fee.

Required:

   1. Calculate the proceeds of the discounted note.
   2. Prepare entries in general journal form for the following:
      (a) Wetzel's receipt of the O'Donnell note
      (b) The discounting of the note
      (c) The payment of the dishonored note

Problem 12A3   Journal Entries for Notes and Interest Payable; Notes Payable Register

M.D. Steider operates a retail business. Occasionally short-term notes are issued to suppliers in return for an extension of time on payment of their account balances. During certain seasons of the year Steider finds it necessary to borrow funds at the bank to meet current expenses and to provide additional working capital. Following is a narrative of transactions involving notes issued during the current year.

It is recommended that the required entry in the notes payable register be made immediately after the related transaction has been entered in the general journal.

   Apr. 16   Borrowed $6,000 at the American National Bank of St. Louis, MO, on a 90-day, 11% note, (note No. 21).

   June 14   Issued an $875, 90-day, 10% note to Barber & Moloney, in payment of an account payable, (note No. 22).

   July 15   Paid $6,165 to American National Bank for note due today, including interest.

   Aug. 13   Issued an $880, 60-day, 9% note to Anita Rao, in payment of an account payable, (note No. 23).

   Sept. 12   Paid $896.88 to Barber & Moloney for note due today including interest.

   Oct. 12   Paid Anita Rao $13.20 for interest due today. Issued a new $880, 60-day 9% note in settlement of the note due today, (note No. 24).

   Nov. 19   Borrowed $10,000 from the American National Bank of St. Louis, MO on a 30-day, 11% note, (note No. 25).

   Dec. 11   Paid Anita Rao $893.20 for note due today, including interest.

   Dec. 19   Paid $10,091.67 to the American National Bank of St. Louis, MO for note due today plus interest.

Required:

As the accountant for M.D. Steider you are required to do the following:

1. Prepare entries in general journal form for the foregoing transactions.
2. Make the required entries in a notes payable register like the one illustrated in the text to provide a detailed auxiliary record of the notes issued by M.D. Steider.

Series B

Problem 12B1   Journal Entries for Notes and Interest Receivable; Notes Receivable Register

Margie Lotz operates a merchandising business. Occasionally short-term notes are accepted from customers who are unable to pay their accounts when due and who seek extensions of time by giving notes. Following is a narrative of transactions involving notes received during the current year.

It is recommended that the required entry in the notes receivable register be made immediately after the related transaction has been entered in the general journal.

Apr. 12	Received a $600, 60-day, 9% note dated April 10 from Shirley Gaskins in payment of an account receivable.
May 10	Received a $700, 90-day, 11% note, dated May 8 from William Guth in payment of an account receivable payable at Fifth Third Bank, Crestwood, MO.
May 18	Received a $900, 60-day, 10% note dated May 15 from Gayle Armbruster in payment of an account receivable.
June 9	Received $609 from Shirley Gaskins for note due today including interest.
July 16	Received $915 from Gayle Armbruster for note due July 14 (weekend), including interest.
Aug. 7	Received $707.25 from Fifth Third Bank in payment of William Guth note due yesterday, including interest, less a $12 collection charge.
Oct. 25	Received an $800, 60-day, 11% note dated October 22 from Lawrence Lees in payment of an account receivable.
Dec. 21	Received $814.67 from Lawrence Lees for note due today, including interest.

Required:

1. Prepare entries in general journal form for the foregoing transactions.
2. Using a notes receivable register like the one illustrated in the text, make the required entries to provide a detailed auxiliary record of the notes received by Margie Lotz. Number the notes consecutively, beginning with No. 1.

Problem 12B2   Journal Entries for Discount and Dishonor of Notes Receivable

Thomas Holling owns and operates a merchandising business. On June 1 of the current year, he received a $15,000, 90-day, 9% note from a customer, Paula

Biehl, in payment of an account receivable, payable at Farmers and Merchants Bank of Bloomington, Illinois.

On July 1 Holling discounted the Biehl note at Farmers and Merchants Bank at a discount rate of 11%.

On August 30 Biehl dishonored the $15,000 note and Holling was obliged to pay the bank the face of the note, plus interest, plus a $12 protest fee.

Required:

    1. Calculate the proceeds of the discounted note.

    2. Prepare entries in general journal form for the following:

        (a) Holling's receipt of the Biehl note

        (b) The discounting of the note

        (c) The payment of the dishonored note

Problem 12B3   Journal Entries for Notes and Interest Payable; Notes Payable Register

T.W. Brockland operates a retail business. Occasionally short-term notes are issued to suppliers in return for an extension of time on payment of their account balances. During certain seasons of the year Brockland finds it necessary to borrow funds at the bank to meet current expenses and to provide additional working capital. Following is a narrative of transactions involving notes issued during the current year.

It is recommended that the required entry in the notes payable register be made immediately after the related transaction has been entered in the general journal.

Mar. 14 Borrowed $8,000 at the First Community Bank, Whitewater, WI, on a 90-day, 12% note, (note No. 31).

May 11 Issued a $950, 90-day, 11% note to Jackes & Evans in payment of an account payable (note No. 32).

June 12 Paid $8,240 to First Community Bank for note due today including interest.

July 10 Issued $775, 60-day, 9% note to Judy Sewing in payment of an account receivable, (note No. 33).

Aug. 9 Paid $976.13 to Jackes & Evans for note due today including interest.

Sept. 8 Paid Judy Sewing $11.63 for interest due today. Issued a new $775, 60-day, 9% note in settlement of the note due today, (note No. 34).

Oct. 18 Borrowed $12,000 from the First Community Bank of Whitewater, WI on a 30-day, 12% note, (note No. 35).

Nov. 7 Paid Judy Sewing $786.63 for note due today, including interest.

Nov. 17 Paid $12,120 to the First Community Bank of Whitewater, WI for note due today including interest.

Required:

    1. Prepare entries in general journal form for the foregoing transactions.

    2. Make the required entries in a notes payable register like the one illustrated in the text to provide a detailed auxiliary record of the notes issued by T.W. Brockland.

Mastery Problem

Eddie Edwards and Phil Bell own and operate The Second Hand Equipment Shop. The following transactions involving notes and interest were completed during the last three months of 19-B.

Oct.   1   Purchased used farm equipment from Mac Farm Equipment by issuing a $6,800, 60-day, 10% note.

Oct. 15   Sold merchandise to R. Chambers. Received $500 plus a $2,000, 60-day, 12% note from R. Chambers.

Nov.   1   Discounted the note received from R. Chambers on October 15 at Merchants National Bank. The bank applied a 14% discount rate.

Nov.   1   Borrowed $5,000 from First National Bank on a 3-month, non-interest-bearing note which was discounted at 10%.

Nov. 20   Received a $4,000, 90-day, 9% note from L. Revsine in payment of an account receivable.

Nov. 30   Issued a check to Mac Farm Equipment in payment of the note issued on October 1 including interest.

Dec. 10   Issued a $3,000, 90-day, 9% note to Remak Tractors to obtain an extension of the time for payment of the amount due them on account.

Dec. 16   Edwards and Bell are notified by Merchants National Bank that R. Chambers has dishonored his note. A check is issued to cover the note plus a $20 penalty that must be paid to the bank.

Required:

1. Prepare general journal entries for the above transactions.
2. Prepare necessary adjusting entries for the notes outstanding on December 31.

CHAPTER 13

Accounting for Inventory and Prepaid Expenses

Chapter Objectives

Careful study of this chapter should enable you to:

- Describe the two principal systems of accounting for inventory—the periodic system and the perpetual system.

- Explain the procedures for determining the end-of-period physical quantity of goods on hand.

- Explain and contrast the specific identification, fifo, weighted average, and lifo methods of cost assignment to inventory.

- Use the lower of cost or market rule in connection with the specific identification, fifo, weighted average, and lifo methods.

- Explain the gross margin and simplified retail methods of estimating the amount to be assigned to the end-of-period inventory.

- Explain and contrast the asset method and the expense method of accounting for prepaid expenses.

Merchandise inventory and prepaid expenses have an important characteristic in common: both represent costs incurred in one accounting period that are expected in part to benefit the following period. Since the benefit is expected to be realized within a relatively short time, these assets are considered to be current rather than long-term. In most cases, the dollar amount of merchandise inventory is much larger than that for prepaid expenses. For this reason, accounting for merchandise inventory poses a much greater challenge and receives much more attention.

Merchandise Inventory

One of the major reasons for processing accounting information is to determine the net income (or net loss) of a business on a periodic basis. If the business purchases and sells merchandise, the cost of all merchandise available for sale during the accounting period (goods on hand at the start of the period plus net purchases) must be apportioned in a reasonable manner between the expense called cost of goods sold (merchandise inventory expense) and the asset commonly called merchandise inventory. Accounting procedures for merchandise, using accounts for purchases, purchases returns and allowances, purchases discounts, and merchandise inventory, were discussed and illustrated in preceding chapters. Procedures for determining the quantity of goods on hand at the end of the period and assigning a cost to these goods will be discussed in this chapter.

Types of Inventory Systems

Describe the two principal systems of accounting for inventory—periodic and perpetual.

There are two principal systems of accounting for inventory: (1) the periodic system and (2) the perpetual system. Under the periodic system, the balance in the merchandise inventory account is merely a record of the most recent physical inventory count, usually taken only once a year. As explained in Chapter 6, the purchases account is debited for the cost of all goods bought at their respective invoice prices. As explained in Chapter 7, the sales account is credited for the respective selling prices of all goods sold. Under this system, the current merchandise inventory and the cost of goods sold are not determined until the end of the accounting period, at which time the following formula is applied:

    Beginning inventory (last year's physical count)
+ Net purchases (account balance at end of this year)
– <u>Ending inventory (this year's physical count)</u>
= Cost of goods sold (for the year)

Net purchases is calculated by subtracting purchases discounts and purchases returns and allowances from the purchases account balance.

Under the perpetual system, the merchandise inventory account is an active account. It is debited for the cost of all goods bought at their respective invoice prices and credited with the assumed cost of all goods sold, as well as the cost of any inventory returns, allowances, or discounts. Thus the balance of the account represents the cost of goods on hand at all times. No purchases or contra purchases accounts are used. When goods are sold a cost of goods sold account is debited for the same amount that the merchandise inventory account is credited.

The following purchases and sales transactions and related journal entries illustrate the difference in accounting procedures under the periodic and perpetual inventory systems.

Purchases and Sales Transactions

Jan.   2   *Purchased 100 cans of lubricant for $400 on account.*
     17   *Sold 30 cans of lubricant for $150 on account. The total cost of the 30 cans of lubricant was $120 (30 cans × $4).*

Journal Entries

	Periodic			*Perpetual*		
Purchases:	Purchases	400		Merchandise Inventory	400	
	Accounts Payable		400	Accounts Payable		400
Sales:	Accounts Receivable . . .	150		Accounts Receivable	150	
	Sales		150	Sales		150
				Cost of Goods Sold	120	
				Merchandise Inventory		120

Taking a Physical Inventory

Explain the procedures for determining the end-of-period physical quantity of goods on hand.

As explained above, under the periodic inventory system, businesses do not maintain a record that shows the quantity and the cost of the merchandise currently on hand. Therefore, to apportion merchandise costs between sold and unsold goods, first the goods that are on hand at the end of the period must be counted or measured. This process is called taking a physical inventory.

Taking a physical inventory of a stock of merchandise can be a sizable task. Frequently it is done after regular business hours. Some firms cease operations for a few days to take inventory. The ideal time to count the goods is when the quantity on hand is at its lowest level. A fiscal year that starts and ends at the time the stock of goods is normally at its lowest level is known as a natural business year. Such a year is used by many businesses for accounting purposes.

It is desirable for all goods on hand to be inventoried in as short a time as possible. Extra help may be employed in order to take the inventory. Even if this is done, however, the taking of an inventory may require several days. If regular business is carried on during this time, special records must be kept of additions to and subtractions from the stock during the inventory-taking period. In this way, the quantities of goods that are on hand at the end of the last day of the fiscal period can be determined.

Various procedures are followed in taking an inventory to ensure that no items are missed and that no items are included more than once. Frequently persons taking inventory work in pairs: one counts the items and the other records the information. Usually this information is entered on a special form called an inventory sheet, such as the one illustrated below. The inventory sheet is arranged with columns for recording the description of each item, the quantity on hand, the cost per unit, and the extension. The extension is the amount that results from multiplying the quantity by the unit cost. The cost per unit usually is determined and the extensions completed after the count is finished. Two extension columns are provided so that subtotals can be separated from totals.

Only goods that are the property of the firm should be included in a physical inventory. Two special situations in which care must be taken to determine ownership are (1) goods acquired and later sold on consignment and (2) goods in transit. The important thing to remember about

INVENTORY Aug. 31 19 -A   Page 1

Sheet No. ___1___

Called by *L.M.M.* Department ___A___

Entered by *K.N.* Location ___Storeroom___

Costed by ___C.M.H.___

Extended by ___C.M.H.___

Examined by ___C.J.C.___

Description	Quantity	Unit	Unit Cost	Extensions	
Table lamp	20	ea.	62.80	1,256.00	
Wall rack	18	ea.	19.70	354.60	
Bookcase	7	ea.	88.10	616.70	
End table	13	ea.	53.20	691.60	
Desk	6	ea.	158.30	949.80	
Total					6,465.10

Inventory Sheet

goods on consignment is that they remain the property of the shipper (**consignor**) and should not be included in the inventory of the company holding the goods (**consignee**). Thus if a company has acquired goods on consignment, they should not be included in that company's inventory. If a company has shipped goods on consignment for later sale, they should be included in that company's inventory.

To determine whether goods in transit at year end should be included in inventory, it is necessary to know the FOB terms. If goods are shipped FOB shipping point, the goods are the property of the buying company as soon as they are shipped. If goods are shipped FOB destination, the goods are the property of the selling company until they are received by the buying company.

Assigning Cost to Inventory Under the Periodic System

Explain and contrast the specific identification, fifo, weighted average, and lifo methods of cost assignment to inventory.

After the quantities of goods owned have been calculated at the end of the accounting period, the next step is to determine how much cost should be assigned to the inventory. In determining the cost to be assigned, it is proper to include a fair share of any transportation costs that were incurred when the goods were purchased. Therefore, cost means all cost accumulated by the time the goods reach the buyer's place of business, not cost at the supplier's shipping point. Transportation charges can be a major part of the total cost of merchandise acquired. In addition, costs should be reduced by the amount of any purchases returns, allowances, or discounts taken.

If all purchases of the same item were made at the same price per unit, the unit cost times the number of units in the inventory would give the total cost to be assigned to those units. Frequently, however, identical items are purchased at different times and at different costs per unit. The question then arises as to which unit costs should be assigned to the goods in the inventory. If it is possible to separately identify and price items on hand when they are sold, an approach to cost assignment called specific identification costing can be used. Often it is impossible or impractical to determine exactly which price was paid for the specific goods that are on hand. If so, one of three other methods of cost assignment can be adopted. These other methods are (1) first-in, first-out costing, (2) weighted average costing, and (3) last-in, first-out costing.

Specific Identification Costing. A method of assigning merchandise cost which requires that each item sold and each item remaining in inventory be separately identified with respect to its purchase cost is called the **specific identification** method. This method is practical only for businesses in which sales volume is relatively low, inventory unit value is relatively high, and items can be distinguished easily from each other. Otherwise, record keeping becomes expensive and time consuming, if not totally impractical.

To illustrate how specific identification costing works, assume the following data for an inventory of children's bicycles:

	Units	Unit Price	Total Cost
On hand at start of period	40	$62	$ 2,480
Purchased during period:			
1st purchase	60	$65	3,900
2nd purchase	80	$67	5,360
3rd purchase	70	$68	4,760
Number of units available for sale	250		$16,500
On hand at end of period	50		
Number of units sold during period	200		

Of the 200 units sold during the period, it is determined from the bicycle serial numbers that 30 were from the beginning inventory, 50 were from the first purchase, 60 were from the second purchase, and 60 were from the last purchase. The cost of goods sold and the cost of inventory at the end of the period are determined as follows:

	Cost of Goods Sold			Cost of Ending Inventory		
Beginning inventory	30 units @ $62 =	$ 1,860		10 units @ $62 =	$ 620	
From 1st purchase	50 units @ $65 =	3,250		10 units @ $65 =	650	
From 2nd purchase	60 units @ $67 =	4,020		20 units @ $67 =	1,340	
From 3rd purchase	60 units @ $68 =	4,080		10 units @ $68 =	680	
Total	200 units	$13,210		50 units	$3,290	

First-In, First-Out Costing. Another widely used method of allocating merchandise cost is called the **first-in first-out** or **fifo** method. This costing method assumes that the first goods bought were the first goods sold and that, therefore, the latest goods bought remain in inventory. Applying this method to the bicycle inventory data, the cost of goods sold and the cost of inventory at the end of the period are determined as follows:

	Cost of Goods Sold			Cost of Ending Inventory	
Beginning inventory	40 units @ $62 =	$ 2,480		-0-	
From 1st purchase	60 units @ $65 =	3,900		-0-	
From 2nd purchase.	80 units @ $67 =	5,360		-0-	
From 3rd purchase	20 units @ $68 =	1,360	50 units @ $68 =	$3,400	
Total	200 units	$13,100	50 units	$3,400	

Note that the 50 items on hand at the end of the period are considered to be those most recently purchased. The term "fifo" relates to the goods sold during the accounting period and not to the goods in inventory at the end of the period.

Whenever the flow of merchandise can be controlled, a business will sell the older goods first. First-in, first-out costing is, therefore, widely used (1) because it usually follows the actual movement of goods, and (2) because it assigns the most recent purchase costs to the ending inventory shown in the balance sheet. The fifo costing method satisfies those accountants who contend that inventory should be shown on the balance sheet at the most current cost possible.

Another reason for the continuing widespread use of fifo costing is the fact that firms have used this method for a long time. Accountants are reluctant to change a long-followed method of accounting when such a change would affect the comparability of their income calculations over a period of years. Consistency based on comparability is important in accounting.

■■■■ **Weighted Average Costing.** Another method of allocating merchandise cost is called the **weighted average cost** method, also known as the **average cost** method. This costing method is based on the average cost of identical units.

Using the bicycle inventory data, the average cost of identical units is determined by dividing the total cost of units available for sale ($16,500) by the total number of units available for sale (250).

$$\frac{\$16,500 \text{ (cost of units available for sale)}}{250 \text{ (units available for sale)}} = \$66 \text{ weighted average cost per unit}$$

The cost of goods sold and the cost of the end-of-period inventory are calculated as follows:

Cost of goods sold	200 units @ $66 =	$13,200
Cost of ending inventory.	50 units @ $66 =	3,300
Total	250 units	$16,500

There is a logical appeal to the use of the weighted average basis to allocate cost between goods sold and goods on hand. In this example, one fifth (50) of the total units available (250) were unsold. The average cost basis assigns one fifth ($3,300) of the total cost ($16,500) to these goods.

■■■■ **Last-In, First-Out Costing.** A fourth method of allocating merchandise cost is called the **last-in, first-out** or **lifo** method. It assumes that the sales in the period were made from the most recently purchased goods and that, therefore, the earliest goods bought remain in inventory. Applying this method to the bicycle inventory data, the cost of goods sold and the cost of inventory at the end of the period are determined as follows:

	Cost of Goods Sold	Cost of Ending Inventory
Beginning inventory	-0-	40 units @ $62 = $2,480
From 1st purchase	50 units @ $65 = $ 3,250	10 units @ $65 = 650
From 2nd purchase.	80 units @ $67 = 5,360	-0-
From 3rd purchase	70 units @ $68 = 4,760	-0-
Total	200 units $13,370	50 units $3,130

Note that the 50 units on hand at the end of the period are considered to be the 40 units that were on hand at the start of the period plus 10 of the units from the first purchase. The term "lifo" relates to the goods sold during the accounting period and not to the goods in inventory at the end of the period.

The lifo method has been justified on the grounds that the physical movement of goods in some businesses is actually last-in, first-out. This is rarely the case, but the method has become popular for other reasons. One persuasive argument for the use of the lifo method is that it matches the most current cost of items purchased against the current sales revenue. When the most current costs of purchases are subtracted from sales revenue, the impact of changing prices on the resulting gross margin figure is minimized. In the opinion of many accountants, this is proper and desirable.

Probably the major reason for the popularity of the lifo method is the fact that when prices are rising, net income calculated by using the lifo method will be less than net income calculated by using either the fifo or the weighted average method. Since the net income amount under lifo will be less, the related income tax will be less. The reverse would be true if prices were falling, but periods of falling prices over the past two centuries have been few and of short duration.

Opponents of the lifo method contend that its use causes old, out-of-date inventory costs to be shown on the balance sheet. The theoretical and practical merits of fifo versus lifo are the subject of much professional debate.

■■■■ **Physical Flows and Cost Flows.** It is important to recognize that of the four inventory costing methods described, only the specific identification costing method will necessarily reflect cost flows that match physical flows of goods. Each of the other three methods— fifo, weighted average, and lifo—is based on assumed cost flows which are not required to reflect the actual physical movement of goods within the company. Any one of the three assumed cost flow methods can be used under any set of physical flow conditions.

Comparison of Methods. To compare the results obtained by the use of the four cost assignment methods discussed, assume that the 200 bicycle units in our example were sold for $18,000. The following tabulation contrasts the cost assigned to the ending inventory and to the cost of goods sold and the resultant gross margin under each of the four methods.

	Specific Identification	Fifo	Weighted Average	Lifo
Sales	$18,000	$18,000	$18,000	$18,000
Cost of goods sold:				
Beginning inventory	$ 2,480	$ 2,480	$ 2,480	$ 2,480
Purchases	14,020	14,020	14,020	14,020
Merchandise available for sale	$16,500	$16,500	$16,500	$16,500
Less ending inventory	3,290	3,400	3,300	3,130
Cost of goods sold	$13,210	$13,100	$13,200	$13,370
Gross margin	$ 4,790	$ 4,900	$ 4,800	$ 4,630

Note that in all cases the total cost of merchandise available for sale ($16,500) is the same. It is the apportionment between goods sold and goods on hand at the end of the period that differs. For example, under fifo costing, $13,100 is apportioned to cost of goods sold and $3,400 to ending inventory. Under conditions of rising prices, the gross margin is lowest if lifo is used because the most recent, and therefore the highest, purchase costs are matched against sales revenue. Under conditions of falling prices, the gross margin would be lowest if fifo were used because the earliest, and therefore the highest, purchase costs would be matched against sales revenue.

It is common practice to describe the methods that have been discussed as methods of inventory valuation. It should be apparent, however, that this process also values the cost of goods sold. The term "valuation" is somewhat misleading, since what is involved is really cost apportionment.

The Perpetual Inventory System and Cost Assignment

Describe the perpetual system of accounting for inventory.

When a firm uses a perpetual inventory system, **perpetual inventory records** are kept that provide a continuous record of the quantities and costs of goods on hand at all times. The general ledger account for Merchandise Inventory under such a system is somewhat like the account for Cash in that a chronological record of each addition (purchase) and subtraction (sale) is maintained. The balance of the account at any time shows the cost of goods that should be on hand.

When perpetual inventory records are kept, the merchandise inventory account in the general ledger is usually a control account. A subsidiary ledger is maintained with an account for each type of goods. These accounts are often recorded on cards or in computer files which are designed to handle additions and subtractions, and determine the new balance after each change. Goods sold usually are assigned cost on either a fifo, weighted average, or lifo basis. Procedures for applying the fifo method in a perpetual inventory system are similar to those illustrated for a periodic system. The first merchandise purchased simply is treated as the first merchandise sold. The specific techniques used to apply the weighted average and lifo methods in a perpetual system are more complicated and are illustrated in more advanced texts.

Many types of businesses maintain perpetual inventory records in quantities only, using supplementary or auxiliary records of inventory items, called **stock records**. Stock records serve as a guide in purchasing operations, may help to reveal any shortages, and may be helpful in assigning merchandise cost to inventory and cost of goods sold for interim-statement purposes.

Perpetual inventories do not eliminate the need for taking periodic physical inventories. The perpetual records must be compared with the physical inventory from time to time to discover and correct any errors. However, it is not always necessary to count everything at the same time. The stock can be counted and the records verified by groups of items, by departments, or by sections as time permits.

If a difference is found between the physical count and the amount in the perpetual inventory records, the records must be corrected by an appropriate adjusting entry, normally using an account called Inventory Short and Over. For example, if the book balance is $3,840 and the physical count shows $3,710, the $130 shortage would be entered as follows:

Inventory Short and Over............................	130	
Merchandise Inventory............................		130
To adjust inventory per physical count.		

Similarly, if the book balance is $3,840 and the physical count shows $3,900, this $60 overage would be entered as follows:

Merchandise Inventory	60	
Inventory Short and Over.........................		60
To adjust inventory per physical count.		

The balance in the Inventory Short and Over account at the end of the year may be reported as miscellaneous expense or miscellaneous revenue on the income statement.

A business that sells a wide selection of comparatively low-cost goods (such as a limited-price variety store) may not find it practical to keep a perpetual inventory. In contrast, a business that sells a relatively few high-cost items (an automobile dealer, for example) can maintain such a record without incurring excessive processing cost. The increasing use of the microcomputer and "point-of-sale" recording probably will cause more businesses to switch from periodic to perpetual inventories.

Lower of Cost or Market Method of Inventory Valuation

Use the lower of cost or market rule in connection with the specific identification, fifo, weighted average, and lifo methods.

It is a well-established tradition in accounting that, except in very unusual cases, gains should not be recognized unless a sale has occurred. If the value of an asset increases while it is being held, no formal entry of the gain is made on the books because it has not been actually realized. On the other hand, if the value or usefulness of an asset declines while it is being held, it is generally considered proper to recognize and enter the loss, even though it has not yet been realized. This is in keeping with the practice of conservatism, which states that gains should not be anticipated, but that all potential losses should be recognized.

As applied to inventory, conservatism means that if the value of inventory declines while it is being held, the loss should be recognized in the period of the decline. The purpose of the lower of cost or market method is to see that such losses are recognized.

In applying the lower of cost or market method, "cost" means the amount calculated using one of the four cost assignment methods described in the previous section (except that lower of cost or market may not be used with lifo for tax purposes). "Market" means the cost to replace. It is the prevailing price in the market in which goods are purchased—not the prevailing price in the market in which they are normally sold. The lower of cost or market method assumes that a decline in the purchase (replacement) price of inventory generally is accompanied by a decline in the selling price. In this sense, a decline in the purchase (replacement) price signals a decline in the value of the inventory. Accountants have assigned upper and lower limits to the market value that may be used in particular cases. The meaning and calculation of these limits is a topic for a more advanced course.

To illustrate the application of the lower of cost or market rule, assume the following end-of-period data with respect to an inventory consisting of three items:

Item	Recorded Purchase Cost	End-of-Period Market Value	Lower of Cost or Market
1	$ 8,000	$ 7,000	$ 7,000
2	9,000	10,000	9,000
3	7,000	6,500	6,500
	$24,000	$23,500	$22,500

The illustration demonstrates two possible ways of making the lower of cost or market calculation. First, the lower of cost or market rule can be applied to the total inventory. In the foregoing illustration, this would involve comparing the $24,000 total cost with the $23,500 total market value. Under the second approach, the rule is applied to each item in inventory. In the foregoing illustration, this would involve comparing the $24,000 total cost with the $22,500 lower of cost or market value determined by comparing cost with market for each item. The approach chosen should be applied consistently between periods.

The difference between the cost and market value is considered a loss due to holding inventory and normally is charged to an account such as "Loss on Write-Down of Inventory." For example, based on application of the method to the total inventory in the above illustration, a $500 loss ($24,000 − $23,500) would need to be recognized as follows:

Loss on Write-Down of Inventory	500	
Merchandise Inventory............................		500
To recognize loss in value of inventory held.		

The loss due to write-down of inventory should be reported on the income statement as an expense, but often is included in cost of goods sold.

The Gross Margin Method of Inventory Estimation

Explain the gross margin method of estimating the amount to be assigned to the end-of-period inventory.

Taking a physical inventory often is such a sizable task that it is attempted only once a year. If interim financial statements are to be prepared, an estimate must be made to allocate the cost of merchandise available for sale between goods sold during the period and goods on hand at the end of the period. One way of doing this is to apply the **gross margin method**, in which the amount of sales during the period is reduced by the normal gross margin (gross profit) percentage to determine the estimated cost of goods sold. Deducting this amount from the total cost of goods available for sale gives the estimated amount of the ending inventory.

To illustrate the gross margin method, assume the following data with respect to a particular firm:

1. Net sales, first month $110,000
2. Normal gross margin as a percentage of sales 40%
3. Inventory, start of period .... $ 80,000
4. Net purchases, first month.................................... $ 70,000

The estimated cost of goods sold for the month and the estimated merchandise inventory at the end of the month would be determined as follows:

1. Estimated cost of goods sold:

Net sales	$110,000
Normal gross margin ($110,000 × 40%)	44,000
Estimated cost of goods sold	$ 66,000

2. Cost of goods available for sale:

Inventory, start of period	$ 80,000
Net purchases, first month	70,000
Cost of goods available for sale	$150,000

3. Estimated inventory at end of month:

Cost of goods available for sale	$150,000
Less estimated cost of goods sold	66,000
Estimated end-of-month inventory	$ 84,000

This computation is applicable only if the normal gross margin on sales has prevailed during the immediate past period and is expected to prevail during the following periods when the goods in the inventory will be sold. This type of calculation also can be used to evaluate the reasonableness of the amount of an inventory that was computed on the basis of a physical count. A sizable difference in the two calculations might indicate a possible mistake in the count, in costing the items, or a marked change in the realized rate of gross margin. The gross margin procedure also can be used to estimate the cost of an inventory that was destroyed by fire or other casualty. Such a calculation might be useful in negotiating an insurance settlement.

The Retail Method of Inventory Estimation

Explain the simplified retail method of estimating the amount to be assigned to the end-of-period inventory.

Many retail merchants use a variation of the gross margin method to calculate cost of goods sold and ending inventory for interim-statement purposes. The procedure employed, called the **retail method** of inventory, requires keeping records of both the cost and selling prices of all goods purchased. This information can be used to compute the ratio between cost and retail (selling) prices. When the amount of retail sales is subtracted from the retail value of all goods available for sale, the result is the estimated retail value of the ending inventory. Multiplying this amount by the ratio of cost to selling price gives the estimated cost of the ending inventory.

Following is an example of the calculation of the estimated cost of merchandise inventory by the retail method:

	Cost	Retail
Inventory, start of period	$ 60,000	$ 85,000
Net purchases during period	126,000	163,000
Merchandise available for sale	$186,000	$248,000
Less sales for period		180,000
Inventory, end of period, at retail		$ 68,000
Ratio of cost to retail prices of merchandise available for sale ($186,000 / $248,000)		75%
Inventory, end of period, at estimated cost (75% of $68,000) ..	$ 51,000	

The foregoing example was simplified by assuming that there were no changes in the prices at which the goods were marked to sell. In practice, such changes as additional markups, markup cancellations, and markdowns are commonplace and the calculation must take such adjustments into consideration.

In addition to using the retail method in estimating the cost of inventory for interim-statement purposes, the ratio of cost to retail that is developed can be used to convert the amount of a physical inventory which originally has been priced at retail to its approximate cost.

Building Your Accounting Knowledge

1. What are the main differences between the periodic system of accounting for inventory and the perpetual system of accounting for inventory?
2. What is the first step in apportioning merchandise costs between sold and unsold goods?
3. If it is assumed that the first units purchased were the first ones sold, what is assumed about the source of the units left at the end of the accounting period?
4. What two factors are taken into account by the weighted average costing method of merchandise cost allocation?
5. If it is assumed that all sales in the accounting period were of the goods most recently purchased, what is assumed about the source of the units left at the end of the accounting period?
6. Under conditions of rising prices, which inventory costing method yields the lowest gross margin? Why?
7. If perpetual inventory records are kept, is it still necessary to take a periodic physical inventory? Why?
8. When "lower of cost or market" is assigned to the items that comprise the ending merchandise inventory, what does "cost" mean? What does "market" mean?
9. For what two major purposes is the gross margin method of inventory estimation utilized?
10. For what two major purposes is the retail method of inventory estimation utilized?

Assignment Box

To reinforce your understanding of the preceding text material, you may complete the following:

Study Guide: Part A
Textbook: Exercises 13A1 through 13A5 and 13B1 through 13B5
Problems 13A1 and 13A2, and 13B1 and 13B2.

Prepaid Expenses

Explain and contrast the asset method and the expense method of accounting for prepaid expenses.

The cost of unused supplies on hand at the close of the accounting period and the portion of prepayments such as insurance, rent and interest that will benefit future periods are known as **prepaid expenses**. Office, store, advertising, and other supplies may not be wholly consumed in the period in which they are acquired. The premiums on insurance policies often are prepaid, but the terms of the policies may extend beyond the current accounting period. Rent and interest may be paid in advance, but the use of the facilities rented or the money borrowed may not occur entirely in the same accounting period.

When accounts are kept on the accrual basis, it is necessary to adjust for prepaid items at the close of each accounting period. There are two acceptable methods of accounting for prepaid items: (1) the asset method and (2) the expense method.

Asset Method of Accounting for Prepaid Expenses

Explain the asset method of accounting for prepaid expenses.

Under the **asset method** of accounting for prepaid expenses, supplies and services that may not be wholly consumed in the period in which they are purchased are entered as assets at the time of purchase. Under this method, it is necessary to adjust the accounts at the end of each accounting period to record the used supplies and services as expenses.

Supplies. Supplies such as office supplies, store supplies, and advertising supplies, which may not be wholly consumed in the accounting period in which they are acquired, are usually entered as assets at the time of purchase. Office supplies include paper, envelopes, pencils, adding machine tape, computer diskettes, printer ribbons, and other miscellaneous supplies that are normally consumed in the operation of an office. When supplies are purchased, the transactions are entered by debiting the appropriate supplies account and crediting Accounts Payable if the purchase is on account or Cash if the purchase is for cash. For example, the purchase of $180 of supplies on account would be entered as follows:

```
Office Supplies ...................................    180
    Accounts Payable ..............................           180
    Purchase of office supplies on account.
```

At the end of each accounting period, an inventory of the office supplies on hand is taken, and an adjusting entry is made for the amount consumed during the period. For example, assume that at the end of the accounting period, the office supplies account shows a debit balance of $984.26 and a physical inventory count reveals that the cost of supplies on hand amounts to $340. The supplies expense for the period can be calculated as $644.26 ($984.26 − $340). The adjusting entry is as follows:

Office Supplies Expense	644.26	
Office Supplies		644.26
Office supplies consumed during period.		

As shown in the T accounts below, after this entry is posted, the office supplies account will have a debit balance of $340, which is reported in the balance sheet as a current asset. The office supplies expense account will have a debit balance of $644.26, which is reported in the income statement as an operating expense.

Office Supplies		Office Supplies Expense	
984.26	644.26	644.26	
340.00			

Store supplies include wrapping paper, twine, tape, bags, containers, and other miscellaneous supplies that are normally consumed in the operation of a store. Advertising supplies include catalogs, circulars, price lists, order blanks, and other miscellaneous supplies that are normally consumed in an advertising program. The purchase of such supplies should be entered in the same manner as the purchase of office supplies. The end-of-period adjusting process and resulting treatment of asset and expense elements on the financial statements are similar.

Postage. A business can meet its postage requirements by (1) buying postage stamps, (2) making a deposit under the postal permit system for a certain amount of postage, or (3) using a postage meter. In the third case, a certain amount of postage is paid for, and the meter is set so that the postage may be used as needed. The cost of postage purchased is usually entered by debiting Postage and crediting the cash account. Some of the postage may be used on packages mailed to customers and some on ordinary mail. If postage used on packages is billed to the customer, the entry for the sale will include a credit to the postage account, such as the following:

Accounts Receivable	122	
Sales		120
Postage		2

Usually no entry is made when postage is used on ordinary mail each day, but periodically the postage on hand is counted (or valued, if a postage meter is used). The difference between the amount of the unused postage on hand and the debit balance of the postage account represents the amount of postage used and not billed to customers. This requires an adjusting entry to the postage account.

To illustrate, assume that the postage account (1) had a debit balance for the amount of postage on hand at the beginning of the month, $76, (2) is debited for the amount of postage purchased during the month, $261.80, and (3) is credited for the amount of postage used on packages during the month, $95. In this case, the account will have a debit balance of $242.80 at the end of the month, as shown in the following T account.

Postage

76.00	95.00
261.80	
242.80	

If, at that time, the actual amount of postage on hand is found to be $62.40, the difference of $180.40 ($242.80 − $62.40) represents the amount of postage that was used and not billed to customers during the month. The following adjusting entry would be made:

Postage Expense...............................	180.40	
Postage......................................		180.40
Amount of postage used on ordinary mail.		

As shown in the T accounts below, after this entry is posted, the postage account will have a debit balance of $62.40, which is reported in the balance sheet as a current asset. The postage expense account will have a debit balance of $180.40, which is reported in the income statement as an operating expense.

Postage		**Postage Expense**	
76.00	95.00	180.40	
261.80	180.40		
62.40			

Insurance. A variety of risks are assumed in the operation of a business. Property such as buildings, furniture, machinery, and merchandise inventory may be damaged or destroyed by fire, water, earthquake, windstorm, or other natural disaster. Many types of property, especially money, may be stolen. State laws impose liability on an employer for employee injury or death arising out of the employees' work. The hazards connected with the ownership and operation of motor vehicles are well known. Accidents to persons unconnected with the business but occurring on business premises pose the threat of lawsuits and possibly large settlements. Loss of income as a result of the interruption of business operations because of a fire or a flood is a possibility.

It is possible to obtain insurance against these types of losses and others. A separate insurance policy relating to each type of risk can be obtained, but the practice of obtaining one policy covering most or all of the risks has become commonplace. The cost of such multi-risk policies is lower than the total of a collection of policies for separate risks.

A contract under which an insurance company (the insurer) agrees to protect the business (the insured) from loss is known as an **insurance policy** The amount that the insured is required to pay for insurance protection is known as the **premium**. The premium is usually stated as a specified rate per $1,000 of insurance. Workers' compensation, automobile, fire and theft insurance policies may be purchased as a comprehensive policy or independent of each other at various times of the year. The amount of the premium will vary according to the item insured. The premium is paid in advance by the insured and the amount paid is usually charged to a prepaid insurance account. This account is classified as a current asset.

The prepaid insurance account gradually decreases in value as the life of the insurance policy grows shorter. At the close of each accounting period the total amount of prepayment that expired during the period is entered as an expense. The expired amount can be determined by referring to the policy (or policies) and calculating the portion of the premium that relates to the year just ended.

If the management of the business does not need a detailed breakdown of the insurance expense, an end-of-year adjusting entry such as the following would suffice:

Insurance Expense	xxx	
Prepaid Insurance		xxx
Insurance expired during the year.		

If more detail about the insurance expense is wanted, it would be possible to analyze the total and to classify it into, perhaps, delivery equipment insurance expense, fire insurance expense (with subclassifications relating to building, furniture and fixtures, and merchandise), and workers' compensation insurance expense. Separate accounts can be established to provide as much detail as needed.

If a business has several insurance policies, it may be useful to maintain an auxiliary record known as an Insurance Policy Register. This record provides spaces to show the date and number of each policy, name of the insurer, type and amount of coverage, total term, expiration date, total premium, and columns to show the premium applicable to each month.

Prepaid Rent. When business property is rented for more than one accounting period on the basis of a lease agreement, and the lease payment is made in advance, the amount of the lease payment usually is treated as prepaid rent. Prepaid rent is classified as a current asset.

At the end of the accounting period, the amount of rent expense relating to the period just ended should be determined, and an adjusting entry made to transfer that portion of the lease payment from the prepaid rent account to the rent expense account. For example, assume that on July 1, an office building was leased by the business for a 2-year period, and a lease payment of $36,000 was made in advance. The entry for the lease payment is as follows:

July 1	Prepaid Rent	36,000	
	Cash		36,000
	Two-year lease of office building.		

By December 31 one-fourth of the lease had expired; therefore, the following adjusting entry was made:

Dec. 31	Rent Expense	9,000	
	Prepaid Rent		9,000
	Prepaid rent transferred to rent expense.		

As shown in the T accounts below, after the foregoing entry is posted, the prepaid rent account will have a debit balance of $27,000, which represents 1 1/2 years that the lease will remain active. The $27,000 of prepaid rent is reported in the balance sheet as a current asset. The $9,000 debit balance of the rent expense account is reported in the income statement under the heading "Operating expenses."

Prepaid Rent		Rent Expense	
36,000	9,000	9,000	
27,000			

One advantage of using the asset method of accounting for prepaid expenses is that the adjusting entries required at the end of the period are of the write-off type. Such adjustments do not need to be reversed at the start of the new period.

Expense Method of Accounting for Prepaid Expenses

Explain the expense method of accounting for prepaid expenses.

Under the **expense method** of accounting for prepaid expenses, supplies and services that may not be wholly consumed in the period in which they are purchased are entered as expenses at the time of purchase. Under this method, it is necessary to adjust the accounts at the end of each accounting period to record the unused portions as assets. For example, if office supplies purchased during an accounting period are charged to the office supplies expense account, it will be necessary to adjust the account at the end of the period for the cost of the supplies on hand. To illustrate, assume that Office Supplies Expense had been charged for a total of $425 during the period and an inventory taken at the end of the period shows that supplies on hand amount to $150. The following adjusting entry is made for supplies on hand:

Office Supplies	150	
Office Supplies Expense		150
Office supplies on hand.		

As shown in the T accounts below, after this entry is posted, the office supplies expense account will have a debit balance of $275, which is reported in the income statement as an operating expense. The office supplies account will have a debit balance of $150, which is reported in the balance sheet as a current asset.

Office Supplies		Office Supplies Expense	
150		425	150
		275	

The adjusting entry for office supplies illustrated above represents a delay in the recognition of the expense portion of a payment already made. This delay is known as a **deferral**. When the expense method of accounting is used, the adjustments made at the end of the period are called **deferral adjustments**, because they defer expenses to the next period. To simplify accounting procedures in the following period, adjustments of this type should be reversed at the start of the new period. In the foregoing example relating to office supplies, the reversing entry would be:

Office Supplies Expense	150	
Office Supplies		150
Reversing entry for supplies.		

The effect of the adjusting, closing, and reversing procedure under the expense method is (1) to remove the unused or unexpired amount from the expense account at the end of the period, (2) to transfer the remaining amount to the expense and revenue summary account, and (3) at the start of the new period, to transfer back to the expense account the amount of expense that previously had been deferred. The following T accounts illustrate the effect of this procedure.

Office Supplies				Office Supplies Expense		
(1)	150	(3)	150	Bal.	425	(1) 150
						(2) 275
						425
				(3)	150	

By reversing the adjusting entry from the prior period, the procedure for determining the appropriate adjusting entry at the end of the new period is simplified. The amount of supplies on hand at the end of the period simply needs to be determined and an adjusting entry made debiting Office Supplies and crediting Office Supplies Expense for that amount. If the prior period's adjusting entry had not been reversed at the beginning of the new period, it would have been necessary to perform three steps: (1) determine the amount of supplies on hand at the end of the period; (2) determine the balance currently in the supplies account; and (3) calculate the adjustment necessary to bring the supplies account balance into agreement with the amount of supplies on hand.

The asset and expense methods of accounting for prepaid expenses give the same final result. In the asset method, an amount that will eventually become the expense of current and future periods is first put into an asset account, and at the end of each period, a proper portion is transferred to an expense account. In the expense method, the original amount is first put into an expense account. At the end of each accounting period, the portion that will be an expense of future periods is moved into an asset account and subsequently brought back into the related expense account by a reversing entry at the start of the new period.

Building Your Accounting Knowledge

1. What are the two methods of entering the amounts of supplies or services purchased when accounts are kept on the accrual basis?
2. How is the value of supplies or postage on hand at the end of the accounting period determined?
3. Under what heading should supplies or postage on hand be reported in the balance sheet?
4. Under what heading should supplies or postage expense be reported in the income statement?
5. Why has the practice of obtaining a single multi-risk insurance policy become commonplace in recent years?
6. Under what heading should prepaid insurance be reported in the balance sheet? Prepaid rent?

7. What type of end-of-period adjusting entries are required when the asset method of accounting for prepaid expenses is used? Do such adjustments need to be reversed?

8. What type of end-of-period adjusting entries are required when the expense method of accounting for prepaid expenses is used? Do such adjustments need to be reversed?

Assignment Box

To reinforce your understanding of the preceding text material, you may complete the following:

      Study Guide: Part B
      Textbook: Exercises 13A6 through 13A7 and 13B6 through 13B7
               Problems 13A3 through 13A5 and 13B3 through 13B5

Expanding Your Business Vocabulary

What is the meaning of each of the following terms?

asset method (p. 522)
average cost (p. 514)
consignee (p. 512)
consignment (p. 511)
consignor (p. 512)
cost (p. 518)
cost apportionment(p. 516)
deferral (p. 527)
deferral adjustments (p. 527)
expense method (p. 526)
first-in, first-out (fifo) (p. 513)
gross margin method (p. 519)
insurance policy (p. 525)
in transit (p. 511)
inventory sheet (p. 511)

last-in, first-out (lifo) (p. 515)
lower of cost or market (p. 518)
market (p. 518)
natural business year (p. 511)
periodic system (p. 510)
perpetual inventory records (p. 516)
perpetual system (p. 510)
practice of conservatism (p. 518)
premium (p. 525)
prepaid expenses (p. 522)
retail method (p. 520)
specific identification (p. 513)
stock records (p. 517)
taking a physical inventory (p. 511)
weighted average cost (p. 514)

Demonstration Problem

The Fialka Company's beginning inventory and purchases during the fiscal year ended October 31, 19-B, were as follows:

	Units	Unit Price	Total Cost
November 1, 19-A, beginning inventory	500	$25.00	$12,500
November 12, 19-A, 1st purchase.....................	600	$26.25	15,750
December 28, 19-A, 2nd purchase	400	$27.50	11,000
March 29, 19-B, 3rd purchase	1,000	$28.00	28,000
May 31, 19-B, 4th purchase..........................	750	$28.50	21,375
July 29, 19-B, 5th purchase	350	$29.00	10,150
August 30, 19-B, 6th purchase	675	$30.00	20,250
October 21, 19-B, 7th purchase	225	$31.00	6,975
	4,500		$126,000

There are 1,600 units of inventory on hand at October 31, 19-B.

Required:

1. Calculate the total amount to be assigned to the ending inventory on October 31, 19-B under each of the following methods:
    (a) First-in, first-out.
    (b) Last-in, first-out.
    (c) Weighted average (round unit costs to two decimal places).
2. Assume that the market price per unit (cost to replace) of the Fialka Company's inventory on October 31, 19-B was $29. Calculate the total amount to be assigned to the ending inventory on October 31, 19-B, under each of the following methods:
    (a) Fifo lower of cost or market.
    (b) Weighted average lower of cost or market.
3. Assume that during the fiscal year ended October 31, 19-B, net sales of $134,000 were made at a normal gross margin rate of 40%. Use the gross margin method to estimate the cost of goods sold for the fiscal year ended October 31, 19-B, and the inventory at October 31, 1991.

Solution

1. (a) First-in, first-out method:

225 units @ $31...	$ 6,975
675 units @ $30...	20,250
350 units @ $29...	10,150
350 units @ $28.50	9,975
1,600 units	$47,350

   (b) Last-in, first-out method:

500 units @ $25...	$12,500
600 units @ $26.25	15,750
400 units @ $27.50	11,000
100 units @ $28.00	2,800
1,600 units	$42,050

   (c) Weighted average method:
   Average cost per unit: $126,000 ÷ 4,500 units = $28.
   Inventory, October 31, 19-B:
   1,600 units @ $28 = $44,800

2. (a) Fifo lower of cost or market:

Fifo cost	$47,350
Market 1,600 @ $29	$46,400
Choose market,	$46,400

(b) Weighted average lower of cost or market:
    Weighted average cost $44,800
    Market 1,600 @ $29 $46,400
    Choose weighted
        average cost, $44,800

3. Estimated cost of goods sold:

Net sales	$134,000
Normal gross margin ($134,000 × 40%)	53,600
Estimated cost of goods sold	$ 80,400

Estimated inventory at October 31, 19-B:

Inventory, Nov. 1, 19-A	$ 12,500
Net purchases, Nov. 1, 19-A-Oct. 31, 19-B	113,500
Cost of goods available for sale	$126,000
Less estimated cost of goods sold	80,400
Estimated inventory at October 31, 19-B	$ 45,600

*Note: Now that you have reviewed the Demonstration Problem and Solution you may complete the **Mastery Problem** at the end of the chapter activities.

Applying Accounting Concepts

Series A

Exercise 13A1—Cost of Goods Sold and Ending Inventory; Specific Identification, Fifo, Weighted Average, Lifo. Assume the following data for a single item of merchandise sold by Oka Company:

	Units	Unit Price	Total Cost
On hand at start of period	500	$8.00	$ 4,000
Purchased during the period:			
1st purchase	400	$8.20	3,280
2nd purchase	700	$8.40	5,880
Number of units available for sale	1,600		$13,160
On hand at end of period	600		
Number of units sold during period	1,000		

Compute the cost of goods sold and ending inventory for Oka Company under each of the following methods:

(a) Specific identification. (Of the 1,000 units sold, 400 were from the beginning inventory, 300 were from the first purchase, and 300 were from the last purchase.)

(b) First-in, first-out.

(c) Weighted average.

(d) Last-in, first-out.

Exercise 13A2—Lower of Cost or Market; Total Inventory and Item by Item. Assume that Vyson Company has three items of inventory with costs and market values at year end as follows:

Item	Cost	Market value
1	$12,000	$10,000
2	$18,000	$20,000
3	$24,000	$22,000

Compute the amount of Vyson's inventory at year end using (a) the lower of cost or market rule applied to the total inventory, and (b) the lower of cost or market rule applied to each item in the inventory.

Exercise 13A3—Gross Margin Method of Estimating Cost of Goods Sold and Ending Inventory. Assume the following data for Simeon Company:

Net sales, February	$240,000
Normal gross margin as a percentage of sales	30%
Inventory, February 1	$180,000
Net purchases, February	$160,000

Use the gross margin method to estimate the cost of goods sold for February and the inventory at February 28.

Exercise 13A4—Retail Method of Estimating Inventory. Assume the following data for Sparks Company:

	Cost	Retail
Inventory, April 1	$100,000	$140,000
Net purchases, April....................................	208,000	300,000
Merchandise available for sale..........................	$308,000	$440,000
Less sales, April.......................................		340,000
Inventory, April 30, at retail		$100,000

Use the retail method to estimate the cost of inventory at April 30.

Exercise 13A5—Entries for Sale Under Perpetual Inventory System. On September 15, Neice Company sold inventory with a cost of $1,400 for $2,100 cash. Prepare the necessary entries for this sale under a perpetual inventory system.

Exercise 13A6—Asset Method of Accounting for Prepaid Expenses. Use the asset method to account for the following prepaid expenses of Locke Company, a new business.

(a) Office supplies were purchased for $1,700 cash.
(b) Rent was paid in advance for a two-year period, $40,000.

At the end of the accounting period, prepare adjusting entries for the following:

(c) Office supplies on hand, $320.
(d) Six months rent has expired.

Exercise 13A7—Expense Method of Accounting for Prepaid Expenses. Assume the same economic events as in Exercise 13A6. Use the expense method to account for the four economic events of Locke Company.

Series B

Exercise 13B1—Cost of Goods Sold and Ending Inventory; Specific Identification, Fifo, Weighted Average, Lifo. Assume the following data for a single item of merchandise sold by Gitel Company:

	Units	Unit Price	Total Cost
On hand at start of period	300	$4.00	$1,200
Purchased during the period:			
1st purchase................................	200	$4.10	820
2nd purchase	500	$4.20	2,100
Number of units available for sale	1,000		$4,120
On hand at end of period	400		
Number of units sold during period	600		

Compute the cost of goods sold and ending inventory for Gitel Company under each of the following methods.

(a) Specific identification. (Of the 600 units sold, 200 were from the beginning inventory, 100 were from the first purchase, and 300 were from the last purchase.)
(b) First-in, first-out.
(c) Weighted average.
(d) Last-in, first-out.

Exercise 13B2—Lower of Cost or Market; Total Inventory and Item by Item. Assume that Flowers Company has three items of inventory with costs and market values at year end as follows:

Item	Cost	Market value
1	$ 9,000	$ 8,000
2	$12,000	$14,000
3	$18,000	$16,000

Compute the amount of Flowers' inventory at year end using (a) the lower of cost or market rule applied to the total inventory, and (b) the lower of cost or market rule applied to each item in the inventory.

Exercise 13B3—Gross Margin Method of Estimating Cost of Goods Sold and Ending Inventory. Assume the following data for Ankney Company:

Net sales, March	$180,000
Normal gross margin as a percentage of sales.....................	30%
Inventory, March 1	$135,000
Net purchases, March	$120,000

Use the gross margin method to estimate the cost of goods sold for March and the inventory at March 31.

Exercise 13B4—Retail Method of Estimating Inventory. Assume the following data for Harre Company:

	Cost	Retail
Inventory, May 1	$30,000	$ 45,000
Net purchases, May	64,500	90,000
Merchandise available for sale..........................	$94,500	$135,000
Less sales, May		100,000
Inventory, May 31, at retail		$ 35,000

Use the retail method to estimate the cost of inventory at May 31.

Exercise 13B5—Entries for Sale Under Perpetual Inventory System. On October 15, Friel Company sold inventory with a cost of $400 for $650 cash. Prepare the necessary entries for this sale under a perpetual inventory system.

Exercise 13B6—Asset Method of Accounting for Prepaid Expenses. Use the asset method to account for the following prepaid expenses of Osterhout Company, a new business.

(a) Office supplies were purchased for $525 cash.
(b) Rent was paid in advance for a two-year period, $12,000.

At the end of the accounting period, prepare adjusting entries for the following:

(c) Office supplies on hand, $95.
(d) Six months' rent has expired.

Exercise 13B7—Expense Method of Accounting for Prepaid Expenses. Assume the same economic events as in Exercise 13B6. Use the expense method to account for the four economic events of Osterhout Company.

Series A

Problem 13A1   Ending Inventory and Gross Margin under Fifo, Weighted Average, and Lifo

The sales of Department B of the Hellweg Supply Company for the year ended September 30, 19--, were as follows:

9,437 units of Item A @ $12.50	....	$117,962.50
3,419 units of Item B @ $25.80	....	88,210.20
2,315 units of Item C @ $23.00	....	53,245.00
Total		$259,417.70

Other information relative to merchandise handled during the year follows:

	ITEM A	ITEM B	ITEM C
Inventory at start of year	2,347 units @ $6.70	895 @ $14.70	810 @ $9.20
1st purchase	3,500 units @ $6.80	3,000 @ $14.90	2,000 @ $9.30
2nd purchase	2,500 units @ $6.90	500 @ $15.20	
3rd purchase	2,500 units @ $7.00		
Ending inventory	1,410 units	976 units	495 units

Required:

1. Calculate the total amount to be assigned to the ending inventory of Department B under each of the following methods:
   (a) Fifo cost.
   (b) Weighted average cost (round unit costs to two decimal places).
   (c) Lifo cost.
2. Use the amounts calculated in part 1 in the format shown at the top of the next page to show the resulting gross margin using:
   (a) The fifo cost basis.
   (b) The weighted average cost basis.
   (c) The lifo cost basis.

Sales
Cost assigned to goods sold:
  Beginning inventory
  Purchases
  Cost of goods available for sale
  Less ending inventory
  Cost of goods sold
Gross margin

Problem 13A2   Ending Inventory and Gross Margin Under Fifo Lower of Cost or Market and Weighted Average Lower of Cost or Market

Refer to Problem 13A1. The sales, inventory, and purchases data of the Hellweg Supply Company remain the same. In addition, the following market price information is available.

	ITEM A	ITEM B	ITEM C
Market price per unit (cost to replace) at end of period	$6.80	$15.40	$9.20

Required:

1. Calculate the total amount to be assigned to the ending inventory of Department B under each of the following methods. (Apply the lower of cost or market method to each item in the inventory.)
  (a) Fifo lower of cost or market.
  (b) Weighted average lower of cost or market.
2. Use the amounts calculated in part 1 in the format shown below to show the resulting gross margin using:
  (a) Fifo lower of cost or market.
  (b) Weighted average lower of cost or market.

Sales
Cost assigned to goods sold:
  Beginning inventory
  Purchases
  Cost of goods available for sale
  Less ending inventory
  Cost of goods sold
Gross margin

Problem 13A3   Journal and Ledger Account Entries Using Asset Method of Accounting for Supplies and Prepayments

The Freedman Company is a wholesale merchandising business. Following are transactions that occurred during the year:

Jan.   8   Received an invoice from Premium Printers for letterheads and envelopes for office use, $572; terms, 30 days.

Mar.   3 Received an invoice from Port Edwards Paper Co. for corrugated board to be used in the store, $420; terms, 30 days.

15 Paid cash for postage stamps, $800.

April 1 Paid the Catastrophic Insurance Co. $578, premium for 1 year on fire insurance policy No. 90167 for $24,000.

May 18 Received an invoice from The Dura-Kraft Paper Co. for wrapping paper to be used in the store, $290; terms, 30 days.

July 12 Received an invoice from the McLean Manufacturing Co. for miscellaneous office supplies, $230; terms, 30 days.

Sept. 1 Paid cash for postage stamps, $800.

Oct. 1 Paid the Svenska Insurance Co. $760, premium for 1 year on fire insurance policy No. 78659 for $25,000.

Dec. 31 To prepare for closing the books for the year, make the proper adjusting entries for the following:
Inventory of store supplies on hand, $864.
Inventory of office supplies on hand, $968.
Inventory of postage stamps on hand, $824.
Insurance expired during year, $1,824.

Required:

Using the asset method of accounting for supplies and prepayments, prepare the proper general journal entries for the above transactions and post to the appropriate four-column ledger accounts. The balances of the accounts as of January 1 are as follows:

Cash, No. 111	$8,256	Store Supplies Expense,	
Store Supplies, No. 151	2,314	No. 543	$ -0-
Office Supplies, No. 152	2,378	Office Supplies Expense,	
Postage Stamps, No. 154	1,274	No. 544	-0-
Prepaid Insurance, No. 155	1,794	Insurance Expense, No. 548	-0-
Accounts Payable, No. 218	16,016	Postage Expense, No. 556	-0-

---

Problem 13A4   Journal Entries Using Expense Method of Accounting for Supplies and Prepayments

Refer to Problem No. 13A3.

Required:

Using the expense method of accounting for supplies and prepayments, prepare the proper adjusting entries in general journal form at Dec. 31, based on the same information provided at Dec. 31 in Problem 13A3.

Problem 13A5   Comprehensive Problem; Journal Entries for Prepaid Insurance and Adjustment of Ledger Account.

The Schleper Company is in the wholesale jewelry business. In accounting for insurance, the following accounts are used:

Prepaid Insurance
Merchandise Insurance Expense
Store Equipment Insurance Expense
Office Equipment Insurance Expense

All premiums paid for insurance are charged to the prepaid insurance account. At the end of each month, the expired insurance is charged to the proper expense accounts and credited to Prepaid Insurance. In addition to the insurance accounts, the firm keeps an auxiliary record of insurance in the form of an insurance policy file. Information from the insurance policy file on 3 policies in effect December 31 of the previous year (19-A) is given below. All of these policies will expire during the current year.

Date of Policy	Policy No.	Insurer	Property Insured	Amount	Expiration Date	Unexpired Premium Dec. 31, 19-A
Mar. 1 19-A	32772	Global Ins. Co.	Mdse.	52,000	Mar. 1, 19-B	67.20
May 1, 19-A	96495	Black Ins. Co.	Mdse.	38,000	May 1, 19-B	144.80
June 1, 19-A	75399	Wholesaler Ins. Co.	Store Equipment	30,000	June 1, 19-B	124.00

Following is a record of the insurance transactions completed during the current year (19-B).

Jan.   3   Paid the premiums on the following additional insurance policies:

No. 76488 dated January 1, 19-B, Wholesaler Insurance Co.; merchandise, $194,000; one year; premium, $1,620.
No. 97292 dated January 1, 19-B, Black Insurance Co.; merchandise, $52,000; three years; premium, $1,080.
No. 52869 dated January 1, 19-B, Global Insurance Co.; office equipment, $34,000; one year; premium, $168.

Feb.   5   Paid $204 premium on insurance policy No. 74569 dated February 1, 19-B, Tranquil Insurance Co.; merchandise, $24,000; term, 1 year.

June 11   Paid $312 premium on insurance policy No. 85426 dated June 1, 19-B, Wholesaler Insurance Co.; Store equipment, $28,000; term, one year. (Renewal of policy expired June 1, 19-B.)

Required:

1. Prepare general journal entries for the transactions involving the premiums paid on new policies purchased during January.
2. Prepare a journal entry for the amount of the insurance premiums expired during January, according to type of insurance.
3. Continue with the work required each month from January through June to enter any premiums paid on new insurance purchased during the month and to enter the total insurance premiums expired during the month.
4. Open a four-column ledger account for Prepaid Insurance, Account No. 155, and debit it for the beginning balance representing the unexpired insurance premiums as of the end of the prior year. (See above.) Post from the general journal all debit and credit entries affecting the prepaid insurance account. After completing each posting to the prepaid insurance account, determine the balance and enter it in the proper balance column.

5. Prove the June 30 balance of the prepaid insurance account by computing the total unexpired premium on the five unexpired policies: No. 76488 (6 mos. remaining); No. 52869 (6 mos. remaining); No. 85426 (11 mos. remaining); No. 97292 (30 mos. remaining); and No. 74569 (7 mos. remaining). Show the proof under the prepaid insurance account.

Series B

Problem 13B1   Ending Inventory and Gross Margin under Fifo, Weighted Average, and Lifo

The sales of Department C of the Calhoun Supply Company for the year ended November 30, 19--, were as follows:

4,718 units of Item A @ $6.25	$29,487.50
1,709 units of Item B @ $12.90	22,046.10
1,157 units of Item C @ $11.50	13,305.50
Total	$64,839.10

Other information relative to merchandise handled during the year follows:

	ITEM A	ITEM B	ITEM C
Inventory at start of year	1,173 units @ $3.35	447 @ $7.35	405 @ $4.60
First purchase	1,750 units @ $3.40	1,500 @ $7.45	1,000 @ $4.65
Second purchase	1,250 units @ $3.45	250 @ $7.60	
Third purchase	1,250 units @ $3.50		
Ending inventory	705 units	488 units	247 units

Required:
1. Calculate the total amount to be assigned to the ending inventory of Department C under each of the following methods:
   (a) Fifo cost.
   (b) Weighted average cost (round unit costs to two decimal places).
   (c) Lifo cost.
2. Use the amounts calculated in part 1 in the format shown below to show the resulting gross margin using:
   (a) The fifo cost basis.
   (b) The weighted average cost basis.
   (c) The lifo cost basis.

   Sales
   Cost assigned to goods sold:
     Beginning inventory
     Purchases
     Cost of goods available for sale
     Less ending inventory
     Cost of goods sold
   Gross margin

Problem 13B2	**Ending Inventory and Gross Margin under Fifo Lower of Cost or Market and Weighted Average Lower of Cost or Market**

Refer to Problem 13B1. The sales, inventory, and purchases data of the Calhoun Supply Company remain the same. In addition, the following market price information is available.

	ITEM A	ITEM B	ITEM C
Market price per unit (cost to replace) at end of period	$3.40	$7.70	$4.60

Required:

1. Calculate the total amount to be assigned to the ending inventory of Department C under each of the following methods. (Apply the lower of cost or market method to each item in the inventory.)
   (a) Fifo lower of cost or market.
   (b) Weighted average lower of cost or market.
2. Use the amounts calculated in part (1) in the format shown below to show the resulting gross margin using:
   (a) Fifo lower of cost or market
   (b) Weighted average lower of cost or market

   Sales
   Cost assigned to goods sold:
      Beginning inventory
      Purchases
      Cost of goods available for sale
      Less ending inventory
      Cost of goods sold
   Gross margin

Problem 13B3	**Journal and Ledger Account Entries Using Asset Method of Accounting for Supplies and Prepayment**

The Dugle Company is a wholesale merchandising business. Following are transactions that occurred during the year:

Jan. **10** Received an invoice from Consistent Printers for letterheads and envelopes for office use, $429; terms, 30 days.

Mar. **5** Received an invoice from Manalow Paper Co. for corrugated board to be used in the store, $315; terms, 30 days.

17 Paid cash for postage stamps, $600.

Apr. **1** Paid the Accurate Insurance Co. $435, premium for 1 year on fire insurance policy No. 67019 for $18,000.

May 20 Received an invoice from The Creative Paper Co. for wrapping paper to be used in the store, $215; terms, 30 days.

July 14 Received an invoice from the Moksnes Manufacturing Co. for miscellaneous office supplies, $175; terms, 30 days.

Sept. **3** Paid cash for postage stamps, $600.

Oct. 1 Paid the Dansk Insurance Co. $570, premium for 1 year on fire insurance policy No. 69785 for $18,500.

Dec. 31 To prepare for closing the books for the year, make the proper adjusting entries for the following:

Inventory of store supplies on hand, $648.

Inventory of office supplies on hand, $726.

Inventory of postage stamps on hand, $618.

Insurance expired during year, $1,368.

Required:

Using the asset method of accounting for supplies and prepayments, prepare the proper general journal entries for the above transactions and post to the appropriate four-column ledger accounts. The balances of the accounts as of January 1 are as follows:

Cash, No. 111	6,192	Store Supplies Expense, No.	
Store Supplies, No. 151	1,736	543	-0-
Office Supplies, No. 152	1,784	Office Supplies Expense, No.	
Postage Stamps, No. 154	956	544	-0-
Prepaid Insurance, No. 155 . . .	1,346	Insurance Expense, No. 548 . .	-0-
Accounts Payable, No. 218 . . .	12,014	Postage Expense, No. 556	-0-

---

Problem 13B4   Journal Entries Using Expense Method of Accounting for Supplies and Prepayments

Refer to Problem No. 13B3.

Required:

Using the expense method of accounting for supplies and prepayments, prepare the proper adjusting entries in general journal form at Dec. 31, based on the same information provided at Dec. 31 in Problem 13B3.

Problem 13B5   Comprehensive Problem; Journal Entries for Prepaid Insurance and Adjustment of Ledger Account

The Cohen Company is in the wholesale jewelry business. In accounting for insurance, the following accounts are used:

Prepaid Insurance

Merchandise Insurance Expense

Store Equipment Insurance Expense

Office Equipment Insurance Expense

All premiums paid for insurance are charged to the prepaid insurance account. At the end of each month, the expired insurance is charged to the proper expense accounts and credited to Prepaid Insurance. In addition to the insurance accounts, the firm keeps an auxiliary record of insurance in the form of an insurance policy file. Information from the insurance policy file on 3 policies in effect December 31 of the previous year (19-A) is given below. All of these policies will expire during the current year.

Date of Policy	Policy No.	Insurer	Property Insured	Amount	Expiration Date	Unexpired Premium Dec. 31, 19-A
Mar. 1 19-A	22737	World-wide Ins. Co.	Mdse.	39,000.00	Mar. 1, 19-B	50.40
May 1, 19-A	59649	Green Ins. Co.	Mdse.	28,000.00	May 1, 19-B	108.60
June 1, 19-A	75939	Jeweler's Ins. Co.	Store Equipment	22,500.00	June 1, 19-B	93.00

Following is a record of the insurance transactions completed during the current year (19-B).

Jan. 2 Paid the premiums on the following additional insurance policies:

No. 78648 dated January 1, 19-B, Jarrod's Insurance Co.; merchandise, $145,500; one year; premium, $1,215.

No. 59922 dated January 1, 19-B, Black Insurance Co.; merchandise, $39,000; three years; premium, $810.

No. 29865 dated January 1, 19-B, Worldwide Insurance Co.; office equipment, $25,500; one year; premium, $126.

Feb. 4 Paid $153 premium on insurance policy No. 64597 dated February 1, 19-B, Capital Insurance Co.; merchandise, $18,000; term, 1 year.

June 10 Paid $234 premium on insurance policy No. 84562 dated June 1, 19-B, Jarrod's Insurance Co.; store equipment, $21,000; term, one year. (Renewal of policy expired June 1, 19-B.)

Required:

1. Prepare general journal entries for the transactions involving the premiums paid on new policies purchased during January.

2. Prepare a journal entry for the amount of the insurance premiums expired during January, according to type of insurance.

3. Continue with the work required each month from January through June to enter any premiums paid on new insurance purchased during the month and to enter the total insurance premiums expired during the month.

4. Open a four-column ledger account for Prepaid Insurance, Account No. 155, and debit it for the beginning balance representing the unexpired insurance premiums as of the end of the prior year (see above). Post from the general journal all debit and credit entries affecting the prepaid insurance account. After completing each posting to the prepaid insurance account, determine the balance and enter it in the proper balance column.

5. Prove the June 30 balance of the prepaid insurance account by computing the total unexpired premium on the five unexpired policies: No. 78648 (6 mos. remaining); No. 29865 (6 mos. remaining); No. 84562 (11 mos. remaining); No. 59922 (30 mos. remaining); and No. 64597 (7 mos. remaining). Show the proof under the prepaid insurance account.

**Mastery
Problem**

Jim Kitchell opened a new business on July 1, 19-A. Financial statements were prepared as of December 31, 19-A. Kitchell uses the asset method of accounting for insurance and supplies, and the expense method of accounting for rent. He employs the periodic method of accounting for inventory. Selected account balances are reported below for January 1, 19-B.

Merchandise Inventory	$50,000	
Prepaid Insurance	4,500	(Paid $6,000 for a 2-year policy on July 1, 19-A.)
Supplies	800	
Prepaid Rent	6,000	(Paid $12,000 for 1 year's rent on July 1, 19-A.)

The following summary transactions occurred during 19-B:

(a) Purchased supplies at a cost of $2,800.
(b) Paid one year's rent in advance on July 1, 19-B, $13,200.
(c) Beginning and ending inventory as well as purchases are listed below.

	Units		Unit Price	Total Cost
Inventory (1/1/B)	500	@	$100	$ 50,000
Purchase #1	400	@	$110	44,000
Purchase #2	800	@	$120	96,000
Purchase #3	1,000	@	$130	130,000
Purchase #4	1,500	@	$140	210,000
Purchase #5	300	@	$150	45,000
Ending Inventory	1,000			

Required:

1. Prepare any necessary reversing entries on January 1, 19-B.
2. Prepare general journal entries for payments made for supplies, rent, and inventory.
3. Prepare adjusting entries for insurance, supplies and rent. An inventory of supplies reveals that there are $700 in supplies on hand.
4. Compute the cost of the ending inventory and cost of goods sold under the fifo, lifo and weighted average methods. (To avoid large rounding errors, you may want to carry out the weighted average calculations to several decimal places.)
5. Assume that the market price per unit of the ending inventory was $130. Calculate the total amount to be assigned to the ending inventory under fifo lower of cost or market.

CHAPTER 14

Accounting for Property, Plant, and Equipment

Chapter Objectives	Careful study of this chapter should enable you to:

- Determine the cost of property, plant, and equipment.

- Explain the nature and purpose of depreciation.

- Explain how to apply the following depreciation methods:

    1. Straight-line
    2. Declining-balance
    3. Sum-of-the-years digits
    4. Units-of-output

- Explain the possible effects of different depreciation methods on the balance sheet and income statement.

- Describe acceptable depreciation methods for federal income tax purposes.

- Explain the nature and purpose of depletion and the methods of accounting for depletion for financial reporting and tax purposes.

- Account for the acquisition, depreciation, and disposition of property, plant, and equipment.

- Prepare a property, plant, and equipment record.

- Describe the reporting of depreciation in financial statements.

- Account for the depletion of wasting assets.

- Describe the reporting of depletion in financial statements.

A ssets that are expected to provide benefits for a number of accounting periods are called **long-term assets**. Long-term assets that are **tangible** (have physical substance), that are used in the operations of the business, and that are not held for sale in the ordinary course of business are called **property, plant, and equipment; plant assets;** or **fixed assets.** Some examples of these tangible assets are land, buildings, furniture, and equipment. Properties whose physical substance consists of natural resources that are consumed in the operation of the business are called **wasting assets.** Some examples of wasting assets are mines, stands of timber, and oil and gas wells. Long-term assets that have no physical substance are called **intangible** assets. Common examples of intangible assets are patents, copyrights, and trademarks.

All long-term assets except land gradually wear out or are used up as time passes. In determining net income, a portion of the cost of such assets is charged off as expense in the periods benefited by the assets. A different term is used to describe this expense for the different types of long-term assets identified above, but the concept remains the same. For plant assets, the expense is called **depreciation**; for wasting assets, the expense recognized as the natural resources are removed or exhausted is known as **depletion**; and for intangible assets, the expense is called **amortization**.

In this chapter, proper accounting for plant assets and wasting assets will be described and illustrated. Both the determination of the original cost of these assets and the expensing of the cost over time will be addressed.

Property, Plant, and Equipment

In accounting for property, plant, and equipment, two major issues need to be addressed: (1) what elements should be included in the cost of an asset, and (2) how the cost should be allocated or apportioned to those future accounting periods that will benefit from the use of the asset.

Determining Cost

Determine the cost of property, plant, and equipment.

Long-term assets may be purchased for cash or on account. The amount at which long-term assets should be entered is the total of all outlays needed to put them in use. This total may include the purchase price, transportation charges, installation costs, and any other costs that are incurred up to the point of placing the asset in service. Legal costs incurred in acquiring land or natural resources should be treated as part of the cost of those assets. If money is borrowed for the purpose of constructing a building or other facility, the interest incurred during the period of construction should be added to the cost of such building or facility. It is important that the total cost of a long-term asset be properly accounted for, because this cost becomes the basis for the periodic expense write-off.

Transactions involving the purchase of long-term assets are entered by debiting the proper asset account and crediting the cash account for the amount paid, or by crediting the proper liability account, such as Accounts Payable, Notes Payable, or Mortgage Payable, for the obligation incurred. Additions or improvements increase the usefulness of the assets and should be entered by debiting the proper asset account and crediting the cash account or the proper liability account. For example, if there is an addition to a building, the total cost incurred should be debited to the building account. In the same manner, the cost of improvements, such as the installation of partitions, shelving, hardwood or tile floors, sprinkler systems, or air conditioning systems, should be debited to the building or building improvements account.

Costs incurred in connection with land may be charged to the land or land improvements account, depending on the nature of the item. When land is purchased, the costs of removing old buildings or of grading the land to prepare it for its intended use should be charged to the land account. Special tax assessments for streets, sewers, flood prevention, or parks also should be charged to the land account. Costs related to the land that are less permanent in nature are normally charged to the land improvements account. Common examples of these less permanent improvements include the costs of planting trees and shrubs, installing fences, and paving parking areas. Items charged to the land improvements account are depreciated over their expected useful lives.

Depreciation

Explain the nature and purpose of depreciation.

Under the accrual basis of accounting, net income is determined by matching the revenues earned during a period with the expenses incurred (or assigned to that period) as a result of the efforts made to produce the revenues. Plant assets last for many years and help produce revenues over these periods. The purpose of depreciation is to try to match the cost of the plant asset with the revenues it helps to produce in the current and future accounting periods.

It should be emphasized that depreciation is a process of cost allocation, not a process of valuation. Many factors cause the market values of plant assets to change over time. The recognition of depreciation on these assets is not intended to produce market values. The net amounts reported on the balance sheet are merely the portions of the original costs which have not yet been allocated to expense.

Causes of Depreciation. The allocation of the cost of a plant asset over the periods expected to benefit from its use is called depreciation. There are two major types of depreciation: physical and functional.

Physical depreciation refers to the loss of usefulness because of deterioration from age and from wear. It is generally continuous, though not necessarily uniform from period to period. Assets exposed to the elements may wear out at a fairly regular rate. Assets not exposed to the elements may slowly deteriorate whether in use or not, but the speed at which they deteriorate often is related to the extent to which they are used.

Functional depreciation refers to the loss of usefulness because of inadequacy or obsolescence. The growth of a business may result in some of its plant assets becoming inadequate. The assets remain capable of doing the job for which they were acquired, but the job has become too big for them. Assets may become obsolete because of a change in the demand for products or services, or because of the development of new methods, equipment, or processes which can either reduce costs, increase quality, or both.

Explain how to apply different depreciation methods.

▰▰▰ **Calculating the Amount of Depreciation for a Period.** The depreciable cost of an asset should be apportioned over the periods the asset is expected to benefit. **Depreciable cost** means original cost less scrap or salvage value. Scrap or salvage value is quite difficult to predict in most cases. Unless such value is expected to be a significant fraction of original cost, it often is ignored (considered to be zero). Although the estimation of salvage value can be difficult, the major challenge in depreciation accounting is attempting to predict either how many periods the asset will serve or how many units of service the asset will provide. If it were possible to know that a machine could operate a total of 100,000 hours, it would be easy to decide that 5% of its net cost should be charged to the first year if, during that year, the machine operated 5,000 hours. Likewise, prior knowledge that an asset would last 10 years and equally serve each of those years would help solve the problem of how to apportion its cost. Unfortunately, there is no way of knowing exactly how long an asset will last or exactly what its output will be; therefore, it becomes necessary to make estimates based upon past experience. In attempting to make such estimates, the accountant may be assisted by information relating to assets previously owned by the business or be guided by the experience of others. Utilization of statistics supplied by trade associations and government agencies (such as the Internal Revenue Service) and the opinions of engineers or appraisal companies may be helpful. Past experience with respect to physical depreciation may be a very good guide for the future but it is not much help in attempting to predict depreciation caused by inadequacy or obsolescence. Uncertainty surrounds all depreciation calculations.

▰▰▰ **Methods of Calculating Depreciation.** There are several different ways of calculating the amount of depreciation for each period. The most commonly used methods for financial reporting purposes are the following:

1. Straight-line method
2. Declining-balance method
3. Sum-of-the-years-digits method
4. Units-of-output method

Explain how to apply the straight-line depreciation method.

Straight-Line Method. The depreciation method in which the depreciable cost of an asset is apportioned equally over its estimated useful life in terms of months or years is called the **straight-line method**. For example, assume that a new asset with a cost of $10,000, an expected life of 4 years, and a $1,000 estimated salvage value at the end of its useful life, is to be depreciated on a straight-line basis. The amount of depreciation apportioned to each year would be $2,250, computed as follows:

$$\frac{\$10,000 \ (cost) \ - \ \$1,000 \ (salvage \ value)}{4 \ years} = \$2,250 \ annual \ depeciation$$

The annual rate of depreciation would be 25% (100% / 4 years) of the depreciable cost.

A month is usually the shortest period that is used in depreciation accounting. An asset purchased on or before the fifteenth of the month is considered to have been owned for the full month. An asset purchased after the fifteenth of the month is considered to have been acquired the first of the next month.

The difference between the cost of an asset and the total amount charged off as depreciation as of a certain date is its **undepreciated cost** (often called **book value**). In the foregoing illustration, the undepreciated cost of the asset after the first year, assuming it was in use for 12 months, would be $7,750 [$10,000 (cost) − $2,250 (depreciation)]. When the straight-line method is used, the undepreciated cost of the asset decreases uniformly period by period. As shown on the following graph, the undepreciated cost over a number of periods is a downward-sloping, perfectly straight line. That is how the method got its name.

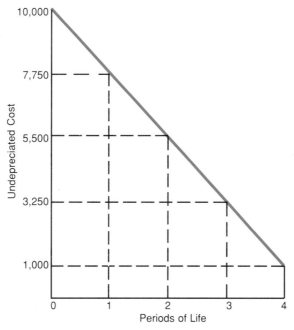

Straight-Line Method

The straight-line method's outstanding advantage is its simplicity. Since depreciation is based upon estimates, many accountants believe that the use of more complicated procedures is not warranted. The calculation of depreciation on a straight-line basis is still a widely followed practice when other methods offer no particular advantage.

Explain how to apply the declining-balance depreciation method.

Declining-Balance Method. Many plant assets require repairs and replacement of parts to keep them in service. Such expenses usually increase as the assets get older. Some accountants believe that depreciation expense therefore should be higher in early years to offset the higher repair and maintenance expenses of the later years. Another reason offered for charging higher depreciation in early years is the contention that assets contribute proportionately more to the business during the years that the assets are comparatively new. For these reasons, it may be desirable to calculate depreciation in a way that will give larger write-offs in the early years of the life of the asset. Depreciation methods that provide for a higher depreciation charge in the first year of an asset's life and gradually decreasing charges in subsequent years are called accelerated depreciation methods.

One popular accelerated method is the declining-balance method. Under this method, a fixed rate is applied to the undepreciated cost of the asset each year, resulting in successively smaller depreciation charges as the undepreciated cost declines year by year. The most common rate used is double the straight-line rate. For this reason, this technique is sometimes referred to as the double-declining-balance method.

To illustrate the application of this method, consider the same asset that was used in explaining the straight-line method. The asset cost $10,000, had an expected life of 4 years and a $1,000 estimated salvage value. Using the double-declining-balance method, the depreciation rate to be applied to the undepreciated cost of the asset each year would be 50%, computed as follows:

> Straight-line rate = 25% (100% ÷ 4 years)
> Double-declining-balance rate = 50% (2 × 25%)

The annual depreciation and the undepreciated cost at the end of each year would be as follows:

Year	Undepreciated Cost Beginning of Year	Rate	Annual Depreciation	Accumulated Depreciation End of Year	Undepreciated Cost End of year
1	$10,000	50%	$5,000	$5,000	$5,000
2	5,000	50	2,500	7,500	2,500
3	2,500	50	1,250	8,750	1,250
4	1,250	50	250	9,000	1,000

Note that although salvage value is not considered directly in the determination of the depreciation amount, the asset should not be depreciated below its estimated salvage value. Thus the amount of depreciation actually recorded in the final year (Year 4) is limited to $250 ($1,250 − $1,000).

As shown on the following graph, when the declining-balance method is used, the undepreciated cost declines rapidly in the early years and more slowly in the later years of an asset's life.

If the asset in the above illustration were acquired at some time other than the beginning of the year, a slight change would be necessary in the

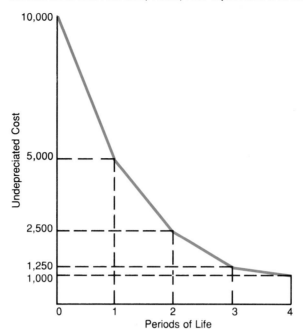

Declining-Balance Method

computation of depreciation for the year. For example, if the asset were acquired on April 1, the depreciation for Year 1 would be calculated as follows:

$$\text{Year 1: } \$10,000 \times 50\% = \$5,000 \times 9/12 = \underline{\$3,750}$$

Depreciation for years 2 through 4 would then be calculated by applying the 50% depreciation rate to the undepreciated cost of the asset at the beginning of each year, as follows:

$$\text{Year 2: } \$6,250 \times 50\% \quad = \underline{\$3,125.00}$$
$$\text{Year 3: } \$3,125 \times 50\% \quad = \underline{\$1,562.50}$$
$$\text{Year 4: } \$1,562.50 - \$1,000 \text{ (salvage value)} = \underline{\$562.50}$$

Depreciation in Year 4 is limited to $562.50 because the asset should not be depreciated below its estimated salvage value.

Sum-of-the-Years-Digits Method. Another commonly used accelerated depreciation method is the sum-of-the-years-digits method. With this method, a steadily decreasing rate is applied to the depreciable cost (original cost less salvage value) of the asset, resulting in successively smaller depreciation charges over the life of the asset. This method is similar in effect to the declining-balance method. However, with the sum-of-the-years-digits method, a write-down to the exact amount of estimated salvage value (which might be zero) is possible. The write-off each year is

Explain how to apply the sum-of-the-years-digits depreciation method.

based on a schedule of fractions. The denominator for all fractions is determined by listing the digits that represent the years of the estimated life of the asset and adding these digits. The numerator in any year is the number of years of remaining life for the asset, measured from the beginning of the year. For example, suppose that the estimated life of an asset is 4 years. The sum of the digits (4 + 3 + 2 + 1) equals 10 (the denominator). A formula can also be used to determine the denominator, as follows:

$$S = N \frac{(N + 1)}{2}$$

S = sum of the digits
N = number of years of estimated life

If the life of the asset is 4 years:

$$S = 4 \frac{(4 + 1)}{2} = 4(2\ 1/2) = 10$$

The denominator equals 10. Therefore, the fractions used for an asset with a 4-year life would be:

Year 1: 4/10 write-off of cost less salvage
Year 2: 3/10 write-off of cost less salvage
Year 3: 2/10 write-off of cost less salvage
Year 4: 1/10 write-off of cost less salvage

If these fractions were applied to the asset used to illustrate the straight-line and declining-balance depreciation methods (cost of $10,000, with a 4-year expected life and $1,000 estimated salvage value), the results would be as follows:

Year	Depreciable Cost	Rate	Annual Depreciation	Accumulated Depreciation End of Year	Undepreciated Cost End of Year
1	$9,000	4/10	$3,600	$3,600	$6,400
2	9,000	3/10	2,700	6,300	3,700
3	9,000	2/10	1,800	8,100	1,900
4	9,000	1/10	900	9,000	1,000

As shown on the following graph, the pattern of decline in the undepreciated cost using the sum-of-the-years-digits method is similar to that under the declining-balance method.

As was the case with the declining-balance method, if an asset was acquired at some time other than the beginning of an accounting period, a modification would be necessary in the sum-of-the-years-digits depreciation calculation. For example, if the $10,000 asset described above was

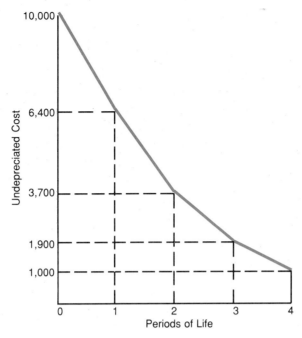

Sum-of-the-Years-Digits Method

acquired on April 1, the depreciation for years 1 and 2 would be calculated as follows:

$$
\begin{array}{llll}
\text{Year 1: } \$9,000 \times 4/10 = \$3,600 \times 9/12 = & \underline{\$2,700} \\
\text{Year 2: } \$9,000 \times 4/10 = \$3,600 \times 3/12 = & \$\ \ 900 \\
\phantom{\text{Year 2: }} 9,000 \times 3/10 = 2,700 \times 9/12 = & \underline{\ \ 2,025} \\
& \underline{\$2,925}
\end{array}
$$

Depreciation for years 3-5 would be calculated in a similar manner.

Explain how to apply the units-of-output depreciation method.

Units-of-Output Method. The depreciation method that estimates the number of units of service or output that can be provided by an asset and allocates the depreciable cost of the asset on the basis of the use or output during each period is called the **units-of-output** or **units-of-production method**. This method is used less often than any of the three methods discussed previously, because this measurement of service is not possible for many assets.

The units-of-output method can be used for certain types of machinery, equipment, and vehicles. For example, assume that a company finds from experience that it can obtain 80,000 miles of service from certain types of vans before they become so worn out that the need for extensive repairs and replacements makes it advisable to dispose of them. The company purchases a new van of this type at a cost of $10,000 and expects that it can be sold for $2,000 after 80,000 miles of service. The estimated depreciable cost to be charged to operations during the life of the van, the depreciation per mile, and the first-year depreciation, assuming the van is driven 24,000 miles, are therefore:

Depreciable cost = $10,000 cost − $2,000 salvage = $8,000
Depreciation per mile = $\frac{\$8,000 \text{ depreciable cost}}{80,000 \text{ total miles}}$ = 10¢
First-year depreciation = 24,000 miles × 10¢/mile = $2,400.

Comparison of Methods

Explain the possible effects of different depreciation methods on the balance sheet and income statement.

Under the units-of-output method, depreciation charges can vary greatly from year to year, depending on the amount of usage of the asset. Under the straight-line, declining-balance, and sum-of-the-years-digits methods, the amount of usage of the asset has no effect on the depreciation charges. Once one of these three methods has been chosen, depreciation charges over time are set, regardless of the extent of use of the asset. It is therefore interesting to compare the effects of the latter three methods on both the balance sheet and income statement. The balance sheet is affected because different undepreciated cost amounts result from the different depreciation methods. The income statement is affected because of the role that the different depreciation charges play in the periodic determination of net income.

Depreciation Pattern and Undepreciated Costs. The following tabulation contrasts the results of using straight-line, declining-balance, and sum-of-the-years-digits depreciation methods. The asset in the illustration is the same one used to demonstrate the application of these depreciation methods in the previous sections. The asset cost $10,000, had a 4-year estimated life and an estimated salvage value of $1,000.

	Depreciation Expense			Undepreciated Cost		
Year	Straight-Line	Declining-Balance	Sum-of-the-Years-Digits	Straight-Line	Declining-Balance	Sum-of-the-Years-Digits
1	$2,250	$5,000	$3,600	$7,750	$5,000	$6,400
2	2,250	2,500	2,700	5,500	2,500	3,700
3	2,250	1,250	1,800	3,250	1,250	1,900
4	2,250	250	900	1,000	1,000	1,000

Note that the declining-balance method provides the most rapid write-off of the asset and therefore the lowest undepreciated cost on the balance sheet.

Effect on Net Income Calculation. Over a number of years, the total of the amounts of the calculated annual net income will be about the same regardless of the method of depreciation. For any one year, however, the method of depreciation used can make a significant difference in the amount of the calculated net income. For example, assume that for the first year of operation a business had revenue of $40,000 and all costs and expenses other than depreciation amounted to $22,000. Further assume that the asset described in the previous illustration was the only depreciable asset of the business. Following is a comparison of three very condensed income statements of the new business showing the net income for the first year after applying the three depreciation methods:

	Straight-Line Depreciation Method Used		Double-Declining-Balance Depreciation Method Used		Sum-of-the-Years-Digits Depreciation Method Used	
Revenue		$40,000		$40,000		$40,000
Costs and expenses other than						
depreciation	$22,000		$22,000		$22,000	
Depreciation...............	2,250	24,250	5,000	27,000	3,600	25,600
Net income		$15,750		$13,000		$14,400

Note that the calculated amount of net income using the straight-line method is over one fifth greater than the amount using the declining-balance method. In contrast, the effect on net income will reverse itself in later years. During those years the reported net income will be larger for the accelerated methods than for the straight-line method. Clearly significant differences in net income may result from the choice of depreciation methods.

In the preceding chapter, the effects of the choice of inventory method on net income were noted. It is apparent that periodic business income calculation is not an exact science, but rather an art involving careful judgment based on an understanding of acceptable alternatives and the consequences of their use.

Depreciation for Federal Income Tax Purposes

Describe acceptable depreciation methods for federal income tax purposes.

A business is allowed to deduct depreciation expenses in calculating taxable income. Allowable depreciation methods for tax purposes vary depending on when the asset was acquired. For plant assets acquired prior to 1981, any of the four methods described in the previous sections is permitted. For plant assets acquired between 1981 and 1986, either the straight-line method or the Accelerated Cost Recovery System (ACRS) must be used. ACRS classifies all business plant assets into four different useful life categories. Most business assets fall into one of three categories: 3-year, 5-year, or 18-year property. ACRS defines depreciation rates for each of these categories. For example, the rates for 3-year and 5-year property are shown below. In using these rates, salvage value is ignored.

ACRS Depreciation Rates

Year	3-year Property	5-year Property
1	25%	15%
2	38	22
3	37	21
4		21
5		21
	100%	100%

For plant assets acquired after 1986, either the straight-line method or the Modified Accelerated Cost Recovery System (MACRS) must be used. MACRS identifies eight categories of useful life for plant assets. Most business assets other than real estate fall into one of two categories: 5-year or 7-year property. MACRS defines depreciation rates for each category. The rates for 5-year property are shown below. In using these rates, salvage value is ignored. The rates assume that an asset was acquired at mid-year and disposed of at mid-year, regardless of the actual month of acquisition or disposal.

MACRS Depreciation Rates

Year	5-year Property
1	20.0%
2	32.0
3	19.2
4	11.5
5	11.5
6	5.8
	100.0%

Depletion

Explain the nature and purpose of depletion and the different methods of accounting for depletion for financial reporting and tax purposes.

The consumption or exhaustion of wasting assets is called depletion. Apart from income tax considerations, the accounting problem is to apportion the cost of such assets to the periods in which they are consumed. The procedure called cost depletion is very similar to that used in computing depreciation on a units-of-output basis. The cost of the property less the estimated salvage or residual value, if any, is divided by the estimated number of units that the property contains. The result is the depletion expense per unit. This amount times the number of units removed and sold during the period is the depletion expense for the period.

To illustrate the computation of depletion, consider the following example. A coal mine is acquired at a cost of $1,000,000. No salvage value is expected. The estimated recoverable amount of coal in the mine is 1,000,000 tons. During the current year, 180,000 tons of coal are mined and sold. The computation of the amount of depletion expense is as follows:

$$\frac{\$1,000,000}{1,000,000 \text{ tons}} = \$1 \text{ per ton}$$

$$180,000 \text{ tons} \times \$1 \text{ per ton} = \$180,000 \text{ depletion expense}$$

From time to time the estimate of the quantity of the resource that remains in the property has to be changed. When this happens, a new calculation should be made of the depletion per unit, starting with the most recently determined undepleted cost of the property and dividing that amount (less estimated salvage value, if any) by the number of units extracted during the current year plus the current estimate of the number of units remaining. For example, the mine mentioned above had an un-depleted cost of $820,000 at the start of the second year. Assume that during that year, 275,000 tons were extracted, and at the end of the year the engineers estimate that 925,000 tons remain. The calculation of the revised depletion expense per unit and depletion expense for the second year would be as follows:

$$\frac{\$820,000}{275,000 \text{ tons } + \text{ 925,000 tons}} = \$0.6833 \text{ (or } 68.33\text{¢) per ton}$$

$$275,000 \text{ tons } \times \$0.6833 = \$187,907.50 \text{ depletion expense}$$

Depletion Expense for Federal Income Tax Purposes. Special rules govern the amount of depletion expense that can be deducted for federal income tax purposes. A business can compute the amount using the cost depletion method explained in the preceding paragraphs. However, certain businesses that own and operate oil and gas wells (basically where the resource is regulated or sold under a fixed contract) and certain types of mines can use percentage depletion. Under this method, depletion is equal to certain specified percentages (which vary from 5% to 22%) of the amount of the sales of the period subject to stated maximum and minimum limits. The dollar amount deductible is limited to 50% of the taxable income exclusive of any depletion deduction.

Building Your Accounting Knowledge

1. What costs should be included in the total amount at which long-term assets are entered?
2. How should additions or improvements representing an increase in the use-fulness of plant assets be entered?
3. How should the cost of such activities as planting trees and shrubs be entered?
4. What are the two major causes of depreciation?
5. What is meant by the "depreciable cost" of a plant asset?
6. What are the four most commonly used methods of calculating depreciation for financial reporting purposes, and how do they differ in their application?
7. Why can the units-of-output method of depreciation not be applied to all depreciable assets?
8. Explain how the depreciation method selected affects both the balance sheet and income statement.
9. For assets acquired after 1986, what depreciation methods are allowed for federal income tax purposes?
10. What depreciation method is very similar to cost depletion? How does per-centage depletion differ from cost depletion?

Assignment Box

To reinforce your understanding of the preceding text material, you may complete the following:

> Study Guide: Part A
> Textbook: Exercises 14A1 through 14A4 or 14B1 through 14B4
> Problems 14A1 through 14A2 or 14B1 through 14B2

Accounting Procedures

The number of accounts for long-term assets that will be kept in the general ledger will depend mainly upon the number of assets and the type of information required by management. If there are very few long-term assets and management requires only a limited amount of information regarding them, a separate account for each one with a related depreciation account can be kept in the general ledger. If there are many long-term assets, subsidiary records are needed to provide details regarding each asset, with summary accounts in the general ledger for each major type of asset.

Entering Depreciation

Account for the depreciation of property, plant, and equipment.

Depreciation usually is entered at the end of the period, along with other necessary adjusting entries. One or more depreciation expense accounts may be debited, and one or more accumulated depreciation accounts may be credited. Often there is one depreciation expense account for each major type of asset, such as Depreciation Expense—Buildings, Depreciation Expense—Furniture and Fixtures, and Depreciation Expense—Delivery Equipment. A business that classifies expenses on a departmental basis may use a large number of depreciation expense accounts.

Usually, the only entries in the accumulated depreciation accounts are those made at the end of each period to enter the depreciation for that period. When a plant asset is disposed of (such as by sale, exchange, or retirement), depreciation should be entered for the interval between the date of the last regular adjustment of the accounts and the date of the disposition of the asset. Usually, the depreciation is calculated to the nearest full month.

To illustrate the depreciation accounting process, assume that the asset described in the first half of this chapter was a delivery truck acquired on January 3, with a cost of $10,000, an estimated useful life of 4 years, and an estimated salvage value of $1,000. The annual depreciation using the straight-line method would be $2,250, calculated as follows:

$$\frac{\$10,000 \text{ cost } - \$1,000 \text{ salvage}}{4\text{-year life}} = \$2,250 \text{ annual depreciation}$$

The following journal entry would be made for the annual depreciation on the truck as of December 31.

Depreciation Expense—Delivery Equipment	2,250	
Accumulated Depreciation—Delivery Equipment		2,250
Annual depreciation on truck.		

The foregoing entry would be repeated each succeeding December 31 until the truck was either fully depreciated or disposed of.

Assume that the truck was sold on May 1 of the following year. The entry for the depreciation through the date of the sale of the asset would be as follows:

Depreciation Expense—Delivery Equipment	750	
Accumulated Depreciation—Delivery Equipment		750
Depreciation on truck for 1/3 year.		

Disposition of Plant Assets

Account for the disposition of property, plant, and equipment.

A plant asset can be disposed of in any one of the following ways:

1. It may be discarded or retired.
2. It may be sold.
3. It may be exchanged or traded in for property of like kind or for other property.

Discarding or Retiring Plant Assets. A plant asset may be discarded or retired whether or not it has been fully depreciated. If it has been fully depreciated, no gain or loss will be realized. If it has not been fully depreciated, the undepreciated cost of the discarded asset will represent a loss. Such a loss may be the result of underestimating the depreciation of the asset for the period of time that it has been in use, or it may be the result of obsolescence.

To illustrate, assume that a printer that cost $800 and had an accumulated depreciation balance of $800 was discarded. Because the printer is fully depreciated, its undepreciated cost is zero and no gain or loss results from this transaction. The amounts for the asset and the related accumulated depreciation would be eliminated from the accounts as follows:

Accumulated Depreciation—Office Equipment	800	
Office Equipment		800
Discarded printer.		

If at the time it was discarded, the accumulated depreciation on this same asset was $720, the undepreciated cost would be $80 and a loss would result. The amounts for the asset and the related accumulated depreciation would be eliminated from the accounts and the loss recognized as follows:

Accumulated Depreciation—Office Equipment	720	
Loss on Discarded Office Equipment.	80	
Office Equipment		800
Discarded printer.		

Losses of this type are shown in the income statement as "Other expense."

■■■■ **Selling Plant Assets.** If a plant asset is sold, it is necessary to know its undepreciated cost before the proper amount of any gain or loss resulting from the transaction can be determined. When a plant asset is sold at its undepreciated cost, no gain or loss results from the transaction; when it is sold for more than its undepreciated cost, the difference represents a gain; when it is sold for less than its undepreciated cost, the difference represents a loss.

To illustrate, assume the printer in the previous illustration was sold for $80 at the time its undepreciated cost was $80. This transaction would be entered as follows:

Cash.	80	
Accumulated Depreciation—Office Equipment	720	
Office Equipment		800
Sold printer.		

No gain or loss results from this transaction because the printer was sold for the same net amount at which it was being carried on the books.

If the same printer was sold for $120 at the time its undepreciated cost was $80, there would be a gain of $40, the difference between the selling price and the undepreciated cost of the printer. The following journal entry would be made to remove the asset and its related accumulated depreciation from the accounts, to increase Cash, and to recognize the gain on the sale:

Cash..	120	
Accumulated Depreciation—Office Equipment	720	
Office Equipment		800
Gain on Sale of Printer		40
Sold printer.		

Gains of this type are shown in the income statement as "Other revenue."

If the printer was sold for $50, there would be a loss of $30 and the following journal entry would be made:

Cash..	50	
Accumulated Depreciation—Office Equipment	720	
Loss on Sale of Printer	30	
Office Equipment		800
Sold printer.		

Exchange or Trade-In of Plant Assets. A plant asset may be exchanged or traded in for another asset. Accepted financial accounting treatment, in most cases, is based on the fair market value of the asset exchanged. **Fair market value** is a value that is agreed upon in a current sales transaction by a willing buyer and a willing seller. On the other hand, tax regulations often allow the asset acquired to be assigned a cost based on the undepreciated cost of the asset given up.

If one asset is traded in on the purchase of another, a **trade-in allowance** frequently is granted which may be equal to, greater than, or less than the undepreciated cost of the asset traded in. Trade-in allowances based on the list prices of new assets frequently do not reflect fair market values. Therefore, the fair market value of the asset traded in or of the new asset must be determined to correctly calculate the gain or loss on exchange transactions.

In financial accounting, plant assets are classified into two categories for purposes of exchange or trade-in: similar (the tax laws refer to these as "of like kind") and dissimilar (the tax laws refer to these as "not of like kind"). In accounting for exchanges of similar assets, financial accounting recognizes all losses but no gains. For tax purposes, neither gains nor losses are recognized on such exchanges. In contrast, in accounting for exchanges of dissimilar assets, both financial accounting and the tax laws recognize gains and losses on the exchanges.

To illustrate proper accounting for the exchange or trade in of similar assets ("like kind"), assume that a delivery truck that cost $8,000 and has been owned for 3 years is traded in for another delivery truck which is to be used for a similar purpose. Depreciation in the amount of $2,300 has been taken each year—a total of $6,900. Thus the undepreciated cost of the truck is $1,100 ($8,000 − $6,900). If the new truck has a fair market value of $10,000 and the trade-in value of the old truck is $1,500, $8,500 would be paid in cash ($10,000 − $1,500). This $8,500 balance paid to the supplier is known as boot. The transaction would be entered as follows:

Delivery Equipment (new truck)	9,600	
Accumulated Depreciation—Delivery Equipment	6,900	
Delivery Equipment (old truck)....................		8,000
Cash		8,500
Purchased a new truck.		

The new truck's cost ($9,600) is the sum of the undepreciated cost of the old truck ($1,100) and the boot paid ($8,500). This cost becomes the basis for future depreciation charges. Note that this journal entry does not recognize the $400 gain, which is the difference between the undepreciated cost of $1,100 and the trade-in value of the old truck of $1,500. When this entry is posted, the cost of the old truck will be eliminated from the delivery equipment account and that account will be charged with the cost of the new truck. The accumulated depreciation on the old truck will also be eliminated from the accumulated depreciation account, and no gain will be recognized in recording the transaction. This method of accounting also conforms to the tax laws.

Assume instead that the new truck had a fair market value of $9,500, and that the trade-in value of the old truck was only $1,000. In this case, the old truck plus $8,500 (boot) still would be given to the supplier, and the following journal entry would be required:

Delivery Equipment (new truck)	9,500	
Accumulated Depreciation—Delivery Equipment	6,900	
Loss on Exchange of Delivery Equipment..............	100	
Delivery Equipment (old truck)....................		8,000
Cash		8,500
Purchased a new truck.		

Note that in this situation the new truck is entered at its fair market value and that a $100 loss (the excess of the undepreciated cost over the trade-in allowance) on the exchange is charged to a special loss account. This method of accounting does not conform to the tax laws, because losses for tax purposes (like gains for tax purposes) are not recognized in connection with a "like kind" exchange. The proper entry for tax purposes would be the same as the entry previously illustrated above where a gain on the exchange was involved but not entered.

To illustrate proper accounting for the trade-in of dissimilar assets (not of like kind), assume that a typewriter that cost $300 and has been owned for 2 years is traded in for a new cash register. Depreciation in the amount of $60 has been taken each year for a total of $120. Thus the undepreciated cost of the typewriter is $180 ($300 − $120). If the cash register has a fair market value of $625 and the trade-in value of the typewriter is $200, $425 would be paid in cash ($625 − $200). Since this transaction involves an exchange of dissimilar assets, any gain or loss should be recognized. Because $200 trade-in value was allowed for an asset that had an undepreciated cost of $180 ($300 cost of asset − $120 accumulated depreciation), the transaction involved a gain of $20. The transaction would be entered as follows:

Office Equipment	625	
Accumulated Depreciation—Office Equipment	120	
Office Equipment		300
Cash		425
Gain on Exchange of Office Equipment		20
Purchased a new cash register.		

Assume instead that the new cash register had a fair market value of $590, and that the trade-in value of the typewriter was only $165. In this case, the typewriter plus $425 still would be given to the supplier, and the following journal entry would be required:

Office Equipment	590	
Accumulated Depreciation—Office Equipment	120	
Loss on Exchange of Office Equipment	15	
Office Equipment		300
Cash		425
Purchased a new cash register.		

Note that in this situation the new cash register is entered at its fair market value, and that the $15 loss (the excess of the undepreciated cost over the trade-in allowance) is recognized. This method of accounting also conforms to the tax laws, because the exchange involves dissimilar ("not of like kind") assets.

The following chart summarizes the financial accounting and income tax accounting rules for recognition of gain or loss in "like kind" and "not of like kind" exchanges of plant assets.

	Asset			
	Like Kind		Unlike Kind	
	Recognition of		Recognition of	
	Gain	Loss	Gain	Loss
Financial Accounting	No	Yes	Yes	Yes
Tax Accounting	No	No	Yes	Yes

Property, Plant, and Equipment Records

If a business has a large number of depreciable assets, it is likely that a summary general ledger account will be kept for each major class of assets, such as one account for buildings, one for machinery and equipment, one for office furniture and equipment, and one for delivery trucks. Each of these summary accounts will have a related accumulated depreciation account. Such summary accounts will be supported by some sort of supplementary or subsidiary records. Such records commonly take the form of cards or computer disks. Space is provided on each card or disk to record the details about the asset, including the cost of the unit (which supports the debit in the general ledger asset account) and the amount of depreciation taken each period (which supports the credits in the general ledger accumulated depreciation account). Space is also provided to enter the disposition of the asset. A typical property, plant, and equipment record is shown on the following page. Note that salvage value was considered in arriving at the amount of annual depreciation, $520 [($3,000 original cost − $400 estimated salvage value) / 5 years]. Also note that the 20% rate (100% / 5 years) is applied to the original cost of $3,000, less the $400 estimated salvage value.

Following is a narrative of the transactions that were entered on the record:

Jan. 9, 19-A. Purchased ABC DE/3, Model 50, Serial No. 8403637, from Northern Micro, for $3,000.

Dec. 31, 19-A. Depreciation of computer at annual rate of $520 [($3,000 cost − $400 salvage value) × .20].

Dec. 31, 19-B. Depreciation of computer at annual rate of $520.

July 1, 19-C. Depreciation of computer for one-half year, $260. Sold computer for $1,750 cash.

Note that before the sale of the computer on July 1, 19-C, was entered, depreciation for the half year, amounting to $260, was entered on the record. The sale was also entered, after which the record was transferred from a file of assets owned to a file of assets sold, exchanged, or discarded. (In a computer-based accounting system, the record would be transferred electronically from an "active asset" file to an "inactive asset" file.) Such an asset record should provide all the information needed to determine the proper amount of depreciation to claim on each plant asset as a deduction from gross income in the annual income tax returns.

Fully Depreciated Plant Assets

A plant asset is said to be fully depreciated when the accumulated depreciation is equal to the cost of the asset. When an asset is fully depreciated, no further depreciation should be entered. Since the rate of depreciation is based on its estimated useful life, an asset may still be used after it is fully depreciated. In this case, the cost of the asset and an equal amount of accumulated depreciation are usually retained in the accounts. When the asset eventually is disposed of, then the cost and accu-

PROPERTY, PLANT, AND EQUIPMENT RECORD

Description   *Computer*

Age when acquired   *New*

Estimated life   *5 years*

Account   *Office Equipment*

Estimated salvage value   *$400*

Rate of annual depreciation based on cost less salvage value   *20%*

COST					DEPRECIATION RECORD				
Date Purchased		Description	Amount		Year	Rate	Amount		Total To Date
1988 *Jan.*	*9*	*ABC DE/3 MODEL 50*	*3,000*	*00*	19 *88*	*20%*	*520*	*00*	*520*	*00*
		Serial No. 8403637			19 *89*	*20%*	*520*	*00*	*1,040*	*00*
		American Micro			19 *90*	*20%*	*260*	*00*	*1,300*	*00*
		Less estimated salvage value	*400*	*00*	19					
		Depreciable cost	*2,600*	*00*	19					
					19					
					19					
					19					
					19					

SOLD, EXCHANGED, OR DISCARDED								
Date		Explanation	Amount Realized		More than ✓ ⎰ Undepr. Less than ⎱ Cost		Accum. Depr.	
1990 *July*	*1*	*Sold*	*1,750*	*00*	*50*	*00*	*1,300*	*00*

Property, Plant, and Equipment Record

mulated depreciation should be removed from the accounts, as illustrated in previous sections.

In some states a taxable value is placed on a fully depreciated asset if the asset is still in use. Under such circumstances, a notation of the taxable value of the fully depreciated asset should be made in the property, plant, and equipment record as a guide in preparing the property tax schedule. The taxable values of fully depreciated plant assets and the undepreciated costs of other plant assets should be listed so that the total taxable value of the plant assets can be determined.

Depreciation in the Financial Statements

Describe the reporting of depreciation in financial statements.

Depreciation normally is classified as an operating expense in the income statement. There can be as much subclassification as management desires. Depreciation of delivery equipment, for example, may be classified as a selling expense, while depreciation of office furniture and equipment may be classified as an office or general administrative expense.

In view of the close relationship between plant asset accounts and their accumulated depreciation accounts, the accepted practice in the preparation of balance sheets is to show the amount of the accumulated depreciation as a deduction from the cost of the asset. The difference, representing undepreciated cost, is extended to be included in the asset total.

Accumulated depreciation accounts, like allowances for doubtful accounts, are sometimes called asset valuation accounts. An accumulated depreciation account, however, only values the asset in a very limited and remote sense. The difference between the cost of the asset and the balance of the accumulated depreciation account is not expected to have any relation to the market value of the asset. Such assets are not intended for sale. What they might bring, if sold, is usually of small consequence. The difference between the gross amount of the plant assets and the related accumulated depreciation accounts simply represents costs not yet charged to operations. Some companies so describe this difference in their balance sheets.

Entering Depletion

Account for the depletion of wasting assets.

Depletion usually is entered at the end of the period, along with other necessary adjusting entries. Usually, the only entries in the accumulated depletion accounts are those made at the end of the period to enter the depletion for that period.

To illustrate the depletion accounting process, consider the coal mine that was described in the first half of the chapter. The mine cost $1,000,000 and was estimated to produce 1,000,000 tons of coal. In the current year, 180,000 tons of coal were mined and sold, so that $180,000 of depletion expense was calculated, as follows:

$$\frac{\$1,000,000}{1,000,000 \text{ tons}} = \$1 \text{ per ton}$$

$$180,000 \text{ tons} \times \$1 \text{ per ton} = \$180,000 \text{ depletion expense}$$

The depletion is entered as follows:

Depletion Expense	180,000	
Accumulated Depletion—Coal Mine		180,000
Depletion based on 180,000 tons of coal @ $1 a ton.		

The difference between the cost of the mine and the amount of the accumulated depletion is the undepleted cost of the property:

Cost of coal mine	$1,000,000
Less accumulated depletion	180,000
Undepleted cost of mine	$ 820,000

Depletion in the Financial Statements

Describe the reporting of depletion in financial statements.

Depletion expense should be reported as an operating expense in the income statement. It can be subclassified by type of wasting asset if desired.

Accumulated depletion should be reported in the balance sheet as a deduction from the related asset account, with the difference identified as undepleted cost of the asset. As was explained for depreciation, this undepleted cost of the wasting asset simply represents the cost not yet charged to operations. It is not intended to reflect the market value of the asset.

Building Your Accounting Knowledge

1. For what time interval should depreciation be entered when a depreciable asset is disposed of?
2. What are the three major ways in which a plant asset may be disposed of?
3. From what two major causes may a loss result when a plant asset is discarded or retired? Will a gain or loss result if a discarded or retired asset has been fully depreciated?
4. When a plant asset is sold, what must be known about the asset in order to determine the proper amount of gain or loss on the sale?
5. Describe the major differences between accounting for a "similar" (or "like kind") exchange of plant assets, and accounting for a "dissimilar" (or "not of like kind") exchange. Indicate the ways in which financial accounting and income tax procedures differ in dealing with plant asset exchanges.
6. What details about a particular asset are provided by a property, plant, and equipment record?
7. What does the difference between the gross amount of plant assets and the related accumulated depreciation or accumulated depletion accounts represent to accountants?

Assignment Box

To reinforce your understanding of the preceding text materials, you may complete the following:

       Study Guide: Part B
       Textbook: Exercises 14A5 through 14A9 or 14B5 through 14B9
                Problems 14A3 through 14A5 or 14B3 through 14B5

Expanding Your Business Vocabulary

What is the meaning of each of the following terms?

accelerated depreciation methods (p. 548)
ACRS (p. 553)
amortization (p. 544)
book value (p. 547)
boot (p. 560)
cost allocation (p. 545)
cost depletion (p. 554)
declining-balance method (p. 548)
depletion (p. 554)
depreciable cost (p. 546)
depreciation (p. 545)
double-declining-balance method (p. 548)
fair market value (p. 559)
fixed assets (p. 543)

functional depreciation (p. 545)
intangible (p. 544)
long-term assets (p. 543)
MACRS (p. 554)
percentage depletion (p. 555)
physical depreciation (p. 545)
plant assets (p. 543)
property, plant, and equipment (p. 543)
straight-line method (p. 546)
sum-of-the-years-digits method (p. 549)
tangible (p. 543)
trade-in allowance (p. 559)
undepreciated cost (p. 547)
units-of-output (production) method (p. 551)
wasting assets (p. 543)

Demonstration Problem

The Stillman Company purchased a new machine at the start of their current accounting year at a cost of $37,500. The machine is expected to serve for 5 years and to have a salvage value of $3,000. Ronald L. Stillman, the CEO, has asked for information as to the effects of alternative depreciation methods.

Required:

1. Calculate the annual depreciation expense for each of the five years of expected life of the machine, the accumulated depreciation at the end of each year, and the undepreciated cost at the end of each year using the:
   (a) Straight-line method
   (b) Double declining-balance method
   (c) Sum-of-the-years-digits method
2. Assume that in Year 2 and Year 4 of the 5-year life of this machine, revenues are $45,000 and costs and expenses other than depreciation are $25,000. Calculate the net income for Year 2 and Year 4, using the same three depreciation methods used in Requirement 1.
3. Assume that Mr. Stillman chose the double-declining-balance method of depreciation for this machine. Then, in the first week of Year 5, the machine was exchanged (traded in) for similar equipment costing

$45,000. The trade-in allowance on the old machine was $4,000 and cash boot was paid for the balance.

(a) Prepare the necessary journal entry to record this exchange.

(b) What value would be given to the replacement machine for income tax purposes (the basis for future income tax depreciation)?

Solution

		Year	Annual Depreciation Expense	Accumulated Depreciation, End of Year	Undepreciated Cost End of Year
1.	(a)	1	$6,900	$ 6,900	$30,600
		2	6,900	13,800	23,700
		3	6,900	20,700	16,800
		4	6,900	27,600	9,900
		5	6,900	34,500	3,000
	(b)	1	$15,000	$15,000	$22,500
		2	9,000	24,000	13,500
		3	5,400	29,400	8,100
		4	3,240	32,640	4,860
		5	1,860*	34,500	3,000
	(c)	1	$11,500	$11,500	$26,000
		2	9,200	20,700	16,800
		3	6,900	27,600	9,900
		4	4,600	32,200	5,300
		5	2,300	34,500	3,000

* The machine is not depreciated below its estimated salvage value of $3,000.

2.	Year 2	(a) Straight-line Method	(b) Double-Declining-Balance Method	(c) Sum-of-the Years Digits Method
Revenue		$45,000	$45,000	$45,000
Costs and expenses other than depreciation		25,000	25,000	25,000
Depreciation		6,900	9,000	9,200
Net income		$13,100	$11,000	$10,800
	Year 4			
Revenue		$45,000	$45,000	$45,000
Costs and expenses other than depreciation		25,000	25,000	25,000
Depreciation		6,900	3,240	4,600
Net income		$13,100	$16,760	$15,400

3. (a)

Accumulated Depreciation—Equipment	32,640	
Equipment (new machine)	45,000	
Loss on Exchange of Equipment	860	
Equipment (old machine)		37,500
Cash		41,000

(b) Undepreciated cost of old machine	$ 4,860
Cash boot given	41,000
Value of replacement machine for income tax purposes	$45,860

or

Cost of new equipment	$45,000
Add unrecognized loss on old machine	860
Value of replacement machine for income tax purposes	$45,860

*Note: Now that you have reviewed the Demonstration Problem and Solution you may complete the **Mastery Problem** at the end of the chapter activities.

Applying Accounting Concepts

Series A

Exercise 14A1—Depreciation Expense Calculation; Straight-Line, Double-Declining-Balance, Sum-of-Years-Digits. A light truck is purchased on January 1 at a cost of $21,000. It is expected to serve for 5 years and to have a salvage value of $3,000. Calculate the depreciation expense for the first and third years of use of the truck using the

1. straight-line method.
2. double-declining-balance method.
3. sum-of-the-years-digits method.

Exercise 14A2—Depreciation Expense Calculation; Units of Output. The truck purchased in Exercise 14A1 is expected to be used for 80,000 miles over its 5-year life. Using the units-of-output method, calculate the depreciation expense for the first and third years of use if the truck is driven 20,000 miles in year 1 and 18,000 miles in year 3.

Exercise 14A3—Depreciation Expense Calculation; Five-Year MACRS Property. The truck purchased in Exercise 14A1 is classified as 5-year property according to MACRS depreciation. Using the MACRS depreciation rates provided in the chapter, calculate the depreciation expense for tax purposes in the first and third years of use of the truck.

Exercise 14A4—Depletion Expense Calculation; Cost Depletion. A gravel pit was acquired at a cost of $600,000. It is estimated that the pit will produce 400,000 cubic yards of gravel. During the first year 120,000 cubic yards of gravel were mined and sold.

(a) Calculate the proper depletion expense for Year 1.
(b) During the second year 150,000 cubic yards of gravel were mined and sold. At the end of the year, it is estimated that 225,000 cubic yards of gravel remain to be mined. Calculate the proper depletion expense for Year 2.

Exercise 14A5—Journal Entry for Discarding Depreciable Assets. On Jan. 4, 19--, shelving units which had cost $5,600 and had accumulated depreciation of $5,160 were discarded. Prepare the journal entry for this transaction.

Exercise 14A6—Journal Entries for Selling Depreciable Assets at a Gain and at a Loss. A delivery truck which had cost $22,000 and had accumulated depreciation of $17,800 was sold for $5,600.

1. Prepare the journal entry for this transaction.
2. Assuming that the truck was sold for $3,800, prepare the journal entry for this transaction.

Exercise 14A7—Journal Entries for Exchanging Similar Depreciable Assets at a Gain and at a Loss. A drill press which had cost $40,000 and had accumulated depreciation of $22,800 was traded in for a new drill press with a fair market value of $46,000. The old drill press and $26,000 in cash were given for the new drill press.

1. Prepare the journal entry for this transaction.
2. Assuming that the old drill press and $30,000 in cash were given for the new drill press, prepare the journal entry for this transaction.

Exercise 14A8—Journal Entry for Exchanging Dissimilar Depreciable Assets at a Gain. On June 30, 19--, office partitions which had cost $4,800 and had accumulated depreciation of $3,800 were traded in on new typewriters with a fair market value of $4,200. The partitions and $2,300 were given for the typewriters. Prepare the journal entry for this transaction.

Exercise 14A9—Journal Entry for Cost Depletion. A silver mine was acquired at a cost of $1,500,000, and estimated to contain 300,000 tons of ore. During the current year 90,000 tons of ore were mined and sold. Prepare the journal entry on Dec. 31, 19--, for the year's depletion expense.

Series B

Exercise 14B1—Depreciation Expense Calculation; Straight-Line, Double-Declining-Balance, Sum-of-Years-Digits. A machine is purchased on January 1 at a cost of $16,000. It is expected to serve for 10 years and to have a salvage value of $2,000. Calculate the depreciation expense for the second and sixth years of use of the truck using the

1. straight-line method.
2. double-declining-balance method (round to nearest dollar).
3. sum-of-the-years-digits method (round to nearest dollar).

Exercise 14B2—Depreciation Expense Calculation; Units of Output. The machine purchased in Exercise 14B1 is expected to produce 70,000 units of product over its 10-year life. Using the units-of-output method, calculate the depreciation expense for the second and sixth years of use if the machine produces 10,000 units in year 2 and 6,000 units in year 6.

Exercise 14B3—Depreciation Expense Calculation; Five-Year MACRS Property. The truck purchased in Exercise 14B1 is classified as 5-year property according to MACRS depreciation. Using the MACRS depreciation rates provided in the chapter, calculate the depreciation expense for tax purposes in the second and sixth years of use of the truck.

Exercise 14B4—Depletion Expense Calculation; Cost Depletion. A coal mine was acquired at a cost of $1,800,000. It is estimated that the mine will yield 900,000 tons of coal. During the first year 220,000 tons of coal were mined and sold.

(a) Calculate the proper depletion expense for Year 1.
(b) During the second year, 200,000 tons of coal were mined and sold. At the end of the year, it is estimated that 600,000 tons of coal remain to be mined. Calculate the proper depletion expense for Year 2.

Exercise 14B5—Journal Entry for Discarding Depreciable Assets. On June 1, 19--, a hand truck which had cost $1,400 and had accumulated depreciation of $1,290 was discarded. Prepare the journal entry for this transaction.

Exercise 14B6—Journal Entries for Selling Depreciable Assets at a Gain and at a Loss. Office equipment which had cost $16,500 and had accumulated depreciation of $13,350 was sold for $4,200.

1. Prepare the journal entry for this transaction.
2. Assuming that the office equipment was sold for $2,850, prepare the journal entry for this transaction.

Exercise 14B7—Journal Entries for Exchanging Similar Depreciable Assets at a Gain and at a Loss. A lathe which had cost $30,000 and had accumulated depreciation of $17,100 was traded in for a new lathe with a fair market value of $34,500. The old lathe and $19,500 in cash were given for the new lathe.

1. Prepare the journal entry for this transaction.
2. Assuming that the old lathe and $22,500 in cash were given for the new lathe, prepare the journal entry for this transaction.

Exercise 14B8—Journal Entry for Exchanging Dissimilar Depreciable Assets at a Gain. On Sept. 1, 19--, cash registers which had cost $3,600 and had accumulated depreciation of $2,850 were traded in on new typewriters with a fair market value of $3,150. The cash registers and $1,725 were given for the typewriters. Prepare the journal entry for this transaction.

Exercise 14B9—Journal Entry for Cost Depletion. A timber tract was acquired at a cost of $2,000,000, and estimated to contain 800,000 board feet. During the current year, 120,000 board feet of timber were cut and sold. Prepare the journal entry on Dec. 31, 19--, for the year's depletion expense.

Series A

Problem 14A1 Depreciation Expense Calculation and Schedule; Straight-Line, Double-Declining-Balance, Sum-of-Years-Digits

A machine is purchased on January 1 at a cost of $58,000. It is expected to serve for 10 years and to have a salvage value of approximately $9,000.

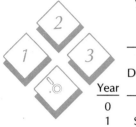

Required:

Calculate the depreciation for each year and the undepreciated cost at the end of each year using the:

1. Straight-line method
2. Double-declining-balance method
3. Sum-of-the-years-digits method

Show the results in a schedule like the one below. The amounts for the first year are given.

	(1) Straight-Line Method		(2) Double-Declining-Balance Method		(3) Sum-of-the-Years-Digits Method	
Year	Depreciation Charge	Undepreciated Cost End of Year	Depreciation Charge	Undepreciated Cost End of Year	Depreciation Charge	Undepreciated Cost End of Year
0		$58,000.00		$58,000.00		$58,000.00
1	$4,900.00	53,100.00	$11,600.00	46,400.00	$8,909.09	49,090.91

Problem 14A2   Depreciation Expense Calculation and Net Income Determination for Two Different Years; Straight-Line, Double-Declining Balance, Sum-of-Years-Digits

Refer to Problem 14A1. Assume that in Year 2 and Year 6 of the 10-year life of the machine purchased in Problem 14A1, revenues are $40,000 and costs and expenses other than depreciation are $27,000.

Required:

Calculate the net income for each year using the following depreciation methods:

1. Straight-line method.
2. Double-declining-balance method.
3. Sum-of-the-years-digits method.

Show the results for each of the years (2 and 6) in a separate schedule such as the one shown on page 553 of the text.

Problem 14A3   Journalizing and Posting Depreciable Asset Transactions; Property, Plant and Equipment Record Preparation

On January 1 of the current year, Massie and Scaggs go into the wholesale merchandise business as partners. In accounting for their plant assets, the following accounts are to be used:

181   Store Equipment
181.1 Accumulated Depreciation—Store Equipment
185   Delivery Equipment

185.1 Accumulated Depreciation—Delivery Equipment
191   Office Equipment
191.1 Accumulated Depreciation—Office Equipment
547   Depreciation Expense—Store Equipment
548   Depreciation Expense—Delivery Equipment
549   Depreciation Expense—Office Equipment

Transactions involving the purchase of plant assets are entered in a general journal from which they are posted to the proper general ledger accounts. A card record is kept of each individual depreciable asset.

The following transactions involve the purchase of plant assets during the current year.

Jan. 1 Invoice No. 431 from Copying Concepts was used to record the purchase of a new electronic typewriter, No. 44221120-15, for $1,045 cash. Its estimated useful life is 12 years with a salvage value of $95 at the end of that period.

April 1 Invoice No. 459 from Motor Transport Co. is used to record the purchase of a small new delivery truck for $15,000 cash. Its estimated useful life is 4 years with a salvage value of $2,000 at the end of that period.

May 2 Invoice No. 542 from the A-1 Lock & Safe Co. is used to record the purchase of a new office safe for $1,274 cash. Its estimated useful life is 30 years with an estimated salvage value of $74 at the end of that period.

June 6 Invoice No. 559 from Storage Systems, Inc. is used to record the purchase of a new showcase for $1,700 cash. Its estimated useful life is 20 years with no estimated salvage value at the end of that period.

July 1 Invoice No. 588 from Copying Concepts is used to record the purchase of a new typewriter desk for $900 cash. Its estimated useful life is 20 years with no salvage value.

Aug. 1 Invoice No. 632 from Warehouse of Fixtures is used to record the purchase of a new storeroom table for $450 cash. Its estimated useful life is 10 years with no estimated salvage value.

Required:

1. Enter the above transactions in a general journal.
2. Complete the individual posting from the Debit column (only) of the general journal to the following ledger accounts:

> Store Equipment, Account No. 181
> Delivery Equipment, Account No. 185
> Office Equipment, Account No. 191

In posting to the plant asset accounts, it is important that each asset be described in the "item" column of the account so that it may be identified with the record card that is kept.

3. Prepare the record of each depreciable asset purchased, using the format for the property, plant, and equipment record illustrated in the textbook on page 563. It will be necessary to calculate the rate of depreciation applicable to each asset (using the straight-line method). Take into consideration (a) the cost of the asset, (b) its estimated useful life, and (c) its salvage value, if any.

Problem 14A4	**Computing Year-End Depreciation from Property, Plant and Equipment Records; Journalizing in Compound Entry Form**

Refer to Problem 14A3. Massie and Scaggs keep their accounts on the calendar year basis and close their books on December 31. In connection with the adjusting entries at the end of the current year, you are required to compute the amount of the depreciation expense on the plant assets purchased during the year. The plant asset records should supply all the information needed in computing the depreciation. In the case of assets acquired on or before the 15th day of the month, depreciation should be computed for the full month; in the case of assets acquired after the 15th day of the month, no depreciation should be considered for the month in which acquired.

Required:

Compute the depreciation and prepare a compound journal entry for the depreciation, using a general journal. Also enter the depreciation of each asset in the plant asset records prepared in Problem 14A3.

Problem 14A5	**Calculating and Journalizing Cost Depletion in Two Successive Years**

Mineralex Co. acquired a coal mine at a cost of $1,600,000. The estimated number of units available for production is 1,000,000 tons.

(a) During the first year 200,000 tons of coal are mined and sold.
(b) During the second year, 260,000 tons of coal are mined and sold. At the end of the year, it is estimated that 700,000 tons of coal remain to be mined. (Compute the depletion expense per unit to four decimal places.)

Required:

Use general journal paper to prepare the entry for (a) the depletion of the Mineralex Co. coal mine in Year 1, and (b) the depletion of the mine in Year 2.

Series B

Problem 14B1	**Depreciation Expense Calculation and Schedule; Straight-Line, Double-Declining-Balance, Sum-of-Years-Digits**

A truck is purchased on January 1 at a cost of $19,000. It is expected to serve for 5 years and to have a salvage value of approximately $4,000.

Required:

Calculate the depreciation for each year and the undepreciated cost at the end of each year using the:

1. Straight-line method
2. Double-declining-balance method
3. Sum-of-the-years-digits method

Show the results in a schedule like the one below. The amounts for the first year are given.

	(1) Straight-Line Method		(2) Double-Declining-Balance Method		(3) Sum-of-the-Years-Digits Method	
Year	Depreciation Charge	Undepreciated Cost End of Year	Depreciation Charge	Undepreciated Cost End of Year	Depreciation Charge	Undepreciated Cost End of Year
0		$19,000.00		$19,000.00		$19,000.00
1	$3,000.00	16,000.00	$7,600.00	11,400.00	$5,000.00	14,000.00

Problem 14B2   Depreciation Expense Calculation and Net Income Determination for Two Different Years; Straight-Line, Double-Declining-Balance, Sum-of-Years-Digits

Refer to Problem 14B1. Assume that in Year 3 and Year 5 of the 5-year life of the machine purchased in Problem 14B1, revenues are $18,000 and costs and expenses other than depreciation are $9,000.

Required:
Calculate the net income for each year using the following depreciation methods:

1. Straight-line method.
2. Double-declining-balance method.
3. Sum-of-the-years-digits method.

Show the results for each of the years (3 and 5) in a separate schedule such as the one shown on page 553 of the text.

Problem 14B3   Journalizing and Posting Depreciable Asset Transactions; Property, Plant and Equipment Record Preparation

On July 1 of the current year, Rolfe and Smith go into the wholesale hardware business as partners. In accounting for their plant assets, the following accounts are to be used:

181   Store Equipment
181.1 Accumulated Depreciation—Store Equipment
185   Delivery Equipment
185.1 Accumulated Depreciation—Delivery Equipment
191   Office Equipment
191.1 Accumulated Depreciation—Office Equipment
547   Depreciation Expense—Store Equipment
548   Depreciation Expense—Delivery Equipment
549   Depreciation Expense—Office Equipment

Transactions involving the purchase of plant assets are entered in a general journal from which they are posted to the proper general ledger accounts. A card record is kept of each individual depreciable asset.

The following transactions involve the purchase of plant assets during the current year:

July 3   Invoice No. 214 from Enterprise Office Products, Inc. is used to record the purchase of a new electronic typewriter, No. 2211440-16, for $975 cash. Its estimated useful life is 10 years with estimated salvage value of $75 at the end of that period.

Aug. 1   Invoice No. 259 from Hogan Motor Co. is used to record the purchase of a small new delivery truck for $12,500 cash. Its estimated useful life is 4 years with estimated salvage of $1,500 at the end of that period.

Sept. 1   Invoice No. 322 from American Safe Co. is used to record the purchase of a new office safe for $974 cash. Its estimated useful life is 25 years with a salvage value of $74 at the end of that period.

Oct. 5   Invoice No. 359 from Marc Interiors is used to record the purchase of a new showcase for $1,275 cash. Its estimated useful life is 20 years and it is expected to have no salvage value.

Nov. 1   Invoice No. 377 from Enterprise Office Products, Inc. is used to record the purchase of a new typewriter desk for $675 cash. Its estimated useful life is 15 years and it is estimated to have no salvage value.

Dec. 1   Invoice No. 432 from National Furniture Co. is used to record the purchase of a new storeroom table for $335 cash. Its estimated useful life is 10 years with no expected salvage value.

Required:

1. Enter the above transactions in a general journal.
2. Complete the individual posting from the Debit column (only) of the general journal to the following four-column ledger accounts:

> Store Equipment, Account No. 181
> Delivery Equipment, Account No. 185
> Office Equipment, Account No. 191

In posting to the plant asset accounts, it is important that each asset be described in the "item" column of the account so that it may be identified with the record card that is kept.

3. Prepare the record of each depreciable asset purchased, using the format for the property, plant, and equipment record illustrated in the textbook on page 563. It will be necessary to calculate the rate of depreciation applicable to each asset (using the straight-line method). Take into consideration (a) the cost of the asset, (b) its estimated useful life, and (c) its salvage value, if any.

Problem 14B4   Computing Year-End Depreciation from Property, Plant and Equipment Records; Journalizing in Compound Entry Form

Refer to Problem 14B3. Rolfe and Smith keep their accounts on the calendar year basis and close their books on December 31. In connection with the adjusting entries at the end of the current year, you are required to compute the amount of the depreciation expense on the plant assets purchased during the year. The plant asset records should supply all the information needed in computing the depreciation. In the case of assets acquired on or before the 15th day of the month, depreciation should be computed for the full month; in the case of assets acquired after the 15th of the month, no depreciation should be considered for the month in which acquired.

Required:

Compute the depreciation and prepare a compound journal entry for the depreciation, using a general journal. Also enter the depreciation of each asset in the plant asset records prepared in Problem 14B3.

Problem 14B5   Calculating and Journalizing Cost Depletion in Two Successive Years

Monarch Metals Co. acquired a copper mine at a cost of $1,200,000. The estimated number of units available for production is 800,000 tons.

(a) During the first year, 180,000 tons of copper ore are mined and sold.
(b) During the second year, 215,000 tons of copper ore are mined and sold. At the end of the year, it is estimated that 250,000 tons of copper ore remain to be mined.

Required:

Use general journal paper to prepare the entry for (a) the depletion of the Monarch Metals Co. copper mine in Year 1, and (b) the depletion of the mine in Year 2.

Mastery Problem

On April 1, 19-A, Kwik Kopy Printing purchased two copying machines (A and B) for $25,000 each. The estimated life of each machine is 5 years and each has a salvage value of $2,500. The machines were used until July 1, 19-D.

Required:

1. Assuming that Kwik Kopy uses straight-line depreciation, prepare the following entries.
   (a) Adjusting entries for depreciation at the end of 19-A through 19-C.
   (b) Adjusting entry for depreciation on June 30, 19-D, just prior to trading the assets.
   (c) On July 1, 19-D, copying machine "A" was traded for a delivery van. The market value of the van is $19,000. Kwik Kopy must trade the copying machine and pay $11,000 for the new van.
   (d) On July 1, 19-D, copying machine "B" was traded for a newer copying machine. The market value of the new machine is $19,000. Kwik Kopy must trade the old copying machine and pay $11,000 for the new machine.

2. Assuming that Kwik Kopy uses sum-of-the-years-digits depreciation, prepare the following entries.

(a)   Adjusting entries for depreciation at the end of 19-A through 19-C.

(b)   Adjusting entry for depreciation on June 30, 19-D, just prior to trading the assets.

(c)   On July 1, 19-D, copying machine "A" was traded for a delivery van. The market value of the van is $19,000. Kwik Kopy must trade the copying machine and pay $11,000 for the new van.

(d)   On July 1, 19-D, copying machine "B" was traded for a newer copying machine. The market value of the new machine is $19,000. Kwik Kopy must trade the old copying machine and pay $11,000 for the new machine.

CHAPTER 15

Accounting Concepts and Accepted Practices

Chapter
Objectives

Careful study of this chapter should enable you to:

- Describe and explain the basic accounting concepts of:

  1. The business entity
  2. The going concern
  3. The monetary unit
  4. Transaction-based records and historical cost
  5. Periodicity, realization, and matching
  6. The accrual basis

- Describe and explain the widely accepted accounting practices of:

  1. Consistency and comparability
  2. Adequate disclosure
  3. Objectivity and verifiability
  4. Materiality and practicality
  5. Conservatism
  6. Legality

In Chapters 6 through 14 numerous applications of the accrual basis of accounting have been illustrated. Accrual accounting is used instead of the cash or modified cash basis by most businesses because it should provide better measures of the performance and current condition of the business in the financial statements. For these financial statement measures to be reliable, there is a need for a set of concepts and practices to serve as guidelines in preparing the statements. The purpose of this chapter is to describe that set of concepts and practices.

The framework that underlies financial accounting today is a blend of various assumptions, conventions, requirements, practical compromises, and constraints. Because these factors are so interrelated, it is not possible to list them in an unquestioned order of importance. You should remember this in the discussion that follows. In the organization of this chapter, the various matters are grouped according to (1) those that can be regarded as concepts and (2) those that can be classified as accepted practices. However, it will soon become apparent that there is some overlap between the categories.

Basic Financial Accounting Concepts

The basic concepts in financial accounting include: (1) the business entity, (2) the going concern, (3) the monetary unit, (4) transaction-based records and the related concept of historical cost, (5) periodicity and the related concepts of realization and matching, and (6) the accrual basis.

The Business Entity

Describe and explain the business entity concept.

As applied to financial accounting, the entity concept assumes that a business is treated as a separate and identifiable economic unit. This economic unit can be defined in various ways without regard to legal considerations of who actually owns the property and who is liable for the debts. In connection with the discussions and illustrations of the accounts of a single-owner business (a sole proprietorship), it was stressed that while the owner might possess various properties, only the property used in the business was taken into account. Likewise, the record of liabilities excluded any of the proprietor's debts of a non-business or personal nature. Consequently, there was no accounting for any type of revenue and expense not connected with business operations. Of course, a business could be considered to include other, perhaps wholly unrelated, profit-seeking activities if the owner so desires. Or, the accounting entity could consist of the assets used by the business and the liabilities incurred on behalf of the business, even though, legally, the property belonged to the owner who was personally liable for the debts.

In the case of business partnerships, the separate entity is almost a legal reality. Property can be owned by a partnership. However, with limited exceptions, the debts of the firm may become personal liabilities of each of the partners. In the case of business corporations, the business entity is a legal reality, even though corporations are owned by their shareholders or stockholders. Corporations can own property, incur debt, sue, and be sued. The debts of a corporation are debts of the corporate entity, not personal debts of its owners (stockholders). This is one of the reasons for the wide popularity of the corporate form of business organization.

Probably the greatest extension of the entity concept occurs when one corporation owns most or all of another (or perhaps several others). While each corporation is a legal entity and each has a separate set of records, their individual financial statements are combined to present what is known as a consolidated income statement and a consolidated balance sheet. From the viewpoint of the stockholders of the parent corporation (the corporation that controls the other corporations in the consolidated group), there is, in effect, just one entity.

The Going-Concern

Describe and explain the going concern concept.

A well-established tradition in business accounting is to assume that in most cases a business will have a continuing, indefinite life. This is called the going concern concept, or concept of continuity. Several arguments are offered in support of this concept. Corporations can have virtually perpetual existence. Sole proprietorships and partnerships can also have continuing lives if when proprietors and partners die, the businesses involved are continued by others—perhaps by those who inherit the business, by remaining partners, or by those to whom the business may be sold. In most cases, the owners and managers of a business intend and hope that the business will continue indefinitely. They usually make decisions with a view to maintaining the existence of the business, often in the hope of expanding it.

The reality of the economic world does not give full support to the going concern concept. Business failures are commonplace, especially among new businesses. However, the alternative to assuming that a business will continue indefinitely would be to make an estimate of its probable life. This type of estimate could cause many problems for a business. For example, the acquisition of a depreciable asset with a potential useful life greater than the expected life of the business might seem inadvisable. Also, the nature of depreciation calculations for long-term assets could be affected. The estimated life of the business rather than the estimated useful life of the asset might become the controlling element. In addition, the longer a business survives, the greater its chance for continued existence; thus some depreciation rates might have to be revised and re-revised. Since this alternative to a continuity concept is so unattractive (perhaps unworkable), the going concern concept seems the more sensible alternative.

The Monetary Unit

Describe and explain the monetary unit concept.

The monetary unit concept means that business transactions are measured in terms of money and that the purchasing power of money is assumed to be stable. Note that there are two important aspects of this concept. The first is that accounting recognizes only those events and transactions that can be accurately measured in terms of money. The second is that for those events and transactions that are recognized, the money measure used is assumed to have the same value over time. Both of these aspects of the monetary unit concept must be considered in evaluating financial statements.

By reporting only events and transactions that can be measured in terms of money, accounting reports necessarily are limited in scope. Such matters as competitive advantage or disadvantage, employee attitudes, management talents, and working conditions are important in evaluating a business, but they cannot be stated adequately in money terms. Major changes in top management positions or new government regulations are perhaps even more important to a business, but once again measurement in money terms would be quite difficult. Accountants are aware of these limitations but they feel that the measurement and interpretation of the effects of such matters should be made by the users of the accounting reports rather than by the accountants.

Another limitation of the information contained in accounting reports is the assumption that the purchasing power of money is stable. In America the monetary unit used to measure financial transactions is the dollar; in Great Britain, the pound; and in West Germany, the mark. Whatever form of monetary unit is used, it is not as reliable a measuring unit as is a physical measure, such as the meter or kilogram, because the value of money fluctuates. This can cause the monetary unit to have different values at different points in time.

For several decades, the question of whether changes in the value of the dollar should be recognized in the accounting process has been discussed and debated. It is well known that the purchasing power of the dollar is constantly changing—nearly always declining. The impact of this on the financial statements is greatest in the case of long-term assets. The problem is that the amounts shown as the costs of long-term assets may be a mixture of some dollars spent perhaps 25 years ago, some 20 years ago, some 10 years ago, and some more recently. Almost certainly, the value of the dollar was not the same at those different times. The amount charged to depreciation expense would be, in consequence, a mixture of different-valued dollars. To a lesser extent, this may apply to shorter-term assets whose costs become expenses within a shorter period of time, as in the case of inventories. Another point is that the dollars of revenue for a single period generally represent similar purchasing power, while the dollars of expense deducted may be a diverse mixture.

The effects of the instability of the dollar on accounting reports can be illustrated as follows. Assume that a business bought equipment for $50,000 ten years ago and that the equipment now costs $100,000 to replace because of inflation. If the old equipment is fully depreciated and the net income of the business over the ten-year period was equal to $50,000, then the cost of the old equipment has been recovered and the firm has had a profit of $50,000. However, the firm has not really had a profit at all, because it will require both the recovered cost of the old equipment ($50,000) and the $50,000 of reported net income to purchase the new equipment for $100,000. Thus, the reported net income might be misleading.

The monetary unit concept continues to be accepted, because money is still a common ingredient of all business transactions. Money provides a practical measurement unit capable of lending objectivity and uniformity to financial data. Nevertheless, there is a continuing interest by some firms in reporting accounting information either adjusted for general price level changes or in terms of replacement costs.

Transaction-Based Records and Historical Cost

Describe and explain the transaction-based records and historical cost concepts.

Fundamental to business accounting is the idea that there is nothing to account for until a transaction occurs. When the transaction involves the acquisition of an asset, then the amount to be entered is the acquisition cost, or historical cost, of that asset. The historical cost concept states that, generally, no adjustment will be made to this amount in later periods, except to allocate the original cost of the asset to periodic expense as the asset is consumed.

Accountants do not deny that changes in the values of assets occur over time. But accountants generally insist on objective, verifiable evidence before they are willing to enter information in the accounts. This evidence is available whenever a transaction occurs. (Objective, verifiable evidence is discussed in a later section of this chapter.) Differences between the historical cost of a business's assets and the various market values of those assets that may exist at some later date may be difficult to measure and may never materialize. Consequently, accountants are reluctant to enter such value changes in the accounts. This concept is furthered strengthened by the application of the realization concept discussed in the next section.

Periodicity, Realization, and Matching

Describe and explain the periodicity, realization, and matching concepts.

Central to financial accounting is the concept that income determination can be made on a periodic basis, known as the **periodicity concept**. This means that income should always be determined annually, and in addition, sometimes for shorter periods, such as quarterly or monthly. Any period shorter than a year is described as an **interim period**. The requirement that income be determined on a periodic basis causes most of the problems associated with income measurement.

In order to determine income on a periodic basis, the accountant must decide when to recognize revenue and expenses. In accordance with the realization concept, revenue is generally considered to be realized when there is a receipt of cash or a claim to cash in exchange for goods or services. For example, assume a car is taken to a service station for gasoline (goods) and a car wash (services). The dealer may either receive cash or make the sale on account. In either event, the dealer is considered to have realized revenue, even though the sale on account would create an account receivable on the dealer's books.

Once a decision is made regarding when to recognize revenue (using the realization concept), the expenses must next be recognized in accordance with the matching concept. The **matching concept** states that expenses incurred to generate particular revenues should be matched with those revenues that they helped to generate. For example, if the dealer in the previous example recorded the sale of gasoline, the cost of the gasoline sold should be matched against the revenue realized from the sale. Uncollectible accounts receivable represent a potential problem if revenue is considered realized when a claim to cash is created. The usual solution is the periodic estimation of uncollectible accounts expense. This estimation becomes part of the income calculation for the same period in which the revenue and receivables were recorded.

It is in attempting to perform the matching process that the periodic-income-determination requirement poses the largest problem. Two outstanding examples of expense-matching problems are: (1) the apportionment of merchandise cost between cost of goods sold and end-of-period inventory, and (2) the allocation of the cost of plant and equipment by means of depreciation. Considerable judgment and estimation are necessary in each of these cases. Nonetheless, the matching of revenues and expenses is a fundamental part of the accrual accounting process.

The Accrual Basis

Describe and explain the accrual basis concept.

According to the accrual basis concept, revenue is recognized in the accounting period in which it is earned, and expenses are recognized in the accounting period in which they are incurred, regardless of whether the receipt or disbursement of cash takes place in the same period. The accrual basis involves the periodic matching of revenue with the expenses related to its realization. Revenue from sales must be matched with the cost of goods sold and the various other expenses incidental to conducting a business. The simple matching of cash receipts for a particular period with the cash paid for goods or services acquired in that period is meaningless for the most part. Collections may relate to sales of the current period and payments may relate to purchases during a previous period or vice versa. The expenses related to most long-term assets occur as the assets lose their usefulness. The accrual basis recognizes changes in a variety of assets and liabilities in determining periodic net income—not just cash changes.

It is the combined effect of the realization and matching concepts coupled with the accrual basis concept, that provides some assurance that income is accurately measured and reported each period.

Building Your Accounting Knowledge

1. Does the business entity concept identify only the legal property and legal debts of the business enterprise or is it broader than this? Discuss.
2. What attribute of corporations supports the going-concern concept? What experiences of proprietors and partners support it?
3. Since the realities of the economic world do not fully support the going-concern concept, how is it justified by accountants? Discuss.
4. How do accountants justify the use of the monetary unit as a measuring device?
5. How is the historical cost concept related to transaction-based records?
6. How do the realization and matching concepts relate to the periodicity concept? Give two examples of this relationship.
7. When is revenue considered to be earned on the accrual basis? When is expense considered to be incurred on this basis?
8. What problems are created by a simple matching of cash received from customers during an accounting period with the cash paid for goods or services purchased in that same period?

Assignment Box

To reinforce your understanding of the preceding text materials, you may complete the following:

Study Guide: Part A
Textbook: Exercises 15A1 through 15A5 or 15B1 through 15B5
Problems 15A1 through 15A2 or 15B1 through 15B2

Accepted Accounting Practices

Several practices concerning financial statements have become widely accepted in the accounting profession to help make accounting data more useful. Some of these practices have grown out of the concepts that have been discussed. Others are intended to help make accounting reports easier to understand. Many involve a compromise between partially-conflicting objectives. Six of the most important of these practices are discussed in the paragraphs that follow.

Consistency and Comparability

Describe and explain the consistency and comparability practices.

It has already been noted that the problems posed by the periodicity and matching concepts (which are fundamental to business accounting) make it impossible to achieve absolute accuracy in the calculation of periodic income. Nevertheless, the users of financial statements invariably want to make comparisons between current and past results. This combination of circumstances makes it necessary to have a degree of consistency (the use of the same accounting method from period to period) in accounting methods which makes comparability (the ability to identify similarities and differences in performance) between periods possible. One example of this need is found in the choice of an accounting method for merchandise inventory. Regardless of whether lifo or fifo is considered best, it is not difficult to imagine the possible consequence of switching from one to the other each year. This switching might make any comparison of the results of operations for several years almost meaningless. Frequent changes of the depreciation method could produce a similar undesirable result. Stated loosely, the rule is: "If you cannot be completely certain of your choice of method, at least use it consistently."

The consistency practice must not be carried to such an extreme that it is taken to mean that a method of accounting once adopted must never be changed. Changing circumstances or new accounting standards may require a change in accounting method, but it is not expected that numerous and substantial changes will be needed each year. When important changes are made, it is essential that the financial statements clearly indicate (by footnote or otherwise) the changes made and the reasons therefor. Sometimes data are included in the explanation to show what the result would have been if the change had not been made. The act of providing an explanation of what was done, and why, is an example of compliance with the practice of adequate disclosure

Adequate Disclosure

Describe and explain the adequate disclosure practice.

The practice of adequate disclosure must be followed in the preparation of accounting reports for several reasons:

1. Financial statement users want to know which of the various generally accepted accounting principles and practices have been used.
2. There is a danger that significant facts about what has taken place during the period under review will somehow get "buried" among all the other information that the report contains or else remain undisclosed.
3. There has been an increasing demand from users of financial reports for more information about the business.

To meet the adequate disclosure requirement, a number of procedures have evolved. The use of explanatory notes, either in the body of financial statements or as footnotes, has become widespread. What is termed the "all inclusive" type of income statement has become widely used. Such a statement not only shows the composition of the income (loss) from regular operations for the period, but, in addition, any unusual gains or losses that have occurred.

The annual reports of large corporations often include an assortment of tables and graphs intended to emphasize significant trends in the corporate business affairs. Often statistical data of a non-financial nature are included, such as the number of employees or the number of units produced. Annual reports of this type always include a message from the company president or board chairperson. This message attempts to draw attention to important things that happened during the year, including any major changes in management personnel and a general forecast for the year or years ahead.

In the interest of adequate disclosure, multiproduct-line companies are now required to provide information about major segments or product lines of the business by both the Securities and Exchange Commission and the Federal Trade Commission. It has also been proposed that annual reports should include a financial budget (forecast) so that interested parties can have an idea of "what's coming." Just how far adequate disclosure should go is an unsettled issue. Nevertheless, the inclusion of forecast data in published annual reports is increasing.

Objectivity and Verifiability

Describe and explain the objectivity and verifiability practices.

Data that are entered in the accounting records and later reported in the financial statements of a business generally should be supported by source documents or other records. These records should be both objective and verifiable forms of evidence that certain transactions occurred.

This is the practice of objectivity and verifiability. Sales tickets, purchase invoices, and employee paychecks are examples of source documents that provide objective evidential matter. When evidence is not completely objective, as in the case of doubtful accounts receivable or long-term asset depreciation, the most objective evidence available should be used. Records of past experience in collecting accounts receivable are an example of objective evidence for entering doubtful accounts expense.

The notion of **objectivity** is that such source documents or records of past experience provide unbiased, factual evidence of real transactions and events that have occurred. The notion of **verifiability** is that any two accountants looking independently at the same evidence probably would make the related entry in the same way.

Materiality and Practicality

Describe and explain the materiality and practicality practice.

In the field of law, there is a maxim of *de minimis non curat lex*, which means that the law is not concerned with trifles. The same can be said of accounting. In accounting, the practice of **materiality and practicality** means that the concepts of accrual accounting need not be followed for amounts that are too small to make any real difference. For example, even though a waste basket that cost $5 may be expected to be useful for many years, it is not necessary to account for it as an asset to be depreciated. Instead the expenditure could be treated as miscellaneous expense. It is an almost universal practice for each business to establish some "cut-off point" that the accountant should follow in entering such expenditures. In the case of a small business, the point might be $25 or $50; larger businesses may have a higher limit. Consistency of treatment is, of course, necessary.

In the handling of certain year-end adjustments, the amount involved may dictate whether an adjustment should be made. For example, it may be unnecessary to bother with accrued interest payable or receivable in the amount of $2.65 or to enter the fact that $15 of the supplies expense account balance (amounting to more than $600) actually relates to supplies that are still on hand.

Probably the most important application of the practice of materiality is in connection with the financial statements. Adequate disclosure does not require that a petty cash fund of $100 be shown by itself rather than being lumped together with cash in bank. It also does not require the detail for prepaid expenses, whose total is equal to one percent of total assets, to be shown. In fact, the interests of adequate disclosure are best served by preparing financial statements and schedules that are not so filled with detail that the significant matters are obscured.

The use of rounded amounts on the financial statements is another widespread practice that is followed in the interest of eliminating the immaterial aspects of financial statements. Depending on the size of the company, financial statement amounts are rounded to the nearest dollar, $100, $1,000, and even more for very large companies.

Conservatism

Describe and explain
the conservatism
practice.

The customs, concepts, and conventions of financial accounting involve a tendency (some say a bias) toward **conservatism**. Generally, this means that when two or more acceptable ways of allocating the cost of an asset between benefiting periods can be used, the one that causes reported assets and periodic income to be smaller usually is chosen. The widely used "cost or market, whichever is lower" method for assigning a value to the end-of-period merchandise inventory will cause both the inventory and the income of the period just ended to be smaller than otherwise. As applied to depreciation, if equally good reasons exist to use either a ten-year or a twelve-year estimated life for a depreciable asset, most accountants would use the shorter life. For the years the asset is used, both the income of each of the periods and the undepreciated cost of the asset at the end of each period will be smaller than if the longer life were used. When the question arises whether to charge the total cost of an item to expense immediately or to treat it as an asset to be amortized, the "expense-it-now" option usually is followed.

Probably the most extensive example of the practice of conservatism stems from the historical-cost and realization concepts. These concepts do not permit "writing up" assets (changing the amount of an asset on the balance sheet to account for the increase in value) even if they are thought at a later date to be worth more than the accounts show. Some accountants contend that refusing to show market values for all assets causes many balance sheets to have very little meaning. However, if such write-ups were to become accepted practice, either accountants would have to be trained as appraisers or appraisers would have to be employed. It is questionable whether the values thus determined would qualify as objective, verifiable evidence. Historical costs, generally, do meet this test. Further, either the amount of the write-up would have to be considered as revenue even though there were no inflows of cash or receivables (or other assets), or provision would have to be made in the accounts for **unrealized revenue**. In the opinion of many accountants and business executives, so-called unrealized revenue is not revenue at all.

The conservatism practice is thought to have become deeply imbedded in accounting for two major reasons: (1) If unquestioned absolute accuracy in accounting is not possible, there is probably less danger of damaging the interests of existing and prospective owners and creditors by following conservative practices. (2) Conservative accounting practices lead to lower reported income for tax purposes and therefore lower taxes. Income tax laws do not require that most items be handled in the same way for tax purposes as they are in the accounts. Nevertheless, businesses typically find it easier to account for their activities in the same way for financial reporting purposes as for tax purposes. Further, a tax approach is easier to defend if it corresponds to what is done in the accounts.

Legality

Describe and explain
the legality practice.

Accounting records and reports must conform with certain legal requirements, such as tax regulations, contract provisions, and state incorporation laws, that relate to specific business transactions. This is the practice of legality. For example, it is illegal to evade taxes or reduce the required tax payments by ignoring or flaunting the law. It is also illegal to fail or refuse to enter payroll tax deductions when keeping employee payroll records. The structure of the equity section of a corporation balance sheet often is affected by the laws of the state in which the firm is incorporated. In addition, the ability of a corporation to pay dividends can be determined by state incorporation laws. The accounting system must be maintained in such a way that compliance with applicable laws can be determined.

Building Your Accounting Knowledge

1. How are consistency and comparability related in business accounting?
2. If an important change occurs in the accounting method used, how should it be indicated to users of financial statements?
3. Give three reasons for observing the practice of adequate disclosure.
4. How are source documents related to achieving objectivity and verifiability?
5. Explain why materiality is closely associated with practicality.
6. What is the relationship between materiality and adequate disclosure?
7. Give two examples of the application of the practice of conservatism.
8. Give two examples of legal requirements to which accounting records and reports must conform.

Assignment Box

To reinforce your understanding of the preceding text materials, you may complete the following:

       Study Guide: Part B
       Textbook: Exercises 15A6 through 15A7 or 15B6 through 15B7
               Problems 15A3 through 15A4 or 15B3 through 15B4

Expanding Your Business Vocabulary

What is the meaning of each of the following terms?

accrual basis concept (p. 583)
adequate disclosure (p. 585)
concept of continuity (p. 580)
conservatism (p. 587)
consistency and comparability (p. 584)

consolidated balance sheet (p. 579)
consolidated income statement (p. 579)
entity concept (p. 579)
going-concern concept (p. 580)
historical cost concept (p. 581)

Demonstration Problem

Mohr and Jones, partners in a wholesale hardware business, completed the following transactions during the last half of 19--:

July 10 Ordered 50 heavy-duty lock sets from Sure Locks at $95 each.

Aug. 6 Ordered 30 double-section 3' × 5' prefabricated windows from Arch-View Energy Products at $195 each.

9 Received the lock sets ordered from Sure Locks on July 10.

13 Received the invoice from Sure Locks, dated August 9, for $4,750, terms n/30.

Sept. 4 Received the windows ordered from Arch-View Energy Products on Aug. 6.

7 Received the invoice from Arch-View Energy Products dated Sept. 4 for $5,850, terms n/30.

12 Paid $4,750 to Sure Locks in settlement of Aug. 13 invoice.

18 Sold 10 heavy-duty lock sets received Aug. 9 to Essen Hardware Co. for $110 each.

Oct. 6 Paid $5,850 to Arch-View Energy Products in settlement of Sept. 7 invoice.

11 Sold 12 double-section 3' × 5' windows received Sept. 4 to Lincoln Lumber Co. for $225 each.

15 Paid Echo Express $130 for delivery services rendered during the past month.

Nov. 12 Sold 10 double-section 3' × 5' windows received Sept. 4 to Cooper Exteriors for $225 each.

Dec. 9 Sold 20 heavy-duty lock sets received Aug. 9 to Century Hardware Co. for $110 each.

14 Paid Echo Express $120 for delivery services rendered during the past month.

Required:

1. Compute the amount of gross margin on the Sept. 18 lock set sale.
2. Compute the amount of gross margin on the Oct. 11 double-section window sale.
3. Determine the income of Mohr and Jones for the period July 1-Oct. 31, 19--.
4. Compute the amount of gross margin on the Nov. 12 double-section window sale.

5. Compute the amount of gross margin on the Dec. 9 heavy-duty lock set sale.
6. Determine the income of Mohr and Jones for the last half of 19--.
7. Identify the concept of accounting which has been utilized throughout this problem.

Solution

1. Gross margin on Sept. 18 lock set sale:

Sales (10 heavy-duty lock sets at $110)	$1,100
Cost of sales (10 heavy-duty lock sets at $95)	950
Gross margin	$ 150

2. Gross margin on Oct. 11 double-section window sale:

Sales (12 windows at $225)	$2,700
Cost of sales (12 windows at $195)	2,340
Gross margin	$ 360

3. Income of Mohr and Jones for the period July 1—Oct. 31, 19--:

Gross margin on Sept. 18 sale	$ 150
Gross margin on Oct. 11 sale	360
	$ 510
Less delivery expenses	130
Income for four months	$ 380

4. Gross margin on Nov. 12 double-section window sale:

Sales (10 windows at $225)	$2,250
Cost of sales (10 windows at $195)	1,950
Gross margin	$ 300

5. Gross margin on Dec. 9 lock set sale:

Sales (20 heavy duty lock sets at $110)	$2,200
Cost of sales (20 heavy duty lock sets at $95)	1,900
Gross margin	$ 300

6. Income of Mohr and Jones for the last half of 19--:

Income July 1—Oct. 31	$ 380
Gross margin on Nov. 12 sale	300
Gross margin on Dec. 9 sale	300
	$ 980
Less delivery expenses	120
Income for last half of 19--	$ 860

7. matching

Note: Now that you have reviewed the Demonstration Problem and Solution you may complete the **Mastery Problem** at the end of the chapter activities.

Applying Accounting Concepts

Series A

Exercise 15A1—Journal Entries—Business Related. Nancy Sachar, who owns and operates N.S. Locksmiths, completed the following transactions during the past month.

(a) Received $170 for repairing lock on customer safe.
(b) Paid $124 shop electric bill.
(c) Paid $74 dental bill for daughter.
(d) Received $280 for installing new deadbolt locks on customer doors.
(e) Received $134 from sale of son's bicycle.
(f) Paid $140 for cleaning service at shop.

Prepare general journal entries for each of the above transactions that should be considered part of N.S. Locksmiths' operations.

Exercise 15A2—Calculation of Depreciation Expense. Gordon Wilson purchased new office equipment for $6,000. The equipment is expected to last 10 years and have no salvage value. Wilson plans to sell the business in which the equipment is used in three years.

Compute depreciation expense for the equipment for the first year of use, using the straight-line method.

Exercise 15A3—Journal Entries—Transaction Related. Prepare appropriate general journal entries for each of the following events and transactions that should be reflected in the accounting records.

(a) Purchased manufacturing equipment for $6,800 on account.
(b) Purchased merchandise for $3,100 cash.
(c) Determined that the equipment in transaction (a) could now be purchased for $6,300.
(d) Determined that the merchandise in transaction (b) could now be sold for $3,650.
(e) Sold the merchandise in transaction (b) for $3,600 cash.

Exercise 15A4—Gross Margin and Net Income Computation. P.J. Orthwein, who runs a used car lot, completed the following transactions:

(a) Acquired a used Cutlass at auction for $6,200.
(b) Acquired a used Taurus at auction for $7,500.
(c) Sold the Cutlass for $7,050.
(d) Acquired a used Celebrity at auction for $5,880.
(e) Sold the Taurus for $8,900.
(f) Paid lot rental and utilities of $720.

1. Compute the amount of gross margin on the sale of the Cutlass.
2. Compute the amount of gross margin on the sale of the Taurus.
3. Compute the net income from operating the lot during this time period.

Exercise 15A5—Effect of Adjustments on Net Income. Wasley Company has completed its first year of operations and the new accountant has prepared an income statement showing net income of $106,200 for the year ended December 31, 19-A. You have reviewed the accountant's work and discovered the following items which the accountant failed to consider in calculating net income:

(a) Supplies inventory at year end was $1,940. All purchases of supplies during the year were charged to Supplies Expense.
(b) The rent expense account includes $4,800 of rent paid that pertains to 19-B.

(c) Unpaid employee salaries total $6,220.

(d) Auto repairs performed in December and costing $760 have not yet been entered or paid for.

(e) Kathy Wasley, the owner, withdrew $4,000 during November. The amount was charged to Accounts Receivable.

(f) Straight-line depreciation on office equipment costing $16,000 has not been recorded. The equipment is expected to last 10 years and have a salvage value of $1,000.

(g) Accrued interest of $1,120 on a note receivable has not been entered.

(h) Uncollectible accounts are estimated at $800.

For each item listed, indicate the amount, if any, that should be added to (+) or subtracted from (−) the reported net income. Then, calculate the corrected net income.

Exercise 15A6—Change in Accounting Method—Effect on Net Income. Last Co. is considering making three accounting changes in the current year:

(a) Change in inventory method. The ending inventory cost under the present fifo method of valuation is $14,000; under the proposed lifo method it would be $10,400. (Hint: Ending inventory and net income vary directly; a decrease in one would cause a similar decrease in the other.)

(b) Change in depreciation method. Presently, depreciation under the straight-line method is $13,200; under the double-declining-balance method it would be $17,800. (Hint: An increase in depreciation expense would cause a corresponding decrease in net income.)

(c) Change in the estimated allowance for doubtful accounts. The uncollectible accounts expense presently is $1,180; after the change in estimate, this expense would be $1,420. (Hint: An increase in uncollectible accounts expense would cause a corresponding decrease in net income.)

If Last Co.'s net income is $24,600 under present conditions, determine what the net income would be if the three proposed accounting changes were made.

Exercise 15A7—Net Income after Adjustments. Walton Co. reported net income of $76,000 for the current year. In reviewing Walton's records, you discover the following items for which no adjustments were made at the end of the period.

(a) Supplies of $54 were on hand.

(b) Interest revenue of $10 had accrued for four days on a note receivable.

(c) Delivery charges of $26 on packages received in the current period were not entered until paid in the following period.

(d) Petty cash expenditures of $14 were not entered because reimbursement of petty cash was not made at the end of the period.

(e) Interest expense of $20 had accrued for six days on a note payable.

Compute the net income of Walton Co. for the year if adjustments were made for these items. What accounting practice would support Walton's not making these adjustments?

Series B

Exercise 15B1—Journal Entries—Business Related. Charles Shock, who owns and operates Shock Electric Service, completed the following transactions during the past month.

(a) Received $125 for replacing control panel in customer's home.
(b) Paid $93 shop electric bill.
(c) Paid $55 doctor bill for son.
(d) Received $210 for installing new fixtures in customer's home.
(e) Received $100 from sale of daughter's clarinet.
(f) Paid $120 for cleaning service at shop.

Prepare general journal entries for each of the above transactions that should be considered part of Shock Electric Service's operations.

Exercise 15B2—Calculation of Depreciation Expense. Helen Thompson purchased new office equipment for $4,500. The equipment is expected to last 10 years and have no salvage value. Thompson plans to sell the business in which the equipment is used in five years.

Compute the appropriate depreciation expense for the equipment for the first year of use, using the straight-line method.

Exercise 15B3—Journal Entries—Transaction Related. Prepare appropriate general journal entries for each of the following events and transactions that should be reflected in the accounting records.

(a) Purchased manufacturing equipment for $5,100 on account.
(b) Purchased merchandise for $2,325 cash.
(c) Determined that the merchandise in transaction (b) could now be sold for $2,800.
(d) Determined that the equipment in transaction (a) could now be purchased for $4,500.
(e) Sold the merchandise in transaction (b) for $2,700 cash.

Exercise 15B4—Gross Margin and Net Income Computation. S.G. Murphy, who runs a used car lot, completed the following transactions:

(a) Acquired a used Accord at auction for $4,500.
(b) Acquired a used Reliant at auction for $5,250.
(c) Sold the Accord for $6,075.
(d) Acquired a used Celica at auction for $4,410.
(e) Sold the Reliant for $7,200.
(f) Paid lot rental and utilities of $540.

1. Compute the amount of gross margin on the sale of the Accord.
2. Compute the amount of the gross margin on the sale of the Reliant.
3. Compute the net income from operating the lot during this time period.

Exercise 15B5—Effect of Adjustments on Net Income. Laine Company has completed its first year of operations and the new accountant has prepared an income statement showing net income of $79,650 for the year ended December 31, 19-A. You have reviewed the accountant's work and discovered the following items which the accountant failed to consider in calculating net income:

(a) Supplies inventory at year end was $1,455. All purchases of supplies during the year were charged to Supplies Expense.

(b) The rent expense account includes $3,600 of rent paid that pertains to 19-B.

(c) Unpaid employee salaries total $4,665.

(d) Auto repairs performed in December and costing $570 have not yet been entered or paid for.

(e) Steven Laine, the owner, withdrew $3,000 during November. The amount was charged to Accounts Receivable.

(f) Straight-line depreciation on office equipment costing $12,000 has not been recorded. The equipment is expected to last 10 years and have a salvage value of $2,000.

(g) Accrued interest of $840 on a note receivable has not been entered.

(h) Uncollectible accounts are estimated at $600.

For each item listed, indicate the amount, if any, that should be added to (+) or subtracted from (−) the reported net income. Then, calculate the corrected net income.

Exercise 15B6—Change in Accounting Method—Effect on Net Income. Adams Co. is considering making the following changes in the current year:

(a) Change in inventory method. The ending inventory cost under the present lifo method is $7,800; under the proposed fifo method it would be $10,500. (Hint: Ending inventory and net income vary directly; an increase in one would cause a similar increase in the other.)

(b) Change in depreciation method. Depreciation under the sum-of-years-digits method is $12,350; under the proposed straight-line method it would be $9,900. (Hint: A decrease in depreciation expense would cause a corresponding increase in net income.)

(c) Change in the estimated allowance for doubtful accounts. The uncollectible accounts expense presently is $1,060; after the change in estimate, this expense would be $890. (Hint: A decrease in the uncollectible accounts expense would cause a corresponding increase in net income.)

If Adams Co.'s net income is $18,500 under present conditions, determine what the net income would be if the three proposed accounting changes were made.

Exercise 15B7—Net Income after Adjustments. Sanchez Co. reported net income of $57,000 for the current year. In reviewing Sanchez' records, you discover the following items for which no adjustments were made at the end of the period.

(a) Supplies of $40 were on hand.

(b) Interest revenue of $8 had accrued for four days on a note receivable.

(c) Delivery charges of $19 on packages received in the current period were not entered until paid in the following period.

(d) Petty cash expenditures of $10 were not entered because reimbursement of petty cash was not made at the end of the period.

(e) Interest expense of $15 had accrued for six days on a note payable.

Compute the net income of Sanchez Co. for the year if adjustment were made for these items. What accounting practice would support Sanchez' not making these adjustments?

Series A

Problem 15A1   Choosing Items to Prepare Balance Sheet in Report Form

---

Eisenman Electronic Typewriter Sales and Service, owned and operated by Shira Eisenman, is in the process of separating the assets and liabilities of the business enterprise from Eisenman's personal assets and liabilities as of December 31, 19--. Eisenman has solicited your help.

Cash in business bank account in Shays Bank	$ 15,200
Cash in personal bank account in Fortress Savings	40,280
Accounts receivable owed to Eisenman Typewriter	35,980
Allowance for doubtful accounts:	
on Eisenman Typewriter Accounts Receivable	2,200
Merchandise inventory of Eisenman Typewriter	148,780
Prepaid insurance:	
Eisenman Typewriter	800
Shira Eisenman	600
Supplies:	
Eisenman Typewriter	350
Shira Eisenman	50
Store equipment	8,240
Accumulated depreciation—store equipment	4,120
Business delivery truck	17,790
Accumulated depreciation—delivery truck	8,000
Eisenman's personal automobile	16,800
Notes receivable owed to S. Eisenman	10,000
Store building, net value (owned by Eisenman as a personal asset)	75,800
Notes payable to outsiders by Eisenman Typewriter	12,000
Notes payable to outsiders by Eisenman	8,000
Accrued interest payable on above notes:	
Eisenman Typewriter	300
Shira Eisenman	200
Accounts payable to outsiders by:	
Eisenman Typewriter	29,000
Shira Eisenman	2,000
Sales tax owed by Eisenman Typewriter	3,780
FICA tax payable	600
Employees' income tax payable	1,300
FUTA tax payable	160
State unemployment tax payable	90
Mortgage due on Eisenman's home	73,980
Net income of Eisenman Typewriter for 19--	52,980
Eisenman's withdrawals from Eisenman Typewriter	48,000

(handwritten margin notes:)
Income
Ex & Rev

Owners Equity.
Capital
Income
Withdrawals

Balance
Assets.
Liability
Capital

Required:

1. From the list of assets, liabilities, income, and withdrawals given above, separate those that clearly relate to Eisenman Electronic Typewriter Sales and Service and prepare a statement of owner's equity and a balance sheet as of December 31, 19--. Use the report form of balance sheet as defined and illustrated in Chapter 4.
2. The separation of Eisenman Electronic Typewriter Sales and Service's assets and liabilities from Shira Eisenman's assets and liabilities is an adaptation of what concept of accounting?

Problem 15A2   Gross Margin and Income Determination

Mohamad Noor and Mohammed Salleh, partners in a wholesale carpet and rug business, completed the following selected transactions during the first half of 19--.

Jan. 17 Ordered 1,000 square yards of carpeting material from Wonder-Weave Co. at $9.75 per square yard.

Feb. 14 Ordered ten 9' × 12' rugs from Islam Co. at $177.90 each.
16 Received carpeting ordered from Wonder-Weave Co. on January 17.
19 Received invoice from Wonder-Weave Co., dated February 16, for $9,750, terms n/30.

Mar. 12 Received rugs ordered from Islam Co. on February 14.
15 Received invoice from Islam Co., dated March 12, for $1,779, terms n/30.
19 Paid $9,750 to Wonder-Weave Co. in settlement of February 16 invoice.
21 Sold 200 square yards of carpeting material received February 16 to Carpetime, for $13.05 per square yard.

Apr. 11 Paid $1,779 to Islam Co. in settlement of March 12 invoice.
12 Sold four 9' × 12' rugs received March 12 to Floors With Flair for $265.50 each.
16 Paid Daniels Delivery $65 for delivery services rendered during the past month.

May 11 Sold three 9' × 12' rugs received March 12 to Mid-West Floor Co. for $265.50 each.

June 8 Sold 400 square yards of carpeting material received February 16 to Carpet Shop for $13.05 per square yard.
14 Paid Daniels Delivery $85 for delivery services rendered during the past month.

Required:

Answer the following questions (show any necessary calculations):

1. What was the amount of the gross margin on the March 21 carpeting sale?
2. What was the amount of the gross margin on the April 12 rug sale?
3. On the basis of the transactions given, what was the income of Mohamad Noor and Mohammed Salleh for the first four months of 19--?
4. What was the amount of the gross margin on the May 11 rug sale?

5. What was the amount of the gross margin on the June 8 carpeting sale?
6. On the basis of the transactions given, what was the income of Mohamad Noor and Mohammed Salleh for the first six months of 19--?

Problem 15A3   Effect of Change in Accounting Method on Reported Net Income

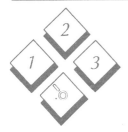

Condensed income statement data for the Dwarf Co. for the first two years of operation are presented below. Additional information related to the report is as follows:

1. Data reported in columns (a) and (b) are based on the fifo inventory method and the straight-line depreciation method.
2. Ending inventory using lifo would be $14,000 in Year 1 and $17,000 in Year 2.
3. Depreciation expense using the double-declining-balance method would be $30,000 in Year 1 and $28,000 in Year 2.

Dwarf Co.
Condensed Income Statements
For Years 1 and 2

	(a) Year 1	(b) Year 2	(c) Year 2	(d) Year 1	(e) Year 2
Sales...................	$160,000	$180,000	$180,000	$160,000	$180,000
Cost of goods sold:					
Beginning inventory	-0-	$ 16,000	$ 16,000	-0-	14,000
Purchases	$106,000	104,000	104,000	$106,000	104,000
Goods available........	$106,000	$120,000	$120,000	$106,000	118,000
Ending inventory	16,000	20,000	17,000	14,000	17,000
Cost of goods sold	$ 90,000	$100,000	103,000	92,000	101,000
Gross margin	$ 70,000	$ 80,000	77,000	68,000	79,000
Depreciation expense.....	20,000	22,000	28,000	30,000	28,000
Other operating expenses	28,000	30,000	30,000	28,000	30,000
Net income	$ 22,000	$ 28,000	19,000	10,000	21,000

Required:

1. Recompute net income by completing columns (c), (d), and (e) of the schedule as follows:
   (c) Assume that Dwarf Co. changed to the lifo and double-declining-balance methods during Year 2.
   (d) and (e) Assume that Dwarf Co. changed both its inventory and depreciation methods as indicated in (c) above in Years 1 and 2.
2. Calculate the increase (decrease) in net income from Year 1 to Year 2 in each of the following situations:
   (a) The fifo inventory and straight-line depreciation methods were used in Years 1 and 2.
   (b) Dwarf Co. changed to the lifo and double-declining-balance methods during Year 2.
   (c) Dwarf Co. changed both its inventory and depreciation methods as indicated in (b) above in Years 1 and 2.

Problem 15A4   Net Income—Cash Basis versus Accrual Basis

Sherry Jordan completed the following partial list of transactions during December, 19-A and January, 19-B.

(a) Dec. 5, 19-A Purchased merchandise for $2,600 on account, terms net 30 days.
(b) Dec. 8, 19-A Sold merchandise for $3,300 on account, terms net 30 days.
(c) Dec. 11, 19-A Purchased merchandise for $1,800 cash.
(d) Dec. 14, 19-A Sold merchandise for $2,200 cash.
(e) Dec. 31, 19-A Made adjusting entry for accrued wages payable to part-time employee, $120.
(f) Jan. 4, 19-B Paid for merchandise purchased Dec. 5, 19-A, $2,600
(g) Jan. 4, 19-B Paid weekly wages of part-time employee, $600.
(h) Jan. 8, 19-B Collected $3,300 on sale of Dec. 8, 19-A.

Required:
Determine the effect of each item on net income for 19-A and 19-B using

(a) the accrual basis concept
(b) the cash basis concept.

Show the total effect on net income for two years combined under each concept as a means of proof. (Assume no beginning or ending inventories and fifo flow.)

Series B

Problem 15B1   Choosing Items to Prepare Balance Sheet in Report Form

---

Parker PC Sales and Service, owned and operated by Sandra Parker, is in the process of separating the assets and liabilities of the business enterprise from Parker's personal assets and liabilities as of December 31, 19--. Parker has solicited your help.

Cash in business bank account in Regal Bank......................	$ 11,400
Cash in personal bank account in Bohemian Savings	30,120
Accounts receivable owed to Parker PC	26,985
Allowance for doubtful accounts:	
on Parker PC Accounts Receivable.............................	1,650
Merchandise inventory of Parker PC	111,585
Prepaid insurance:	
Parker PC	600
Sandra Parker..	450
Supplies:	
Parker PC	262
Sandra Parker..	38
Store equipment	6,180
Accumulated depreciation—store equipment	3,090
Business delivery truck	13,342

Accumulated depreciation—delivery truck.........................	6,000
Parker's personal automobile	12,600
Notes receivable owed to S. Parker	7,500
Store building, net value (owned by Parker as a personal asset)......	56,850
Notes payable to outsiders by Parker PC	9,000
Notes payable to outsiders by Parker.............................	6,000
Accrued interest payable on above notes:	
Parker PC	225
Sandra Parker...	150
Accounts payable to outsiders by:	
Parker PC	21,750
Sandra Parker...	1,500
Sales tax owed by Parker PC.....................................	2,835
FICA tax payable	450
Employees' income tax payable..................................	975
FUTA tax payable...	120
State unemployment tax payable.................................	68
Mortgage due on Parker's home	55,485
Net income of Parker PC for 19--	39,735
Parker's withdrawals from Parker PC	36,000

Required:

1. From the list of assets, liabilities, income, and withdrawals given above, separate those that clearly relate to Parker PC Sales and Service and prepare a statement of owner's equity and a balance sheet as of December 31, 19--. Use the report form of balance sheet as defined and illustrated in Chapter 4.

2. The separation of Parker PC Sales and Service's assets and liabilities from Sandra Parker's assets and liabilities is an adaptation of which concept of accounting?

Problem 15B2   Gross Margin and Income Determination

Lawry and Margolis, partners in a wholesale curtain and drapery business, completed the following selected transactions during the first half of 19--:

Jan. 10 Ordered 500 square yards of drapery material from Designer's Workroom Co. at $7.25 per square yard.

Feb. 7 Ordered ten pairs of 35" × 60" curtains from Hilson, Inc. at $29.95 each.

10 Received drapery material ordered from Designer's Workroom Co. on January 10.

12 Received invoice from Designer's Workroom Co., dated February 10, for $3,625, terms n/30.

Mar. 5 Received curtains ordered from Hilson, Inc. on February 7.

8 Received invoice from Hilson, Inc. dated March 5, for $299.50, terms n/30.

12 Paid $3,625 to Designer's Workroom Co. in settlement of February 10 invoice.

14 Sold 100 square yards of drapery material received February 10 to Proctor Drapery for $9.50 per square yard.

Apr. **4** Paid $299.50 to Hilson, Inc., in settlement of March 5 invoice.

5 Sold four pairs of 35" × 60" curtains received March 5 to Curtains Etc. for $44.95 each.

7 Paid Flanagan Delivery $50 for delivery services rendered during the past month.

May **4** Sold three pairs of 35" by 60" curtains received March 5 to Calico Corners for $44.95 each.

June **1** Sold 200 square yards of drapery material received February 10 to Draperyland, for $9.50 per square yard.

7 Paid Flanagan Delivery $70 for delivery services rendered during the past month.

Required:

Answer the following questions (show any necessary calculations):

1. What was the amount of the gross margin on the March 14 sale of drapery material?
2. What was the amount of the gross margin on the April 5 sale of curtains?
3. On the basis of the transactions given, what was the income of Lawry and Margolis for the first four months of 19--?
4. What was the amount of the gross margin on the May 4 sale of curtains?
5. What was the amount of the gross margin on the June 1 sale of drapery material?
6. On the basis of the transactions given, what was the income of Lawry and Margolis for the first six months of 19--?

Problem 15B3   Effect of Change in Accounting Method on Reported Net Income

Condensed income statement data for the Small Co. for the first two years of operation are presented below. Additional information related to the report is as follows:

1. Data reported in columns (a) and (b) are based on the lifo inventory method and the double-declining-balance depreciation method.
2. Ending inventory using fifo would be $14,000 in Year 1 and $17,000 in Year 2.
3. Depreciation expense using the straight-line method would be $12,000 in Year 1 and $14,000 in Year 2.

Required:

1. Recompute net income by completing columns (c), (d), and (e) of the schedule as follows:

    (c) Assume that Small Co. changed to the fifo and straight-line methods during Year 2.

    (d) and (e) Assume that Small Co. changed both its inventory and depreciation methods as indicated in (c) above in Years 1 and 2.

2. Calculate the increase (decrease) in net income from Year 1 to Year 2 in each of the following situations:

(a) The lifo inventory and double-declining-balance depreciation methods were used in Years 1 and 2.
(b) Small Co. changed to the fifo and straight-line methods during Year 2.
(c) Small Co. changed both its inventory and depreciation methods as indicated in (b) above in Years 1 and 2.

Small Co.
Condensed Income Statements
For Years 1 and 2

	(a) Year 1	(b) Year 2	(c) Year 2	(d) Year 1	(e) Year 2
Sales..................	$120,000	$135,000	$135,000	$120,000	$135,000
Cost of goods sold:					
Beginning inventory	-0-	$ 12,000	$ 12,000	-0-	?
Purchases	$ 79,500	78,000	78,000	$ 79,500	78,000
Goods available........	$ 79,500	$ 90,000	$ 90,000	$ 79,500	
Ending inventory	12,000	15,000	?	?	?
Cost of goods sold	$ 67,500	$ 75,000	?	?	?
Gross margin	$ 52,500	$ 60,000	?	?	?
Depreciation expense	15,000	16,500	?	?	?
Other operating expenses	21,000	22,500	22,500	21,000	22,500
Net income	$ 16,500	$ 21,000	?	?	?

Problem 15B4 Net Income—Cash Basis versus Accrual Basis

Randy Nitz completed the following partial list of transactions during December 19-C and January 19-D.

(a) Dec. 4, 19-C Purchased merchandise for $3,900 on account, terms net 30 days.
(b) Dec. 7, 19-C Sold merchandise for $4,950 on account, terms net 30 days.
(c) Dec. 12, 19-C Purchased merchandise for $2,700 cash.
(d) Dec. 15, 19-C Sold merchandise for $3,300 cash.
(e) Dec. 31, 19-C Made adjusting entry for accrued wages payable to part-time employee, $360.
(f) Jan. 3, 19-D Paid for merchandise purchased Dec. 4, 19-C, $3,900.
(g) Jan. 3, 19-D Paid weekly wages of part-time employee, $900.
(h) Jan. 6, 19-D Collected $4,950 on sale of Dec. 7, 19-C.

Required:

1. Determine the effect of each item on net income for 19-C and 19-D using
   (a) the accrual basis concept
   (b) the cash basis concept.
2. Show the total effect on net income for two years combined under each concept as a means of proof. (Assume no beginning or ending inventories and fifo flow.)

Mastery Problem

The Daley Company was organized on January 5, 19-A. During the first three years of operations, the company employed the following accounting techniques.

(1) Straight-line depreciation.
(2) Direct write-off method for uncollectible accounts.
(3) First-in, first-out for costing inventory.

The amounts of net income reported and the expenses recognized as a result of the above accounting techniques are shown below.

	19-A	19-B	19-C
Net income	$59,500	$91,125	$107,100
Depreciation expense..........................	28,500	29,850	31,350
Uncollectible accounts expense................	1,575	3,525	6,375
Ending merchandise inventory	74,625	81,000	87,225

Barbara Daley, the owner, is considering changing to the following methods in determining net income for the fourth and subsequent years.

(1) Double-declining-balance method for depreciation.
(2) Allowance method of recognizing uncollectible accounts.
(3) Last-in, first-out for costing inventory.

To evaluate the future effects of these accounting changes on net income, Daley has requested that net income for the past three years be recomputed on the basis of the proposed methods. The depreciation expense, uncollectible accounts expense, and ending inventory under the proposed accounting treatments are listed below.

	19-A	19-B	19-C
Depreciation expense..........................	$57,000	$48,000	$41,280
Uncollectible accounts expense................	2,438	4,350	6,000
Ending merchandise inventory	65,280	69,866	75,000

Required:

Recompute the net income for each of the three years. Assume that purchases were $400,000 each year. (Hint: The change in inventory method affects the ending inventory in Year 19-A, and both the beginning and ending inventories in Years 19-B and 19-C.)

CHAPTER 16

Internal Accounting Control

Careful study of this chapter should enable you to:

- Define internal accounting control and to explain its importance in operating a business.

- Identify the basic elements of good internal accounting control.

- Explain the application of internal accounting control concepts in the expenditure cycle, including use of

1. The voucher system.
2. The voucher register.
3. The check register.

- Explain the application of internal accounting control concepts in the revenue cycle.

There are enormous variations in size, type of operation, and product lines of companies. Each of these factors affects the type of control system appropriate for a particular company. For example, a very small business often uses only a limited number of formal control procedures and has little segregation of duties because there are so few employees to perform those duties. The key internal control element for a small business is the owner-manager who personally supervises the activities of the business. As the size and nature of a business become larger and more complex, it becomes impossible for the owner to maintain such close contact with all the activities of the business. Consequently, the owner must rely on a more formal internal accounting control system to ensure that the activities of the business are conducted properly and that errors or fraud are prevented or promptly detected. It is important to recognize that it is impossible to define the "correct" system of internal accounting control for all businesses.

In this chapter, certain basic internal accounting control concepts are explained and many aspects of the application of these concepts are illustrated. Some of the internal accounting controls, such as the use of prenumbered documents, are relevant for virtually every business. Other controls, such as an ideal segregation of duties, are not feasible for very small firms. Clearly, the system of internal accounting control developed for a given firm should be based on that firm's particular needs and the business environment.

Internal Accounting Control Concepts

In order to appreciate why many documents, records and procedures exist and are used in particular ways in accounting, an understanding is needed of the concept and the key elements of internal accounting control.

Meaning and Importance of Internal Control

Define internal accounting control and explain its importance in operating a business.

An **internal accounting control system** is defined as all the procedures, documents, and records used by a business to protect its assets and to ensure that the activities of the business are properly performed and documented. The system should provide assurance that (1) all transactions are properly authorized and accounted for, (2) access to assets is permitted only to authorized parties for authorized purposes, and (3) records of assets are verified periodically by examining the related assets.

Internal accounting control is essential to the functioning of a business. Virtually every aspect of a business is affected by it. For example, the system must ensure that purchases are made only of goods to be used in the business and that bills are paid only for goods and services actually purchased and received by the business. Similarly, when shipments are made to customers, the system must ensure that the customers are billed and the related amounts collected. Then, the system must ensure that cash receipts from sales are received and entered into the records of the business and that they are not kept by an employee. In addition, management decisions often are based on accounting information; the control system must ensure that this information is accurate and up to date.

Internal accounting control systems can take many different forms in different businesses; they can be quite simple or very complex. Regardless of their form, however, internal accounting controls are critical to the efficient functioning of a business.

Key Elements of Internal Control

Identify basic elements of good internal accounting control.

Before looking at specific applications of internal accounting control in individual areas of a business, it will help to examine the basic elements or principles underlying the entire concept. Four key elements of internal accounting control can be identified:

1. Segregation of duties
2. Authorization procedures and related responsibilities
3. Accounting procedures
4. Independent checks on performance

Segregation of Duties. Segregation of duties involves the assigning of duties in such a way that (1) different employees are responsible for different parts of a transaction, and (2) that employees who maintain accounting records do not have custody of the firm's assets. Appropriate segregation of duties helps to detect errors promptly and reduces the possibility of employee fraud. For example, assume that one employee is responsible for ordering goods, a second employee for receiving goods, a third employee for paying for goods based on proper evidence of purchase, and a fourth employee for making the accounting entries for the purchase and payment of the goods. Such a segregation of duties provides a built-in check of one employee on another in that the amounts ordered, received, paid for, and entered in the accounting records must agree. Similarly, no one of these four employees can obtain goods for personal use or make improper payments for goods without being caught.

The duties of accounting and asset custody should be segregated in order to prevent employees from stealing business assets and concealing their theft by modifying the accounting records. For example, assume that one employee is responsible for receiving customer remittances on account, and a second employee is responsible for entering sales and customer remittances in the accounting records. This segregation of duties prevents the first employee from keeping the customers' remittances because the customer would complain if billed by the second employee for amounts that already had been remitted. Similarly, the second employee has no incentive to make improper entries in the accounting records because of lack of access to cash receipts.

Authorization Procedures and Related Responsibility. Sound authorization procedures involve the assigning of responsibilities so that only properly authorized activities take place in the business and that persons responsible for these activities, and related assets, are identified at every step in the process. Basically, this element of internal accounting control should ensure that transactions do not occur without sufficient authorization. For some transactions this authorization can be general. For example, a sales clerk in a department store has general authorization to make sales of particular goods using a particular cash register and perhaps keying in a specific clerk number. For other transactions, the authorization is likely to be specific. For example, major production equipment of a business normally is bought or sold only if specific written authorization is obtained from management at a relatively high level. Whether the authorization is general or specific, the control concept remains the same: Someone should be responsible for every activity in which a business engages. Unless someone has authorized and assumed responsibility for an action, that action should not be taken by the business. Correspondingly, after some activity has occurred, it should be possible to determine who authorized it and who, therefore, is held responsible.

▩ **Accounting Procedures.**   Proper **accounting procedures** include use of accounting records and documents in such a way that whenever business activities occur, the accounting system reacts. A major dimension of this internal accounting control element is the use of pre-numbered documents that must be promptly generated when an activity occurs. These pre-numbered documents must also be accounted for and this procedure can be simplified by entering the data and filing the documents in numerical order. This element of internal accounting control helps ensure that all valid activities of the business are included in the records and that only valid activities are included. For example, assume that pre-numbered sales receipts are used, that one copy of the receipt is issued to a customer whenever a sale occurs and the other copy is retained in the firm's files. In this situation, if the numerical sequence of receipts is complete and there are no duplicate receipts entered, it is reasonable to assume that all sales transactions are accounted for and only valid sales transactions are entered.

▩ **Independent Checks on Performance.**   This last key element of internal accounting control consists of the various methods used by a business to ensure that management's accounting rules and regulations are being followed. Perhaps the most easily recognized type of **independent check** on performance is that provided by the internal audit department of a business. The **internal audit department** has broad responsibility to see that the internal accounting control system is effective. This includes responsibilities for determining (1) that the system is properly designed and (2) that there is compliance with the segregation of duties, authorization, and accounting procedures dictated by the system. The first responsibility is fulfilled primarily by making sure that the system is characterized by the key elements of internal control described in this section. The second responsibility is fulfilled by testing and analyzing the business activities that occur during the year. For example, the numerical sequence of sales invoices or checks can be accounted for by maintaining numerical order. The sum of the balances in the accounts receivable ledger can be verified by comparing it with the general ledger accounts receivable balance. A bank reconciliation can be prepared. Canceled checks can be traced to appropriate supporting documents.

In addition to the specific performance checks provided by the internal audit department, a system of independent checks is built into many phases of the business. For example, if the accounts receivable records, sales journal, and general ledger are maintained by three different people in the accounting department, each of these employees provides an automatic independent check on a part of the work of the other two employees. If any one of these employees does not perform the prescribed procedures correctly, the accounting records will not agree. Another type of independent check built into the system literally involves some duplication of work. This happens whenever an employee is responsible for verifying the work of a fellow employee, such as when the price, quantity, and total dollar amount of a sales invoice must be verified by a second employee before it is mailed to a customer. Many of these built-in checks can exist throughout a company's accounting system and can help provide assurance that various procedures are being properly performed.

Building Your Accounting Knowledge

1. Why is it impossible to define the "correct" system of internal accounting control for all businesses?
2. What assurance should be provided by an internal accounting control system?
3. How would appropriate segregation of duties prevent an employee responsible for receiving customer remittances on account from keeping the customers' remittances?
4. How do sound authorization procedures contribute to internal accounting control?
5. Why should documents be pre-numbered and subsequently accounted for?
6. What are the responsibilities of an internal audit department?
7. Give an example of an independent check built into an accounting system.

Assignment Box

To reinforce your understanding of the preceding text materials, you may complete the following:
> Study Guide: Part A
> Textbook: Exercises 16A1 through 16A2 and 16B1 through 16B2

Application in the Expenditure Cycle

Explain the application of internal accounting control concepts in the expenditure cycle.

The expenditure cycle includes all of the functions involved in acquiring and receiving goods from suppliers and in making payments for the goods purchased. Diagramming and briefly explaining the expenditure cycle will assist in understanding internal accounting control in the expenditure cycle. A flowchart of the basic elements of the expenditure cycle appears on the following page. Many variations of the expenditure cycle are possible for different businesses. For example, in a small business, all the purchasing and payment activities might be performed by a single owner/manager. Purchases might be made directly from sales representatives who visit the store, perhaps with the goods ready for delivery. At the other extreme, in very large firms more than one level of authorization might be required in order to make expenditures above a specified dollar amount. The flowchart presented here assumes a medium-sized business that purchases tangible products.

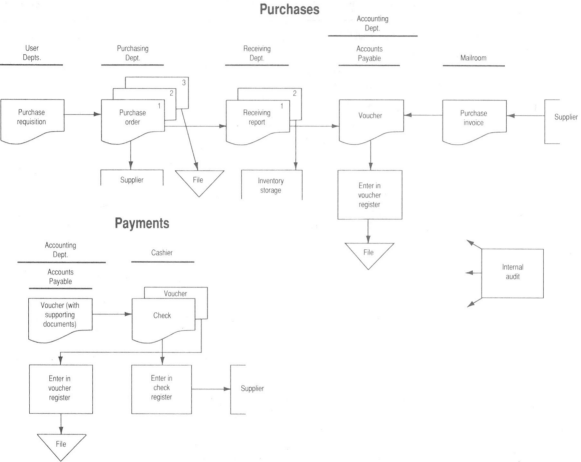

Flowchart of Expenditure Cycle

The Purchases portion of the flowchart shows that any department or person in the firm wanting to purchase goods must prepare an authorized purchase requisition and forward it to the purchasing department. The purchasing department examines the purchase requisition, prepares a purchase order and sends it to the appropriate supplier. When the goods arrive from the supplier, a receiving report is prepared in the receiving department. This receiving report and a copy of the purchase order are sent to the accounting department where eventually they are matched with the purchase invoice received from the supplier. The purchase order, receiving report, and purchase invoice provide the basis for preparing a voucher, which is a document used to authorize payments for goods and services. The voucher is entered in the voucher register, an accounting record similar to a purchases journal.

The "Payments" portion of the flowchart indicates that the voucher and supporting documents are used by the cashier as a basis for preparing a check. The cashier enters in the check register the date, amount, and payee of the check, and sends the check to the supplier in payment for the goods received. The voucher and supporting documents are then returned to the accounts payable section where they are used to enter, in the voucher register, the fact that the voucher has been paid.

The Internal Audit Department has responsibility to oversee and monitor the entire system of internal accounting control shown in the flowchart. Its functions might include seeing that purchases are made only on the basis of authorized purchase orders or that all payments are properly entered.

Internal accounting control over the expenditure cycle will now be discussed in some detail. The partial records of Mitchell & Jenkins, a partnership engaged in selling golf and tennis equipment, are illustrated. The organization of this discussion follows the outline suggested by the expenditure flowchart.

Acquisition of Goods

An internal accounting control system should ensure that a firm purchases only those goods and services that are necessary for the efficient and effective operation of the business. Documents and procedures that are relevant for controlling the purchasing process are illustrated and explained in the following sections.

Purchase Requisition. The purchase requisition is a document requesting that the purchasing department order specific goods. The purchase requisition used by Mitchell & Jenkins is shown on page 610. Purchase requisitions should be pre-numbered and subsequently accounted for by number. This practice ensures that all requisitions are properly handled by the purchasing department and that the individual responsible for requesting that any merchandise be purchased can be subsequently identified if necessary.

The purchase requisition itself does not authorize a purchase. The requisition must first be approved. For a minor purchase, the approval might come from a department supervisor, whereas a major purchase should be approved at a higher level of management. When approved, the purchase requisition authorizes the purchasing department to generate a purchase order.

Purchase Order. The purchase order is an explicit request by the firm to buy goods from a supplier. The purchase order prepared by Mitchell & Jenkins illustrated on page 611 was based on the purchase requisition illustrated on page 610. Purchase orders should be pre-numbered and

```
┌─────────────────────────────────────────────────────────────────────┐
│                                                                       │
│   [racket logo]  Mitchell & Jenkins Sporting Goods   Purchase Requisition  No.  218
│                  2200 E. Washington St.                               │
│                  Indianapolis, IN 46201-3216                          │
│                                                                       │
│                                        Date issued:    May 1, 19--    │
│   Order from:                          Date required:  May 6, 19--    │
│   Sportime Corp.                       Dept.:          Tennis         │
│   6825 Kentucky Ave.                   Deliver to:     D. Baker       │
│   Louisville, KY 40258-4111                                           │
│                                                                       │
├──────────────────────────┬────────────────────────────────────────────┤
│        Quantity           │              Description                    │
├──────────────────────────┼────────────────────────────────────────────┤
│          12               │        Prince Spectrum rackets              │
├──────────────────────────┴────────────────────────────────────────────┤
│                                                                       │
│   Purchasing Dept. Memorandum          Placed by:  D. Baker           │
│   Date:        May 1, 19--             Approved by: J. Jenkins        │
│                Sportime Corp.          Purchase Order No.:  302       │
│   Issued to:   6825 Kentucky Ave.                                     │
│                Louisville, KY 40258-4111                              │
│                                                                       │
└─────────────────────────────────────────────────────────────────────┘
```

Purchase Requisition

subsequently accounted for by number, to ensure either that all of the goods on an order are received or that the order is canceled, and that only goods that have been ordered are received and paid for subsequently. The number of copies of the purchase order that are prepared depends on the particular accounting information system. There are likely to be at least three copies. One copy is sent to the supplier, a second copy goes to the accounting department, and the third copy is retained by the purchasing department for its files. A fourth copy could be sent to the individual who requisitioned the goods, and a fifth copy could be sent to the receiving department for use as a receiving report.

▬ **Receiving Report.** Whether or not a copy of the purchase order is used for this purpose, a document called a **receiving report** should be prepared promptly by the receiving department for all goods received by the firm. Receiving reports should be pre-numbered and subsequently accounted for by number to ensure that all goods received are properly entered. There are normally two copies of the receiving report. One copy is sent to the accounting department, and the other remains with the goods for forwarding to the inventory storage area.

Payment for Goods Using the Voucher System

Explain the use of the voucher system.

Much of the material covered thus far in this chapter was addressed previously in other sections of the text. For example, basic features of accounting for purchases and payments were explained in Chapter 6, and

```
                                                    Purchase Order No. 302

        Mitchell & Jenkins Sporting Goods
        2200 E. Washington St.
        Indianapolis, IN 46201-3216

                                        Date:        May 1, 19--
   To:  Sportime Corp.                  Delivery by: May 6, 19--
        6825 Kentucky Ave.              Terms:       Net
        Louisville, KY 40258-4111
```

Quantity	Description	Unit Price
12	Prince Spectrum rackets	130.00

J. Jenkins

Purchase Order

accounting for sales and collections was addressed in Chapter 7. For this reason, data entry procedures in these areas generally have not been explained and illustrated in detail in this chapter. However, the accounting system used to control payments for items purchased by the business warrants further attention. Therefore, the data entry aspects of internal accounting control over payments will be explained in greater detail in this section.

A system for controlling expenditures, used by many businesses, is known as a **voucher system**. This system is very useful for controlling cash payments, because written authorization is required for each payment. A voucher system usually involves the use of vouchers, a voucher register, a vouchers payable account in the general ledger, voucher checks, and a check register. There are several alternative accounting procedures that may be used in a voucher system. For instance, ordinary checks may be used and entered in either a simple cashbook or in a cash payments journal. Like most accounting processes, the voucher system is flexible and readily adaptable to various situations.

The use of the voucher system of accounting is not advisable under all conditions, but it usually may be used to advantage when one or more of the following circumstances exist:

1. When the volume of transactions is large enough to require a system of control over expenditures.

2. When the nature of the business is such that it is desirable to enter invoices at the time that they are received rather than when payment is made.

3. When it is the custom of the firm to pay all invoices in full at maturity instead of making partial or installment payments.

There are generally five key documents in a voucher system: a purchase order, a receiving report, a purchase invoice, a voucher, and a check. Purchase orders and receiving reports were described previously. The purchase invoice and voucher will now be explained.

Purchase Invoice. A purchase invoice is the supplier's bill for goods or other assets purchased or for services rendered. The following is a purchase invoice received by Mitchell & Jenkins for the purchase of tennis rackets from Sportime Corp. When the purchase invoice is received by the accounts (or vouchers) payable section of the accounting department, it should be compared with the purchase order and receiving report on file in that department. This comparison is made to verify that the invoice is for the quantity ordered and subsequently received and that it reflects the proper price. In addition, the accounting department should verify the mathematical accuracy of the invoice and should determine which account to charge for the purchase.

Sportime Corp. **6825 Kentucky Ave.** **Louisville, KY 40258-4111**			Invoice No. **163**

Sold to

Mitchell & Jenkins Sporting Goods
2200 E. Washington St.
Indianapolis, IN 46201-3216

Date   May 6, 19--

Terms   Net

Quantity	Description	Unit Price	Total
12	Prince Spectrum rackets	$130.00	$1,560.00

Received by *S. Miller*
Date 5/7/--

Purchase Invoice

An alternative approach to purchase invoice verification used by some firms is to have the different employees responsible for ordering and receiving goods participate in the verification process. The receiving clerk would verify receipt of the assets purchased and the purchasing agent would verify the quantities, prices, and terms of the order. The accounting department would then verify the mathematical accuracy of the invoice and determine the account distribution.

▬▬ **Voucher.** Based on the verified purchase invoice, receiving report, and purchase order, a voucher is prepared by the vouchers payable section. The **voucher** is a key internal accounting control document which provides authorization for payment of goods or services. The voucher normally provides space to enter the invoice date, the goods or services purchased, accounts to be charged, authorization for payment, date of payment, and number of the check issued. There is no standard form of voucher; it varies depending on the nature of the business, the classification of accounts, and the distribution desired. Regardless of its form, however, for good internal accounting control the voucher should be prenumbered and subsequently accounted for by number to ensure that all payments are properly entered and that payments are made only for authorized purchases.

A voucher that was prepared by the voucher clerk for Mitchell & Jenkins is shown on page 614. The information entered on this voucher was obtained from the invoice shown on page 612. All of the information on the front and the account distribution on the back of this voucher would be entered when the voucher is prepared. The payment information would be entered when the voucher is paid.

▬▬ **Entering Vouchers.** There are two accounting records involved in entering vouchers: the voucher register and the general ledger. All vouchers should be entered in the voucher register. The **voucher register** is basically an expanded purchases journal that is used to enter purchases of all types of assets and services. The voucher register represents the first point at which purchases activities are reflected in the accounting records. In addition, each entry in the voucher register is a key step leading to the payment of a specific amount. This makes the voucher register particularly important from a control standpoint. To the extent feasible, vouchers should be entered in the voucher register in numerical order to facilitate accounting for the numerical sequence of the vouchers.

Explain the use of the voucher register.

The columnar headings of a voucher register depend upon the nature of the business and the desired classification of purchases and expenses. The form of voucher register used by Mitchell and Jenkins is shown on page 616. There are three debit columns—for Purchases, Operating Expenses, and Sundry Accounts; and two credit columns—for Sundry Accounts and Vouchers Payable. The Purchases Dr. column is used to enter all merchandise purchases. Mitchell & Jenkins have two departments, golf and tennis, and a separate column is provided for each.

Mitchell & Jenkins Sporting Goods
2200 E. Washington St.
Indianapolis, IN 46201-3216

Voucher No. 164

Date Issued May 7 **19** -- **Terms** Net **Due** May 7 **19** --

To Sportime Corp.

Address 6825 Kentucky Ave.
Louisville, KY 40258-4111

Invoice Date	Description	Amount	
May 6	12 Prince Spectrum rackets	1,560	00

Authorized by

J. Jenkins

Prepared by

B. Zimmer
Voucher Clerk

Voucher *(front)*

DISTRIBUTION

Purchases		Operating Expenses		Sundry Accounts	
Golf	Tennis	Acct. No.	Amount	Acct. No.	Amount
	1,560 00				

PAYMENT

Date of Payment May 7 **19** -- **Check No.** 519 **Amount $** 1,560.00

CERTIFICATION

This voucher has been audited carefully and is correct in every respect.

J. Goally
Accountant

Voucher *(back)*

The Operating Expenses Dr. column is used to enter all administrative and selling expenses. Note that both the amount of the transaction and the operating expense subsidiary ledger account number are entered in this column. The operating expense subsidiary ledger functions in a manner similar to an accounts receivable subsidiary ledger. There are control accounts in the general ledger for administrative and selling expenses, and an operating expense subsidiary ledger is maintained for each of these control accounts. The use of the operating expense subsidiary ledger will be explained and illustrated more fully in Chapter 19.

The Sundry Accounts Dr. column of the voucher register is used to enter all transactions other than merchandise purchases and operating expenses. The Vouchers Payable Cr. column is used to enter credits for most transactions. Occasionally a transaction also involves a credit to some other account, and the Sundry Accounts Cr. column is used for that purpose. Voucher No. 164, which is illustrated on page 614, was entered in the voucher register as a debit to Purchases—Tennis and a credit to Vouchers Payable.

Following is a description of selected vouchers that have been entered in the voucher register:

May 1 Vou. No. 161, Capital Leasing Co.; store and office rent, Acct. No. 5443, $2,000, and Acct. No. 5406, $1,000.

    5 Vou. No. 162, Golf World; merchandise, Acct. No. 511, $5,120.

    5 Vou. No. 163, Hoosier Supply; office supplies, Acct. No. 152, $198.

    7 Vou. No. 164, Sportime Corp.; merchandise, Acct. No. 521, $1,560.

    8 Vou. No. 165, Indianapolis Star; advertising, Acct. No. 5433, $286.

  16 Vou. No. 169, Payroll, May 1-16, $11,239. Distribution: Store Clerks Wage Expense, Acct. No. 5431, $3,418; Truck Drivers Wage Expense, Acct. No. 5432, $3,615; Office Salaries Expense, Acct. No. 5401, $3,050; Robert Mitchell, Salary Expense, Acct. No. 5402, $1,500; Jessica Jenkins, Salary Expense, Acct. No. 5434, $1,900. Taxes withheld: FICA Tax Payable, Acct. No. 211, $718; Employees Income Tax Payable, Acct. No. 214, $1,526.

Voucher No. 169 was based on a report of the payroll clerk. The amount payable ($11,239) is the net amount of the payroll after deducting the taxes withheld. Note that five lines were required to enter the payroll transaction. This was because of the five entries in the Operating Expenses Dr. column.

To prove the voucher register, it is only necessary to determine that the sum of the debit footings is equal to the sum of the credit footings. The footings should be proved before the totals are forwarded and before the summary posting is completed.

Both individual posting and summary posting from the voucher register to the general ledger are required. In addition, individual posting from the voucher register to the operating expense ledger is required. The individual posting involves posting each item entered in the Sundry Accounts Dr. and Cr. Amount columns to the proper account in the general ledger, and posting each item in the Operating Expense Dr. Amount column to the proper account in the operating expense subsidiary ledger. As each item is posted, a check mark should be placed beside it in the check ($\sqrt{}$)

VOUCHER REGISTER FOR MONTH OF May 19 --

PAGE 13

	DAY	VOU. NO.	TO WHOM ISSUED	PURCHASES DR. GOLF	PURCHASES DR. TENNIS	OPER. EXP. DR. ACCT. NO.	OPER. EXP. DR. AMOUNT	SUNDRY DR. ACCT. NO.	SUNDRY DR. AMOUNT	VOUCHERS PAYABLE CR.	SUNDRY CR. ACCT. NO.	SUNDRY CR. AMOUNT	DISPO. DATE	CK. NO.
1	1	161	Capital Leasing Co.			5443	2 000 00			3 000 00			5/1	511
2						5406	1 000 00							
3														
4	5	162	Golf World	5 120 00						5 120 00			5/7	514
5	5	163	Hoosier Supply					152	1 98 00	1 98 00			5/7	515
6	7	164	Sportime Corp.		1 560 00					1 560 00			5/7	516
7	8	165	Indianapolis Star			5433	2 86 00			2 86 00			5/8	517
11	16	169	Payroll			5431	3 418 00			11 239 00	211	7 18 00	5/16	520
12						5432	3 615 00				214	1 526 00		
13						5401	3 050 00							
14						5402	1 500 00							
15						5434	1 900 00							
16														
28				62 940 00	41 143 00		48 824 00		4 917 00	152 699 00		5 125 00		
29				(511)	(521)		(541)		(✓)	(218)		(✓)		

column of the voucher register. The page number of the voucher register should also be entered in the Posting Reference column of the ledger account to which the amount is posted.

The summary posting of the voucher register required each month involves the following procedures:

1. The total of the column headed Purchases—Golf should be posted as a debit to the purchases—golf account in the general ledger.
2. The total of the column headed Purchases—Tennis should be posted as a debit to the purchases—tennis account in the general ledger.
3. The total of the column headed Operating Expenses Dr. should be posted as a debit to the operating expenses account in the general ledger, which is the control account for the operating expense subsidiary ledger.
4. The total of the column headed Vouchers Payable Cr. should be posted as a credit to the vouchers payable account in the general ledger.

As the total of each column is posted from the voucher register, the account number should be entered in parentheses immediately below the total. The page number of the voucher register should also be entered in the Posting Reference column of the ledger account to which it is posted. Check marks in parentheses should be entered below the totals of the Sundry Accounts Dr. and Cr. amount columns in the voucher register to indicate that these totals should not be posted.

Paying Vouchers. After the vouchers are entered in the voucher register, they may be filed either by due date or alphabetically by supplier name in an unpaid vouchers file. Regardless of the way in which the vouchers are filed, they should be paid according to the terms stated in the invoice. Delay in payment may result in discounts being lost or in the loss of credit standing.

When they become due, the vouchers and supporting documents should be presented to the cashier or other proper disbursing officer for payment. The disbursing officer should review each voucher and supporting documents for propriety of the expenditure, prepare and sign the check, and mail it directly to the supplier. In no case should a check be written without a supporting voucher and documentation. Ordinary checks may be used. In some cases, however, a **voucher check** is used, which is a check with space for entering data from the invoice or other sources of information concerning the voucher to which the check relates. In the following illustration, a voucher check issued to Sportime Corp. in payment of its invoice of May 6 is reproduced. The statement attached to it provides space for details of the invoice, including its date, number, description, amount, deductions, if any, and net amount. The information given on the statement attached to the check is for identification purposes and serves as a remittance advice to the payee of the check. Whether an ordinary check or a voucher check is used, the checks should be pre-numbered and subsequently accounted for by number to ensure that no unauthorized payments occur.

No. 519	**Mitchell & Jenkins Sporting Goods** 2200 E. Washington St. Indianapolis, IN 46201-3216		3-4 740
Date May 7, 19--	May 7 19 --		**No. 519**
To Sportime Corp.	**Pay to the order of** Sportime Corp.	**$**	1,560.00
	Fifteen hundred sixty 00/100----------------------- **Dollars**		
Voucher No. 164	**FIRST** **NATIONAL**	*Jessica Jenkins*	
Amount of **Voucher** $1,560.00	**BANK** Indianapolis, Indiana ⑆074000009⑆ 926418⑈		Treasurer
Discount	Detach this statement before depositing check		
Amount of **Check** $1,560.00	**Date** May 7, 19--		
Remarks	Attached voucher check is full settlement of the following:		

Invoice		Description	Invoice Amount	Deductions		Net Amount
Date	No.			For	Amount	
May 7	163	12 Prince Spectrum Rackets	1560 00			1560 00

Voucher Check

After the voucher has been paid, the disbursing officer should cancel the voucher and supporting documents to indicate payment. This ensures that a voucher will not be processed again to generate a duplicate payment. The canceled voucher and supporting documents are then returned to the vouchers payable section for filing either numerically or alphabetically in a paid vouchers file. In either case, the numerical sequence should be strictly controlled for possible missing or duplicate vouchers.

Entering Checks. Three accounting records are affected by the check entering process: the check register, voucher register, and general ledger. All checks issued in payment of vouchers can be entered in a **check register**. A check register is an accounting record of all checks written by a firm. When the charges pertaining to each voucher have been entered in the voucher register, it is not necessary to make provision for distribution of charges in the check register. It is not unusual, however, to find columns provided in the check register for entering deductions, such as purchases discounts, that may be made at the time of payment. The form of check register shown below does not have such a column. After checks are entered in the check register, an entry should also be made in the "Disposition" columns of the voucher register to show that the voucher has been paid, as illustrated in the disposition columns of the voucher register on page 616. This entry, which would be made by the vouchers payable clerk based on a canceled voucher, serves the same purpose as a debit entry in a supplier's ledger account.

Explain the use of the check register.

CHECK REGISTER FOR MONTH OF *May* 19 -- PAGE *13*

| | VOUCHERS PAYABLE DR. | | DAY | DRAWN TO THE ORDER OF | CHK. NO. | CASH CR. | |
	NO.	AMOUNT				AMOUNT	
1	161	3 0 0 0 00	1	Capital Leasing Co.	511	3 0 0 0 00	1
2	156	2 5 5 00	2	Ace Office Supply	512	2 5 5 00	2
3	154	9 5 00	5	Sherman's Garage	513	9 5 00	3
4	162	5 1 2 0 00	7	Golf World	514	5 1 2 0 00	4
21		141 0 1 9 00				141 0 1 9 00	21
22		(2 1 8)				(1 1 1)	22

Following is a description of the checks that have been entered in the check register illustrated above.

May 1 Check No. 511, Capital Leasing Co., $3,000, in payment of Voucher No. 161.

2 Check No. 512, Ace Office Supply, $255, in payment of Voucher No. 156.

5 Check No. 513, Sherman's Garage, $95, in payment of Voucher No. 154.

7 Check No. 514, Golf World, $5,120, in payment of Voucher No. 162.

To prove the check register, it is only necessary to determine that the footing of the Cash Cr. column is equal to the footing of the Vouchers Payable Dr. column. The footings should be proved before the totals are forwarded and before the summary posting is completed.

No individual posting from the check register is required. The summary posting required each month involves the following procedures:

1. The total of the column headed Vouchers Payable Dr. should be posted as a debit to the vouchers payable account in the general ledger.

2. The total of the column headed Cash Cr. should be posted as a credit to the cash account in the general ledger.

As the total of each column is posted from the check register, the account number in parentheses should be entered immediately below the total. The page number of the check register should also be entered in the Posting Reference column of the ledger account to which the amount is posted.

■ **Proving Vouchers Payable.** When the voucher system is used, it is possible to dispense with a subsidiary accounts payable ledger. The file of unpaid vouchers serves as the detail to support the balance of the vouchers payable account after all posting has been completed. The voucher register itself partially performs this function. Every blank in the Disposition column of the register shows that the indicated voucher is unpaid.

The unpaid vouchers file can be consulted if more detail about any item is needed.

When a trial balance is prepared at the end of a period, the balance of the vouchers payable account should be verified by preparing a list of the vouchers contained in the unpaid vouchers file. The total amount of this list should be equal to the balance of the account.

Note that if no subsidiary accounts payable ledger is maintained and if unpaid vouchers are filed by due date, there will be no ongoing record of the total amount owed to each supplier. Fortunately, such information generally is considered to be of limited importance. Businesses tend to think in terms of the total amount of unpaid invoices and when the amounts are due, not in terms of total amounts due to individual suppliers. If the latter information is needed, copies of the vouchers can be filed by supplier name.

Purchases Returns and Allowances. When a voucher system of accounting is used, purchases returns and allowances must be entered in such a way that the amount of the affected unpaid voucher is reduced, the voucher register shows the proper amounts payable, and the accounts properly reflect such transactions. A commonly used procedure involves three steps:

1. A notation of the return or allowance is made on the affected voucher and the credit memo is attached to it.
2. A notation of the reduction is made in the voucher register beside the amount of the affected voucher.
3. The transaction is formally entered in the general journal.

A return or allowance relating to a merchandise purchase would require a debit to Vouchers Payable and a credit to Purchases Returns and Allowances. If the return or allowance is related to a purchase of a long-term asset or to some expense, the credit in the entry would be to the asset or expense account.

Partial Payments. When a business using the voucher system makes partial payments on invoices, special handling is required. If it is known at the outset that an invoice will be paid in installments, a separate voucher for each installment should be prepared. If it is decided to make a partial payment on an invoice already vouchered and entered, the original voucher should be canceled and two or more new ones issued. The total amount of the new vouchers should be equal to that of the old voucher. The vouchers would be entered in the voucher register by a debit to Vouchers Payable in the Sundry Accounts-Dr. column for the amount of the old voucher, and by a credit to Vouchers Payable in the Vouchers Payable Cr. column for the amounts of the new vouchers. A note should be entered in the Disposition column of the voucher register indicating that the old voucher has been canceled and showing the numbers of the new vouchers issued. Payments of the vouchers should then be entered in the usual manner.

Building Your Accounting Knowledge

1. What functions are included in the expenditure cycle?
2. Purchase orders are typically prepared in multiple-copy form. What is done with the different copies of the purchase order?
3. Why is a voucher system very useful for controlling cash payments?
4. Under what circumstances is there usually an advantage in using a voucher system?
5. What two accounting records are involved in entering vouchers?
6. What are the appropriate procedures for paying vouchers?
7. Why should the disbursing officer cancel a voucher and supporting documents to indicate payment after the voucher is paid?
8. When a voucher system is used, how is the vouchers payable account balance verified at the end of a period?

Assignment Box

To reinforce your understanding of the preceding text materials, you may complete the following:

Study Guide: Part B
Textbook: Exercises 16A3 through 16A5 and 16B3 through 16B5
Problems 16A1 through 16A2 and 16B1 through 16B2

Application in the Revenue Cycle

Explain the application of internal accounting control concepts in the revenue cycle.

The revenue cycle includes all the functions involved in receiving customer orders, providing goods and services, billing customers, and collecting payments—either on account or for cash sales. Diagramming and briefly explaining the revenue cycle will assist in understanding internal accounting control in the revenue cycle. A flowchart of the basic elements of the revenue cycle appears on the following page. Many variations of the revenue cycle are possible for different businesses. The flowchart shown here illustrates a medium-sized business that deals in a tangible product.

The Credit Sales portion of the flowchart shows that a customer who purchases merchandise on account usually sends a purchase order to a particular business. In response to this order, a sales order would be generated by the business. This sales order is the basis for preparing a shipping order which causes goods to be shipped to the customer. One copy of the shipping order is sent to the customer with the goods and a second copy is sent to the Billing section so that a bill, the sales invoice, will be sent to the customer. A second copy of the sales invoice is sent to the General Accounting and Accounts Receivable sections for entry in the accounting system.

The Collections and Cash Sales portion of the flowchart depicts the processing of both collections on account and collections from cash sales. Collections on account generally are received by mail from customers. Normally included with the check is a remittance advice, which is a document indicating the purpose of the payment, that is, the bill that is being paid. Remittance advices are sent to the General Accounting and Accounts Receivable sections for entering in the accounting records and the checks are sent to the cashier, who prepares a deposit slip and sends it with the checks to the bank. The bank returns a validated deposit slip to the Accounting Department.

Sales clerks normally use cash registers to handle cash sales. Customer remittances of cash or checks are forwarded to the cashier, who prepares a deposit slip and sends the deposit to the bank. The cash register tape is sent to the Accounting Department for entering in the accounting records. A validated deposit slip is returned to the Accounting Department by the bank.

The Internal Audit Department has responsibility to oversee or monitor the entire system of internal accounting control depicted in the flowchart. Its functions might include making sure that goods are shipped only on the basis of authorized shipping orders or that all collections on account are properly entered in the accounting records.

Internal accounting control over the revenue cycle will now be discussed in some detail. The partial records illustrated are those of Mitchell & Jenkins. The merchandise accounts are kept on a departmental basis— one for golf and one for tennis. Since internal accounting controls relevant for cash sales differ significantly from those relevant for credit sales, cash sales and credit sales are discussed separately here.

Cash Sales

Most businesses make at least a portion of their sales for cash rather than on account. Regardless of the percentage of sales made for cash, certain basic internal accounting control procedures should be employed.

Cash Register Tapes and Sales Tickets. Receipts from cash sales generally are controlled by the use of a cash register that generates a cash register tape in duplicate; one copy for the customer and one copy to be retained for the firm's records. At the end of each day, the cash and any checks received from customers are sent to the cashier for preparation of the bank deposit, and the cash register tapes are either picked up by or sent to the accounting department for entry in the accounting records.

An alternative system for handling cash sales that is used by many businesses is the preparation of a separate sales ticket for each transaction. A salesclerk prepares a sales ticket in duplicate for each sale, and these tickets and the related cash receipts are then handled in a manner similar to that used for cash register tapes and related cash receipts. The only additional control necessary when sales tickets are used is that the

FLOWCHART OF REVENUE CYCLE

Credit Sales

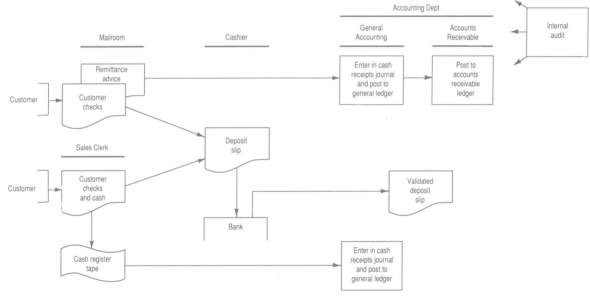

Collections and Cash Sales

Flowchart

tickets should be pre-numbered and subsequently accounted for by number.

Deposit Slip. The cashier prepares a deposit slip in duplicate for the cash and checks received from the salesclerks and sends both copies with the deposit to the bank. The validated deposit slip should be returned by the bank to the firm's accounting department.

Accounting Procedures for Cash Sales. The first accounting record affected by cash sales is the cash receipts journal. The cash register tapes, the sales tickets, or a listing of the tickets are the basis for the entries in the cash receipts journal. Examples of entries of cash sales are shown in the portion of the cash receipts journal of Mitchell & Jenkins illustrated on page 631.

The second accounting record affected by cash sales is the general ledger. At the end of each month, a summary posting is made from the cash receipts journal to the general ledger cash and sales accounts.

When each validated deposit slip is returned by the bank to the firm's accounting department, the amount deposited is compared with the amount entered in the cash receipts journal based on the cash register tapes or sales tickets. This procedure ensures that all cash sales collected by the salesclerks and forwarded to the cashier were in fact properly deposited.

This system appears to control adequately what happens to cash once a proper cash register or sales ticket record is made of each cash sale. A question might be raised, however, as to the control that exists over the salesclerks to see that a valid cash register entry or sales ticket is prepared in the first place. The answer essentially is the customer. Any customer purchasing merchandise expects to receive some kind of receipt for the amount remitted. In order to provide such a receipt, the salesclerk must generate either a cash register entry or a sales ticket. It would still be possible for the salesclerk to alter a sales ticket subsequently, but if these documents are reviewed by the accounting department or internal audit staff, frequent alterations in sales tickets would be questioned.

Credit Sales

Internal accounting control procedures for credit sales typically are more complicated than those for cash sales. By their nature, credit sales involve more documents, more people, and more accounting records.

Customer Purchase Order.　The customer's purchase order initiates a sales transaction. Since the customer intends to purchase goods from another business, clearly one firm's purchase is another firm's sale. Customer orders can be received either by mail or by telephone. If an order is received by telephone, the customer order document usually is generated internally by the seller. Based on the customer order, a sales order is prepared.

Sales Order.　The sales order is a document prepared by the sales order department which authorizes sales of merchandise to a customer. It would be possible to use the customer order as a sales order, but control and handling efficiency are improved if a separate sales order is generated. The following is a sales order prepared by Mitchell & Jenkins for a sale to Fleetwood Country Club. Sales orders should be pre-numbered and, subsequently, all numbers should be accounted for. If any numbers are missing, this would suggest that some orders have been lost and not properly processed. Sales orders are often prepared in duplicate so that the sales order department can retain one copy for its files. Many companies also have a separate credit department. If a credit department exists, the sales order is sent to the credit department to obtain approval of a sale to any charge customer. Note the credit approval that appears on the Mitchell & Jenkins sales order. After credit is approved, the sales order is sent to the shipping department.

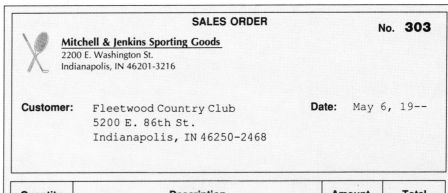

Sales Order

■■■ **Shipping Order.** The shipping order is the document that provides authorization to ship merchandise. It is an important control document in a firm's information system. An example of a shipping order for a shipment from Mitchell & Jenkins to Fleetwood Country Club is shown on page 626. This shipping order was prepared based on the preceding sales order. Shipping orders should be pre-numbered and subsequently accounted for by number to ensure that all shipments are properly entered and that all goods shipped are billed to the purchasers. One copy of the shipping order is sent to the customer with the goods and the other copy is sent to the billing section so that a sales invoice can be prepared.

■■■ **Sales Invoice.** A multiple-copy sales invoice, which is the company's bill to the customer, is prepared in the billing section of the accounting department as soon as the copy of the shipping order has been received, indicating that the goods have been shipped. A copy of a sales invoice that was generated based on the shipping order discussed above is

SHIPPING ORDER	No. **295**

Mitchell & Jenkins Sporting Goods
2200 E. Washington St.
Indianapolis, IN 46201-3216

Date: May 6, 19--

Customer:

Fleetwood Country Club
5200 E. 86th St.
Indianapolis, IN 46250-2468

Shipping instructions: Our truck

To be delivered: May 7, 19--

Quantity	Description	Amount	Total
2	Sets Precision Clubs-Men's @ $390	$780	
2	Sets Elite Clubs-Women's @ $370	740	$1,520

Shipping Order

shown on page 627. This document is extremely important from a control standpoint. In conjunction with the shipping order, the sales invoice provides assurance that all goods shipped are also billed. Sales invoices should be pre-numbered and subsequently accounted for by number in order to provide this assurance of proper billing. If any sales invoice number is missing from the sequence, it would suggest that some shipment was not billed or perhaps that the billing was not entered in the accounting records. In addition, each sales invoice should be supported by a shipping order to make certain that sales are entered only for goods actually shipped to customers. One copy of the sales invoice is sent to the customer and a second copy is sent to accounting. Other copies of the sales invoice might also be used in an accounting information system but the two copies described above are the minimum necessary. Before they are mailed to customers, the sales invoices should be verified as to price, quantity, and extended amounts.

Accounting Procedures for Credit Sales. Accounting procedures for entering sales were explained to a great extent in Chapter 7. That discussion is expanded here in order to emphasize the internal accounting control aspects of the data entry process.

The first accounting record affected by sales transactions is a firm's **sales journal**. The following is a portion of the sales journal for Mitchell & Jenkins. The individual sales invoices represent the basis for entries in

SALES INVOICE		No. **491**

Mitchell & Jenkins Sporting Goods
2200 E. Washington St.
Indianapolis, IN 46201-3216

Customer: **Date:**   May 7, 19--

          Fleetwood Country Club
          5200 E. 86th St.
          Indianapolis, IN 46250-2468

Description	Amount	Total
2 Sets Precision Clubs-Men's @ $390	$780	
2 Sets Elite Clubs-Women's @ $370	740	$1,520

Sales Invoice

the sales journal. In most accounting information systems, entries in such a journal represent the first point at which sales activities are reflected in the accounting records. Neither the customer order, nor the sales order, nor the shipping order, nor the preparation of the sales invoice directly affects any accounting record. This makes the sales journal particularly important from a control standpoint. Note that the sales invoices are entered in the sales journal not only in chronological order but also in numerical order. This feature of the data entry process makes the sales journal a convenient place to account for the numerical sequence of sales invoices.

A second accounting record affected by sales transactions is the accounts receivable ledger. An account from the accounts receivable ledger for Mitchell & Jenkins is reproduced on page 628. For good internal accounting control, the individual sales invoices should be used to post to the individual customer accounts in the accounts receivable ledger. As each invoice is posted, a check mark is entered in the Check ($\sqrt{}$) column following the Accounts Receivable Dr. column of the sales journal.

Posting to the individual customer accounts from the sales invoices rather than from the sales journal provides an independent check on the posting process. If the postings of customer accounts were made from the sales journal, any error in posting the sales journal would automatically be carried forward to the accounts receivable ledger. On the other hand, if both the sales journal and the customer accounts are posted from individual sales invoices by different accounting department employees, a posting error by either employee would cause the records to disagree, unless of course, both employees made exactly the same error. The posting error would be discovered at the end of the month because at that time, the individual customer account balances in the accounts receivable ledger would be scheduled, totaled, and compared with the general ledger accounts receivable control, which is posted from the total of the sales journal entries.

SALES JOURNAL FOR MONTH OF *May*   19 --   PAGE *9*

	ACCOUNTS RECEIVABLE DEBIT	✓	DAY	NAME	SALE NO.	SALES CREDIT GOLF	TENNIS	
1	1 4 8 5 00	✓	5	Court Side	489		1 4 8 5 00	1
2	4 2 7 3 00	✓	5	Lakeside Country Club	490	3 8 1 0 00	4 6 3 00	2
3	1 5 2 0 00	✓	5	Fleetwood Country Club	491	1 5 2 0 00		3
4	5 0 4 0 00	✓	7	Swing Shop	492	3 1 0 0 00	1 9 4 0 00	4
5	9 1 2 00	✓	7	The Tennis Racket	493		9 1 2 00	5
29	126 8 2 7 00 126 8 2 7 00					74 8 8 4 00 74 8 8 4 00	51 9 4 3 00 51 9 4 3 00	29
30	(1 3 1)					(4 1 1)	(4 2 1)	30

NAME *Fleetwood Country Club*   TERMS *Net*

ADDRESS *5200 E. 86th. St., Indianapolis, IN 46250*

DATE		ITEM	POST. REF.	DEBIT	CREDIT	BALANCE
19-- May	1	Balance	✓			9 7 6 00
	5		S491	1 5 2 0 00		2 4 9 6 00

Note that the individual posting for sales invoice No. 491 appears in the customer account, just as it appeared in the preceding sales journal. This approach to coding the posting reference in the customer account differs from that illustrated in Chapter 7. In Chapter 7, the posting reference consisted of the journal page preceded by the initial "S" for sales journal, to provide a cross-reference between the sales journal and the customer accounts. The approach illustrated here also provides a proper cross-reference because the same sales invoice number appears for both the journal entry in the sales journal and the posting in the customer account. Either approach to cross-referencing the journal entries and subsidiary ledger postings can provide good internal control.

The third accounting record affected by sales transactions is the general ledger. As explained in Chapter 7, at the end of the month a summary posting would be made from the sales journal to the appropriate general ledger accounts. The accounts and amounts posted for May are indicated at the bottom of the columns in the sales journal on page 628. As each total is posted to the appropriate general ledger account, the account number is entered in parentheses at the bottom of the column in the sales journal, and the journal page and "SJ" for sales journal are entered in the Post. Ref. column of the general ledger account.

The posting of particular interest here is the one to accounts receivable for $126,827. The following illustration shows the general ledger accounts receivable control account. After posting from the sales journal, the account has a balance of $333,653. This represents the total balances in all accounts receivable as of the end of May, after posting all charge sales made during May.

ACCOUNT *Accounts Receivable*   ACCOUNT NO. *131*

DATE		ITEM	POST. REF.	DEBIT	CREDIT	BALANCE	
						DEBIT	CREDIT
19-- May	1	Balance				206 8 2 6 00	
	31		SJ9	126 8 2 7 00		333 6 5 3 00	

▨ **Remittance Advice and Check.** When a customer makes a remittance by mail, the customer normally includes a remittance advice with the check. The **remittance advice** is a form showing the customer's name and address and the purpose and amount of the remittance. An example of a remittance advice is shown on page 630. For good internal accounting control, the checks and remittance advices should be separated in the mailroom; the checks should be sent to the cashier and the remittance advices to the accounting department. If a customer remittance arrives without a remittance advice, a remittance advice should be prepared in the mailroom for forwarding to the accounting department.

The processing of the checks and remittance advices is designed to ensure that customer remittances on account are properly received, deposited, and entered in the firm's records. If employees in the mailroom attempt to retain any customer remittances for their own use, the fraud will be discovered because mailroom employees do not have access to the accounting records. Consequently, the customer will undoubtedly be billed again for the amount previously remitted but intercepted by the mailroom employees. When the customer complains about the billing, the theft will be discovered. The actions of the cashier who receives the remittances from the mailroom are similarly controlled. The accounting department employees have access to the accounting records and can fraudulently alter them, but these employees have no access to the remittances and therefore, no incentive to modify the accounting records.

▨ **Deposit Slip.** The cashier prepares a deposit slip in duplicate for the checks and cash received from the mailroom, and sends both copies

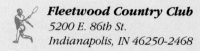

Fleetwood Country Club
5200 E. 86th St.
Indianapolis, IN 46250-2468

Date   May 25, 19--

Enclosed is our payment of the following:

Invoice		Description	Amount
Date	No.		
5/7	491	2 Sets Precision Clubs-Men's @ $390	$ 780.00
		2 Sets Elite Clubs-Women's @ $370	740.00
		Deductions	-0-
		Net	$1,520.00

Remittance Advice

along with the checks and cash to the bank. The following is a common form of deposit slip. These deposit slips are often pre-numbered. The bank validates the deposit slip and returns it to the depositing firm.

Mitchell & Jenkins Sporting Goods
2200 E. Washington St.
Indianapolis, IN 46201-3216

DEPOSIT SLIP		3-4
		740

Date _____ May 12 _____ **19** _____ --

**FIRST
NATIONAL
BANK**   Indianapolis, Indiana

Currency	2,452	20
Coin	139	80
Checks		
Total from other side		
Total	2,592	00

⑆074000009⑆ 926418⑈

Deposit Slip

▨▨▨▨ **Accounting Procedures for Collections.**   The first accounting record affected by collections on account is the **cash receipts journal**, a special journal used to enter all cash receipts. The individual remittance advices are the basis for entries in this record. A portion of the cash receipts journal for Mitchell & Jenkins is shown below.

CASH RECEIPTS JOURNAL FOR MONTH OF *May*   **19 --**   **PAGE** *12*

	DEBIT			CREDIT								
							SALES			GENERAL LEDGER		
	CASH	DAY	RECEIVED FROM DESCRIPTION	ACCOUNTS RECEIVABLE	√	GOLF		TENNIS		ACCT. NO.	AMOUNT	√
1	1 368 00	1	Cash sales			896 00		472 00				1
2	2 592 00	2	Cash sales			1 434 00		1 158 00				2
3	1 941 00	5	Cash sales			1 571 00		370 00				3
4	1 260 00	6	Cash sales			798 00		462 00				4
5	976 00	6	Fleetwood Country Club	976 00	√							5
6	3 977 00	6	Court Side	3 977 00	√							6
7	2 650 00	6	Swing Shop	2 650 00	√							7
27	170 720 00 170 720 00			130 500 00 130 500 00		22 451 00 22 451 00		17 186 00 17 186 00			583 00 583 00	27
28	(1 1 1)			(1 3 1)		(4 1 1)		(4 2 1)			(√)	28

A second accounting record affected by the collections is the accounts receivable ledger. The receipts are posted to the accounts receivable ledger in chronological order and the source of each receipt is indicated. For good internal accounting control, the individual remittance advices should be used to post to the individual customer accounts in the accounts receivable ledger. As each item is posted, a check mark is entered in the Check (√) column following the Accounts Receivable Credit column in the cash receipts journal. The journal page and "CR" for cash receipts journal are entered in the Post. Ref. column of the individual customer account in the accounts receivable ledger. The individual remittance advices are not used as posting references because no remittance advice reference numbers are available.

The account from the accounts receivable ledger illustrated on page 628 is reproduced on page 632, with one additional item, the remittance on account by the customer during May. Note that using the remittance advices to post the accounts receivable ledger provides control over the cash receipts posting process in the same way that using the individual sales invoices to post the accounts receivable ledger provided control over the sales posting process. If an error was made in posting either to the general ledger or to the accounts receivable ledger, the error would be discovered at the end of the month when the total of the balances in the accounts receivable ledger is compared with the general ledger accounts receivable control account balance.

NAME Fleetwood Country Club						TERMS Net	
ADDRESS 5200 E. 86th. St., Indianapolis, IN 46250							

DATE		ITEM	POST. REF.	DEBIT	CREDIT	BALANCE
19-- May	1	Balance	✓			9 7 6 00
	5		S491	1 5 2 0 00		2 4 9 6 00
	6		CR12		9 7 6 00	1 5 2 0 00

Another accounting record affected by the collections is the general ledger. At the end of each month, a summary posting would be made from the cash receipts journal to the appropriate general ledger accounts. The accounts and amounts posted for May are indicated at the bottom of the columns in the cash receipts journal on page 631. As each total is posted to the appropriate general ledger account, the account number is entered in parentheses at the bottom of the column in the cash receipts journal, and the journal page and "CR" for cash receipts journal are entered in the Post. Ref. column of the general ledger account.

The general ledger accounts receivable control account shown on page 629 is reproduced below, with one additional item, the credit total of $130,500 from the May cash receipts journal. After this posting, the account has a balance of $203,153. This represents the total of the balances in all individual customer accounts receivable as of the end of May, after crediting the customer accounts for all remittances received.

ACCOUNT Accounts Receivable							ACCOUNT NO. 131	
DATE		ITEM	POST. REF.	DEBIT	CREDIT	BALANCE		
						DEBIT	CREDIT	
19-- May	1	Balance	✓			206 8 2 6 00	
	31		S9	126 8 2 7 00		333 6 5 3 00	
	31		CR12		130 5 0 0 00	203 1 5 3 00	

In the previous discussion of deposit slips, it was noted that validated deposit slips are returned by the bank to the firm. Internal control is strengthened if these deposit slips are returned to the accounting department of the firm rather than to the cashier. An accounting department employee should compare the amount shown on the validated deposit slip with the amounts entered in the cash receipts journal as remittances on account. This procedure ensures that customer remittances on account as indicated on the remittance advices and entered in the cash receipts journal were in fact deposited by the cashier.

Building Your Accounting Knowledge

1. What functions are included in the revenue cycle?
2. What control exists over sales clerks to see that a valid cash register entry is made or a sales ticket is prepared when a sale occurs?
3. What purpose is served by the shipping order?
4. Why should postings to individual customer accounts receivable be made from the sales invoices rather than from the sales journal?
5. Why are checks and remittance advices separated in the mailroom, with the checks being sent to the cashier, and the remittance advices to the accounting department?
6. What three accounting records are affected by collections on account?
7. Why should validated deposit slips be returned by the bank to the accounting department of the firm rather than to the cashier?

Assignment Box

To reinforce your understanding of the preceding text material, you may complete the following:
Study Guide: Part C
Textbook: Exercises 16A6 through 16A7 and 16B6 through 16B7
Problems 16A3 through 16A4 and 16B3 through 16B4

Expanding Your Business Vocabulary

What is the meaning of each of the following terms:

accounting procedures (p. 606)
authorization procedures (p. 605)
cash receipts journal (p. 630)
check register (p. 609)
customer's purchase order (p. 624)
independent check (p. 606)
internal accounting control system
  (p. 604)
internal audit department (p. 606)
purchase invoice (p. 612)
purchase order (p. 609)
purchase requisition (p. 609)

receiving report (p. 610)
remittance advice (p. 629)
sales invoice (p. 625)
sales journal (p. 626)
sales order (p. 624)
segregation of duties (p. 605)
shipping order (p. 625)
voucher (p. 608)
voucher check (p. 617)
voucher register (p. 609)
voucher system (p. 611)

Demonstration Problem

The following selected transactions were completed by the Donovan and Donovan Drug Co. during the month of April. Donovan uses the gross-price method of accounting for cash discounts on purchases and sales of merchandise. Donovan and Donovan does business in a state which has no sales taxes.

(a)   **Apr. 1**   Issued Check No. 1501 in payment of April rent, $1,800 (Voucher No. 263).

(b)   **2**   Sold merchandise on account to Webster, Inc., terms, 2/EOM, n/60, Invoice No. 81, $6,750.

(c)   **4**   Issued Check No. 1503 for office supplies purchased, $675 (Voucher No. 266).

(d)   **8**   Purchased merchandise on account from MacDougall Co., $5,400, terms 2/10-n/30 (Voucher No. 270).

(e)   **9**   Issued Check No. 1505 to Allied Van Lines in payment of freight charges on merchandise purchased on April 8, $480 (Voucher No. 272).

(f)   **10**   Sold merchandise on account to Roswell Co., terms, 30 days. Invoice No. 88, $12,000.

(g)   **11**   Issued credit memorandum No. 901 for $600 to Webster, Inc. for merchandise returned.

(h)   **12**   Purchased office equipment on account from Faulstich Office Products, $22,500 (Voucher No. 275).

(i)   **12**   Received cash for office supplies sold to employees at cost, $180.

(j)   **16**   Hugh Donovan, one of the owners, invested an additional $150,000 cash in the business.

(k)   **18**   Issued Check No. 1510 in payment for merchandise purchased from MacDougall Co. on April 8, less discount, $5,292 (Voucher No. 270).

(l)   **20**   Issued Credit Memorandum No. 902 for $330 to Roswell Co. as a price reduction on spoiled merchandise sold to them on April 10.

(m)   **23**   Sold merchandise for cash, $23,850.

(n)   **24**   Sold merchandise on account to Fulton Hospital, terms, 2/10-n/30, Invoice No. 95, $9,500.

(o)   **28**   Received $6,027 from Webster, Inc. in settlement of April 2 invoice, less return of April 11 and discount.

(p)   **29**   Issued Check No. 1550 in payment of utility bills for gas and electricity, $1,035 (Voucher No. 276).

(q)   **30**   Issued Check No. 1551 to Hugh Donovan, $2,500 and Check No. 1552 to James Donovan, $2,500; representing withdrawals by the two owners of the business (Voucher Nos. 280 and 281).

(r)   **30**   Issued Check No. 1553 in payment of office and sales salaries for April, $23,700 (Voucher No. 282).

(s)   **30**   Entered adjustments from the work sheet for the company's fiscal year ended April 30.

Donovan and Donovan maintains a voucher register, a check register, a sales journal, a cash receipts journal, and a general journal. In addition, accounts receivable and accounts payable subsidiary ledgers are used.

Required:

1. Name the journal in which each of the preceding transactions (a) through (s) would be entered.
2. Tell whether an account in the accounts receivable subsidiary ledger would be affected for each of the preceding transactions.
3. Enter transactions (b), (d), (e), (g), (k), and (o) in the proper journals.

Solution

1.

(a) Check register
(b) Sales journal
(c) Check register
(d) Voucher register
(e) Check register
(f) Sales journal
(g) General journal
(h) Voucher register
(i) Cash receipts journal
(j) Cash receipts journal
(k) Check register
(l) General journal
(m) Cash receipts journal
(n) Sales journal
(o) Cash receipts journal
(p) Check register
(q) Check register
(r) Check register
(s) General journal

2.

(b) Accounts receivable ledger

(f) Accounts receivable ledger
(g) Accounts receivable ledger

(l) Accounts receivable ledger

(n) Accounts receivable ledger
(o) Accounts receivable ledger

3. Transaction (b):

Sales Journal for Month of April   19--   **Page 25**

Accounts Receivable Debit	(√)	Day	Name	Sale No.	Sales Credit
6,750.00		2	Webster, Inc.	81	6,750.00

Transaction (d):

Voucher Register for Month of April 19--   **Page 17**

Purchases Dr.	Operating Expenses Dr. Acct. No.	Amount	√	Sundry Accounts Dr. Acct. No.	Amount	√	Day	Vou. No.	To Whom Issued	Sundry Accounts Cr. Acct. No.	Amount	√	Vouchers Payable Cr.	Disposition Date	Ck. No.
5,400.00							8	270	MacDougall Co.				5,400.00	18	1510

Transactions (e) and (k)

| | | | | | Purchases | Cash Cr. | |
| Vouchers Payable Dr. | | | | | Discount | Ck. | |
No.	Amount	Day	Drawn to the Order of		Cr.	No.	Amount
272	480.00	9	Allied Van Lines			1505	480.00
270	5,400.00	18	MacDougall Co.		108.00	1510	5,292.00

Check Register for Month of April   19--   Page 29

Transaction (g)

Journal   Page 37

Date	Description	Post. Ref.	Debit	Credit
April 11	Sales Returns & Allowances		600.00	
	Accounts Receivable—Webster, Inc.			600.00
	Credit memo No. 901			

Transaction (o)

Cash Receipts Journal for Month of April   19--   Page 19

| Debit | | | Received from- | Credit | | General Ledger Acct. | |
Sales Discounts	Cash Net Amount	Day	Description	Accounts Receivable √	Sales	No.	Amount
123.00	6,027.00	28	Webster, Inc.	6,150.00			

Note: Now that you have reviewed the Demonstration Problem and Solution you may complete the **Mastery Problem** at the end of the chapter activities.

Applying Accounting Concepts

Series A

Exercise 16A1—Journal Enteries; Post to T-Accounts; Schedule of Accounts Payable. Selected acquisition and payment transactions of Fritz Co. for the first month of operations are as follows:

(a) Purchased equipment on account from Slater Co., $2,594.
(b) Purchased merchandise for cash, $1,606.
(c) Purchased merchandise on account from Stokes Co., $1,830.
(d) Paid $1,400 on account to Slater Co.
(e) Purchased merchandise on account from Varvil Co., $1,096.
(f) Paid $1,000 on account to Stokes Co.
  1. Prepare appropriate general journal entries for the above transactions.
  2. Post appropriate entries to the accounts payable subsidiary ledger and to the accounts payable account. (Use T-account forms.)
  3. Prove the balance of the accounts payable account by preparing a schedule of accounts payable.

Exercise 16A2—Journal Entries; Post to T-Accounts; Schedule of Accounts Receivable. Selected sales and collection transactions of Burnett Co. for the first month of operations are as follows:

(a) Sold merchandise on account to M. Causey, $838.

(b) Sold merchandise for cash, $1,220.

(c) Sold merchandise on account to R. Cline, $528.

(d) Collected $600 on account from M. Causey.

(e) Sold merchandise on account to L. Pelly, $634.

(f) Collected $300 on account from R. Cline.

1. Prepare appropriate general journal entries for the above transactions.
2. Post appropriate entries to the accounts receivable subsidiary ledger and to the accounts receivable account. (Use T-account forms.)
3. Prove the balance of the accounts receivable account by preparing a schedule of accounts receivable.

Exercise 16A3—Entries in Voucher Register. The following transactions occurred during the first month of operations of Lawler Co.

Sept. 3 Received an invoice for $1,600 from Kuhn Realty Co. for rent. (Rent Expense, Account No. 5443)

5 Received an invoice for $3,041.70 from Crow Supply House for merchandise.

10 Received an invoice for $1,821.80 from Reitz Equipment Co. for office furniture. (Office Equipment, Account No. 191)

17 Received a bill for $220.14 for telephone service and installation from Inland Telephone Co. (Telephone Expense, Account No. 5409)

19 Received an invoice for $175.00 from the Daily Banner for advertising. (Advertising Expense, Account No. 5433)

26 Received an invoice for $2,221.10 from Ladd Co. for merchandise.

Enter the foregoing transactions in a voucher register similar to the one on page 616 but use only one purchases column.

Exercise 16A4—Entries in Check Register. Refer to Exercise 16A3. The following payments were made during the first month of operations of Lawler Co.

Sept. 4 Issued Check No. 1 in payment of invoice from Kuhn Realty Co.

17 Issued Check No. 2 in payment of invoice from Crow Supply House.

18 Issued Check No. 3 in payment of invoice from Reitz Equipment Co.

26 Issued Check No. 4 in payment of invoice from the Daily Banner.

Enter the foregoing transactions in a check register similar to the one on page 619.

Exercise 16A5—Total and Post Voucher Register; Schedule of Unpaid Vouchers. Refer to Exercises 16A3 and 16A4.

1. Foot, prove, total, and rule the amount columns of the voucher register and the check register. Open a T account for Vouchers Payable and post the appropriate totals to it.
2. Prove the balance of the vouchers payable account by preparing a schedule of unpaid vouchers from the voucher register.

Exercise 16A6—Entries in Sales Journal. The following selected charge sales transactions occurred during the first month of operations of the Roberts Co.

May 4 Made charge sale No. 1 to D. Irby, $621.00.
   11 Made charge sale No. 2 to J. Weiland, $566.78.
   14 Made charge sale No. 3 to B. McGill, $804.00.
   28 Made charge sale No. 4 to P. Fehnel, $663.42.
   30 Made charge sale No. 5 to D. Irby, $408.26.

Enter the preceding transactions in a sales journal similar to the one on page 628 but use only one sales column.

Exercise 16A7—Entries in Cash Receipts Journal. Refer to Exercise 16A6. Enter the following cash receipts transactions of Roberts Co. in a cash receipts journal similar to the one on page 631.

May 7 Made cash sales of $2,824.90.
   18 Received $400 on account from D. Irby.
   21 Made cash sales of $1,808.50.
   24 Received $566.78 on account from J. Weiland.

Exercise 16A8—Total and Post Sales Journal and Cash Receipts Journal; Schedule of Accounts Receivable. Refer to Exercises 16A6 and 16A7.

(a) Foot, prove, total, and rule the sales journal in Exercise 16A6 and the cash receipts journal in Exercise 16A7.
(b) Post the journal entries to an accounts receivable subsidiary ledger, and the appropriate journal totals to an accounts receivable account. Use T-account forms. Insert posting references.
(c) Prove the accounts receivable balance by preparing a schedule of accounts receivable.

Series B

Exercise 16B1—Journal Entries; Post to T-Accounts; Schedule of Accounts Payable. Selected acquisition and payment transactions of Harris Co. for the first month of operations are as follows:

(a) Purchased equipment on account from Basler Co., $1,945.
(b) Purchased merchandise for cash, $1,205.
(c) Purchased merchandise on account from Braun Co., $1,372.
(d) Paid $1,000 on account to Basler Co.
(e) Purchased merchandise on account from Downs Co., $822.
(f) Paid $800 on account to Braun Co.
   1. Prepare appropriate general journal entries for the above transactions.
   2. Post appropriate entries to the accounts payable subsidiary ledger and to the accounts payable account. (Use T-account forms.)
   3. Prove the balance of the accounts payable account by preparing a schedule of accounts payable.

Exercise 16B2—Journal Entries; Post to T-Accounts; Schedule of Accounts Receivable. Selected sales and collection transactions of Nissing Co. for the first month of operations are as follows:

(a) Sold merchandise on account to G. Pearl, $628.
(b) Sold merchandise for cash, $915.
(c) Sold merchandise on account to E. Pickles, $396.

(d) Collected $500 on account from G. Pearl.

(e) Sold merchandise on account to M. Quail, $475.

(f) Collected $250 on account from E. Pickles.

    1. Prepare appropriate general journal entries for the above transactions.

    2. Post appropriate entries to the accounts receivable subsidiary ledger and to the accounts receivable account. (Use T-account forms.)

    3. Prove the balance of the accounts receivable account by preparing a schedule of accounts receivable.

Exercise 16B3—Entries in Voucher Register. The following transactions occurred during the first month of operations of Keyser Co.

Oct. **2** Received an invoice for $1,200 from O'Brien Realty Co. for rent. (Rent Expense, Account No. 5443)

    4 Received an invoice for $2,281.28 from Page Supply House for merchandise.

    10 Received an invoice for $1,366.35 from Prince Equipment Co. for office furniture. (Office Equipment, Account No. 191)

    15 Received a bill for $165.10 for telephone service and installation from Sangamon Telephone Co. (Telephone Expense, Account No. 5409)

    18 Received an invoice for $131.25 from the Daily Register for advertising. (Advertising Expense, Account No. 5433)

    25 Received an invoice for $1,665.82 from Rodis Co. for merchandise.

Enter the foregoing transactions in a voucher register similar to the one on page 616 but use only one purchases column.

Exercise 16B4—Entries in Check Register. Refer to Exercise 16B3. The following payments were made during the first month of operations of Keyser Co.

Oct. **3** Issued Check No. 1 in payment of invoice from O'Brien Realty Co.

    16 Issued Check No. 2 in payment of invoice from Page Supply House.

    17 Issued Check No. 3 in payment of invoice from Prince Equipment Co.

    25 Issued Check No. 4 in payment of invoice from the Daily Register.

Enter the foregoing transactions in a check register similar to the one on page 619.

Exercise 16B5—Total and Post Voucher Register; Schedule of Unpaid Vouchers. Refer to Exercises 16B3 and 16B4.

    1. Foot, prove, total, and rule the amount columns in the voucher register and in the check register. Open a T account for Vouchers Payable and post the appropriate totals to it.

    2. Prove the balance of the voucher payable account by preparing a schedule of unpaid vouchers from the voucher register.

Exercise 16B6—Entries in Sales Journal. The following selected charge sales transactions occurred during the first month of operations of the Ryan Co.

June **3** Made charge sale No. 1 to C. Izard, $465.75.

    11 Made charge sale No. 2 to T. Wilder, $425.08.

12 Made charge sale No. 3 to J. Matcuk, $603.00.

26 Made charge sale No. 4 to G. Franken, $497.57.

28 Made charge sale No. 5 to C. Izard, $306.20.

Enter the preceding transactions in a sales journal similar to the one on page 628 but use only one sales column.

Exercise 16B7—Entries in Cash Receipts Journal. Refer to Exercise 16B6. Enter the following cash receipts transactions of Ryan Co. in a cash receipts journal similar to the one on page 631.

June 6 Made cash sales of $2,118.68.

18 Received $300 on account from C. Izard.

19 Made cash sales of $1,356.38.

25 Received $425.08 on account from T. Wilder.

Exercise 16B8—Total and Post Sales Journal and Cash Receipts Journal; Schedule of Accounts Receivable. Refer to Exercises 16B6 and 16B7.

1. Foot, prove, total, and rule the sales journal in Exercise 16B6 and the cash receipts journal in Exercise 16B7.
2. Post the transactions from Exercise 16B6 to an accounts receivable subsidiary ledger, and the journal totals to an accounts receivable account. Use T-account forms. Insert posting references.
3. Prove the accounts receivable balance by preparing a schedule of accounts receivable.

Series A

Problem 16A1   Entries in Voucher Register

The following transactions were completed by the Olympia Foundry on June 4:

(a) Received an invoice from the American Mining Co. for raw materials, $1,300. Prepared Voucher No. 472.

(b) Received a statement from the Midwest Telephone Company for exchange and toll service, $89.72. Prepared Voucher No. 473.

(c) Issued a voucher (No. 474) to C. McCarter an attorney, for $1,600 representing a retainer for legal services. (Debit Prepaid Legal Services, Account No. 157)

(d) Received an invoice from the Dennis Paper Supply Co. for office supplies purchased on May 28, $144.60. Prepared Voucher No. 475.

(e) Received an invoice from Bond Insurance Agency for insurance on merchandise and office equipment, $373.42. Prepared Voucher No. 476.

(f) Issued a payroll voucher (No. 477) for the week ended June 2. Total payroll for week, $4,431.33 (Yard Salaries Expense, $3,184.33; Drivers Wage Expense, $1,247.00). FICA tax withheld, $292.62. Employees income tax withheld, $1,058.62.

(g) Received an invoice from the Imperial Oil Co. for gasoline and oil, $1,874. Prepared Voucher No. 478.

Following is a list of the accounts affected by these transactions:

Operating Expense Accounts		Selected General Ledger Accounts	
No.	Title	No.	Title
5401	Yard Salaries Expense	152	Office Supplies
5409	Telephone Expense	155	Prepaid Insurance
5432	Drivers Wage Expense	157	Prepaid Legal Services
5441	Gas and Oil Expense	211	FICA Tax Payable
		214	Employees Income Tax Payable

Required:

Enter the transactions in a voucher register. Foot the amount columns and prove the footings. Total and rule the register.

Problem 16A2   Entries in Check Register

The following checks were issued by the treasurer for The Hanenkamp Co.:

July 3 Check No. 521 to Regency Auto Co., on Voucher No. 626, $1,380.00.

3 Check No. 522 to Whitmire Co., on Voucher No. 594, $1,470.00 less 2% discount.   *29.40   1440.60*

3 Check No. 523 to Forshaw Heating Co., on Voucher No. 620, $1,626.40.

5 Check No. 524 to Fletcher Typewriter Co., on Voucher No. 627, $558.00.

6 Check No. 525 to Crestside Furnace Co., on Voucher No. 619, $1,500.00 less 3% discount.   *45   1455*

7 Check No. 526 to Payroll, on Voucher No. 621, $4,990.00.

10 Check No. 527, to T.H. Wolff, on Voucher No. 629, $470.00.

10 Check No. 528 to Climate Heating Co., on Voucher No. 616, $2,227.22 less 1% discount.   *22.27   2204.95*

11 Check No. 529 to Devere Printing Co., on Voucher No. 628, $185.20.

12 Check No. 530 to B.C. Elder Co., on Voucher No. 612, $595.00 less 2% discount.   *11.90   583.10*

13 Check No. 531 to Finley Office Supply Co., on Voucher No. 630, $138.60.

14 Check No. 532 to Payroll, on Voucher No. 631, $5,274.00.

Required:

Enter the checks, using a check register. Foot the amount columns and prove the footings. Total and rule the register.

Problem 16A3   Entries in Sales and Cash Receipts Journals; Posting; Schedule of Accounts Receivable

Charles Lapp is the owner of the Lapp Exercise Equipment Store. Following is a list of the general ledger accounts that are affected by the August sales and collections with the August 1 balances indicated:

111 Cash, $8,813.40
131 Accounts Receivable, $12,584.01
411 Sales, $45,985.77

As of August 1, the accounts receivable had debit balances as follows:

Thelma Caskey, 1 McKnight Place, Ladue, MO 63124-5504; $3,647.01
John Dooley, 7121 Stanford, University City, MO 63130-1718; $3,280.32
Dorothy Fleming, 7629 Carrswold Dr., Clayton, MO 63105-2163; $1,929.48
Michael Hudson, 508 Redondo Dr., Ballwin, MO 63135-4712; $1,977.54
Mark Maguire, 2142 Bellevue, Maplewood, MO 63143-3781; $1,749.66

Lapp's August sales and collections transactions are as follows:

Aug. 1 Charge sale No. 162, Michael Hudson, $1,224.00.
       2 Cash sales of $1,536.00.
       3 Collected $3,647.01 on account from Thelma Caskey.
       6 Charge sale No. 163, Mark Maguire, $501.00.
       9 Collected $1,977.54 on account from Michael Hudson.
      10 Charge sale No. 164, John Dooley, $2,490.00.
      13 Cash sales of $1,317.00.
      14 Cash sales of $1,854.00.
      16 Collected $1,749.66 on account from Mark Maguire.
      17 Charge sale No. 165, Dorothy Fleming, $564.00.
      20 Collected $3,280.32 on account from John Dooley.
      23 Cash sales of $882.00.
      24 Charge sale No. 166, Thelma Caskey, $501.00.
      27 Cash sales of $1,827.00.
      29 Collected $1,929.48 on account from Dorothy Fleming.
      31 Charge sale No. 167, Michael Hudson, $1,632.00.

Required:

1. Open the necessary general ledger accounts and enter the August 1 balances, using four-column ledger paper.
2. Open the accounts receivable ledger and enter the August 1 balances, using three-column ledger paper.
3. Journalize each transaction in either the sales or cash receipts journal. Make any necessary individual postings immediately to the customer accounts.
4. Foot, prove the footings, enter the totals, and rule the journals. Complete the summary postings and update the account balances.
5. Prove the balance of the accounts receivable account by preparing a schedule of the accounts receivable as of August 31.

Series B

Problem 16B1   Entries in Voucher Register

The following transactions were completed by the Central States Smelting Company on May 1:

(a) Received an invoice from the National Mining Co. for raw materials, $975. Prepared Voucher No. 724.

(b) Received a statement from the Ozark Telephone Company for exchange and toll service, $67.29. Prepared Voucher No. 725.

(c) Issued a voucher (No. 726) to G. Zafft an attorney, for $1,200 representing a retainer for legal services. (Debit Prepaid Legal Services, Account No. 157)

(d) Received an invoice from the Overland Paper Supply Co. for office supplies, $108.45. Prepared Voucher No. 727.

(e) Received an invoice from Maes Insurance Agency for insurance on merchandise and office equipment, $359.34. Prepared Voucher No. 728.

(f) Issued a payroll voucher (No. 729) for the week ended April 29. Total payroll for week, $3,323.50 (Yard Salaries Expense, $2,388.25; Drivers Wage Expense, $935.25). FICA tax withheld, $219.46. Employees income tax withheld, $793.96.

(g) Received an invoice from the Apex Oil Co. dated April 24, for gasoline and oil, $1,405.50. Prepared Voucher No. 730.

Following is a list of the accounts affected by these transactions:

Operating Expense Accounts		Selected General Ledger Accounts	
No.	Title	No.	Title
5401	Yard Salaries Expense	152	Office Supplies
5409	Telephone Expense	155	Prepaid Insurance
5432	Drivers Wage Expense	157	Prepaid Legal Services
5441	Gas and Oil Expense	211	FICA Tax Payable
		214	Employees Income Tax Payable

Required:

Enter the transactions in a voucher register. Foot the amount columns and prove the footings. Total and rule the register.

Problem 16B2   Entries in Check Register

The following checks were issued by the treasurer for The Applewhite Co.:

June 3 Check No. 611 to Sutton Heating Co., on Voucher No. 826, $1,035.00.

3 Check No. 612 to Essen Auto Co., on Voucher No. 794, $1,102.00.

4 Check No. 613 to Pickett Co., on Voucher No. 820, $1,219.80 less 2% discount.

5 Check No. 614 to Meyer Furnace Co., on Voucher No. 827, $1,125.00 less 3% discount.

6 Check No. 615 to Adler Typewriter Co., on Voucher No. 819, $418.00.

7 Check No. 616 to Payroll, on Voucher No. 821, $3,742.00.

10 Check No. 617 to R.F. Wood, on Voucher No. 829, $353.00.

10 Check No. 618 to Lennox Cooling Co., on Voucher No. 816, $1,670.42 less 1% discount.

11 Check No. 619 to Sterling Office Supply Co., on Voucher No. 828, $103.95.

12 Check No. 620 to M.H. Lane Co., on Voucher No. 812, $446.25 less 2% discount.

13 Check No. 621 to Comfort Printing Co., on Voucher No. 830, $138.90.
14 Check No. 622 to Payroll, on Voucher No. 831, $3,955.00.

Required:

Enter the checks, using a check register. Foot the amount columns and prove the footings. Total and rule the register.

Problem 16B3   Entries in Sales and Cash Receipts Journals; Posting; Schedule of Accounts Receivable

Linda Bowyer is the owner of a radio, television, and stereo equipment store known as Bowyer Electronics. Following is a list of the general ledger accounts that are affected by the September sales and collections with the September 1 balances indicated:

> 111 Cash, $5,875.60
> 131 Accounts Receivable, $8,389.34
> 411 Sales, $61,314.36

As of September 1, the accounts receivable had debit balances as follows:

Ursula Flitner, 122 Main St., Wheaton, IL 60188-1314; $2,431.34
Allen Gist, 1586 Briarcliffe Blvd., Lombard, IL 60148-1819; $2,186.88
Pat Guhin, 542 Kenilworth, Batavia, IL 60510-5732; $1,286.32
Tim Gulstrom, 655 Roosevelt Rd., Glen Ellyn, IL 60139-7121; $1,318.36
Hank Thun, 1512 Blackburn St., Wheaton, IL 60187-3185; $1,166.44

The narrative of September sales and collections transactions is as follows:

Sept.   **2** Charge sale No. 262, Tim Gulstrom, $816.00.
      3 Cash sales of $1,024.00.
      4 Collected $2,431.34 on account from Ursula Flitner.
      6 Charge sale No. 263, Hank Thun, $334.00.
      9 Collected $1,318.36 on account from Tim Gulstrom.
   10 Charge sale No. 264, Allen Gist, $1,660.00.
   11 Cash sales of $878.00.
   13 Cash sales of $1,236.00.
   16 Collected $1,166.44 on account from Hank Thun.
   18 Charge sale No. 265, Pat Guhin, $376.00.
   20 Collected $2,186.88 on account from Allen Gist.
   23 Cash sales of $588.00.
   24 Charge sale No. 266, Ursula Flitner, $334.00.
   25 Cash sales of $1,218.00.
   27 Collected $1,286.32 on account from Pat Guhin.
   30 Charge sale No. 267, Tim Gulstrom, $1,088.00.

Required:

1. Open the necessary general ledger accounts and enter the September 1 balances, using four-column ledger paper.
2. Open the accounts receivable ledger and enter the September 1 balances, using three-column ledger paper.

3. Journalize each transaction in either the sales or cash receipts journal. Make any necessary individual postings immediately to the customer accounts.
4. Foot, prove the footings, enter the totals, and rule the journals. Complete the summary postings and update the account balances.
5. Prove the balance of the accounts receivable account by preparing a schedule of the accounts receivable as of September 30.

Mastery Problem

Bill Keloh owns and operates Classic Collections, a business specializing in the purchase and sale of classic record collections. He travels all over the world acquiring complete record collections. Most sales are made through the mail to collectors. Keloh's accountant has set up the following journals as the basis for the accounting system.

Journals
(a) Voucher Register
(b) Check Register
(c) Sales Journal
(d) Cash Receipts Journal
(e) General Journal

The following representative transactions occurred during the month of March.

Mar. **1** Purchased a collection of Beethoven piano sonatas and a mixture of works of other composers, $3,800. Issued Check No. 381 to John Quatro. (No voucher was issued for this expenditure.)

3 Purchased a collection of Mozart symphonies and other rare classical albums in excellent condition, $4,900. Issued Check No. 382 to Jill Long. (No voucher was issued for this expenditure.)

5 Received American Express bill for airfare to purchase collections, $3,485, and other travel-related expenses (Account No. 5445), $2,395. Issued Voucher No. 555. (Keloh finds it easier to have these expenses entered in the accounting system when the credit card bills are received, rather than when the expenses are initially incurred. This generally results in a one-month lag in the recognition of these expenses.)

7 Received utility bill (Account No. 5408) for month of February, $458. Issued Voucher No. 556 to The Power Company.

10 Issued Voucher No. 557 to CFC Real Estate for March rent (Account No. 5406), $755.

11 Sold collection of albums to Barbara Dean on account, $535. (Sale No. 481)

12 Issued Voucher No. 559 to A. Mallor for legal fees (Account No. 5611), $800.

13 Issued Check No. 384 to American Express in payment of Voucher No. 555.

14 Sold collection of albums to Wayne Smith on account, $625. (Sale No. 482)

15 Issued Check No. 385 to The Power Company in payment of Voucher No. 556.

17 Sold collection of albums to Penny Marquette on account, $3,200. (Sale No. 484)

18 Issued Check No. 386 to CFC Real Estate in Payment of Voucher No. 557.

20 Issued Credit Memorandum No. 111 to Penny Marquette for $320 in response to her complaint concerning the physical condition of some of the albums in her most recent acquisition.

22 Issued Voucher No. 561 to United Express for shipping charges (Account No. 5416), $245.

24 Received remittance from Barbara Dean, $400.

25 Received remittance from Wayne Smith, $500.

27 Received remittance from Penny Marquette, $2,000.

31 Issued Check No. 387 for $2,500 to Bill Keloh for his monthly withdrawal (Account No. 312). (No voucher was issued for this expenditure.

Required:

1. Enter the above transactions in the appropriate journals provided on the following pages. (Hint: Checks issued without a supporting voucher must be entered in the voucher register prior to entering the payment in the check register.)

2. Prepare a schedule of vouchers payable. Are you confident that this schedule represents all current liabilities?

3. What suggestions would you make to Bill Keloh concerning the effectiveness of the internal accounting control techniques used for his business? What changes would you suggest?

Accounting for Partnerships

When two or more individuals engage in an enterprise as co-owners, the organization is known as a partnership. This form of organization is common to practically all types of enterprises. However, it is more popular among personal service enterprises than among merchandise enterprises. For example, the partnership form of organization is quite common in the legal and public accounting professions. In this chapter, the essential features and accounting procedures for the partnership form of business organization will be discussed and illustrated.

Partnership Formation and Distribution of Profits

Explain the manner in which a partnership is formed, and describe the basic provisions of a partnership agreement.

The Uniform Partnership Act states that "a partnership is an association of two or more persons who carry on, as co-owners, a business for profit." The partners may, by agreement, unite their capital, labor, skill, or experience in the conduct of a business for their mutual benefit. While under certain circumstances a partnership may be formed by means of an oral or implied agreement, it is desirable that a partnership agreement be evidenced by a written contract. A written agreement containing the various provisions under which a partnership is to operate is known as a partnership agreement. There is no standard form of partnership agreement, but there are certain provisions that are essential, such as:

1. Date of agreement.
2. Names of the partners.
3. Kind of business to be conducted.
4. Length of time the partnership is to run.
5. Name and location of the business.
6. Investment of each partner.
7. Basis on which profits or losses are to be shared by the partners.
8. Limitation of partners' rights and activities.
9. Salary allowances to partners.
10. Division of assets upon dissolution of the partnership.
11. Signatures of the partners.

A common form of partnership agreement is reproduced on the following page.

Advantages and Disadvantages

Explain the advantages and disadvantages of a partnership.

In comparison with the single proprietorship form of organization, the partnership form offers certain advantages, such as the following:

1. The ability and the experience of the partners are combined in one enterprise.
2. More capital may be raised because the resources of the partners are combined.
3. Credit may be improved because each general partner is personally liable for partnership debts.

There also are some disadvantages that are peculiar to the partnership form of organization, such as the following:

1. Each partner is individually liable for all of the debts of the partnership. The liability of each partner is not limited to a pro rata share of the partnership debts. Each partner is personally liable for all of the debts of the business to the same extent as if the business were a

PARTNERSHIP AGREEMENT

THIS CONTRACT, made and entered into on the first day of July, 19--, by and between Robert Mitchell of Indianapolis, Indiana, and Jessica Jenkins of the same city and state.

WITNESSETH: That the said parties have this day formed a partnership for the purpose of engaging in and conducting a wholesale and retail business in the city of Indianapolis under the following stipulations which are a part of this contract:

FIRST: The said partnership is to continue for a term of twenty-five years from July 1, 19--.

SECOND: The business is to be conducted under the firm name of Mitchell & Jenkins, at 2200 East Washington Street, Indianapolis, Indiana.

THIRD: The investments are as follows: Robert Mitchell, cash, $350,000; Jessica Jenkins, $200,000. These invested assets are partnership property.

FOURTH: Each partner is to devote his/her entire time and attention to the business and to engage in no other business enterprise without the written consent of the other partner.

FIFTH: During the operation of this partnership, neither partner is to become surety or bonding agent for anyone without the written consent of the other partner.

SIXTH: Robert Mitchell is to receive a salary of $36,000 a year, payable $1,500 in cash on the fifteenth day and last business day of each month. Jessica Jenkins is to receive a salary of $48,000 a year, payable $2,000 in cash on the fifteenth day and last business day of each month. At the end of each annual fiscal period, the net income or the net loss shown by the income statement, after the salaries of the two partners have been allowed, is to be shared as follows: Robert Mitchell, 60 percent; Jessica Jenkins, 40 percent.

SEVENTH: Neither partner is to withdraw assets in excess of his/her salary, any part of the assets invested, or assets in anticipation of net income to be earned, without the written consent of the other partner.

EIGHTH: In the case of the death or the legal disability of either partner, the other partner is to continue the operations of the business until the close of the annual fiscal period on the following June 30. At that time the continuing partner is to be given an option to buy the interest of the deceased or incapacitated partner at not more than 10 percent above the value of the deceased or incapacitated partner's proprietary interest as shown by the balance of his/her capital account after the books are closed on June 30. It is agreed that this purchase price is to be paid one half in cash and the balance in four equal installments payable quarterly.

NINTH: At the conclusion of this contract, unless it is mutually agreed to continue the operation of the business under a new contract, the assets of the partnership, after the liabilities are paid, are to be divided in proportion to the net credit of each partner's capital account on that date.

IN WITNESS WHEREOF, the parties aforesaid have hereunto set their hands and affixed their seals on the day and year above written.

Robert Mitchell (Seal)
_____
Robert Mitchell

Jessica Jenkins (Seal)
_____
Jessica Jenkins

Partnership Agreement

sole proprietorship. Under the laws of some states, certain partners may limit their liability. At least one partner, however, must be a general partner who is responsible for all of the debts of the partnership.

2. The interest of a partner in the partnership cannot be transferred without the consent of the other partners.

3. Termination of the partnership agreement, bankruptcy of the firm, or death of one of the partners dissolves the partnership.

Accounting for Initial Investments

Explain and prepare the accounting entries needed for the formation of a partnership.

In accounting for the operations of a partnership, it is necessary to keep a separate capital account for each partner. It is also customary to keep a separate drawing account for each partner. While no new principles are involved in keeping these accounts, care should be used in preparing the opening entry and in entering any transactions thereafter that affect the respective interests of the partners.

Cash Investments. Partners may invest cash and other property in the partnership. Certain liabilities may be assumed by the partnership, such as accounts payable, notes payable, and mortgages payable. In opening the books for a partnership, it is customary to prepare a separate journal entry for the investment of each partner. The proper asset accounts should be debited for the amounts invested, the proper liability accounts should be credited for the amounts of obligations assumed, and each partner's capital account should be credited for the residual equity in the assets. The opening entries for Mitchell & Jenkins based on the partnership agreement reproduced on page 649 are as follows:

Cash..	350,000	
Robert Mitchell, Capital.............................		350,000
R. Mitchell invested $350,000 in cash.		
Cash..	200,000	
Jessica Jenkins, Capital.............................		200,000
J. Jenkins invested $200,000 in cash.		

Investment of Cash and Non-Cash Items. If, instead of investing $200,000 in cash, Jenkins invested inventory valued at $47,500 on which is owed $10,500 in vouchers payable, office equipment valued at $40,000, delivery equipment valued at $92,000 on which is owed $19,000 represented by a note, and $50,000 in cash, the proper opening entry would be as follows:

Cash..	50,000	
Inventory......................................	47,500	
Office Equipment	40,000	
Delivery Equipment	92,000	
Vouchers Payable		10,500
Note Payable...............................		19,000
Jessica Jenkins, Capital......................		200,000
J. Jenkins' investment in partnership.		

Partnerships Formed from Existing Businesses. Two or more individuals who have been engaged in business as sole owners may form a partnership for the purpose of combining their businesses. Their respective balance sheets may be the basis for the opening entries for the investments of such partners. For example, assume that on April 1, S. H. Day and L. A. Knight form a partnership under the firm name of Day & Knight to continue the conduct of the businesses which they have been operating as sole owners. The balance sheets reproduced below and on page 652 are made a part of the partnership agreement. They agree to invest their assets and also agree that the partnership shall assume the liabilities shown in their respective balance sheets. Each partner is to receive credit for the equity in the assets invested, and the profits and losses are to be shared on a 50-50 basis. In case of dissolution, the assets are to be distributed between the partners in the ratio of their capital interests at the time of dissolution.

S.H. Day
Balance Sheet
March 31, 19--

Assets

Cash		$ 6,344
Accounts receivable	$ 5,524	
Less allowance for doubtful accounts.................	430	5,094
Merchandise inventory		24,574
Store equipment	$ 3,840	
Less accumulated depreciation......................	1,000	2,840
Total assets		$38,852

Liabilities

Notes payable	$ 3,600	
Accounts payable	10,082	
Total liabilities		$13,682

Owner's Equity

S.H. Day, capital		25,170
Total liabilities and owner's equity		$38,852

L.A. Knight
Balance Sheet
March 31, 19--

Assets

Cash		$ 3,544
Accounts receivable	$ 5,280	
Less allowance for doubtful accounts	720	4,560
Merchandise inventory		29,692
Supplies		286
Office equipment	$ 4,320	
Less accumulated depreciation	1,100	3,220
Store equipment	$ 4,800	
Less accumulated depreciation	1,200	3,600
Total assets		$44,902

Liabilities

Notes payable	$ 6,000	
Accounts payable	13,238	
Total liabilities		$19,238

Owner's Equity

L.A. Knight, capital		25,664
Total liabilities and owner's equity		$44,902

When two single proprietors decide to combine their businesses, generally accepted accounting principles usually require that non-cash assets (primarily inventories and long-term assets) be taken over at their fair market values as of the date of formation of the partnership. Since it probably cannot be determined as of March 31, 19--, which of the accounts receivable may later prove to be uncollectible in whole or in part, the amount of each accounts receivable balance cannot be adjusted for the currently accumulated allowance for doubtful accounts. It is, therefore, usual practice to enter the full amount of the accounts receivable as a debit and the amount of the allowance for doubtful accounts as a credit in placing each partner's investment in the books of the partnership. In this way, the accounts receivable are entered at their approximate fair market value. Subsequent end-of-period adjustments of the allowance for doubtful accounts on the books of the partnership will reflect future collection experience with respect to the combined accounts receivable of Day & Knight. If any accounts receivable on either set of books had been considered to be uncollectible as of March 31, 19--, it should have been written off by a debit to the Allowance for Doubtful Accounts and a credit to Accounts Receivable before the partnership was formed.

Because both Day & Knight had been using the fifo method of inventory costing, the values shown for merchandise inventories on their respective balance sheets are mutually acceptable as approximations of fair market value as of March 31, 19--. This is because under the fifo method, the most recently purchased inventory is considered to be still on hand. If Day or Knight had been using some other inventory costing method, the merchandise inventory amounts might require restatement to reflect the appropriate fair market value, with effects on the partners' capital accounts similar to those for long-term assets discussed below.

It is determined that the fair market value of Day's store equipment as of March 31, 19--, is $3,600, so this amount should be entered on the books of the new partnership, rather than the undepreciated cost of $2,840 ($3,840 − $1,000) shown on Day's balance sheet as of that date. In like manner, it is determined that the fair market values of Knight's office equipment and store equipment as of March 31, 19--, are $3,850 and $4,200 respectively, so these amounts should be entered on the books of the new partnership, rather than the respective undepreciated costs of $3,220 ($4,320 − $1,100) and $3,600 ($4,800 − $1,200) shown on Knight's balance sheet as of that date. The differences between the fair market values and the undepreciated costs of the long-term assets contributed by each partner are reflected in the respective credits to the partners' capital accounts of $25,930 and $26,894 shown in the following opening entries.

Apr. 1 Cash	6,344	
Accounts Receivable	5,524	
Merchandise Inventory	24,574	
Store Equipment	3,600	
Notes Payable............................		3,600
Accounts Payable.........................		10,082
Allowance for Doubtful Accounts		430
S. H. Day, Capital........................		25,930*
S. H. Day's investment in partnership.		

*S. H. Day, Capital (before partnership)		$25,170
Add: Fair market value of store equipment	$3,600	
Undepreciated cost	2,840	760
		$25,930

Apr. 1 Cash	3,544	
Accounts Receivable	5,280	
Merchandise Inventory	29,692	
Supplies	286	
Office Equipment...........................	3,850	
Store Equipment	4,200	
Notes Payable............................		6,000
Accounts Payable.........................		13,238
Allowance for Doubtful Accounts		720
L. A. Knight, Capital		26,894*
L. A. Knight's investment in partnership.		

*L. A. Knight, Capital (before partnership)			$25,664
Add: Fair market value of office equipment	$3,850		
Undepreciated cost	3,220	$630	
Fair market value of store equipment	$4,200		
Undepreciated cost	3,600	600	1,230
			$26,894

Observe that the ratio of the partners' investments in the partnership ($25,930 to $26,894) is not exactly the same as their profit-and-loss sharing ratio (50% each). The basis on which profits and losses are to be shared is a matter of agreement between the partners, and not necessarily the same as their investment ratio. There are factors other than the assets invested that may enter into a profit-and-loss sharing agreement. For example, one partner may contribute most of the assets but render no services, while the other partner may contribute less in assets but devote full time to the activities of the partnership.

Compensation of Partners

Explain and prepare the accounting entries needed for the compensation of partners.

The compensation of partners (other than their share of profits) may be in the form of salaries, royalties, commissions, bonuses, or other compensation. The amount of each partner's compensation and the method of accounting for it should be stated in the partnership agreement. The partnership agreement between Mitchell & Jenkins shown on page 649 states that Mitchell and Jenkins are to receive salaries of $1,500 and $2,000 respectively on the fifteenth day and last business day of each month. If partners' salaries and other forms of compensation are treated as operating expenses, it is usually advisable to keep a separate salary expense account for each partner as shown in the following entry.

Salary Expense, R. Mitchell	1,500	
Salary Expense, J. Jenkins.	2,000	
Cash		3,500
Semi-monthly salaries.		

Instead of paying partners' salaries regularly in cash, they may be credited to the partners' drawing accounts. The partners may then draw against such salaries at will. Under this procedure, the proper entries for salaries on each payday are as follows:

Salary Expense, R. Mitchell	1,500	
R. Mitchell, Drawing		1,500
Salary Expense, J. Jenkins.	2,000	
J. Jenkins, Drawing		2,000

If partners' salaries are not treated as an expense of the partnership, it is not necessary to keep a salary expense account for each partner. Thus, amounts withdrawn by the partners as compensation for services may simply be charged to their respective drawing accounts, as follows:

R. Mitchell, Drawing	1,500	
J. Jenkins, Drawing	2,000	
Cash		3,500

Allocation of Partnership Profits and Losses

Explain and prepare the accounting entries needed for the allocation of partnership profits and losses.

The partnership agreement should specify the basis on which profits and losses are to be shared by the partners. In the absence of any agreement between the partners, profits and losses must be shared equally regardless of the ratio of the partners' investments. If the partnership agreement specifies how profits are to be shared but does not specify how losses are to be shared, the losses must be shared on the same basis as that indicated for the profits.

Allocation when Salaries are Recognized as Expense. Mitchell and Jenkins have agreed that salaries are to be recognized as expenses in the determination of net income and that 60% of the remaining profits or losses are to be allocated to Mitchell and 40% to Jenkins. Expense and revenue accounts, including the salary expense accounts, are closed to Expense and Revenue Summary at the end of the accounting period. As discussed for single proprietors, a credit balance in the expense and revenue account represents the net income for the period and a debit balance represents a net loss. If the closing entries resulted in a credit balance of $106,800, the account would be closed to the Partners' capital accounts in accordance with the partnership agreement as follows.

Expense and Revenue Summary	106,800	
R. Mitchell, Capital*		64,080
J. Jenkins, Capital*		42,720
*(60% of 106,800 = 64,080)		
(40% of 106,800 = 42,720)		

Prepare an income statement reporting the allocation of partnership income.

This allocation of profits may be reported on the income statement as illustrated on the next page.

Allocation when Salaries are not Recognized as Expense. Many firms choose not to recognize salary expense for the partners on the grounds that salary expense should represent wages earned by employees. Since the partners are not employees, it is argued that payments made to the

---

Mitchell and Jenkins
Income Statement (Partial)
For the Year Ended December 31, 19--

Salary expense, Mitchell	36,000		
Salary expense, Jenkins..........................	48,000		
Net income			$106,800

Allocation of net income:	R. Mitchell	J. Jenkins	Total
	$64,080	$42,720	$106,800

---

partners should not be reported as expenses. Instead, salary payments (or allowances) are charged to the partners' drawing accounts. Under this approach, net income is higher than what would be reported if the partners' salaries were recognized as expenses on the income statement. However, if proper allocation procedures are followed, there will be no effect on the partners' total share of the partnership earnings or on their capital accounts.

Rather than simply allocating net income on the 60-40 basis described in the partnership agreement, an allocation for the agreed salaries, $36,000 for Mitchell and $48,000 for Jenkins, first must be made as reported below.

Mitchell and Jenkins
Income Statement (Partial)
For the Year Ended December 31, 19--

Net income ($106,800 + $84,000 of salaries not treated as expense)............................			$190,800

Allocation of net income:	R. Mitchell	J. Jenkins	Total
Salary allowance	$ 36,000	$48,000	$ 84,000
Remaining income	64,080	42,720	106,800
	$100,080	$90,720	$190,800

The total allocation to each partner under this approach is thus the same as when the salaries were treated as expenses. In that case, the salaries of $36,000 and $48,000 were deducted to determine net income of $106,800 to be distributed. In the above illustration, the salary allowances of $36,000 and $48,000 are deducted from net income to determine the "Remaining income" of $106,800 to be distributed.

Based on the above allocation process, the following closing entry is made.

Expense and Revenue Summary	190,800	
R. Mitchell, Capital		100,080
J. Jenkins, Capital................................		90,720

Assuming that Mitchell and Jenkins withdrew their salaries as described in the partnership agreement, the balances in the drawing accounts at year-end would be $36,000 and $48,000 respectively. The drawing accounts would be closed to the partners' capital accounts at year-end by making the following closing entry.

R. Mitchell, Capital	36,000	
R. Mitchell, Drawing		36,000
J. Jenkins, Capital	48,000	
J. Jenkins, Drawing		48,000

Note that the net effect of the above entries on the partners' capital accounts are the same as that illustrated when the salaries were expensed. Under both methods, the partners' capital accounts increased by $64,080 and $42,720.

R. Mitchell, Capital			J. Jenkins, Capital		
		100,080			90,720
36,000	Bal.	64,080	48,000	Bal.	42,720

Allocation of Salaries and Interest. Partners may agree that the most equitable method of allocating profits and losses is to base salaries on the services rendered by each partner and also to provide interest on capital investments. The remainder is then shared equally, or according to a predefined ratio. Assume that B. K. Kelly and S. B. Arthur form a partnership on January 1 of the current year. Kelly will devote full time to operating the business, invests $50,000, and will draw a salary of $35,000 per year. Arthur will devote about 10 hours per week, invests $150,000, and will draw a salary of $10,000 per year. It is also agreed that the partners will be allowed interest at 10% on capital balances on January 1 of the current year and that the balance of earnings will be divided equally. Partnership net income of $80,000 during the first year of operation would be allocated as reported below.

Kelly and Arthur
Income Statement (Partial)
For the Year Ended December 31, 19--

	B.K. Kelly	S.B. Arthur	Total
Net income			$80,000
Allocation of net income:			
Salary allowance	$35,000	$10,000	$45,000
Interest allowance	5,000	15,000	20,000
Remaining income	7,500	7,500	15,000
	$47,500	$32,500	$80,000

Based on the above allocation procedure, the following closing entry would be made.

Expense and Revenue Summary	80,000	
B.K. Kelly, Capital		47,500
S.B. Arthur, Capital		32,500

Statements for Partnerships

The allocation of net income and its impact on the partners' equity balances should be disclosed in the financial statements. All three financial statements are affected: the income statement, the statement of owners' equity and the balance sheet. The details of the allocation process are often reported in the lower portion of the income statement as illustrated in the preceding section for Kelly and Arthur. In addition, the statement of owners' equity, which reflects the equity of each partner, summarizes the allocation of net income for the year. For example, recall that the capital balances for Kelly and Arthur on January 1, 19-- were $50,000 and $150,000 respectively. Further, assume that Arthur invested an additional $10,000 and that the partners withdrew only the salary portion of their compensation ($35,000 and $10,000) during the first year of operation. The following statement is prepared based on the income allocations applied above.

Note that the effect of the income allocation process detailed in the lower portion of the income statement is summarized on the line "Net income for the year." In addition, the impact of this allocation process and the withdrawals for the year on each partner's capital balance are reported.

Finally, the owners' equity section of the balance sheet should also report the equity of each partner as illustrated below.

Prepare the owners' equity section of a partnership balance sheet.

Prepare the statement
of owners' equity for a
partnership.

Kelly and Arthur
Statement of Owners' Equity
For Year Ended December 31, 19--

	B.K.Kelly	S.B.Arthur	Total
Capital, January 1, 19--	$50,000	$150,000	$200,000
Additional investments during the			
year	-0-	10,000	10,000
	$50,000	$160,000	$210,000
Net income for the year	47,500	32,500	80,000
	$97,500	$192,500	$290,000
Withdrawals (salary during the year) . .	35,000	10,000	45,000
Capital, December 31, 19--	$62,500	$182,500	$245,000

Owners' Equity

B. K. Kelly, capital.	$ 62,500
S. B. Arthur, capital	182,500
Total owners' equity	$245,000

Building Your Accounting Knowledge

1. Identify eleven essential provisions of a partnership agreement.
2. Identify three advantages of a partnership in comparison with a single proprietorship.
3. Identify three disadvantages of a partnership form of business organization.
4. When two single proprietors decide to combine their businesses, at what values do generally accepted accounting principles usually require that non-cash assets be taken over by the partnership?
5. In the absence of any agreement between the partners, how must profits and losses be shared? If the partnership agreement specifies how profits are to be shared, but there is no agreement as to how losses are to be shared, what must be true with respect to losses?
6. What two factors generally are considered in determining the allocation of profits and losses?

▇▇ **Assignment Box**

To reinforce your understanding of the preceding text materials, you may complete the following:

        Study Guide: Part A

        Textbook: Exercises 17A1 through 17A4 and 17B1 through 17B4

                Problems 17A1 through 17A2 and 17B1 through 17B2

Dissolution and Liquidation

One of the primary characteristics of the partnership form of organization is its limited life. Any change in the members of the partnership results in dissolution.

Dissolution of a Partnership

Describe the actions that result in the dissolution of a partnership.

Dissolution of a partnership may be brought about through the addition of a new partner, the death or withdrawal of one of the partners or bankruptcy. No partner can retire from the partnership without the consent of the remaining partners. To do so would constitute a violation of the partnership agreement and would make the retiring partner liable to the remaining partners for any loss resulting from the retirement.

Dissolution of the partnership does not necessarily imply that business operations will halt. For example, a new partner might be added. Similarly, if one of the partners elects to withdraw from the business, the remaining members may continue operations. Both situations require the dissolution of the old partnership and the creation of a new one.

▇▇ **Admitting a New Partner.** A new partner may be admitted to a partnership by agreement among the existing partners. The admission of a new partner calls for the dissolution of the old partnership and the creation of a new partnership. A new partnership agreement that includes all of the necessary provisions should be prepared. For example, assume that Day and Knight admit H. I. Noon as a new partner as of July 1, 19--, and agree to share profits and losses on the basis of their capital interests. If Noon's investment consisted of cash only, the proper entry to admit Noon to the partnership would involve a debit to the cash account and a credit to Noon's capital account for the amount invested. If Noon has been operating a business as a sole owner and the business is taken over by the partnership, Noon's balance sheet reproduced below can serve as a basis for preparing the opening entry. The assets listed in the balance sheet are taken over, the liabilities are assumed, and Noon is given credit for the equity in the assets of the business.

H.I. Noon
Balance Sheet
June 30, 19--

Assets

Cash		$ 5,000
Accounts receivable	$14,290	
Less allowance for doubtful accounts	1,078	13,212
Merchandise inventory		27,290
Total assets		$45,502

Liabilities

Notes payable	$ 9,048	
Accounts payable	7,550	
Total liabilities		$16,598

Owner's Equity

H.I. Noon, capital		28,904
Total liabilities and owner's equity		$45,502

Explain and prepare the accounting entries needed for the admission of a new partner, including the possible accounting for goodwill.

The proper entry in general journal form to admit Noon as a partner is as follows:

July 1 Cash	5,000	
Accounts Receivable	14,290	
Merchandise Inventory	27,290	
Notes Payable		9,048
Accounts Payable		7,550
Allowance for Doubtful Accounts		1,078
H.I. Noon, Capital		28,904
H.I. Noon admitted to partnership.		

Because Noon has no knowledge of any uncollectible accounts receivable as of June 30, 19--, and has been using the fifo method of inventory costing, no fair market value adjustments of the non-cash asset account balances were made for purposes of this entry.

Goodwill. Some business organizations earn profits that are very large in relation to the stated amounts of the assets. The unique earning power of a business, which may be due to exceptional management, good location, reputation, or other factors, is called goodwill. Since goodwill is difficult to measure and may not prove to be permanent, accountants do not permit its formal recognition as an asset unless it has been purchased.

For example, assume that Day & Knight purchased the business of H. I. Noon for $30,000 cash, acquiring all of the business assets except cash and assuming the business liabilities. If the book values of Noon's net accounts receivable and merchandise inventory were considered to be reasonable approximations of their fair market values ($13,212 + $27,290 = $40,502), and Noon's total liabilities of $16,598 were assumed, Day & Knight paid $30,000 for assets with net values of $23,904 ($40,502 − $16,598). The $6,096 difference between the $30,000 paid and the $23,904 market value of specific assets acquired may be considered to be the price paid for the goodwill of Noon's business. The transaction may be entered as follows:

July 1 Accounts Receivable	14,290	
Merchandise Inventory.........................	27,290	
Goodwill	6,096	
Notes Payable		9,048
Accounts Payable		7,550
Allowance for Doubtful Accounts		1,078
Cash		30,000
Purchased H.I. Noon's business.		

It is also permissible to recognize goodwill if a new partner is taken into a firm and is allowed a capital interest in excess of the net assets that were invested. For example, suppose that instead of purchasing Noon's business, Day and Knight had agreed to give Noon a capital interest of $35,000 in exchange for Noon's business assets and liabilities (including the business cash). Also assume that, as in the previous case, the book values of Noon's non-cash assets were considered to be reasonable approximations of their fair market values. Noon's investment may be entered as follows:

July 1 Cash	5,000	
Accounts Receivable	14,290	
Merchandise Inventory.........................	27,290	
Goodwill	6,096	
Notes Payable		9,048
Accounts Payable		7,550
Allowance for Doubtful Accounts		1,078
H.I. Noon, Capital		35,000
H.I. Noon admitted to partnership.		

Goodwill is considered to be an intangible long-term asset. It is usually reported in the balance sheet as the last item in the asset section. Under present accounting rules, it may be amortized over a future period not to exceed 40 years.

■■■■ **Withdrawal of Partner.** By agreement, a partner may retire and be permitted to withdraw assets equal to, less than, or greater than the amount of the retiring partner's interest in the partnership. The book value of a partner's interest is shown by the credit balance of the partner's capital account after all profits or losses have been allocated, in accordance with the partnership agreement, and the books have been closed. If, upon retirement, cash or other assets equal to the credit balance of the retiring partner's capital account are withdrawn, the transaction will have no effect upon the capital of the remaining partners.

Suppose, for example, that sometime after H. I. Noon had been taken into the partnership of Day & Knight, Noon expressed a desire to retire and the partners agreed to the withdrawal of cash equal to the amount of Noon's equity in the assets of the partnership. After closing the temporary owners' equity accounts into Expense and Revenue Summary, and after allocating the net income and closing the partners' drawing accounts, assume that the partners' capital accounts had credit balances as follows:

S. H. Day $55,000
L. A. Knight 45,000
H. I. Noon... 40,000

This indicates that the book value of Noon's interest in the partnership amounts to $40,000. If this amount is withdrawn in cash, the entry in general journal form for the transaction on the books of the partnership is as follows:

H. I. Noon, Capital	40,000	
Cash		40,000
H. I. Noon retired, withdrawing $40,000 in equity settlement.		

While the transaction involves a decrease in cash with a corresponding decrease in the total capital of the partnership, it does not affect the equity of the remaining partners. Day still has an equity of $55,000 and Knight an equity of $45,000 in the partnership assets.

If a retiring partner agrees to withdraw less than the book value of the interest, the effect of the transaction will increase the capital accounts of the remaining partners. To enter such a transaction it is necessary to debit the retiring partner's account for the amount of its credit balance, to credit the assets withdrawn, and to credit the difference to the capital accounts of the remaining partners. Thus, if Noon agreed to withdraw only $30,000 in settlement of the interest, the transaction should be entered in the books of the partnership as follows:

H. I. Noon, Capital	40,000	
Cash		30,000
S.H. Day, Capital		5,500
L.A. Knight, Capital		4,500
H. I. Noon retired, withdrawing $30,000 in equity settlement.		

The difference between Noon's equity in the assets of the partnership and the amount of cash withdrawn is $10,000 ($40,000 − $30,000). This difference is divided between the remaining partners on the basis stipulated in the partnership agreement; i.e., the ratio of their capital interests after allocating net income and closing their drawing accounts. On this basis, Day is credited for 55/100 [$55,000 ÷ ($55,000 + $45,000)] of $10,000, or $5,500, while Knight is credited for 45/100 [$45,000 ÷ ($45,000 + $55,000)] of $10,000, or $4,500.

If a partner is permitted to withdraw more than the book value of the interest, the effect of the transaction will decrease the capital accounts of the remaining partners. Thus, if Day and Knight agreed to the withdrawal of $45,000 in settlement of Noon's interest, the transaction should be entered in the books of the partnership as follows:

H.I. Noon, Capital	40,000	
S.H. Day, Capital	2,750	
L.A. Knight, Capital	2,250	
Cash		45,000
H.I. Noon retired, withdrawing $45,000 in equity settlement.		

The excess of the amount of cash withdrawn over Noon's equity in the partnership ($5,000) is divided between the remaining partners on the basis stipulated in the partnership agreement. Thus, Day's capital account is debited for 55/100 of $5,000 or $2,750, while Knight's capital account is debited for 45/100 of $5,000 or $2,250.

When a partner retires from the business, the partner's interest may be purchased by one or more of the remaining partners or by an outside party. If the retiring partner's interest is sold to one of the remaining partners, the retiring partner's equity is merely transferred to the other partner. Thus, if instead of withdrawing cash in settlement of the equity in the partnership, Noon's equity is sold to Day, the entry for the transaction on the books of the partnership is as follows:

H.I. Noon, Capital..............................	40,000	
S.H. Day, Capital................................		40,000
S.H. Day purchased H.I. Noon's interest in the partnership.		

The amount paid to Noon by Day is a personal transaction not entered on the books of the partnership. Any gain or loss resulting from the transaction is a personal gain or loss of the withdrawing partner and not of the firm. Thus, whatever amount is involved, the credit in Noon's account is to be transferred to Day's account.

Death of a Partner. The death of a partner dissolves the partnership. On the date of death, the accounts may be closed and the net income for the year to date allocated to the partners' capital accounts in accordance with the partnership agreement. The balance of the deceased partner's capital account is then transferred to a liability account with the deceased's estate. The surviving partners may continue the business or liquidate. If the former action is chosen, the procedures for settling with the estate will be the same as those described earlier for the withdrawal of a partner. Liquidation procedures are described in the following section.

Liquidation of a Partnership

Describe the process followed when liquidating a partnership.

Liquidation of a partnership usually means that assets are sold, liabilities are paid and remaining cash or other assets are distributed to the partners. Upon discontinuing normal operations of the partnership, adjusting and closing entries are made. Thus, only the assets, liabilities and owners' equity accounts remain open. As the assets are sold, the cash realized is applied first to the claims of creditors. Once all liabilities are paid, the remaining cash may be distributed to the partners according to their ownership interests as reflected by the balances of their capital accounts.

To illustrate, assume that after several years of operations the partnership of Day, Knight and Noon is to be liquidated. After making closing entries on May 31, 19-- the following accounts remain open. For simplicity, "Other assets" and "Liabilities" are used as account titles below and in the following illustrations. In actual practice several asset, contra asset, and liability accounts would be involved.

	Account Balance	
Account Title	Dr.	Cr.
Cash	$ 10,000	
Inventory	120,000	
Other assets...	220,000	
Liabilities		$ 80,000
S.H. Day, capital....................................		95,000
L.A. Knight, capital		120,000
H.I. Noon, capital...................................		55,000

Based on these account balances, accounting for the liquidation of the partnership is illustrated below. For convenience, it is assumed that all assets are sold in one transaction on June 1, 19-- and all liabilities are paid at once on June 15, 19--. Cash settlements are made with the partners on June 18. It is also assumed that the partners share equally in all profits and losses.

████ **Gain on Sale of Assets.** Assume that the noncash assets are sold for $370,000. Since these assets are carried on the books at $340,000, a gain on the sale of assets must be recognized and allocated to the partners' capital accounts. Next, the liabilities are paid and the remaining cash distributed to the partners according to the balances of their capital accounts. A statement of partnership liquidation, summarizing these transactions, is provided below.

Prepare a statement of partnership liquidation.

Day, Knight and Noon
Statement of Partnership Liquidation
For Period June 1-18, 19--

	Cash	Inventory	Other Assets	Liabilities	Day	Knight	Noon
Balance before sale of assets............	$ 10,000	$120,000	$220,000	$80,000	$ 95,000	$120,000	$55,000
Sale of noncash assets and allocation of gain	370,000	(120,000)	(220,000)	-0-	10,000	10,000	10,000
Balance after sale ...	$380,000	-0-	-0-	$80,000	$105,000	$130,000	$65,000
Payment of liabilities	(80,000)	-0-	-0-	(80,000)	-0-	-0-	-0-
Balance after payment of liabilities	$300,000	-0-	-0-	-0-	$105,000	$130,000	$65,000
Distribution of cash to partners	(300,000)	-0-	-0-	-0-	(105,000)	(130,000)	(65,000)
Final balances	-0-	-0-	-0-	-0-	-0-	-0-	-0-

The entries for these transactions are illustrated below.

Explain and prepare the accounting entries needed for the liquidation of the partnership.

```
19--
June  1 Cash .......................................  370,000
            Inventory....................................          120,000
            Other Assets................................          220,000
            Gain on Sale of Assets ....................           30,000
                Sale of assets.
```

1 Gain on Sale of Assets	30,000	
S.H. Day, Capital		10,000
L.A. Knight, Capital		10,000
H.I. Noon, Capital		10,000
Allocation of gain.		
15 Liabilities	80,000	
Cash		80,000
Payment of liabilities.		
18 S.H. Day, Capital	105,000	
L.A. Knight, Capital	130,000	
H.I. Noon, Capital	65,000	
Cash		300,000
Distribution of cash to partners.		

Loss on Sale of Assets. Using the same information for Day, Knight and Noon as illustrated above, assume that the noncash assets are sold for $295,000, resulting in a loss of $45,000. The Statement of Partnership Liquidation reflecting the allocation of the loss on the sale of assets, payment of the partnership liabilities, and distribution of the cash to the partners is illustrated below.

Day, Knight and Noon
Statement of Partnership Liquidation
For Period June 1-18, 19--

	Cash	Inventory	Other Assets	Liabilities	Day	Knight	Noon
Balance before sale of assets	$ 10,000	$120,000	$220,000	$80,000	$ 95,000	$120,000	$ 55,000
Sale of noncash assets and allocation of loss . .	295,000	(120,000)	(220,000)	-0-	(15,000)	(15,000)	(15,000)
Balance after sale . . .	$305,000	-0-	-0-	$80,000	$ 80,000	$105,000	$ 40,000
Payment of liabilities	(80,000)	-0-	-0-	(80,000)	-0-	-0-	-0-
Balance after payment of liabilities	$225,000	-0-	-0-	-0-	$ 80,000	$105,000	$ 40,000
Distribution of cash to partners	(225,000)	-0-	-0-	-0-	(80,000)	(105,000)	(40,000)
Final balances	-0-	-0-	-0-	-0-	-0-	-0-	-0-

The entries for these transactions are as follows:

June 1 Cash 295,000		
Loss on Sale of Assets 45,000		
Inventory................................		120,000
Other Assets		220,000
Sale of assets.		
1 S.H. Day, Capital 15,000		
L.A. Knight, Capital 15,000		
H.I. Noon, Capital........................ 15,000		
Loss on Sale of Assets		45,000
Allocation of loss.		
15 Liabilities................................ 80,000		
Cash....................................		80,000
Payment of liabilities.		
18 S.H. Day, Capital 80,000		
L.A. Knight, Capital 105,000		
H.I. Noon, Capital........................ 40,000		
Cash....................................		225,000
Distribution of cash to partners.		

Building Your Accounting Knowledge

1. Identify two ways in which a partnership may be dissolved without the consent of the remaining partners. What form of partnership dissolution requires the consent of the remaining partners?
2. When a new partner who has been the sole owner of a business is admitted to a partnership by having the partnership take over the old business, what usually serves as the basis for preparing the opening entry?
3. What is goodwill? How is it measured?
4. Why do accountants not permit the formal recognition of goodwill as an asset unless it has been purchased? Over what maximum future period may goodwill be amortized?
5. Describe the four accounting entries for the liquidation of a partnership.

Assignment Box

To reinforce your understanding of the preceding text materials, you may complete the following:

    Study Guide: Part B
    Textbook: Exercises 17A5 through 17A7 and 17B5 through 17B7
             Problems 17A3 through 17A4 and 17B3 through 17B4

Expanding Your Business Vocabulary

What is the meaning of each of the following terms?

dissolution (p. 660)   partnership (p. 647)
goodwill (p. 661)   partnership agreement (p. 648)
liquidation (p. 665)

Demonstration Problem

Lisa Armbruster, Robert Beck, and Maria Castro are partners in a law firm, and share profits and losses in a 50-30-20 ratio. The partnership agreement calls for annual salaries of $40,000, $35,000, and $30,000 respectively and interest of 12% on their January 1 capital balances.* Any remaining net income (or net loss) is to be divided in accordance with their ratios for sharing profits and losses.

The partners' capital balances as of January 1, 19-A were Armbruster, $120,000; Beck, $75,000; Castro, $50,000. No additional investments were made during the year. The net income of the partnership for the year 19-A was $160,000. Partners' withdrawals for the year were Armbruster, $50,000; Beck, $40,000; and Castro, $35,000.

On March 4, 19-B, the partners decide to liquidate their law firm. On that date, the firm has a cash balance of $46,000, noncash assets of $274,000, and liabilities of $40,000. No additional investments or withdrawals have been made in 19-B. Between March 5 and March 31, the noncash assets are sold for $290,000, the gain is divided in the profit and loss sharing ratio, and the liabilities are paid. The remaining cash is then distributed to the partners.

*The salaries and interest are not recognized as expenses in the determination of net income.

Required:

1. Prepare the lower part of the income statement of the ABC partnership for the year ended December 31, 19-A, showing the division of the partnership net income for the year.
2. Prepare the general journal entry to close the Expense and Revenue Summary Account to the partners' capital accounts as of December 31, 19-A.
3. Prepare a Statement of Owners' Equity for the ABC partnership for the Year Ended December 31, 19-A.
4. Prepare the general journal entries as of March 31, 19-B for:
    (a) The sale of the noncash assets of the partnership.
    (b) The division of any loss or gain on realization.

(c) The payment of partnership liabilities.

(d) The distribution of remaining cash to the partners.

5. Prepare a Statement of Partnership Liquidation for the ABC partnership for the period March 5-31, 19-B.

Solution

1.

Armbruster, Beck & Castro
Partial Income Statement
For Year Ended December 31, 19-A

	Armbruster	Beck	Castro	Total
Net Income				$160,000
Allocation of net income:				
Salary allowance	$40,000	$35,000	$30,000	$105,000
Interest allowance	14,400	9,000	6,000	29,400
Remaining income	12,800	7,680	5,120	25,600
	$67,200	$51,680	$41,120	$160,000

2.

19-A

Dec. 31 Expense and Revenue Summary	160,000	
Lisa Armbruster, Capital		67,200
Robert Beck, Capital.............................		51,680
Maria Castro, Capital		41,120

3.

Armbruster, Beck and Castro
Statement of Owners' Equity
For Year Ended December 31, 19-A

	Armbruster	Beck	Castro	Total
Capital, January 1, 19-A................	$120,000	$ 75,000	$50,000	$245,000
Net income for year	67,200	51,680	41,120	160,000
	$187,200	$126,680	$91,120	$405,000
Withdrawals..........................	50,000	40,000	35,000	125,000
Capital, December 31, 19-A	$137,200	$ 86,680	$56,120	$280,000

4.

(a) Sale of assets:

19-B

Mar. 31 Cash	290,000	
Noncash Assets		274,000
Gain on Sale of Assets		16,000

(b) Division of gain:

19-B

Mar. 31 Gain on Sale of Assets	16,000	
L. Armbruster, Capital		8,000
R. Beck, Capital		4,800
M. Castro, Capital		3,200

(c) Payment of liabilities:

19-B

Mar. 31 Liabilities..	40,000	
Cash		40,000

(d) Distribution of cash to partners:
19-B

Mar. 31	L. Armbruster, Capital	145,200	
	R. Beck, Capital	91,480	
	M. Castro, Capital	59,320	
	Cash		296,000

5.

Armbruster, Beck, and Castro
Statement of Partnership Liquidation
For Period March 5-31, 19-B

	Cash	Noncash Assets	Liabilities	Capital Armbruster (50%)	Beck (30%)	Castro (20%)
Balances before sale of assets ..	$ 46,000	$274,000	$40,000	$137,200	$86,680	$56,120
Sale of noncash assets and division of gain	290,000	(274,000)	-0-	8,000	4,800	3,200
Balances after sale	$336,000	-0-	$40,000	$145,200	$91,480	$59,320
Payment of liabilities	(40,000)	-0-	(40,000)	-0-	-0-	-0-
Balances after payment of liabilities	$296,000	-0-	-0-	$145,200	$91,480	$59,320
Distribution of cash to partners	(296,000)	-0-	-0-	(145,200)	(91,480)	(59,320)
Final Balances ...	-0-	-0-	-0-	-0-	-0-	-0-

*Note: Now that you have reviewed the Demonstration Problem and Solution you may complete the **Mastery Problem** at the end of the chapter activities.

Applying Accounting Concepts

Series A

Exercise 17A1—Opening Entry for Partnership. J.D. Streett and G.R. Matreci agreed on November 1 to go into business as partners. According to the agreement, Streett is to contribute $90,000 in cash. Matreci is to contribute office equipment valued at $6,000 on which $2,000 is owed, delivery equipment valued at $7,000 on which $1,700 is owed in the form of a note, and enough cash to make his capital investment equal to that of Streett.

Provide the opening entry in general journal form for the investment.

Exercise 17A2—Opening Entry for Partners' Investment. Midwest Rugs, owned by Karen Hakimian, and Benda Rug, owned by Stephen Benda, have decided to combine their businesses on January 1. Midwest Rugs has the following assets and liabilities:

Cash..	$ 50,290
Accounts receivable	64,000
Allowance for doubtful accounts................................	3,200

Store equipment	54,000
Accumulated depreciation on store equipment	18,000
Merchandise inventory..	230,000
Notes payable	130,000
Accounts payable	76,000

Benda Rug has the following assets and liabilities:

Cash...	$ 72,724
Accounts receivable	51,000
Allowance for doubtful accounts................................	2,600
Merchandise inventory..	138,000
Office equipment	66,000
Accumulated depreciation on office equipment	22,000
Notes payable	60,000
Accounts payable	115,000

Hakimian and Benda agree that since both have been using the fifo method of valuing inventory, these amounts are stated at fair market value. The fair market value of the store equipment is $32,000 and the fair market value of the office equipment is $40,000.

Prepare the opening entries in general journal form to enter the investments of Hakimian and Benda.

Exercise 17A3—Entries for Allocation of Profits and Losses. Jerry Bennett and Ruth Weber are in business as partners. According to the agreement, Bennett is to receive a salary of $3,500 a month and Weber is to receive a salary of $4,000 a month.

Provide the monthly entries for salaries, assuming that:

(a) The salaries are treated as operating expenses and paid in cash.
(b) The salaries are treated as operating expenses, but not paid in cash.
(c) The amounts withdrawn as partners' compensation are treated as drawings on a monthly basis.

Exercise 17A4—Allocation Portion of Income Statement. Refer to Exercise 17A3. Bennett is to receive a total salary of $42,000 a year, and Weber is to receive a total salary of $48,000 a year. Partners' salaries are not treated as operating expenses. In addition, each partner is to receive interest at 10% of their capital balance on January 1, which were $125,000 for Bennett and $75,000 for Weber. The balance of earnings will be divided equally. The net income for the year was $150,000.

Prepare the lower portion of the income statement for the calendar year, showing the allocation of salaries, interest, and remaining income. Then show the entry to close Expense and Revenue Summary into the partners' capital accounts.

Exercise 17A5—Statement of Owners' Equity and Owners' Equity Section of Partnership Balance Sheet. Refer to Solution for Exercise 17A2. Assume the following end-of-the-year information related to the Hakimian and Benda partnership. Net income for the year was $176,000; Hakimian received 60% of the profits and Benda received 40%; Hakimian withdrew $32,000 during the year and Benda withdrew $24,000.

Prepare a statement of owners' equity and the owners' equity section of the balance sheet for the partnership as of December 31, 19--.

Exercise 17A6—Entry to Admit New Partner. Hakimian and Benda (see Exercises 17A2 and 17A5) decided to admit Jean Emory, owner of another rug store, as a new partner on January 1. Emory's business has the following assets and liabilities:

Cash	$ 61,986
Accounts receivable	36,400
Allowance for doubtful accounts	3,200
Merchandise inventory	171,200
Notes payable	60,000
Accounts payable	20,200

Emory has no knowledge of any uncollectible accounts receivable as of January 1 and has been using the fifo method of inventory costing, so that no fair market value adjustment of the merchandise inventory balance is necessary.

(1) Prepare the entry in general journal form to admit Jean Emory as a partner.
(2) Assume that Emory is to be given a capital interest of $200,000. Prepare the entry in general journal form to admit Jean Emory as a partner.

237,600

Exercise 17A7—Entry to Record Goodwill in Purchase of Another Business. Refer to Exercise 17A6. Assume that Hakimian and Benda purchased the Emory business on January 1 for $154,200 cash, acquiring all of the noncash business assets and assuming the business liabilities. Determine the price paid for the goodwill of Emory's business and show the entry in general journal form to enter the transaction in the accounting records of the Hakimian and Benda partnership.

Series B

Exercise 17B1—Opening Entry for Partnership. H.C. Lee and L.M. Novak agreed on June 1 to go into business as partners. According to the agreement, Lee is to contribute $67,500 in cash. Novak is to contribute office equipment valued at $4,500 on which $1,500 is owed, delivery equipment valued at $5,250 on which $1,275 is owed in the form of a note, and enough cash to make his capital investment equal to that of Lee.
Provide the opening entry in general journal form for the investment.

Exercise 17B2—Opening Entry for Partners' Investment. Far West Draperies, owned by Susan Koffron, and Decorating Den, owned by Barbara Lampe, have decided to combine their businesses on July 1. Far West Draperies has the following assets and liabilities:

Cash	$ 37,750
Accounts receivable	48,000
Allowance for doubtful accounts	2,400
Store equipment	40,500
Accumulated depreciation on store equipment	13,500
Merchandise inventory	172,500
Notes payable	97,500
Accounts payable	57,000

Decorating Den has the following assets and liabilities:

Cash...	$ 54,550
Accounts receivable	38,250
Allowance for doubtful accounts................................	1,950
Merchandise inventory	103,500
Office equipment	49,500
Accumulated depreciation on office equipment	16,500
Notes payable	45,000
Accounts payable	86,250

Koffron and Lampe agree that since both have been using the fifo method of valuing inventory, these amounts are stated at fair market value. The fair market value of the store equipment is $24,000 and the fair market value of the office equipment is $30,000.

Prepare the opening entries in general journal form to enter the investments of Koffron and Lampe.

Exercise 17B3—Entries for Allocation of Profits and Losses. David Farrell and Susan Stark are in business as partners. According to the agreement, Farrell is to receive a salary of $5,000 a month and Stark is to receive a salary of $4,500 a month.

Provide the monthly entries for salaries, assuming that:

(a) The salaries are treated as operating expenses and paid in cash.
(b) The salaries are treated as operating expenses, but not paid in cash.
(c) The amounts withdrawn as partners' compensation are treated as drawings on a monthly basis.

Exercise 17B4—Allocation Portion of Income Statement. Refer to Exercise 17B3. Farrell is to receive a total salary of $60,000 a year, and Stark is to receive a total salary of $54,000 a year. Partners' salaries are not treated as operating expenses. In addition, each partner is to receive interest at 10% of their capital balances on January 1, which were $150,000 for Farrell and $100,000 for Stark. The balance of earnings will be divided 60-40. The net income for the year was $200,000.

Prepare the lower portion of the income statement for the calendar year, showing the allocation of salaries, interest, and remaining income. Then show the entry to close Expense and Revenue Summary into the partners' capital accounts.

Exercise 17B5—Statement of Owners' Equity and Owners' Equity Section of Partnership Balance Sheet. Refer to Solution for Exercise 17B2. Assume the following end-of-the-year information related to the Koffron and Lampe partnership. Net income for the year was $132,000; Koffron received 60% of the profits and Lampe received 40%; Koffron withdrew $24,000 during the year and Lampe withdrew $18,000.

Prepare a statement of owners' equity and the owners' equity section of the balance sheet for the partnership as of June 30, 19--.

Exercise 17B6—Entry to Admit New Partner. Koffron and Lampe (see Exercises 17B2 and 17B5) decided to admit George Kelce, the sole owner of another drapery store, as a new partner on January 1. Kelce's business has the following assets and liabilities:

Cash	$ 46,490
Accounts receivable	27,300
Allowance for doubtful accounts	2,400
Merchandise inventory	128,400
Notes payable	45,000
Accounts payable	15,150

Kelce has no knowledge of any uncollectible accounts receivable as of July 1 and has been using the fifo method of inventory costing, so that no fair market value adjustment of the merchandise inventory account balance is necessary.

(1) Prepare the entry in general journal form to admit George Kelce as a partner.

(2) Assume that Kelce is to be given a capital interest of $150,000. Prepare the entry in general journal form to admit George Kelce as a partner.

Exercise 17B7—Entry to Record Goodwill in Purchase of Another Business.
Refer to Exercise 17B6. Assume that Koffron and Lampe purchased the Kelce business on July 1 for $115,650 cash, acquiring all of the noncash business assets and assuming the business liabilities. Determine the price paid for the goodwill of Kelce's business and show the entry in general journal form to enter the transaction in the accounting records of the Koffron and Lampe partnership.

Series A

Problem 17A1   Opening Entries for Partnership

Claude Remy has been in the retail shoe business for some time as a single proprietor. Remy's balance sheet prepared as of September 30 is shown below.

Claude Remy
Balance Sheet
September 30, 19--

Assets

Cash		$18,688
Accounts receivable	$23,296	
Less allowance for doubtful accounts	3,200	20,096
Merchandise inventory		40,812
Store equipment	$11,000	
Less accumulated depreciation	2,400	8,600
Total assets		$88,196

Liabilities

Notes payable	$16,000	
Accounts payable	10,596	
Total liabilities		$26,596

Owner's Equity

Claude Remy, capital		61,600
Total liabilities and owner's equity		$88,196

On October 1 of the current year, Claude and Karen Remy form a partnership in the business to be conducted under the firm name of Remy & Remy. Under the partnership agreement, Karen Remy is to invest $32,000 in cash. The assets of Claude Remy are to become the property of the partnership and the liabilities are to be assumed by the partnership.

A new set of books is to be used by the partnership. The fair market value of the store equipment contributed by Claude Remy is $11,000 on September 30.

Required:

Prepare the necessary opening entries in general journal form for the investments of the partners.

Problem 17A2   Opening Entries for Partnership

M.C. Kriz and C.J. Meek have been in the video cassette rental business for some time as single proprietors. On January 2 of the current year they form a partnership which is to be conducted under the firm name of Kriz & Meek. Their balance sheets as of December 31 are shown below. It is agreed that the assets of each will be taken over at their fair market values and that the liabilities will be assumed by the partnership. It is also agreed that Meek will contribute a sufficient amount of additional cash to make Meek's investment equal to Kriz's investment in the partnership. It is further agreed that the partners will share profits and losses equally. The fair market values of Kriz's delivery equipment and office equipment on December 31 are $16,600 and $7,800, respectively. The fair market values of Meek's delivery equipment and office equipment on December 31 are $5,400 and $10,200, respectively.

M.C. Kriz
Balance Sheet
December 31, 19--

Assets

Cash		$10,934
Accounts receivable	$ 8,582	
Less allowance for doubtful accounts	1,300	7,282
Merchandise inventory		19,734
Delivery equipment	$17,600	
Less accumulated depreciation	4,400	13,200
Office equipment	$ 9,000	
Less accumulated depreciation	800	8,200
Total assets		$59,350

Liabilities

Notes payable	$16,000	
Accounts payable	8,422	
Total liabilities		$24,422

Owner's Equity

M.C. Kriz, capital		34,928
Total liabilities and owner's equity		$59,350

C.J. Meek
Balance Sheet
December 31, 19--

Assets

Cash...		$ 8,658
Accounts receivable	$ 9,794	
Less allowance for doubtful accounts......................	2,400	7,394
Merchandise inventory		17,934
Delivery equipment	$15,200	
Less accumulated depreciation...........................	13,200	2,000
Office equipment	$11,600	
Less accumulated depreciation...........................	2,000	9,600
Total assets		$45,586

Liabilities

Notes payable	$ 8,000	
Accounts payable	16,784	$24,784

Owner's Equity

C.J. Meek, capital		20,802
Total liabilities and owner's equity		$45,586

Required:

Assuming that a new set of books is used by the partnership, prepare the necessary opening entries in general journal form for the investments of the partners.

Problem 17A3   Dissolution of a Partnership

The Mayes & Mayes Wrecking Company, a partnership, is operating a general demolition business. Ownership of the company is divided among the partners, Perri Mayes, Virginia Mayes, Delcie Merchant, and Richard Proctor. Profits and losses are shared 40-30-20-10. The books are kept on the calendar year basis.

After the business had been in operation for several years, Proctor died on June 15. Mrs. Proctor desired to sell Proctor's interest at 90% of its book value to the nearest dollar as of June 15. After the books were closed, the partners' capital accounts had credit balances as follows:

Perri Mayes	$62,736
Virginia Mayes...	49,848
Delcie Merchant	24,488
Richard Proctor	33,976

Required:

1. As the accountant for the partnership, compute the amount to be paid to Mrs. Proctor under the agreement and prepare the general journal entry required to enter the check issued to her in payment of her deceased husband's interest in the partnership. According to the partnership agreement, the difference between the amount paid to Mrs. Proctor and the book value of Richard Proctor's capital account is allocated to the remaining partners based on their relative profit-sharing ratios.

2. Instead of the foregoing, assume that Mrs. Proctor is paid 115% of the book value of Richard Proctor's capital account. Compute the amount to be paid to Mrs. Proctor and prepare the necessary general journal entry.

3. Instead of the foreoing, assume that one of the partners, Delcie Merchant, (with the consent of the remaining partners) purchased Proctor's interest for $35,000 and gave Mrs. Proctor a personal check for that amount. Prepare the general journal entry that is required in the books of account of the partnership only.

Problem 17A4   Liquidation of Partnership and Statement of Partnership Liquidation with Gain

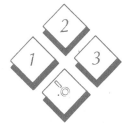

After several years of operations, the partnership of Hawker, Kemper, and Walsh is to be liquidated. After making closing entries on June 30, 19--, the following accounts remain open:

Cash	$ 5,000	
Inventory	60,000	
Other assets	110,000	
Liabilities		$40,000
K.J. Hawker, Capital		47,500
M.S. Kemper, Capital		60,000
A.J. Walsh, Capital		27,500

The noncash assets are sold for $185,000. Profits and losses are shared equally.

Required:

Prepare a Statement of Partnership Liquidation as of July 20, 19--, and show the entries to record:

(1) The sale of the noncash assets on July 1.
(2) The allocation of any gain or loss to the partners on July 1.
(3) The payment of the liabilities on July 15.
(4) The distribution of cash to the partners on July 20.

Problem 17A5   Liquidation of Partnership and Statement of Partnership Liquidation with Loss.

Refer to Problem 17A4. Assume that the noncash assets of Hawker, Kemper, and Walsh were sold for $125,000. Repeat the requirements for Problem 17A4.

Series B

Problem 17B1   Opening Entries for Partnership

Karen Dopuch has been in the retail clothing business for some time as a single proprietor. Dopuch's balance sheet prepared as of April 30 is shown below.

Karen Dopuch
Balance Sheet
April 30, 19--

Assets

Cash..		$14,016
Accounts receivable	$17,472	
Less allowance for doubtful accounts......................	2,400	15,072
Merchandise inventory....................................		30,609
Store equipment	$ 8,250	
Less accumulated depreciation............................	1,800	6,450
Total assets...		$66,147

Liabilities

Notes payable	$12,000	
Accounts payable	7,947	
Total liabilities		$19,947

Owner's Equity

Karen Dopuch, capital..................................		46,200
Total liabilities and owner's equity		$66,147

On May 1 of the current year, Karen and Sharon Dopuch form a partnership in the business to be conducted under the firm name of Dopuch & Dopuch. Under the partnership agreement, Sharon Dopuch is to invest $24,000 in cash. The assets of Karen Dopuch are to become the property of the partnership and the liabilities are to be assumed by the partnership.

A new set of books is to be used by the partnership. The fair market value of the store equipment contributed by Karen Dopuch is $8,250 on April 30.

Required:

Prepare the necessary opening entries in general journal form for the investments of the partners.

Problem 17B2   Opening Entries for Partnership

T.J. Findley and G.H. Martin have been in the formal wear rental business for some time as single proprietors. On January 2 of the current year they form a partnership which is to be conducted under the firm name of Findley & Martin. Their balance sheets as of December 31 are shown below. It is agreed that the assets of each will be taken over at their fair market values and that the liabilities will be assumed by the partnership. It is also agreed that Martin will contribute a sufficient amount of additional cash to make Martin's investment equal to Findley's investment in the partnership. It is further agreed that the partners will share profits and losses equally. The fair market values of Findley's delivery equipment and office equipment on December 31 are $12,500 and $5,900, respectively. The fair market values of Martin's delivery equipment and office equipment on December 31 are $4,100 and $7,700, respectively.

T.J. Findley
Balance Sheet
December 31, 19--

Assets

Cash		$ 8,200
Accounts receivable	$ 6,437	
Less allowance for doubtful accounts	975	5,462
Merchandise inventory		14,800
Delivery equipment	$13,200	
Less accumulated depreciation	3,300	9,900
Office equipment	$ 6,750	
Less accumulated depreciation	600	6,150
Total assets		$44,512

Liabilities

Notes payable	$12,000	
Accounts payable	6,316	
Total liabilities		$18,316

Owner's Equity

T.J. Findley, capital		26,196
Total liabilities and owner's equity		$44,512

G.H. Martin
Balance Sheet
December 31, 19--

Assets

Cash		$ 6,494
Accounts receivable	$ 7,346	
Less allowance for doubtful accounts	1,800	5,546
Merchandise inventory		13,450
Delivery equipment	$11,400	
Less accumulated depreciation	9,900	1,500
Office equipment	$ 8,700	
Less accumulated depreciation	1,500	7,200
Total assets		$34,190

Liabilities

Notes payable	$ 6,000	
Accounts payable	12,588	
Total liabilities		$18,588

Owner's Equity

G.H. Martin, capital		15,602
Total liabilities and owner's equity		$34,190

Required:

Assuming that a new set of books is used by the partnership, prepare the necessary opening entries in general journal form for the investments of the partners.

Problem 17B3   Dissolution of a Partnership

The Piening and Piening Construction Company, a partnership, is operating a general contracting business. Ownership of the company is divided among the partners, R.O. Piening, C.L. Piening, E.J. Wapnick, and T.R. Hellwig. Profits and losses are shared 30-30-20-20. The books are kept on the calendar year basis.

After the business had been in operation for several years, Hellwig died on August 15. Mrs. Hellwig desired to sell Hellwig's interest at 80% of its book value to the nearest dollar as of August 15. After the books were closed, the partners' capital accounts had credit balances as follows:

R.O. Piening	$47,052
C.L. Piening	36,441
E.J. Wapnick	18,366
T.R. Hellwig	25,482

Required:

1. As the accountant for the partnership, compute the amount to be paid to Mrs. Hellwig under the agreement and prepare the general journal entry required to enter the check issued to her in payment of her deceased husband's interest in the partnership. According to the partnership agreement, the difference between the amount paid to Mrs. Hellwig and the book value of T.R. Hellwig's capital account is allocated to the remaining partners based on their relative profit-sharing ratios.

2. Instead of the foregoing, assume that Mrs. Hellwig is paid 115% of the book value of T.R. Hellwig's capital account. Compute the amount to be paid to Mrs. Hellwig and prepare the necessary general journal entry.

3. Instead of the foregoing, assume that one of the partners, E.J. Wapnick, (with the consent of the remaining partners) purchased Hellwig's interest for $26,250 and gave Mrs. Hellwig a personal check for that amount. Prepare the general journal entry that is required in the books of account of the partnership only.

Problem 17B4   Liquidation of Partnership and Statement of Partnership Liquidation with Gain

After several years of operations, the partnership of Fenster, Larkin, and Steele is to be liquidated. After making closing entries on May 31, 19--, the following accounts remain open:

Cash	$ 7,500	
Inventory	90,000	
Other assets	165,000	
Liabilities		$60,000
M.D. Fenster, Capital		71,250
H.A. Larkin, Capital		90,000
A.M. Steele, Capital		41,250

The noncash assets are sold for $277,500. Profits and losses are shared 30-50-20.

Required:

Prepare a Statement of Partnership Liquidation as of June 21, 19--, and show the entries to record:

(1) The sale of the noncash assets on June 1.
(2) The allocation of any gain or loss to the partners on June 1.
(3) The payment of the liabilities on June 16.
(4) The distribution of cash to the partners on June 21.

Problem 17B5   Liquidation of Partnership and Statement of Partnership Liquidation with Loss.

Refer to Problem 17B4. Assume that the noncash assets of Fenster, Larkin, and Steele were sold for $187,500. Repeat the requirements for Problem 17B4.

Mastery Problem

Judy Bond, a plumber, has been working for Fleming's Plumbing Supplies for several years. Judy has been invited to enter a partnership with Fleming. The new partnership will be called Fleming and Bond's Plumbing Supplies. The terms of the partnership are provided below.

(a) Fleming will invest the assets of Fleming's Plumbing Supplies and the partnership will assume all liabilities. The market values of the office and store equipment are estimated to be $18,000 and $8,000 respectively. All other values reported on the balance sheet below are reasonable approximations of market values.

Fleming's Plumbing Supplies
Balance Sheet
December 31, 19-A

Assets

Cash		$ 13,544
Accounts receivable	$15,280	
Less allowance for doubtful accounts	1,720	13,560
Merchandise inventory		89,692
Supplies		1,286
Office equipment	14,320	
Less accumulated depreciation	1,100	13,220
Store equipment	8,800	
Less accumulated depreciation	2,200	6,600
Total assets		$137,902

Liabilities

Notes payable	$36,000	
Accounts payable	18,082	
Total liabilities		$ 54,082

Owner's Equity

I. Fleming, capital		83,820
Total liabilities and owner's equity		$137,902

(b) Bond will invest $50,000 cash.
(c) Fleming will draw a salary allowance of $50,000 per year and Bond will receive $30,000. Salaries will not be reported as expenses on the income statement.

(d) The partners will receive 10% interest on the January 1 balance of their capital accounts.

(e) Profits or losses remaining after allocating salaries and interest will be distributed as follows: 60% to Fleming, 40% to Bond.

Required:

1. Prepare the entries on January 1, 19-B for the formation of the partnership.
2. Net income for the partnership for 19-B was $150,000. Prepare the lower portion of the income statement showing the allocation of the profits to each partner.
3. In December, 19-D, Fleming's daughter, Penny, graduated from business college and asked to join the business as a partner. She has $10,000 to invest and, due to the urgent need for someone to take responsibility for the accounting and business side of operations, it is agreed that Penny will be given a capital interest of $30,000. Profits and losses will be shared as follows: I. Fleming, 50%; J. Bond, 30%; P. Fleming, 20%. Prepare the entry for Penny's investment and the recognition of goodwill on January 1, 19-E.
4. After several years of operations it is decided to liquidate the partnership. After making closing entries on July 31, 19-M the following accounts remain open.

Cash	20,000	
Inventory	150,000	
Office Equipment	30,000	
Accumulated Depreciation—Office Equipment		18,000
Store Equipment	22,000	
Accumulated Depreciation—Store Equipment		15,000
Notes Payable		20,000
I. Fleming, Capital		80,000
J. Bond, Capital		50,000
P. Fleming, Capital		39,000

(a) On August 1, 19-M, the inventory is sold for $130,000.
(b) On August 3, 19-M, the office equipment is sold for $10,000.
(c) On August 5, 19-M, the store equipment is sold for $12,000.
(d) On August 10, 19-M, the Notes Payable are paid.
(e) On August 15, 19-M, the remaining cash is distributed to the partners according to the balances in their capital accounts.

Prepare a statement of partnership liquidation and related journal entries for the period August 1 through August 15, 19-M.

CHAPTER 18

Accounting for Departmental and Branch Operations

Careful study of this chapter should enable you to:

- Describe how departmental reports can be useful to management.

- Describe and compute departmental gross margin, departmental operating income, and departmental direct operating margin.

- Prepare departmental income statements showing (a) departmental gross margin, (b) departmental operating income, and (c) departmental direct operating margin.

- Explain the difference between direct and indirect operating expenses.

- Explain how to assign and allocate departmental operating expenses.

- Explain the possible uses of an income statement showing departmental direct operating margin.

- Describe the various business arrangements known as branches.

- Explain the nature and purpose of reciprocal accounts in accounting for branch operations.

- Explain and perform the accounting procedures for branch operations when the branch maintains its own self-contained accounting records.

- Explain how to prepare financial statements for branch and combined branch and home office operations, including the use of a special combined financial statement work sheet.

Companies often engage in different types of major income-producing activities. For example, a firm might sell different products, such as lawn mowers and bicycles, or provide different services, such as auditing and management consulting. It is common for such businesses to be organized into separate segments or components. By dividing the company into components, both the planning and control of operations, and the evaluation of performance can be improved.

One way to divide a company is by department, according to the type of product or service provided. Another way to divide a company which has portions of its business in physically separate locations is to treat each location as a branch. Whatever approach is selected for organizing the company, there is a need to accumulate accounting information for each part of the business. The purpose of this chapter is to explain and illustrate the accounting for businesses organized into departments and branches.

Departmental Accounting

Describe how departmental reports can be useful to management.

One of the challenges of managing any business, and particularly a large one, is to obtain useful and accurate information concerning the activities of the firm. The income statement might show that the firm as a whole is reasonably profitable, but conceal the fact that one portion of the business is highly successful while another portion is operating at a loss. Departmental accounting helps to overcome this problem by providing separate information regarding the performance of each department.

Departmental reports can be useful to management in various ways. First, they are important for planning purposes. To be successful, management must set goals and develop plans for achieving these goals. The use of departmental reports to identify the strengths and weaknesses of the different parts of the firm is an important part of this planning process. A second major use of departmental reports is for control. By identifying specific areas with revenues or expenses that are out of line, management can focus attention on those areas and take corrective action. Finally, departmental reports are critical for performance evaluation. By assigning responsibility for the functioning of departments to specific managers, top management can evaluate those managers' performance and reward them accordingly.

To illustrate departmental accounting, the firm of Mitchell & Jenkins that was introduced in Chapters 16 and 17 will be used. Mitchell & Jenkins is a partnership engaged in selling golf and tennis equipment. To keep the illustrations manageable, a number of simplifying assumptions will be made, and condensed financial statement information will be used.

Departmental Gross Margin

Describe and compute departmental gross margin.

Departmental gross margin is the difference between a department's net sales and cost of goods sold. To compute departmental gross margin, it is necessary to determine the net sales, purchases, and inventory by department. There are two basic ways of accumulating such information. First, separate general ledger accounts can be maintained by department for each of the elements of gross margin. Second, a single general ledger account can be maintained for each of the elements of gross margin, and the total in each account can be assigned to the appropriate departments at the end of the accounting period. Mitchell & Jenkins uses departmental accounts for each of the elements of gross margin.

Prepare a departmental income statement showing departmental gross margin.

A condensed income statement for the year 19-D showing gross margin by department and in total for Mitchell & Jenkins appears on page 691. In addition to showing that the golf department provides the majority of Mitchell & Jenkins' sales and gross margin, this report can also reveal to management a large difference in the gross margin percentages of the two departments. Mitchell and Jenkins' overall gross margin percentage is 43.7% ($749,120 ÷ 1,715,300), but the gross margin percentage of the golf department is 47.9% ($514,720 ÷ 1,075,000), while the tennis department is only 36.6% ($234,400 ÷ 640,300). Management should attempt to determine the causes of this difference and take appropriate action. If the normal retail markup on golf equipment is higher than that on tennis equipment, then management might want to put more emphasis on the sale of golf equipment. If the normal retail markup on golf and tennis products is about the same, then management should evaluate its pricing policies for tennis equipment. It is possible that the tennis department has been using an inadequate markup percentage on its equipment. Another possibility is that appropriate selling prices are being used for the tennis equipment, but the purchase prices are too high. If this is the case, then the efforts of the purchasing department to obtain the best prices and credit terms from reliable vendors should be evaluated. Whatever the cause of the difference in gross margin percentage between the departments, the departmental report helps make management aware of the situation and prompts appropriate action.

Mitchell & Jenkins Sporting Goods
Income Statement (Condensed)
For the Year Ended December 31, 19-D

	Golf	Tennis	Total
Net sales	$1,075,000	$640,300	$1,715,300
Cost of goods sold	560,280	405,900	966,180
Gross margin	$ 514,720	$234,400	$ 749,120
Operating expenses			658,780
Operating income			$ 90,340

The condensed income statement presented above shows that the golf department obviously earns a much higher gross margin than the tennis department. A higher gross margin or gross margin percentage, however, does not necessarily mean that a department is more profitable overall. To assess overall profitability, departmental operating expenses also must be considered.

Departmental Operating Income

Describe and compute departmental operating income.

Explain the difference between direct and indirect operating expenses.

Explain how to assign and allocate departmental operating expenses.

Departmental operating income is the difference between a department's gross margin and its operating expenses. To compute departmental operating income, it is necessary to determine the elements of gross margin, as explained in the previous section, and the operating expenses of each department. As with departmental gross margin, there are two ways of accumulating operating expense data. Separate general ledger departmental operating expense accounts can be used. Alternatively, a single general ledger account can be maintained for each operating expense, and the total in each account can be assigned or allocated to appropriate departments at the end of the accounting period.

The use of separate general ledger departmental operating expense accounts is not very common, in part because many operating expenses cannot be directly related to specific departments. For departmental reporting purposes, there are two broad categories of operating expenses: direct and indirect. Direct expenses are operating expenses which are incurred for the sole benefit of and are traceable directly to a specific department. For example, the wages of an employee working solely in the golf department would be a direct expense of that department. Indirect expenses are operating expenses which are incurred for the benefit of the business as a whole and which cannot be traced directly to any specific department. For example, the salary of the treasurer of the business would be an indirect expense.

In computing department operating income, direct expenses are assigned to departments on the basis of the actual expenses incurred. If separate general ledger departmental accounts are maintained, the expenses are accumulated there. If no separate departmental accounts are maintained, the expenses are assigned to departments based on information contained in supporting records. For example, the personnel records would show the departments in which employees worked, and their wage expenses would be assigned accordingly. Indirect expenses are allocated to departments on some reasonable basis, such as relative sales or cost of goods sold, or the estimated time spent serving a given department.

To illustrate the computation of departmental operating income, the assignment and allocation of the operating expenses of Mitchell & Jenkins are explained in the following paragraphs. Mitchell & Jenkins does not maintain separate general ledger departmental operating expense accounts. For the sake of simplicity, only selected operating expenses are described, and both the departmental operating expense summary and the income statement are presented in condensed form.

■■■ Store Clerks Wage Expense. Mitchell & Jenkins employs five store clerks; two who work solely in the golf department, one in the tennis department, and two who assist customers in both departments. Their wages are as follows:

Employee Number	Dept.	Wages
1	Golf	$19,000
2	Golf	17,000
3	Tennis	15,250
4	Both	13,000
5	Both	16,000
Total		$80,250

Wages of the clerks who work only in one department are assigned to that department. Wages of the other two clerks are allocated between the departments on the basis of the relative net sales of the departments. Total net sales are $1,715,300. Golf net sales are 62.7% ($1,075,000 ÷ 1,715,300), and tennis net sales are 37.3% ($640,300 ÷ 1,715,300) of the total. The division of the total store clerks' wage expense between departments is therefore as follows:

Dept.	Direct Expense	Indirect Expense (Allocated)			Total
Golf	$36,000	62.7% × ($13,000 + $16,000) =	$18,183	$54,183
Tennis	15,250	37.3 × (13,000 + 16,000) =	10,817	26,067
Total					$80,250

▨ **Truck Drivers Wage Expense.** Mitchell & Jenkins employs three delivery truck drivers, one of whom delivers only golf equipment. Their wages are as follows:

Driver Number	Product Delivered	Wages
1	Golf	$29,000
2	Both	26,500
3	Both	28,400
Total		$83,900

Wages of the driver who delivers only golf equipment are assigned to that department. Wages of the other two drivers are allocated on the basis of the relative dollar amount of golf and tennis equipment delivered by the drivers. Shipping and delivery records are used to estimate the percentages as approximately 70% golf and 30% tennis. The division of the total drivers' wage expense between the departments is therefore as follows:

Dept.	Direct Expense	Indirect Expense (Allocated)			Total
Golf	$29,000	70% × ($26,500 + $28,400) =	$38,430	$67,430
Tennis	-0-	30 × (26,500 + 28,400) =	16,470	16,470
Total					$83,900

■■■■ **Advertising Expense.** Mitchell & Jenkins uses newspaper and radio advertising. Total advertising expense is $79,500; $45,000 for newspaper advertising and $34,500 for radio. Newspaper advertising is classified as golf, tennis, or "mixed" on the basis of number of inches of copy space. Of the $45,000 of newspaper advertising, $17,000 is for golf, $12,000 for tennis, and $16,000 is considered mixed. All radio advertising is classified as mixed. The mixed portion of the newspaper advertising and all radio advertising expenses are allocated between departments according to the relative net sales of the departments. The division of the total advertising expense between the departments is therefore as follows:

Dept.	Direct Expense	Indirect Expense (Allocated)			Total
Golf	$17,000	62.7% × ($16,000 + $34,500) =	$31,664	$48,664
Tennis	12,000	37.3 × (16,000 + 34,500) =	18,836	30,836
Total				$79,500

■■■■ **Depreciation Expense—Delivery Equipment.** Mitchell & Jenkins has three delivery trucks, one of which is used to deliver only golf equipment. Total depreciation on the delivery equipment is $24,000 for the year, $9,000 of which relates to the golf delivery truck. The other $15,000 of depreciation is allocated on the basis of the relative dollar amount of golf and tennis equipment delivered with the other two trucks. These percentages are 70% golf and 30% tennis, as explained for the truck drivers' wage expense. The division of the total depreciation expense on the delivery equipment between the departments is therefore as follows:

Dept.	Direct Expense	Indirect Expense (Allocated)		Total
Golf	$9,000	70% × $15,000 =	$10,500	$19,500
Tennis	-0-	30 × 15,000 =	4,500	4,500
Total				$24,000

■■■■ **Store Rent Expense.** Mitchell & Jenkins rents 5,000 square feet of store space for $22,800 per year. The entire rent expense is an indirect expense that is allocated on the basis of the relative square feet of floor space occupied by each department. The golf department occupies 3,200 square feet, or 64% of the floor space, and the tennis department occupies the remaining 36% of floor space. The division of the rent expense between the departments, therefore, is as follows:

Dept.	Indirect Expense (Allocated)		Total
Golf	64% × $22,800 =	$14,592
Tennis	36 × 22,800 =	8,208
Total		$22,800

■■■■ **Uncollectible Accounts Expense.** Mitchell & Jenkins' uncollectible accounts expense of $17,900 is treated as a direct expense and is assigned to the departments based on experience with accounts written off. For the current year, $9,000 is assigned to the golf department and $8,900 to the tennis department.

▓▓▓▓ **Other Operating Expenses.** Other operating expenses incurred by Mitchell & Jenkins totaled $350,430. This total includes a broad range of expenses, from officers salaries to postage expense. Each of these expenses could be assigned and allocated in ways similar to those illustrated for the operating expenses in the preceding paragraphs. It is assumed in this illustration that the expenses are classified as direct and indirect and are assigned and allocated as follows:

| | Direct | Indirect Expense | |
Dept.	Expense	(Allocated)	Total
Golf	$79,420	$154,380	$233,800
Tennis	36,980	79,650	116,630
			$350,430

The assignment and allocation of departmental operating expenses can be summarized in a **departmental operating expense summary** such as the one on page 691. This summary shows all operating expenses, their classification as direct or indirect, their assignment or allocation to the departments, and the total operating expenses for each department.

▓▓▓▓ **Departmental Income Statement Showing Operating Income.** A condensed income statement for Mitchell & Jenkins for the year 19-D showing operating income by department and in total appears on page 691. Operating expense data on the statement were obtained from the departmental operating expense summary on page 691.

Prepare a departmental income statement showing departmental operating income.

This form of income statement could be used by management to evaluate the overall performance of the two departments. For example, the income statement shows that the operating income of the golf department is almost three times that of the tennis department. But remember that the gross margin and gross margin percentage of the golf department are much higher than those of the tennis department. Perhaps the difference in operating income is attributable to the gross margin differences rather than any differences in the operating expenses. In fact, this appears to be the case. The operating expenses of the golf department are 41.6% ($447,169 ÷ 1,075,000) of net sales, whereas the operating expenses of the tennis department are only 33.0% ($211,611 ÷ $640,300) of net sales. The weak performance of the tennis department compared to the golf department appears to be attributable to the inadequate gross margin percentage rather than to excessive operating expenses.

Management must be cautious in interpreting departmental operating income results. Most of the operating expenses of both departments of Mitchell & Jenkins are indirect, and therefore are allocated between departments based on various approximations and arbitrary methods. Indirect expenses, by definition, are incurred for the benefit of the business

Mitchell & Jenkins Sporting Goods
Departmental Operating Expense Summary
For the Year Ended December 31, 19-D

	Total	Golf Direct	Golf Indirect	Tennis Direct	Tennis Indirect	Dept. Totals Golf	Dept. Totals Tennis
Store clerks wage expense ...	$ 80,250	$ 36,000	$ 18,183	$15,250	$ 10,817	$ 54,183	$ 26,067
Truck drivers wage expense ..	83,900	29,000	38,430		16,470	67,430	16,470
Advertising expense.........	79,500	17,000	31,664	12,000	18,836	48,664	30,836
Depreciation expense— delivery equipment........	24,000	9,000	10,500		4,500	19,500	4,500
Store rent expense	22,800		14,592		8,208	14,592	8,208
Uncollectible accounts expense	17,900	9,000		8,900		9,000	8,900
Other operating expenses	350,430	79,420	154,380	36,980	79,650	233,800	116,630
Total	$658,780	$179,420	$267,749	$73,130	$138,481	$447,169	$211,611

as a whole and cannot be traced directly to any department. Thus the departments have no control over such expenses. Further, although it might be possible to reduce some indirect expenses by eliminating a department, most of these expenses would continue to be incurred. Many accountants argue that to properly evaluate departmental performance, an income measure should be used that considers only the direct expenses of each department.

Mitchell & Jenkins Sporting Goods
Income Statement (Condensed)
For the Year Ended December 31, 19-D

	Golf	Tennis	Total
Net sales	$1,075,000	$640,300	$1,715,300
Cost of goods sold	560,280	405,900	966,180
Gross margin...........................		$514,720	$234,400 $ 749,120
Operating expenses:			
Store clerks wage expense	$ 54,183	$ 26,067	$ 80,250
Truck drivers wage expense	67,430	16,470	83,900
Advertising expense	48,664	30,836	79,500
Depreciation expense—delivery equipment	19,500	4,500	24,000
Store rent expense	14,592	8,208	22,800
Uncollectible accounts expense..........	9,000	8,900	17,900
Other operating expenses	233,800	116,630	350,430
Total operating expenses		447,169	211,611 $ 658,780
Operating income		$ 67,551	$ 22,789 $ 90,340

Departmental Direct Operating Margin

Describe and compute
departmental direct
operating margin.

Departmental direct operating margin is the difference between a department's gross margin and its direct operating expenses. To compute departmental direct operating margin, it is necessary to determine the elements of gross margin, and the direct operating expenses of each department. All of the necessary information for Mitchell & Jenkins was developed in the previous section. To prepare a departmental income statement showing departmental direct operating margin, the information in the departmental operating expense summary on page 691 and in the income statement on page 691 simply needs to be reorganized.

Prepare a departmental
income statement
showing departmental
direct operating
margin.

A condensed income statement for Mitchell & Jenkins for the year 19-D, showing departmental direct operating margins, appears below. To complete the income statement, indirect expenses are subtracted from total departmental direct operating margin to determine operating income. No attempt is made to allocate these expenses to specific departments. Note that the operating income is the same as reported in the income statement on page 691.

Mitchell & Jenkins Sporting Goods
Income Statement (Condensed)
For the Year Ended December 31, 19-D

	Golf	Tennis	Total
Net sales	$1,075,000	$640,300	$1,715,300
Cost of goods sold...................	560,280	405,900	966,180
Gross margin........................	$ 514,720	$234,400	$ 749,120
Direct operating expenses:			
Store clerks wage expense	$ 36,000	$ 15,250	$ 51,250
Truck drivers wage expense	29,000		29,000
Advertising expense	17,000	12,000	29,000
Depreciation expense—delivery			
equipment	9,000		9,000
Uncollectible accounts expense........	9,000	8,900	17,900
Other operating expenses	79,420	36,980	116,400
Total direct operating expenses	$ 179,420	$ 73,130	$ 252,550
Departmental direct operating margin ...	$ 335,300	$161,270	$ 496,570
Indirect operating expenses:			
Store clerks wage expense		$	29,000
Truck drivers wage expense			54,900
Advertising expense			50,500
Depreciation expense—delivery equipment			15,000
Store rent expense			22,800
Other operating expenses			234,030
Total indirect operating expenses......................		$	406,230
Operating income......................................		$	90,340

The income statement showing departmental direct operating margin can be used by management in various ways. First, it permits evaluation of a department on the basis of only those expenses over which it has control and for which it is directly responsible. In the case of Mitchell & Jenkins, it shows that the direct operating expenses of the tennis department are only 11.4% ($73,130 ÷ $640,300) of net sales, whereas those of the golf department are 16.7% ($179,420 ÷ $1,075,000) of net sales. It appears that the direct operating expenses of the tennis department are being controlled quite effectively.

The departmental direct operating margin also permits more thorough analysis of the contribution that a department makes to the overall operating income of the company. For Mitchell & Jenkins, the conventional operating income results imply that the tennis department contributes only $22,789 (see page 691) to the overall profits of the company. The departmental direct operating margin results provide a different message. Specifically, the departmental direct operating margin figures show that the tennis department contributes $161,270 (see page 692) to cover the indirect operating expenses and operating income of the firm.

A third possible use of the departmental direct operating margin data is in deciding whether to discontinue a department. In making this decision, management must focus on the revenues and expenses that will be eliminated if a department is discontinued; not on the operating income of that department. Remember that the indirect expenses that are subtracted in calculating conventional operating income are expenses incurred for the business as a whole. Unless management can reduce these expenses by eliminating a department, such expenses will continue to be incurred even if a department is discontinued.

Consider, for example, the situation of R & R Co., which is deciding whether to discontinue one of its three departments. Operating results for the current year for each department, for the business as a whole, and for departments A and B only, are as follows:

	Dept. A	Dept. B	Dept. C	Total	Depts. A & B only
Net sales	$210,000	$185,000	$170,000	$565,000	$395,000
Cost of goods sold	115,000	110,000	96,000	321,000	225,000
Gross margin	$ 95,000	$ 75,000	$ 74,000	$244,000	$170,000
Direct operating expenses	55,000	45,000	54,000	154,000	100,000
Departmental direct operating margin	$ 40,000	$ 30,000	$ 20,000	$ 90,000	$ 70,000
Indirect operating expenses	27,000	22,000	25,000	74,000	74,000
Operating income	$ 13,000	$ 8,000	$ (5,000)	$ 16,000	$ (4,000)

Department C is operating at a $5,000 loss in terms of operating income, but its elimination actually would reduce rather than increase R & R's total operating income, as shown in the last column for departments A and B only. This reduction in operating income would occur because Department C contributes $20,000 (its departmental direct operating margin) to the coverage of the indirect operating expenses and operating income of the firm. If Department C is eliminated, the indirect operating expenses of $25,000 will have to be absorbed by the remaining departments. This is why indirect operating expenses are listed in the schedule as $74,000 both in the total column and in the Departments A and B only column.

Note that the difference between the total operating income of $16,000 and the operating loss of $4,000 for departments A and B only is $20,000. This $20,000 is Department C's departmental direct operating margin which would be lost if the department were eliminated. In general, if a department has a positive departmental direct operating margin, it should be discontinued only if management has a plan to reduce indirect expenses by at least the amount of that department's departmental direct operating margin.

Building Your Accounting Knowledge

1. In what ways can departmental reports be useful to management?
2. In what two ways can the information necessary to compute departmental gross margin be accumulated?
3. In what two ways can departmental operating expense data be accumulated?
4. What is the difference between direct and indirect operating expenses?
5. On what basis are direct expenses assigned to departments?
6. On what basis are indirect expenses allocated to departments?
7. What information is contained in a departmental operating expense summary?
8. Why must management be cautious in interpreting departmental operating income results?
9. Distinguish between departmental gross margin, departmental operating income, and departmental direct operating margin.
10. In what ways can an income statement showing departmental direct operating margin be used by management?

Assignment Box

To reinforce your understanding of the preceding text materials, you may complete the following:
  Study Guide: Part A
  Textbook: Exercises 18A1 through 18A5 and 18B1 through 18B5
        Problems 18A1 through 18A4 and 18B1 through 18B4

Branch Accounting

In an effort to sell more goods or services in a larger geographical area and to thus increase its profits, a business organization some-

Describe the various business arrangements known as branches.

times establishes one or more branches. The term branch covers a variety of different arrangements. Sometimes such units have many of the characteristics of complete and independent businesses. A branch may have its own bank account, receivables, merchandise inventory, long-term assets, and various liabilities. The manager of a branch may have wide authority in the management of all phases of the unit's operations. In other cases, a branch may be nothing more than a sales office and confine its activities to soliciting orders for goods that will be shipped from the main plant or home office. The branch manager might only have authority to negotiate sales contracts for the company.

The size of a branch, the nature of its operations, and various other factors will determine what type of accounting records it will maintain. A small branch might not keep permanent formal records, but would send daily or weekly summaries of its activities to the home office where all formal records are kept. A larger branch may maintain a complete accounting information system of its operations. The larger branch may keep its own journals, keep at least a general ledger, and prepare its own periodic financial statements.

Reciprocal Accounts

Explain the nature and purpose of reciprocal accounts in accounting for branch operations.

When formal records are kept at a branch office, it is common practice to follow a procedure that causes the general ledger of the branch and the general ledger of the home office to be interlocking or reciprocal to each other. In the ledger of the home office, there is an account entitled Branch Office. This is an asset account representing the net investment by the home office in the branch. In the ledger of the branch, there is an account entitled Home Office. This account is like an owner's equity account representing the ownership of the home office in the branch. The balances of these two accounts are equal, but opposite; the debit balance in the one account offsets the credit balance in the other account. Therefore, the two accounts are reciprocal. The relationship is illustrated by the following T accounts.

Relationship of Branch Office and Home Office Accounts

The assets minus the liabilities of the branch equal $90,000, which is the home office's net investment in the branch. This amount appears as a credit balance in the home office account on the branch books and as a debit balance in the branch office account on the home office books.

Transactions between the home office and the branch require entries in both ledgers, and involve the reciprocal accounts. If, for example, the home office remits $20,000 to the branch, the entry in the home office ledger is:

Branch Office	20,000	
Cash		20,000

In the branch ledger, the entry is

Cash	20,000	
Home Office		20,000

At the end of the period, the branch adjusts its accounts and closes the revenue and the expense accounts into Expense and Revenue Summary. The balance of Expense and Revenue Summary is closed to Home Office, a debit indicating a loss or a credit indicating a profit. When the branch income statement reaches the home office, the home office accountant makes an entry debiting Branch Office and crediting Branch Profit if there was a profit, or debiting Branch Loss and crediting Branch Office if there was a loss.

If the business sells merchandise, there probably will be another pair of reciprocal accounts. In the home office ledger, there is an account entitled Shipments to Branch. This is a contra-asset account representing the merchandise sent by the home office to the branch. In the branch ledger, there is an account entitled Shipments from Home Office. This is like a purchases account representing merchandise obtained from the home office. When the home office sends goods to the branch, the entry in the home office ledger is

Branch Office	xxx	
Shipments to Branch		xxx

In the branch ledger, the entry is

Shipments from Home Office	xxx	
Home Office		xxx

If the branch gets all of its merchandise from the home office, the shipments from home office account replaces a purchases account in the branch's ledger. If the branch purchases goods from outsiders, it may have a purchases account in addition to, or in place of, a shipments from home office account.

Branch Accounting Procedure During the Fiscal Year

Explain and perform the accounting procedures for branch operations when the branch maintains its own self-contained accounting records.

In most respects, the usual accounting procedures are followed by both the home office and the branch. Each uses journals, each has its general ledger, and each may have as many subsidiary ledgers as circumstances warrant. The peculiarities of branch accounting arise in connection with transactions or events that affect both home office and branch office accounts (the reciprocal accounts that have been described). The following example illustrates proper accounting procedures for branch transactions. In each instance, the transaction or event is given first, followed by the entries (all in general journal form) that should be made in the books of the branch and in the books of the home office. Note that for the purpose of illustration each transaction is entered simultaneously in the books of both the home office and the branch office without regard to dates. In actual practice there usually would be some lapse of time between the dates on which the transactions are entered in the books of each office.

1. On January 2, the Hosler Co. established a branch in the town of Boydville. Hosler turned over to the manager of the branch $24,000 in cash, furniture and fixtures costing $6,000, and merchandise costing $21,000. The long-term assets used at a branch can be entered either in the branch ledger or in the home office ledger. In this illustration, the long-term assets used at the branch are entered in the branch ledger.

Branch Office Books:			*Home Office Books:*		
Cash	24,000		Branch Office	51,000	
Furniture and Fixtures	6,000		Cash		24,000
Shipments from Home			Furniture and Fixtures		6,000
Office	21,000		Shipments to Branch		21,000
Home Office		51,000			

2. The branch manager purchased additional furniture and fixtures for $15,000 cash and paid $1,700 rent on the branch store.

Branch Office Books:		*Home Office Books:*
Furniture and Fixtures	15,000	No entry.
Operating Expenses*	1,700	
Cash	16,700	

* For the sake of brevity in this example, all expenses are charged to a single account, Operating Expenses.

3. The home office shipped goods costing $135,000 to the branch.

Branch Office Books:		*Home Office Books:*	
Shipments from Home Office	135,000	Branch Office	135,000
Home Office.............	135,000	Shipments to Branch	135,000

4. During the year, the branch had cash sales of $15,600 and sales on account of $144,000.

Branch Office Books:		*Home Office Books:*
Cash	15,600	No entry.
Accounts Receivable	144,000	
Sales	159,600	

5. The branch incurred additional operating expenses during the year (rent, wages, light, telephone, advertising, etc.) in the amount of $56,100. Total payments on account were $49,500.

Branch Office Books:		*Home Office Books:*
Operating Expenses	56,100	No entry.
Accounts Payable................	56,100	
Accounts Payable	49,500	
Cash	49,500	

6. Cash collections on the branch accounts receivable were $78,000.

Branch Office Books:		*Home Office Books:*
Cash	78,000	No entry.
Accounts Receivable	78,000	

7. The branch returned to the home office for credit, goods costing $1,200.

Branch Office Books:		*Home Office Books:*	
Home Office	1,200	Shipments to Branch	1,200
Shipments from Home Office	1,200	Branch Office	1,200

After posting the foregoing transactions, the branch office accounts would appear as shown in the following T accounts:

Branch Office Accounts

	Cash				Accounts Receivable		
(1)	24,000	(2)	16,700	(4)	144,000	(6)	78,000
(4)	15,600	(5)	49,500		*66,000*		
(6)	78,000		*66,200*				
	117,600						
	51,400						

Furniture and Fixtures				Home Office	
(1)	6,000		(7)	1,200	(1) 51,000
(2)	15,000				(3) 135,000
	21,000				186,000
					184,800

Shipments from Home Office				Sales	
(1)	21,000	(7) 1,200			(4) 159,600
(3)	135,000				
	156,000				
154,800					

Accounts Payable				Operating Expenses	
(5)	49,500	(5) 56,100		(2)	1,700
		6,600		(5)	56,100
					57,800

After posting the transactions, the home office accounts that are reciprocal to the branch accounts would appear as shown in the following T accounts:

Home Office Accounts

Branch Office				Shipments to Branch	
(1)	51,000	(7) 1,200	(7) 1,200	(1)	21,000
(3)	135,000			(3)	135,000
	186,000				156,000
184,800				154,800	

The following trial balance of the branch office accounts was taken at the end of the year:

Hosler Co., Boydville Branch
Trial Balance
December 31, 19--

Account	Dr. Balance	Cr. Balance
Cash	51,400	
Accounts Receivable	66,000	
Furniture and Fixtures	21,000	
Accounts Payable		6,600
Home Office		184,800
Sales		159,600
Shipments from Home Office	154,800	
Operating Expenses	57,800	
	351,000	351,000

Accounting Procedure for Year-End Closing of Branch Office and Home Office Books

The accounting procedure for closing the books of a branch office at the end of the year is similar to that discussed previously for a single location business. The major difference is that the branch net income (or net loss) is transferred to the home office account, which serves as an owner's equity account for the branch office. For example, assume that the Expense and Revenue Summary of the Boydville branch had a balance of $18,000 after all revenue and expense accounts were closed. The credit balance (representing net income) is transferred to the home office account by the following journal entry:

Expense and Revenue Summary	18,000	
Home Office		18,000

The accounting procedure for closing the books of the home office at the end of the year is similar to that discussed previously for a single-location business. The major difference is that the branch net income (or net loss) must be entered on the home office books. For the Boydville branch, this is done with the following journal entry:

Branch Office	18,000	
Branch Profit		18,000

The branch profit account is then closed to Expense and Revenue Summary.

Financial Statements

Explain how to prepare financial statements for branch and combined branch and home office operations, including the use of a special combined financial statement work sheet.

Branch financial statements can be prepared beginning with the trial balance on page 699 or from a conventional work sheet like the ones illustrated in previous chapters. There generally are only two differences between branch financial statements and those of an independent business. First, the shipments from home office account might replace the purchases account on the income statement. Second, the home office account replaces the ordinary owner's equity account on the balance sheet.

Combined financial statements for the home office and branch operations can be prepared with the aid of a special work sheet. A portion of one form of such a work sheet is shown on page 701. The work sheet contains columns for the adjusted trial balances of both the home and branch offices, a pair of elimination columns, and columns for the combined balances of the accounts. The home office data on the work sheet are from home office records not illustrated here. The branch data are from the branch trial balance on page 699, after adjustments for the ending merchandise inventory and depreciation of the furniture and fixtures.

The purpose of the Eliminations columns is to make elimination entries for any reciprocal home office and branch accounts. Combined financial statements for a home office and any branches are intended to provide a financial report for a single entity. Reciprocal accounts represent financial activities between the home office and branches and must be eliminated. Entry (a) eliminates the shipments to branch account against the shipments from home office account, since neither account represents activity with any organization outside of the combined home office-branch entity. Similarly, entry (b) eliminates the reciprocal home office and branch office accounts. These entries are made solely for the purpose of preparing combined financial statements and are entered only on the work sheet.

After the elimination entries are completed, all account balances are extended to the combined columns. The amounts in the combined columns would be extended to the balance sheet and income statement columns (not illustrated here) to facilitate financial statement preparation, as in a conventional work sheet. The combined financial statements are prepared in the normal manner, contain the usual accounts and follow the conventional format.

Work Sheet for Combined Financial Statements

Account	Home Office Debit	Home Office Credit	Branch Debit	Branch Credit	Eliminations Debit	Eliminations Credit	Combined Debit	Combined Credit
Cash	54,000		51,400				105,400	
Accounts receivable	151,500		66,000				217,500	
Merchandise inventory	84,000		73,100				157,100	
Branch office	184,800					(b)184,800		
Land	21,000						21,000	
Building (net)	96,000						96,000	
Furniture and fixtures(net)	8,200		18,900				27,100	
Accounts payable		168,000		6,600				174,600
Home office				184,800	(b)184,800			
J. Hosler, capital		356,700						356,700
Expense and revenue summary	64,000	84,000	73,100				64,000	157,100
Sales		381,000		159,600				540,600
Purchases	385,000						385,000	
Shipments to branch		154,800			(a)154,800			
Shipments from home office			154,800			(a)154,800		
Operating expenses	96,000		59,900				155,900	
	1,144,500	1,144,500	424,100	424,100	339,600	339,600	1,229,000	1,229,000

Building Your Accounting Knowledge

1. What kind of accounting procedure might be followed by a small branch operation? A larger branch operation?

2. What does the branch office account on the home office books represent? The home office account on the branch office books?
3. What entry does the home office accountant make for a profit realized by the branch? A loss realized by the branch?
4. What entry is made by the home office when it sends goods to the branch? What entry is made by the branch office when it receives the goods?
5. What kinds of transactions or events are responsible for the peculiarities of branch accounting?
6. What is the major difference between closing the books of a branch office and closing the books of a single-location business?
7. What is the major difference between closing the books of a home office and closing the books of a single-location business?
8. What generally are the two differences between branch financial statements and those of an independent business?
9. What accounts are eliminated against each other on the work sheet for combined financial statements?

Assignment Box

To reinforce your understanding of the preceding text materials, you may complete the following:

          Study Guide: Part B
          Textbook: Exercises 18A6 through 18A7 and 18B6 through 18B7
                      Problems 18A5 through 18A6 and 18B5 through 18B6

Expanding Your Business Vocabulary

What is the meaning of each of the following terms?

branch (p. 695)
Branch Office (p. 695)
departmental gross margin (p. 685)
departmental direct operating margin (p. 692)
departmental operating expense summary (p. 690)
departmental operating income (p. 687)

direct expenses (p. 687)
Home Office (p. 695)
indirect expenses (p. 687)
interlocking (p. 695)
reciprocal (p. 695)
Shipments to Branch (p. 696)
Shipments from Home Office (p. 696)

Demonstration Problem

Kristen Owen and Stephen Kaplan are partners engaged in the sale of outdoor bicycles and exercise bicycles. They keep accounts and prepare reports on a departmental basis. Direct expenses are assigned and indirect expenses are allocated to departments by various means. Selected operating information for the year ended December 31, 19-A is given below.

	Outdoor Bicycles	Exercise Bicycles
Net sales	$1,612,500	$1,150,600
Cost of goods sold	920,420	806,800
Direct operating expenses:		
Store clerks wage expense	45,000	19,500
Truck drivers wage expense	36,000	-0-
Advertising expense	21,000	15,000
Depreciation expense—delivery equipment	12,000	-0-
Uncollectible accounts expense	12,000	11,700
Other operating expenses	97,080	39,840
Indirect operating expenses:		
Store clerks wage expense	26,400	14,850
Truck drivers wage expense	52,800	32,250
Advertising expense	43,200	25,500
Depreciation expense—delivery equipment	13,800	5,700
Store rent expense	21,600	14,400
Other operating expenses	192,360	116,190

Required:

1. Prepare a condensed income statement showing departmental operating income.
2. Prepare another condensed income statement showing departmental direct operating margins and total direct operating margin, but only company-wide operating income.
3. For the first statement, determine which department has the higher operating income as a percentage of net sales.
4. For the second statement, determine which department has the higher direct operating margin as a percentage of net sales.
5. Which of the two measures is more meaningful for decision-making purposes? Discuss.

Solution:

1.

Owen and Kaplan
Outdoor and Exercise Bicycles
Income Statement (Condensed)
For the Year Ended December 31, 19-A

	Outdoor Bicycles	Exercise Bicycles	Total
Net sales	$1,612,500	$1,150,600	$2,763,100
Cost of goods sold	920,420	806,800	1,727,220
Gross margin	$ 692,080	$ 343,800	$1,035,880
Operating expenses:			
Store clerks wage expense	71,400	34,350	105,750
Truck drivers wage expense	88,800	32,250	121,050
Advertising expense	64,200	40,500	104,700
Depreciation expense—delivery equip.	25,800	5,700	31,500
Store rent expense	21,600	14,400	36,000
Uncollectible accounts expense	12,000	11,700	23,700
Other operating expenses	289,440	156,030	445,470
Total operating expenses	$ 573,240	$ 294,930	$ 868,170
Operating income	$ 118,840	$ 48,870	$ 167,710

2.

Owen and Kaplan
Outdoor and Exercise Bicycles
Income Statement (Condensed)
For the Year Ended December 31, 19-A

	Outdoor Bicycles	Exercise Bicycles	Total
Net sales	$1,612,500	$1,150,600	$2,763,100
Cost of goods sold	920,420	806,800	1,727,220
Gross margin	$ 692,080	$ 343,800	$1,035,880
Direct operating expenses:			
Store clerks wage expense	$ 45,000	$ 19,500	$ 64,500
Truck drivers wage expense	36,000	-0-	36,000
Advertising expense	21,000	15,000	36,000
Depreciation expense—delivery equip.	12,000	-0-	12,000
Uncollectible accounts expense	12,000	11,700	23,700
Other operating expenses	97,080	39,840	136,920
Total direct operating expenses	$223,080	$ 86,040	$309,120
Departmental direct operating margin	$469,000	$257,760	$726,760
Indirect operating expenses:			
Store clerks wage expense			$ 41,250
Truck driver wage expense			85,050
Advertising expense			68,700
Depreciation expense—delivery equip.			19,500
Store rent expense			36,000
Other operating expenses			308,550
Total indirect operating expenses			$559,050
Operating income			$167,710

3. Operating income percentage for outdoor bicycles

$\dfrac{\$ 118,840 \text{ operating income}}{\$1,612,500 \text{ net sales}} = 7.4\%$

Operating income percentage for bicycle exercisers

$\dfrac{\$ 48,870 \text{ operating income}}{\$1,150,600 \text{ net sales}} = 4.2\%$

Outdoor bicycles has the higher percentage of operating income to net sales.

4. Direct operating margin percentage for outdoor bicycles:

$\dfrac{\$ 469,000 \text{ departmental direct operating margin}}{\$1,612,500 \text{ net sales}} = 29.1\%$

Direct operating margin percentage for exercise bicycles:

$\dfrac{\$ 257,760 \text{ departmental direct operating margin}}{\$1,150,600 \text{ net sales}} = 22.4\%$

Outdoor bicycles has the higher direct operating margin as a percentage of net sales.

5.   Most accountants believe that the departmental direct operating margin is more meaningful for decision-making purposes than departmental operating income. This is because the direct operating margin takes into account only the direct expenses of operating each department, while departmental operating income is the result of various approaches to the allocation of indirect operating expenses.

The direct operating margin percentage from sales of outdoor bicycles is nearly 30% greater

$$(\frac{29.1\%}{22.4\%} = 1.299, \text{ or } +29.9\%)$$

than that from sales of exercise bicycles. The departmental operating income percentage from sales of outdoor bicycles is more than 75% greater

$$(\frac{7.4\%}{4.2\%} = 1.762, \text{ or } +76.2\%)$$

than that from sales of exercise bicycles. So, outdoor bicycles clearly looks like the better performer on both counts.

However, exercise bicycles are contributing $257,760 to the indirect operating expenses and operating income of Owen and Kaplan, without which the business would sustain an operating loss of $90,050 ($167,710 present operating income minus $257,760 departmental direct operating margin of exercise bicycles). The direct operating margin percentage is a more meaningful decision-making tool for Owen and Kaplan than the departmental operating income percentage because it does not result from the more or less arbitrary allocation of indirect expenses to the two departments.

Note: Now that you have reviewed the Demonstration Problem and Solution you may complete the **Mastery Problem** at the end of the chapter activities.

Applying Accounting Concepts

Series A

Exercise 18A1—Assignment and Allocation of Store Clerks Wage Expense. Jensen & Jones are partners engaged in selling men's clothing and footwear, and they keep accounts and prepare reports on a departmental basis. Direct expenses are assigned and indirect expenses are allocated to departments by various means. Prepare an analysis of the division of store clerks wage expense for the year just ended from the data given below, using the four columns illustrated on page 688 of the text.

Employee No.	Dept.	Wages
1	Clothing	$18,000
2	Clothing	14,000
3	Footwear	13,500
4	Both	16,000
5	Both	12,000
Total		$73,500

Wages requiring allocation are distributed to the departments on a relative net sales basis. Clothing net sales are 65% of the total and footwear net sales are 35% of the total.

Exercise 18A2—Assignment and Allocation of Truck Drivers Wage Expense. Jensen & Jones have three delivery truck drivers, one of whom delivers only clothing. Their wages for the year are as follows:

	Products	
Driver No.	Delivered	Wages
1	Clothing	$28,000
2	Both	23,000
3	Both	26,800
	Total	$77,800

Wages requiring allocation are distributed to the departments on a relative dollar amount of merchandise delivered basis. Delivery and shipping records indicate about 70% clothing and 30% footwear. Prepare an analysis of the division of truck drivers wage expense for the year, using the same column headings as illustrated on page 688 of the text.

Exercise 18A3—Assignment and Allocation of Advertising Expense. Jensen & Jones uses radio and television advertising. Total advertising expense is $159,000: $90,000 for television advertising and $69,000 for radio. Advertising is classified as clothing, footwear, or mixed on the basis of the product or products advertised. All television advertising is classified as mixed. Radio advertising is classified as $30,000 for clothing, $20,000 for footwear, and $19,000 mixed. All mixed advertising is allocated to departments on the basis of net sales—65% clothing and 35% footwear. Prepare an analysis of the division of advertising expense for the year, using the same column headings as those illustrated on page 689 of the text.

Exercise 18A4—Assignment and Allocation of Depreciation Expense—Delivery Equipment. Jensen & Jones have three delivery trucks, one of which is used exclusively for delivering clothing. Total depreciation on the delivery equipment is $48,000 for the year, $18,000 of which is on the clothing delivery truck. The other $30,000 of depreciation is allocated based on the relative amount of merchandise delivered—70% to clothing and 30% to footwear. Prepare an analysis of the division of delivery equipment depreciation expense for the year, with column headings like those illustrated on page 689 of the text.

Exercise 18A5—Allocation of Store Rent Expense. Jensen & Jones rents 10,000 square feet of store floor space for $45,600 a year. All of the rent expense is classified as an indirect expense and allocated on a square footage basis. Clothing occupies 6,400 square feet (64%) of the floor space, and footwear occupies 3,600 square feet (36%) of the floor space. Prepare an analysis of the division of rent expense for the year, using the following columns:

	Indirect Expense	
Department	(Allocated)	Total

Exercise 18A6—Journal Entry to Transfer Branch Profit to Home Office Account. The Jerseyville Branch of the Foster Company had a credit balance of $36,000 in its expense and revenue summary account after all revenue and expense accounts were closed at year end. Prepare the journal entry to transfer this balance to the home office account on the branch books.

Exercise 18A7—Journal Entry to Record Branch Profit in Home Office Books. Refer to Exercise 18A6. Prepare the journal entry to record the $36,000 profit of the Jerseyville branch in the books of the Foster Company home office.

Series B

Exercise 18B1—Assignment and Allocation of Store Clerks Wage Expense. Crumb & Kildow are partners engaged in selling tile and carpeting, and they keep accounts and prepare reports on a departmental basis. Direct expenses are assigned, and indirect expenses are allocated to departments by various means. Prepare an analysis of the division of store clerks wage expense for the year just ended from the data given below, using the four columns illustrated on page 688 of the text.

Employee No.	Dept.	Wages
1	Tile	$ 28,500
2	Tile	25,500
3	Carpeting	22,875
4	Both	19,500
5	Both	24,000
Total		$120,375

Wages requiring allocation are distributed to the departments on a relative net sales basis. Tile net sales are 60% of the total and carpeting net sales are 40% of the total.

Exercise 18B2—Assignment and Allocation of Truck Drivers Wage Expense. Crumb & Kildow have three delivery truck drivers, one of whom delivers only tile. Their wages for the year are as follows:

Driver No.	Products Delivered	Wages
1	Tile	$33,500
2	Both	29,750
3	Both	32,600
Total		$95,850

Wages requiring allocation are distributed to the departments on a relative dollar amount of merchandise delivered basis. Delivery and shipping records indicate about 65% tile and 35% carpeting. Prepare an analysis of the division of truck drivers wage expense for the year, using the same column headings as those illustrated on page 688 of the text.

Exercise 18B3—Assignment and Allocation of Advertising Expense. Crumb & Kildow uses newspaper and television advertising. Total advertising expense is $119,250: $67,500 for television and $51,750 for newspaper. Advertising is classified as tile, carpeting, or mixed on the basis of the product or products advertised. All television advertising is classified as mixed. Newspaper advertising breaks down $22,500 for tile, $15,000 for carpeting, and $14,250 mixed. All mixed advertising is allocated to departments on the basis of net sales—60% tile and 40% carpeting. Prepare an analysis of the division of advertising expense for the year, using the same column headings as those illustrated on page 689 of the text.

Exercise 18B4—Assignment and Allocation of Depreciation Expense—Delivery Equipment. Crumb & Kildow have three delivery trucks, one of which is used exclusively for delivering tile. Total depreciation on the delivery equipment is $36,000 for the year, $13,500 of which is on the tile delivery truck. The other $22,500 of depreciation is allocated based on the relative amount of merchandise delivered—65% to tile and 35% to carpeting. Prepare an analysis of the division of delivery equipment depreciation expense for the year, with the column headings illustrated on page 689 of the text.

Exercise 18B5—Allocation of Store Rent Expense. Crumb & Kildow rents 15,000 square feet of store floor space for $33,200 a year. All of the rent expense is classified as an indirect expense and allocated on a square footage basis. Tile occupies 10,500 square feet (70%) of the floor space, and carpeting occupies 4,500 square feet (30%) of the floor space. Prepare an analysis of the division of rent expense for the year, using the following columns:

	Indirect Expense	
Department	(Allocated)	Total

Exercise 18B6—Journal Entry to Transfer Branch Profit to Home Office Account. The Collinsville Branch of the Dwyer Company had a credit balance of $27,000 in its expense and revenue summary account after all revenue and expense accounts were closed at year end. Prepare the journal entry to transfer this balance to the home office account on the branch books.

Exercise 18B7—Journal Entry to Record Branch Profit in Home Office Books. Refer to Exercise 18B6. Prepare the journal entry to record the $27,000 profit of the Collinsville branch in the books of the Dwyer Company home office.

Series A

| **Problem 18A1** | Income Statement with Departmental Gross Margins |

McKay and Allen are partners engaged in selling art and drafting materials. They keep accounts and prepare reports on a departmental basis. Direct expenses are assigned and indirect expenses are allocated to departments by various means. Information on departmental net sales and cost of goods sold, and total operating expenses for the year ended December 31, 19-A, is given below.

Net sales—Art Materials	$537,500
Net sales—Drafting Materials	370,200
Cost of goods sold—Art Materials	280,140
Cost of goods sold—Drafting Materials	255,400
Operating expenses	289,390

Required:
1. Prepare a condensed income statement showing departmental gross margin for Art Materials and for Drafting Materials.
2. Calculate the gross margin percentage for each department and for the business as a whole. Show your calculations.

Problem 18A2   Income Statement with Departmental Operating Income

Refer to Problem 18A1. McKay and Allen have prepared the following Departmental Operating Expense Summary for the year ended December 31, 19-A:

McKay and Allen Art & Drafting Materials
Departmental Operating Expense Summary
For the Year Ended December 31, 19-A

Expense	Art Materials	Drafting Materials	Total
Store clerks wage expense	$ 23,800	$11,450	$ 35,250
Truck drivers wage expense	29,600	10,750	40,350
Advertising expense	21,400	13,500	34,900
Depreciation expense—delivery equipment	8,600	1,900	10,500
Store rent expense	7,200	4,800	12,000
Uncollectible accounts expense...............	4,000	3,900	7,900
Other operating expenses	96,480	52,010	148,490
Total operating expenses...................	$191,080	$98,310	$289,390

Required:

1. Prepare a condensed income statement showing departmental operating income.
2. Determine which department has the lower operating expenses as a percentage of its net sales. Also show operating expenses as a percentage of net sales for the business as a whole. Show your calculations.

Problem 18A3   Income Statement with Departmental Direct Operating Margin

Refer to Problems 18A1 and 18A2. McKay and Allen have prepared the following analysis of departmental operating expenses for the year ended December 31, 19-A:

McKay and Allen Art & Drafting Materials
Departmental Operating Expense Summary
For the Year Ended December 31, 19-A

Art Materials Expense	Direct	Indirect	Total
Store clerks wage expense	$15,000	$ 8,800	$ 23,800
Truck drivers wage expense	12,000	17,600	29,600
Advertising expense	7,000	14,400	21,400
Depreciation expense—delivery equipment	4,000	4,600	8,600
Store rent expense	-0-	7,200	7,200
Uncollectible accounts expense................	4,000	-0-	4,000
Other operating expenses	32,360	64,120	96,480
Total Art Materials expense	$74,360	$116,720	$191,080

Drafting Materials Expense	Direct	Indirect	Total
Store clerks wage expense	$ 6,500	$ 4,950	$11,450
Truck drivers wage expense	-0-	10,750	10,750
Advertising expense	5,000	8,500	13,500
Depreciation expense—delivery equipment	-0-	1,900	1,900
Store rent expense	-0-	4,800	4,800
Uncollectible accounts expense	3,900	-0-	3,900
Other operating expenses	13,280	38,730	52,010
Total Drafting Materials expense	$28,680	$69,630	$98,310

Required:

1. Prepare a condensed income statement showing departmental direct operating margins and total direct operating margin, but only company-wide operating income.
2. Determine which department has the lower direct operating expenses as a percentage of its net sales. Also show direct operating expenses as a percentage of net sales for the business as a whole. Show your calculations.

Problem 18A4   Possible Discontinuance of a Department

Sloan & Simpson Company is trying to decide whether to discontinue Department B. Operating results for the year just ended for each of the company's three departments and for the entire operation are given below.

	Dept. A	Dept. B	Dept. C	Total
Net sales	$420,000	$340,000	$370,000	$1,130,000
Cost of goods sold	230,000	192,000	220,000	642,000
Gross margin	$190,000	$148,000	$150,000	$ 488,000
Direct operating expenses	110,000	108,000	90,000	308,000
Departmental direct operating				
margin	$ 80,000	$ 40,000	$ 60,000	$ 180,000
Indirect operating expenses	54,000	50,000	44,000	148,000
Operating income (loss)..........	$ 26,000	$(10,000)	$ 16,000	$ 32,000

Required:

1. Prepare an additional column that combines Departments A and C only.
2. Review all data and decide if Department B should be discontinued. Defend your decision.

Problem 18A5   Journal Entries for Branch Transactions

(a) On January 2, the Hempel Co. established a branch in the town of Denton and turned over to the manager of the branch $48,000 in cash, furniture and fixtures that had just been purchased at a cost of $12,000, and merchandise that cost $42,000.

(b) The branch manager purchased for cash additional furniture and fixtures for $15,000, and paid $1,700 rent on the branch store. (Use a single Operating Expense account to enter all expenses.)

(c)   The home office shipped goods costing $270,000 to the branch.

(d)   During the year, the branch had cash sales of $31,200 and sales on account of $288,000.

(e)   The branch incurred additional operating expenses on account during the year (rent, wages, light, telephone, advertising, etc.) in the amount of $112,200. Total payments on account were $99,000.

(f)   Cash collections on the branch accounts receivable were $156,000.

(g)   The branch returned to the home office for credit, goods costing $2,400.

Required:

Record the above transactions in general journal form as they would appear on the branch office books and on the home office books.

Problem 18A6   Preparation of Work Sheet for Combined Financial Statements

Given below are the year-end adjusted trial balances of the Wheeler Company and its Pascagoula branch office:

Account	Home Office Debit	Home Office Credit	Branch Office Debit	Branch Office Credit
Cash	108,000		102,800	
Accounts receivable	345,000		132,000	
Branch office	369,600			
Merchandise inventory	168,000		124,000	
Land	42,000			
Building (net)	192,000			
Furniture and fixtures (net)	16,400		42,000	
Accounts payable		336,000		13,200
Home office				369,600
B. Wheeler, capital		553,400		
Expense and revenue summary	126,000	168,000		124,000
Sales		762,000		319,200
Purchases	570,000			
Shipments to branch		309,600		
Shipments from home office			309,600	
Operating expenses	192,000		115,600	
	2,129,000	2,129,000	826,000	826,000

Required:

Prepare a work sheet like the one on page 701 of the text for combined home office and branch financial statements for the Wheeler Company as of the end of the current year.

Series B

Problem 18B1   Income Statement with Departmental Gross Margins

Lehn and Robinson are partners engaged in selling home and office furniture. They keep accounts and prepare reports on a departmental basis. Direct expenses are assigned and indirect expenses are allocated to departments by various means. Information on departmental net sales and cost of goods sold, and total operating expenses for the year ended December 31, 19-B, is given below.

Net sales—Home Furniture	$806,250
Net sales—Office Furniture	575,300
Cost of goods sold—Home Furniture	460,210
Cost of goods sold—Office Furniture	403,400
Operating expenses	434,085

Required:

1. Prepare a condensed income statement showing departmental gross margin for Home Furniture and for Office Furniture.
2. Calculate the gross margin percentage for each department and for the business as a whole. Show your calculations.

Problem 18B2   Income Statement with Departmental Operating Income

Refer to Problem 18B1. Lehn and Robinson have prepared the following Departmental Operating Expense Summary for the year ended December 31, 19-B:

Lehn and Robinson Home & Office Furniture
Departmental Operating Expense Summary
For the Year Ended December 31, 19-B

Expense	Home Furniture	Office Furniture	Total
Store clerks wage expense	$ 35,700	$ 17,175	$ 52,875
Truck drivers wage expense	44,400	16,125	60,525
Advertising expense	32,100	20,250	52,350
Depreciation expense—delivery equipment	12,900	2,850	15,750
Store rent expense	10,800	7,200	18,000
Uncollectible accounts expense	6,000	5,850	11,850
Other operating expenses	144,720	78,015	222,735
Total operating expenses	$286,620	$147,465	$434,085

Required:

1. Prepare a condensed income statement showing departmental operating income.
2. Determine which department has the lower operating expenses as a percentage of its net sales. Also show operating expenses as a percentage of net sales for the business as a whole. Show your calculations.

Problem 18B3   Income Statement with Departmental Direct Operating Margin

Refer to Problems 18B1 and 18B2. Lehn and Robinson have prepared the following analysis of departmental operating expenses for the year ended December 31, 19-B:

Lehn and Robinson Home and Office Furniture
Departmental Operating Expense Summary
For the Year Ended December 31, 19-B

Home Furniture Expense	Direct	Indirect	Total
Store clerks wage expense	$ 22,500	$ 13,200	$ 35,700
Truck drivers wage expense	18,000	26,400	44,400
Advertising expense	10,500	21,600	32,100
Depreciation expense—delivery equipment......	6,000	6,900	12,900
Store rent expense	-0-	10,800	10,800
Uncollectible accounts expense...............	6,000	-0-	6,000
Other operating expenses	48,540	96,180	144,720
Total Home Furniture expense..............	$111,540	$175,080	$286,620

Office Furniture Expense	Direct	Indirect	Total
Store clerks wage expense	$ 9,750	$ 7,425	$ 17,175
Truck drivers wage expense	-0-	16,125	16,125
Advertising expense	7,500	12,750	20,250
Depreciation expense—delivery equipment......	-0-	2,850	2,850
Store rent expense	-0-	7,200	7,200
Uncollectible accounts expense...............	5,850	-0-	5,850
Other operating expenses	19,920	58,095	78,015
Total Office Furniture expense..............	$43,020	$104,445	$147,465

Required:

1. Prepare a condensed income statement showing departmental direct operating margins and total direct operating margin, but only company-wide operating income.

2. Determine which department has the lower direct operating expenses as a percentage of its net sales. Also show direct operating expenses as a percentage of net sales for the business as a whole. Show your calculations.

Problem 18B4   Possible Discontinuance of a Department

Castle & Carter Company is trying to decide whether to discontinue Department A. Operating results for the year just ended for each of the company's three departments and for the entire operation are given below.

	Dept. A	Dept. B	Dept. C	Total
Net sales	$510,000	$630,000	$555,000	$1,695,000
Cost of goods sold	288,000	345,000	330,000	963,000
Gross margin	$222,000	$285,000	$225,000	$ 732,000
Direct operating expenses	162,000	165,000	135,000	462,000
Departmental direct operating margin	$ 60,000	$120,000	$ 90,000	$ 270,000
Indirect operating expenses........	75,000	81,000	66,000	222,000
Operating income (loss)..........	$ (15,000)	$ 39,000	$ 24,000	$ 48,000

Required:

1. Prepare an additional column that combines Departments B and C only.

2. Review all data and decide if Department A should be discontinued. Defend your decision.

Problem 18B5   Journal Entries for Branch Transactions

(a) On January 2, the Dawson Co. established a branch in the town of Fairfield and turned over to the manager of the branch $36,000 in cash, furniture and fixtures that had just been purchased at a cost of $9,000, and merchandise that cost $31,000.

(b) The branch manager purchased for cash additional furniture and fixtures for $22,500, and paid $2,400 rent on the branch store. (Use a single Operating Expense account to enter all expenses.)

(c) The home office shipped goods costing $195,000 to the branch.

(d) During the year, the branch had cash sales of $23,400 and sales on account of $216,000.

(e) The branch incurred additional operating expenses on account during the year (rent, wages, light, telephone, advertising, etc.) in the amount of $84,300. Total payments on account were $75,500.

(f) Cash collections on the branch accounts receivable were $117,000.

(g) The branch returned to the home office for credit, goods costing $1,800.

Required:

Record the above transactions in general journal form as they would appear on the branch office books and on the home office books.

Problem 18B6   Preparation of Work Sheet for Combined Financial Statements

Given below are the year-end adjusted trial balances of the Watson Company and its Rolla branch office:

Account	Home Office Debit	Home Office Credit	Branch Office Debit	Branch Office Credit
Cash	81,000		77,100	
Accounts receivable	268,250		99,000	
Merchandise inventory	126,000		82,000	
Branch office	277,200			
Land	31,500			
Building (net)	144,000			
Furniture and fixtures (net)	12,300		31,500	
Accounts payable		252,000		9,900
Home office				277,200
A. Watson, capital		415,050		
Expense and revenue summary	85,000	126,000		82,000
Sales		571,500		239,400
Purchases	427,500			
Shipments to branch		232,200		
Shipments from home office			232,200	
Operating expenses	144,000		86,700	
	1,596,750	1,596,750	608,500	608,500

Required:

Prepare a work sheet like the one on page 701 of the text for combined home office and branch financial statements for the Watson Company as of the end of the current year.

Mastery Problem

Bob's Acme Supermarket has been in operation for many years offering high-quality groceries, produce and meat at reasonable prices. Accounting records are maintained on a departmental basis with assignment of direct expenses and allocation of indirect expenses through the use of various procedures. Selected operating information for the year ended December 31, 19-A is provided below.

	Grocery	Meat	Produce	Total
Net sales	$2,104,890	$660,500	$345,800	$3,111,190
Cost of goods sold	1,683,912	462,350	207,480	2,353,742
Direct operating expenses:				
Store clerks wage expense	125,000	58,000	38,500	221,500
Advertising expense	25,000	38,500	18,400	81,900
Depr. exp.—store equip.	10,800	15,000	12,000	37,800
Other operating expenses	28,200	28,540	35,600	92,340
Indirect operating expenses:				
Store clerks wages expense	12,000	5,000	4,000	21,000
Advertising expense	7,000	2,000	1,000	10,000
Depr. exp.—store equip.	35,000	10,000	5,000	50,000
Store rent	60,000	20,000	20,000	100,000
Other operating expenses	25,500	4,500	18,450	48,450

Required:

1. **(a)** Prepare a condensed income statement showing departmental gross margin, departmental operating income, and results from total operations.
   (b) Compute the gross margin percentage and operating income as a percent of net sales for each department.
2. **(a)** Prepare a condensed income statement showing departmental gross margin, departmental direct operating margin, and results from total operations.
   (b) Compute departmental direct operating margin as a percentage of net sales for each department.
3. Should Bob be concerned about the profitability of the three departments?

CHAPTER 19

Accrual Accounting Applied to a Medium-Scale Wholesale-Retail Business

Chapter Objectives

Careful study of this chapter should enable you to:

- Describe the factors affecting the accounting records used by a wholesale-retail business.

- Describe the accounting records and related procedures for such a business.

- Prepare the following new books of original entry:
  1. Departmental sales journal
  2. Departmental cash receipts journal
  3. General journal with a detail column

- Describe the accounting for temporary investments, using the account for government notes as an example.

- Describe the use of departmental cost of goods sold accounts.

- Prepare an operating expense subsidiary ledger with its own chart of accounts.

- Apply accrual accounting techniques to a medium-size wholesale-retail business with two departments operated as a partnership.

- Prepare a ten-column, end-of-year summary work sheet supplemented by a three-column, end-of-year operating expenses work sheet.

- Use end-of-year departmental summary accounts for cost of goods sold.

- Prepare adjustments affecting both the operating expenses work sheet and the summary work sheet.

This chapter focuses on two major topics. The first half of the chapter provides a discussion of the accounting records generally maintained by a medium-scale wholesale-retail business and illustrates the preparation of entries in special journals. The second half of the chapter explains and illustrates the preparation of the year-end work sheet.

Accounting
Records for a
Wholesale-
Retail Business

In the wholesale portion of a wholesale-retail merchandising enterprise, the merchandise handled is usually purchased directly from manufacturers, importers, or producers. The merchandise is sold to retailers and distributors, who in turn sell to consumers at retail prices. The wholesaler usually buys in sizable quantities and has storage facilities that make it possible to carry a large stock of merchandise. Goods may be purchased for cash or on account and, likewise, the goods may be sold for cash or on account. A large percentage of the wholesale business involves the use of credit. The retail portion of such a business is handled in a manner similar to that explained and illustrated in Chapters 9 and 10.

This chapter illustrates departmental accounting and applies it to a partnership operated as both a wholesaler and a retailer. It also illustrates the use of a departmental sales journal, a departmental cash receipts journal, and a general journal with special columns. The voucher register and check register introduced in Chapter 16 are also utilized here. Temporary investment accounts and departmental cost of goods sold accounts are introduced. Finally, an operating expense subsidiary ledger with a separate chart of accounts is fully illustrated for the first time.

Factors Affecting Accounting Records Used

Describe the factors
affecting the
accounting records
used by a wholesale-
retail business.

The books of account and the auxiliary records of a wholesale-retail business will vary depending upon a number of factors, such as the following:

1. Type of business organization.
2. Volume of business.
3. Office equipment used.
4. Information desired by the management and others concerned with the operation of the business.

Type of Business Organization. A wholesale-retail merchandising enterprise may be conducted as a single proprietorship, a partnership, or a corporation. The type of organization will affect the accounts that are kept. In a single proprietorship, it may be necessary to keep two accounts for the proprietor—one for capital and the other for drawing. In a partnership, it is necessary to keep separate accounts for each partner. In the case of a corporation, it is necessary to keep separate accounts for capital stock, retained earnings, and dividends payable. Accou ·ing for the corporate form of organization will be described and illu: ;ated in Chapters 21 through 23.

▩ **Volume of Business.** The volume of business is an important factor in determining the types of records and the number of accounts to be maintained. Obviously, the records and the accounts of a firm with annual sales of a million dollars or more will differ considerably from one with annual sales of only $50,000. In a business with numerous departments, management may demand more financial statistical information and have a greater need for control.

When manual processing methods are used, there is a fairly direct relationship between the size of a business and the number of persons engaged in keeping its records. When several persons are required, the work must be divided in some logical fashion. This means that a separate record or book of original entry will be kept for each major type of business transaction. For example, one journal may be provided to enter purchases, another to enter sales, another to enter cash receipts, and another to enter checks written. A general journal would be used to enter transactions that cannot be entered in the special journals. The books of final entry (the ledgers) also will be subdivided. It is likely that one or more subsidiary ledgers will be kept to enter more detail than that shown in summary in some of the general ledger accounts. For example, one subsidiary ledger may be used to record individual customers' accounts (accounts receivable) and another may be used to record individual operating expense accounts. (A subsidiary ledger for individual accounts payable would not be necessary if a voucher system is used.) Each employee engaged in an accounting activity may specialize in keeping one of these records.

A functional division of the accounting activity may have many advantages. Some of the more important ones are that the functional division:

1. Becomes an integral part of the internal control system, as discussed in Chapter 16.
2. Makes possible a more equitable distribution of the work load among several employees.
3. Provides for a more detailed classification of transactions in the books of original entry.
4. Makes possible periodic summary posting to the general ledger.

▩ **Office Equipment.** The accounting system is certain to be affected by the use of various types of office equipment. In recent years there has been a great expansion in the use of computer-based accounting systems. In the modern office of a big business enterprise, a large share of the data entry work is done with the aid of electronic data processing equipment. Many companies utilize personal computers and other associated equipment.

Regardless of the extent to which equipment is used in performing the accounting function, the fundamental principles involved in keeping the accounts continue to apply. A knowledge of accounting theory and practice on the part of those employed in accounting positions is just as essential in today's computer-based environment as it was when no machines were used.

▰▰▰▰ Information Desired. The accounting information system must be designed to provide the desired information for management and others concerned with the operation of a business. Accounting may be required to supply information of a statistical nature in addition to the usual accounting reports. For example, accounts must be kept in order to provide all the information needed for the many and varied tax reports required by the federal, state, and local governments. In recent years there has been a tremendous increase in the number of tax reports and in the amount of tax information that must be furnished. Many large firms have found it necessary to establish a tax accounting department separate from the general accounting department.

Accounting Records and Related Procedures

Describe the accounting records and related procedures for such a business.

Robert Mitchell and Jessica Jenkins are partners who conduct a wholesale-retail sporting goods business specializing in golf and tennis equipment. The equipment is purchased on account from various manufacturers. The majority of sales are made on account to retail outlets. However, a substantial amount of cash sales are made to retail customers. In the following sections, the books of account and accounting procedures for Mitchell & Jenkins are explained and illustrated.

The records maintained by Mitchell & Jenkins consist of the following:

1. Books of original entry
    (a) Voucher register
    (b) Sales journal
    (c) Cash receipts journal
    (d) Check register
    (e) General journal
2. Books of final entry
    (a) General ledger
    (b) Subsidiary ledgers:
         Accounts receivable ledger
         Operating expense ledger
3. Auxiliary records
    (a) Petty cash payments record
    (b) Long-term asset record

▰▰▰▰ Voucher Register. The format of Mitchell & Jenkins' voucher register shown on pages 732-733 is identical to the voucher register reproduced on page 616. This form of voucher register was described in detail in Chapter 16.

Prepare a departmental sales journal.

▰▰▰▰ Sales Journal. Mitchell & Jenkins keeps a multi-column sales journal as illustrated on page 730. Since there is no sales tax in the state in which Mitchell & Jenkins operates, no sales tax collections are necessary. A special debit amount column is provided for Accounts Receivable, and special credit columns are provided for (1) Sales, Golf, and (2) Sales, Tennis. A Sale No. column is provided to identify the source document for each entry.

Proving the Sales Journal. The sales journal can be footed and the footings proved daily or periodically by comparing the sum of the debit footings with the sum of the credit footings. When a page is filled and the amount columns footed, the footings should be proved, and the totals carried forward to the top of the next page. It is customary to start a month at the top of a new page.

Posting from the Sales Journal. Completing the posting from the sales journal involves both individual and summary posting. Individual posting may be required from the Accounts Receivable Debit column in some accounting information systems. In Mitchell & Jenkins' system, however, individual posting to the accounts receivable subsidiary ledger is done directly from the sales invoices. This posting usually is done daily. As each item is posted, a check mark is entered in the Check (√) column following the Accounts Receivable Debit column of the sales journal.

The summary posting usually is completed at the end of each month and involves the following procedure.

1. The total of the column headed Accounts Receivable Debit should be posted as a debit to Accounts Receivable in the general ledger.
2. The total of the column headed Sales Credit, Golf, should be posted as a credit to Sales—Golf in the general ledger.
3. The total of the column headed Sales Credit, Tennis, should be posted as a credit to Sales—Tennis in the general ledger.

As the total of each column is posted, the account number should be written in parentheses immediately below the total in the sales journal. The final step for both individual and summary posting to the general ledger is to enter the initials "SJ" and the page number of the sales journal in the Posting Reference column of the proper general ledger account to the left of the amount posted. The final step in individual posting from sales invoices to the accounts receivable subsidiary ledger is to enter the letter "S" and the sales invoice number in the Posting Reference column of the proper customer's account to the left of the amount posted. Firms that post to the accounts receivable subsidiary ledger from the sales journal would enter "SJ" and the page number of the sales journal in the Posting Reference column.

Cash Receipts Journal. Mitchell & Jenkins keeps a multi-column cash receipts journal. In the cash receipts journal reproduced on page 731 a special debit amount column is provided for Cash. All cash and cash items are entered by debiting the cash account immediately. This practice

Prepare a departmental cash receipts journal.

usually is followed when a business deposits all of its cash receipts in a bank on the day they are received and makes all of its payments (other than petty cash) by check. On the credit side, special amount columns are provided for Accounts Receivable, Sales—Golf, and Sales—Tennis.

Proving the Cash Receipts Journal. The cash receipts journal may be footed and the footings proved daily or periodically by comparing the sum of the debit footings with the sum of the credit footings. When a page is filled, the amount columns should be footed, the footings proved, and the totals carried forward to the top of the next page. It is customary to start a month at the top of a new page.

Posting from the Cash Receipts Journal. Completing the posting from the cash receipts journal involves both individual posting and summary posting. Individual posting is required from the General Ledger Credit column. Individual posting to the accounts receivable subsidiary ledger is done directly from the remittance advices. This posting usually is done daily. As each item is posted, a check mark is entered in the Check ($\sqrt{}$) column following the Accounts Receivable Credit, or General Ledger Credit Amount column of the cash receipts journal.

The summary posting usually is completed at the end of each month and involves the following procedure:

1. The total of the column headed Cash should be posted as a debit to Cash in the general ledger.
2. The total of the column headed Accounts Receivable should be posted as a credit to Accounts Receivable in the general ledger.
3. The total of the column headed Sales, Golf, should be posted as a credit to Sales—Golf in the general ledger.
4. The total of the column headed Sales, Tennis, should be posted as a credit to Sales—Tennis in the general ledger.

As the total of each column is posted, the account number should be written in parentheses immediately below the total in the cash receipts journal. The final step in both individual and summary posting to the general ledger is to enter the initials "CR" and the page number of the cash receipts journal in the Posting Reference column of the proper general ledger account to the left of the amount posted. Likewise, the final step in individual posting to the accounts receivable subsidiary ledger is to enter the initials "CR" and the page number of the cash receipts journal in the Posting Reference column of the proper customer's account to the left of the amount posted. A check mark should be placed in parentheses below the total of the General Ledger Credit column to indicate that this total is not posted.

Check Register. The format of Mitchell & Jenkins's check register reproduced on page 734 is identical to the check register reproduced on page 619. This form was described in detail in Chapter 16.

Prepare a general
journal with a detail
column.

General Journal. The general journal is used for entering all transactions that cannot be entered in the special journals. Mitchell & Jenkins uses a general journal (reproduced on page 734) with three amount columns—Detail, Debit, and Credit—as well as an Account No. column. The Detail column is used to enter debits to specific operating expense subsidiary ledger accounts to support each of the debits to the control account, Operating Expenses, in the general ledger. Adjusting, closing, and reversing entries also are entered in the general journal.

Proving the General Journal. The general journal can be footed and the footings proved daily or periodically by comparing the debit footing with the credit footing. When a page is filled, the three amount columns should be footed, the debit and credit footings proved, and the totals carried forward to the top of the next page. It is customary to start a month at the top of a new page.

Posting from the General Journal. Completing the posting from the general journal involves only individual posting from the Detail, Debit and Credit columns. This posting usually is done daily. Since the account numbers normally are entered in the Acct. No. column when the entries are made, posting is indicated by entering a check mark in the Check ($\checkmark$) column following each of the amount columns as each item is posted. The initial "J" and the page number of the general journal then should be entered in the Posting Reference column of the proper general ledger (or operating expense subsidiary ledger) account to the left of the amount posted.

Although no summary posting is required, a check mark should be placed in parentheses below the Detail, Debit, and Credit column totals at the end of each month to indicate that these totals are not posted. Check marks should also be placed in parentheses below the proving totals of the adjusting and closing entries in the general journal after each of these sets of entries has been posted.

General Ledger. Mitchell & Jenkins uses a general ledger with the accounts arranged in numerical order according to the chart of accounts reproduced on page 723. Note that the chart includes some accounts not used previously. A brief discussion of these new accounts follows.

Describe the
accounting for
temporary investments,
using the account for
government notes as
an example.

Government Notes, Account No. 121. This account is used to enter the cost of United States government notes owned by Mitchell & Jenkins. From time to time, the partners find that the firm's bank balance is larger than necessary. To supplement earnings from regular operations, the excess cash is temporarily invested in certain types of government notes which earn a relatively high rate of return. The notes can be sold or redeemed with little risk of loss. Because there is no intention to hold the notes for a long period of time, they are regarded as temporary investments and classified as a current asset on the balance sheet. In the end-of-period adjustment process, any interest accrued on the notes is entered as a debit to Accrued Interest Receivable and a credit to Interest Revenue.

Mitchell & Jenkins
Chart of General Ledger Accounts

Current Assets*
Cash
    111 Cash
    112 Petty Cash Fund
Temporary Investments
    121 Government Notes
Receivables
    122 Accrued Interest Receivable
    131 Accounts Receivable
        131.1 Allowance for Doubtful
            Accounts
Inventories
    141 Merchandise Inventory—Golf
    142 Merchandise Inventory—
        Tennis
Supplies and Prepayments
    151 Store Supplies
    152 Office Supplies
    155 Prepaid Insurance
Property, Plant and Equipment
    181 Store Equipment
        181.1 Accumulated
            Depreciation—Store
            Equipment
    185 Delivery Equipment
        185.1 Accumulated
            Depreciation—Delivery
            Equipment
    191 Office Equipment
        191.1 Accumulated
            Depreciation—Office
            Equipment
Current Liabilities
    211 FICA Tax Payable
    212 FUTA Tax Payable
    213 State Unemployment Tax
        Payable
    214 Employees Income Tax
        Payable
    216 Notes Payable
    217 Accrued Interest Payable
    218 Vouchers Payable

Owners' Equity
    311 Robert Mitchell, Capital
    312 Robert Mitchell, Drawing
    321 Jessica Jenkins, Capital
    322 Jessica Jenkins, Drawing
    331 Expense and Revenue
        Summary
Revenue from Sales
    411 Sales—Golf
        411.1 Sales Returns and
            Allowances—Golf
    421 Sales—Tennis
        421.1 Sales Returns and
            Allowances—Tennis
Other Revenue
    431 Interest Revenue
Cost of Goods Sold
    511 Purchases—Golf
        511.1 Purchases Returns and
            Allowances—Golf
    521 Purchases—Tennis
        521.1 Purchases Returns and
            Allowances—Tennis
    531 Cost of Goods Sold—Golf
    532 Cost of Goods Sold—Tennis
Operating Expenses
    540 Operating Expenses
Other Expenses
    581 Interest Expense

*Words in bold type are not account titles.

Describe the use of departmental cost of goods sold accounts.

Cost of Goods Sold—Golf and Cost of Goods Sold—Tennis, Account Nos. 531 and 532. These two accounts are similar to Expense and Revenue Summary in that they are used at the end of the accounting period in the adjusting and closing process. Further, as explained in Chapters 7 and 10, they are reported on the income statement as part of the calculation of gross margin. Work sheet adjustments using these accounts are illustrated later in this chapter. Closing entries and financial statements for Mitchell and Jenkins are illustrated in Chapter 20.

■■■■ **Accounts Receivable Subsidiary Ledger.** Mitchell & Jenkins uses an accounts receivable subsidiary ledger with customer accounts arranged in alphabetical order. A control account, Accounts Receivable, is kept in the general ledger. At the end of each month, it is customary to prepare a schedule of the accounts receivable, the total of which should be the same as the balance of the accounts receivable control account.

Posting to the customers' accounts in the accounts receivable subsidiary ledger may be done either from the books of original entry or directly from the documents that represent the transactions. The accountant for Mitchell & Jenkins follows the latter practice, using copies of sales invoices, remittance advices, and credit memorandums. A check mark is placed in the Check (√) column next to the Accounts Receivable amount column either in the sales journal or cash receipts journal, or next to the credit column in the general journal, each time an entry is posted.

Prepare an operating expense subsidiary ledger with its own chart of accounts.

■■■■ **Operating Expense Subsidiary Ledger.** Mitchell & Jenkins uses an operating expense subsidiary ledger with the expense accounts arranged in numerical order. A chart of the accounts for Mitchell & Jenkins appears below. A control account, Operating Expenses, is kept in the general ledger. At the end of each month, it is customary to prepare a schedule of the operating expenses, the total of which should be the same as the balance of the operating expenses control account.

Mitchell & Jenkins
Chart of Operating Expense Subsidiary Ledger Accounts

Administrative Expenses	Selling Expenses
5401 Office Salaries Expense	5431 Store Clerks Salary Expense
5402 Robert Mitchell, Salary Expense	5432 Truck Drivers Wage Expense
5403 Office Supplies Expense	5433 Advertising Expense
5404 Depreciation Expense—Office Equipment	5434 Jessica Jenkins, Salary Expense
5405 Insurance Expense—Office Equipment	5435 Depreciation Expense—Delivery Equipment
5406 Office Rent Expense	5436 Insurance Expense—Delivery Equipment
5407 Payroll Taxes Expense	5437 Depreciation Expense—Store Equipment
5408 Heat, Light, and Water Expense	5438 Insurance Expense—Store Equipment
5409 Telephone Expense	5441 Truck Gas and Oil Expense
5416 Postage Expense	5442 Truck Repairs & Maintenance Expense
5417 Uncollectible Accounts Expense	5443 Store Rent Expense
5422 Miscellaneous General Expense	5444 Store Supplies Expense
	5452 Miscellaneous Selling Expense

All posting to the operating expense accounts is done from the books of original entry. As each item is posted, the initials and the page of the journal from which it is posted are entered in the Posting Reference column of the account.

As each entry involving an operating expense account is made in either the voucher register or general journal, the appropriate subsidiary ledger account number is written in the Acct. No. column to the left of the proper amount column. Then, when each of these amounts is posted to the operating expense subsidiary ledger, a check mark is placed in the Check (√) column just to the right of the proper amount column.

Auxiliary Records. Mitchell & Jenkins maintains certain auxiliary records such as a petty cash payments record, a long-term asset record, voucher check stubs, and vouchers.

The format of the petty cash payments record is similar to that of the petty cash payments record illustrated on pages 164 and 165 of Chapter 5. The format of the property, plant and equipment record is similar to the format of the property, plant and equipment record illustrated on page 563 of Chapter 14. The voucher check and voucher formats were illustrated on pages 614 and 618 of Chapter 16. To conserve space, Mitchell & Jenkins' auxiliary records are not illustrated in this chapter.

Accounting Procedure Illustrated

Apply accrual accounting techniques to a medium-size wholesale-retail business with two departments operated as a partnership.

The accounts of Mitchell & Jenkins are kept on the basis of a fiscal year ending December 31. The books of original entry (voucher register, sales journal, cash receipts journal, check register, and general journal) are shown on pages 730-734. The general ledger and subsidiary ledgers are not reproduced in this illustration. Following is a narrative of the December transactions that are shown entered in the illustrations.

Mitchell & Jenkins Sporting Goods
Narrative of Transactions

Monday, December 2

1. Issued Voucher No. 296 to Capital Leasing Co., Indianapolis, for $3,300, of which $2,200 represents store rent expense and $1,100 represents office rent expense.

   Since the type of voucher used by Mitchell & Jenkins was illustrated in Chapter 16, it will not be illustrated in this chapter. Instead, sufficient detail will be given to explain each entry in the voucher register illustrated on pages 732-733. The voucher register illustration begins with three unpaid vouchers from the previous month of November.

2. Issued Check No. 701 in payment of Voucher No. 271, and Check No. 702 in payment of Voucher No. 296.

   The voucher register illustration on page 732 shows the payees and amounts of these two checks. Note that, in addition to the check register entries, the date and number of each check are written in the Disposition columns of the voucher register.

3. Cash sales for the day were $1,425 for Golf and $650 for Tennis.
   Cash sales are entered in the cash receipts journal illustrated on page 731. Note that the golf and tennis cash sales are listed separately.

Tuesday, December 3

1. Received checks from customers on account as follows:
   Fleetwood Country Club, $1,880, for merchandise sold on November 29.
   Courtside, $490, for merchandise sold on November 29.
   Lakeside Country Club, $945, for merchandise sold on November 29.
   Checks sent in by customers are accompanied by remittance advices, which are used to enter the transactions in the cash receipts journal illustrated on page 731 and to post to the individual customer accounts receivable subsidiary ledger (not shown).

2. Cash sales for the day were $1,782 for Golf and $1,675 for Tennis.

3. Issued Voucher No. 297 to Public Service Power & Light, Indianapolis, for November electricity bill, $1,500.

Wednesday, December 4

1. Issued Check Nos. 703 and 704 in payment of Voucher Nos. 294 and 295.

2. Issued Voucher No. 298 to the Indianapolis Star for advertising, $495.

3. Made charge sales as follows:
   The Tennis Racket, tennis equipment, $4,300; Sale No. 397.
   The Swing Shop, golf equipment, $1,345; tennis equipment $685; Sale No. 398.
   Fleetwood Country Club, golf equipment, $1,825; tennis shoes, $525; Sale No. 399.
   Entries in the sales journal and postings to individual customer accounts receivable (not shown) are made from copies of the sales invoices. The sales journal is illustrated on page 730. All sales are numbered consecutively.

4. Cash sales for the day were $1,840 for Golf and $925 for Tennis.

Thursday, December 5

1. Issued Voucher No. 299 to Indiana Bell, for November telephone service, $125.

2. Received checks from customers on account as follows:
   Bradon Tennis Camp, $1,250, for merchandise sold to them on November 30.
   Venturi Pro Shop, $3,240, for merchandise sold to them on November 30.
   Pro Tennis & Golf, $2,456, for merchandise sold to them on November 30.

3. Cash sales for the day were $815 for Golf and $245 for Tennis.

4. Issued Credit Memorandum No. 7 to The Swing Shop, $125, as an allowance for defective golf bags.
   The golf equipment had been billed as a part of Sale No. 398. The allowance transaction was entered in the general journal illustrated on page 734,

after which the credit memorandum was posted immediately as a credit to the account of The Swing Shop in the accounts receivable subsidiary ledger.

Friday, December 6

1. Issued vouchers as follows:

    Voucher No. 300 to Beebok Inc., for tennis shoes, $2,800.

    Voucher No. 301 to Footbliss, $3,700; golf shoes, $2,450; tennis shoes, $1,250.

    Voucher No. 302 to Logan Golf Inc., for golf equipment, $8,250.

    Invoices for the previous week's purchases are received from suppliers on Friday and on the last day of the month for any other purchases through that date.

2. Made charge sales as follows:

    Pro Tennis & Golf, Lexington, Kentucky, golf clubs, $1,526; tennis rackets, $643; Sale No. 400.

    Wimbledon Tennis Club, Bloomington, Indiana, tennis rackets, $1,325; Sale No. 401.

    Crooked Tree Country Club, Indianapolis, golf equipment $2,489; tennis equipment $1,288; Sale No. 402.

3. Cash sales for the day were $1,800 for Golf and $1,250 for Tennis.

Saturday, December 7

1. Cash sales for the day were $2,420 for Golf and $1,560 for Tennis.

End-of-the-Week Work

(a) Footed the amount columns in the books of original entry and proved the footings.

(b) Proved the cash balance in the following manner:

Cash balance, December 1	$ 92,695*
Add receipts December 1-7 per cash receipts journal	26,648
Total	$119,343
Subtract checks issued December 1-7 per check register . .	8,430
Cash balance, December 7	$110,913

*From General Ledger Account No. 111 not shown in this illustration.

(c) Completed the individual posting from the books of original entry to the general ledger and operating expense ledger accounts. Accounts receivable subsidiary ledger accounts were posted directly from the sales invoices and remittance advices.

(Transactions from December 8 through December 14 were similar to those illustrated for December 1 through December 7 and are not illustrated here.)

Monday, December 16

1. Issued Voucher No. 313 to the First National Bank for the payment of the following taxes:

Employees' income tax (withheld during November)		$2,976
FICA tax imposed—		
on employees (withheld during November)	$1,594	
on the employer	1,594	3,188
Total		$6,164

2. Issued Voucher No. 314 to Payroll for the semimonthly wages, $11,918.06.

Mitchell & Jenkins follows the policy of paying employees on the 15th (or the next business day) and the last day of each month. The business is subject to the taxes imposed under the Federal Insurance Contributions Act (for old-age benefits and hospital insurance), and the Federal Unemployment Tax Act (for unemployment insurance purposes), and is required to make contributions to the state unemployment compensation fund. The company is also required to withhold a percentage of employees' wages both for FICA and for income tax purposes. In addition to the wages paid to employees, the partnership agreement provides that Mitchell and Jenkins are to receive salaries of $3,000 and $4,000 per month respectively. The salaries of the partners constitute an operating expense of the business and do not represent "wages" as defined in the social security and income tax laws; hence, their salaries are not subject to the FICA tax imposed upon employers and employees. Neither are such salaries subject to withholding for employees' income tax.

Each payday the accountant is supplied with a report prepared by the payroll clerk showing the total amount of wages and salaries earned during the pay period, the amount of payroll deductions, and the net amount of cash needed for payroll purposes. The report for December 16 appears below.

Payroll Statement
Period Beginning December 1 and Ending December 16

		Deductions		
Classification	Total Earnings	FICA Tax	Employees' Income Tax	Net Amount Payable
Store clerks wages	$ 3,676.00	$275.70	$ 441.12	$ 2,959.18
Truck drivers wages	3,769.00	282.68	527.66	2,958.66
Office salaries	3,185.00	238.88	445.90	2,500.22
Partners' salaries:				
R. Mitchell	1,500.00	none	none	1,500.00
J. Jenkins	2,000.00	none	none	2,000.00
	$14,130.00	$797.26	$1,414.68	$11,918.06

Employer's payroll taxes:
FICA tax, 7.5% of $10,630 .... $797.25
Unemployment compensation taxes:
State unemployment compensation tax (4.0% of $2,100) $84.00
FUTA tax (0.8% of $2,100) 16.80   100.80
                                                                   $898.05

A check made payable to Payroll is issued for the net amount payable and deposited in a special payroll bank account. Individual paychecks are then drawn on that account for the amount due to each employee. The accountant is instructed to deposit Mitchell's and Jenkins' salaries in their individual bank accounts and to furnish them with copies of the deposit tickets. The payroll voucher was entered in the voucher register by debiting the proper salary accounts for the earnings, by crediting the proper liability accounts for the taxes withheld, and by crediting the vouchers payable account for the amount of the check to be subsequently issued.

The payroll taxes imposed on the employer were entered in the general journal by debiting Operating Expenses in the Debit column, by debiting Payroll Taxes Expense in the Detail column, and by crediting the proper liability accounts for the taxes imposed.

3. Issued Check Nos. 715 and 716 in payment of Voucher Nos. 313 and 314.
4. Mitchell reported that interest coupons amounting to $400 from government notes were deposited in the First National Bank. This transaction was entered in the cash receipts journal.
5. Cash sales for the day were $1,520 for Golf and $740 for Tennis.
   (Transactions from December 17 through December 30 were similar to those illustrated for December 1 through December 7 and 16, and are not illustrated here.)

Tuesday, December 31

1. Voucher No. 331 was issued to Petty Cash to replenish the petty cash fund. The following report was submitted by the clerk responsible for the fund.

Statement of Petty Cash Payments for December

Acct. No.	Description	Amount
5409	Telephone Expense	$ 13.00
5422	Miscellaneous General Expense	66.00
5433	Advertising Expense	15.00
5441	Truck Gas & Oil Expense	20.00
5452	Miscellaneous Selling Expense	25.00
Total Disbursements		$139.00

2. Issued Check No. 741 in payment of Voucher No. 331.

End-of-the-Month Work

a. Footed the amount columns, proved the footings, entered the totals, and ruled each of the books of original entry.

b. Proved the cash balance in the following manner:

Cash balance, December 1	$ 92,695*
Total receipts for December per cash receipts journal	198,416
Total	$291,111
Less total checks issued during December per check register	192,418
Cash balance, December 31	$ 98,693

*From General Ledger Account No. 111 not shown in this illustration.

c. Completed the individual posting from the books of original entry to the general ledger and to the operating expense subsidiary ledger accounts.

d. Completed the summary posting from the totals of the special columns in each of the books of original entry to the general ledger accounts.

e. Prepared a trial balance and schedules of accounts receivable, vouchers payable, and operating expenses.

Step (5) would be completed as a part of the normal routine at the end of each month. However, since the end of December is also the end of the fiscal year for Mitchell & Jenkins, the procedure is varied slightly. The preparation of the general ledger trial balance and the schedule of operating expenses is combined with the preparation of the end-of-year work sheets used to assist in producing the income statement for the year and the balance sheet as of December 31. This process is described and illustrated in the following chapter. The schedule of accounts receivable, shown on page 778, verifies the balance reported for the accounts receivable control account. As discussed in Chapter 16, a schedule of vouchers payable (listing of unpaid vouchers) serves a similar purpose for the vouchers payable control account.

SALES JOURNAL FOR MONTH OF December   19-F   PAGE 28

	ACCOUNTS RECEIVABLE DR.	√	DAY	NAME	SALE NO.	SALES CR. GOLF	SALES CR. TENNIS	
1	4 3 0 0 00	√	4	The Tennis Racket	397		4 3 0 0 00	1
2	2 0 3 0 00	√	4	The Swing Shop	398	1 3 4 5 00	6 8 5 00	2
3	2 3 5 0 00	√	4	Fleetwood Country Club	399	1 8 2 5 00	5 2 5 00	3
4	2 1 6 9 00	√	6	Pro Tennis & Golf	400	1 5 2 6 00	6 4 3 00	4
5	1 3 2 5 00	√	6	Wimbledon Tennis Club	401		1 3 2 5 00	5
6	3 7 7 7 00	√	6	Crooked Tree Country Club	402	2 4 8 9 00	1 2 8 8 00	6
7	15 9 5 1 00					7 1 8 5 00	8 7 6 6 00	7
31	140 6 2 5 00					89 0 5 0 00	51 5 7 5 00	31
32	(1 3 1)					(4 1 1)	(4 2 1)	32
33								33
34								34
35								35
36								36

CASH RECEIPTS JOURNAL FOR MONTH OF December 19-F

PAGE 28

	DEBIT CASH	DAY	RECEIVED FROM—DESCRIPTION	✓	ACCOUNTS RECEIVABLE	✓	CREDIT SALES GOLF	TENNIS	ACCT. NO.	GENERAL LEDGER AMOUNT	✓	
1	2 075 00	2	Cash sales				1 425 00	6 50 00				1
2	1 880 00	3	Fleetwood Country Club	✓	1 880 00							2
3	4 90 00	3	Courtside	✓	4 90 00							3
4	9 45 00	3	Lakeside Country Club	✓	9 45 00							4
5	3 457 00	3	Cash sales				1 782 00	1 675 00				5
6	2 765 00	4	Cash sales				1 840 00	9 25 00				6
7	1 250 00	5	Bradon Tennis Camp	✓	1 250 00							7
8	3 240 00	5	Venturi Pro Shop	✓	3 240 00							8
9	2 456 00	5	Pro Tennis & Golf	✓	2 456 00							9
10	1 060 00	5	Cash sales				8 15 00	2 45 00				10
11	3 050 00	6	Cash sales				1 800 00	1 250 00				11
12	3 980 00	7	Cash sales				2 420 00	1 560 00				12
13	26 648 00				10 2 61 00		10 0 82 00	6 3 05 00				13
19	4 0 0 00	16	Interest on Gov. Notes						431	4 0 0 00	✓	19
20	2 2 60 00	16	Cash sales				1 5 20 00	7 40 00				20
27	198 4 1 6 00				146 2 5 8 00		35 8 7 4 00	15 8 8 4 00		4 0 0 00		27
28	(1 1 1)				(1 3 1)		(4 1 1)	(4 2 1)		(√)		28

VOUCHER REGISTER FOR MONTH OF November   19-F   PAGE 25

	DAY	VOU. NO.	TO WHOM ISSUED	PURCHASES DR. GOLF	PURCHASES DR. TENNIS	OP. EXP. DR. ACCT. NO.	OP. EXP. DR. AMOUNT	✓	SUNDRY ACCTS. DR. ACCT. NO.	SUNDRY ACCTS. DR. AMOUNT	✓	SUNDRY ACCTS. CR. ACCT. NO.	SUNDRY ACCTS. CR. AMOUNT	✓	VOUCHERS PAYABLE CR.	DISPO-SITION DATE	CK. NO.	
14	27	271	Peter's Office Supply						152	425 00					425 00	11/2	701	14
15	30	294	Sportime Corp.	1 425 00	860 00										2 285 00	11/4	703	15
16	30	295	Golf World	2 420 00											2 420 00	11/4	704	16

VOUCHER REGISTER FOR MONTH OF December   19-F   PAGE 26

	DAY	VOU. NO.	TO WHOM ISSUED	PURCHASES DR. GOLF	PURCHASES DR. TENNIS	OP. EXP. DR. ACCT. NO.	OP. EXP. DR. AMOUNT	✓	SUNDRY ACCTS. DR. ACCT. NO.	SUNDRY ACCTS. DR. AMOUNT	✓	SUNDRY ACCTS. CR. ACCT. NO.	SUNDRY ACCTS. CR. AMOUNT	✓	VOUCHERS PAYABLE CR.	DISPO-SITION DATE	CK. NO.	
1	2	296	Capital Leasing Co.			5443	2 200 00	✓							3 300 00	12/2	702	1
2						5406	1 100 00	✓										2
3	3	297	Public Service Power &			5408	1 500 00	✓							1 500 00	12/7	705	3
4			Light															4
5	4	298	Indianapolis Star			5433	495 00	✓							495 00	12/7	706	5
6	5	299	Indiana Bell			5409	125 00	✓							125 00	12/7	707	6
7	6	300	Beebok Inc.		2 800 00										2 800 00	12/9	708	7
8	6	301	Footbliss	2 450 00	1 250 00										3 700 00	12/9	709	8
9	6	302	Logan Golf Inc.	8 250 00											8 250 00	12/9	710	9
10				10 700 00	4 050 00		5 420 00								20 170 00			10

Line						Acct.							Acct.			Acct.	
18	6 1 6 4 00	12/16 715					*First National Bank*				3 1 8 8 00	√	211				5431	3 6 7 6 00 √
19		12/16 716								√	2 9 7 6 00		214				5432	3 7 6 9 00 √
20	11 9 1 8 06	12/16 716	7 9 7 26 √	211		*Payroll*	313	16	314						5401	3 1 8 5 00 √
21			1 4 1 4 68 √	214				16							5402	1 5 0 0 00 √
22															5434	2 0 0 0 00 √
23																
24																
39	1 3 9 00	12/31 741				*Petty Cash*	331	31							5409	1 3 00 √
40															5422	6 6 00 √
41															5433	1 5 00 √
42															5441	2 0 00 √
43															5452	2 5 00 √
48	159 7 7 9 00 159 7 7 9 00 (2 1 8)		2 6 0 0 00 2 6 0 0 00 (√)							6 2 8 0 00 6 2 8 0 00 (√)			45 2 1 0 00 45 2 1 0 00 (5 4 1)			45 1 0 0 00 45 1 0 0 00 (5 2 1)	65 7 8 9 00 65 7 8 9 00 (5 1 1)

CHECK REGISTER FOR MONTH OF *December*   19-F   PAGE 26

	VOUCHERS PAYABLE DR.					CASH CR.	
	NO.	AMOUNT	DAY	DRAWN TO THE ORDER OF	CHK. NO.	AMOUNT	
1	271	425 00	2	Peter's Office Supply	701	425 00	1
2	296	3 300 00	2	Capital Leasing Co.	702	3 300 00	2
3	294	2 285 00	4	Sportime Corp.	703	2 285 00	3
4	295	2 420 00	4	Golf World	704	2 420 00	4
5		8 430 00				8 430 00	5
19	313	6 164 00	16	First National Bank	715	6 164 00	19
20	314	11 918 06	16	Payroll	716	11 918 06	20
28	331	139 00	31	Petty Cash	741	139 00	28
32		192 418 00 192 418 00				192 418 00 192 418 00	32
33		(218)				(111)	33

JOURNAL

	DATE	DESCRIPTION	ACCT. NO.	DETAIL	√	DEBIT	√	CREDIT	√	
1	19-F Dec. 5	Sales Returns & Allowances—Golf	411.1			125 00	√			1
2		Accounts Receivable—The Swing Shop	131					125 00	√	2
3		Credit Memo No. 7.								3
17	16	Operating Expenses	540			898 05	√			17
18		Payroll Tax Expense	5407	898 05	√					18
19		FICA Tax Payable	211					797 25	√	19
20		FUTA Tax Payable	212					16 80	√	20
21		State Unemployment Tax Payable	213					84 00	√	21
22		Payroll taxes—December 16 payroll.								22
32				2 578 00		2 874 00		2 874 00		32
33				(√)		(√)		(√)		33

Building Your Accounting Knowledge

1. What are the differences in the owners' equity accounts that are kept in a single proprietorship, a partnership, and a corporation?
2. Name five separate books of original entry and indicate the type of business transaction normally entered in each.
3. Give four advantages of a functional division of the accounting activity.
4. What kinds of equipment often are used to aid the accounting work in the modern office of a big business enterprise?

5. What special information requirement has led to the organization of specialized accounting departments in large firms?
6. Describe the function of each of the five books of original entry kept by Mitchell & Jenkins.
7. Describe the function of each of the two subsidiary ledgers kept by Mitchell & Jenkins.
8. What are the two major auxiliary records that Mitchell & Jenkins maintain? Name two other auxiliary records that are kept in files by Mitchell & Jenkins.

Assignment Box

To reinforce your understanding of the preceding text materials, you may complete the following:
>   Study Guide: Part A
>   Textbook: Exercises 19A1 through 19A6 or 19B1 through 19B6
>   Problem 19A1 or 19B1

Summary and Supplementary Year-End Work Sheets

One reason for maintaining an accounting information system is to make it possible to prepare periodic financial reports, including an income statement and a statement of owners' equity for the fiscal year and balance sheet as of the close of that year. An efficient way to produce these financial statements is (1) to use the information provided by the accounts—as reflected by the year-end trial balance taken after the regular posting has been completed, (2) to determine the needed adjustments, and (3) to bring these amounts together in a manner that facilitates statement preparation. The device most commonly used for these purposes is the summary year-end work sheet.

A simple eight-column work sheet for a personal service enterprise was discussed and illustrated in Chapter 5. A ten-column work sheet for a retail merchandising business was introduced in Chapter 9. Following is a discussion and illustration of Mitchell & Jenkins's ten-column summary work sheet supplemented by a three-column operating expenses work sheet. Earlier in this chapter, a partial narrative of transactions for this firm for the month of December, 19-F (the last month of the fiscal year) was given. These transactions were entered in the books of original entry. The books of original entry were reproduced as they would appear after both the individual and the summary posting had been completed. The general ledger accounts and the accounts in each of the two subsidiary ledgers (accounts receivable and operating expenses) were not reproduced. However, it may be assumed that trial balances of these ledgers were taken. The general ledger was found to be in balance and the total of the account balances in each subsidiary ledger was found to agree with the balance of the related control account in the general ledger.

Summary Year-End Work Sheet

Prepare a ten-column, end-of-year summary work sheet supplemented by a three-column, end-of-year operating expenses work sheet.

The Mitchell & Jenkins work sheet is shown on pages 738 and 739. It is identical to that used for Northern Micro on pages 364-365. The first step in its preparation was to place the proper heading at the top, to insert the proper heading in the space provided at the top of each of the five pairs of amount columns, and to list the general ledger account titles and numbers in the spaces provided at the left. Note that with one exception the title and number of each general ledger account was listed (refer to the chart of accounts given on page 723 for the complete list) even though some of the accounts had no balances at the time the trial balance was taken. The one exception is Expense and Revenue Summary, Account No. 331. This account is used in the formal process of closing the books but is not needed on the work sheet. Expense and Revenue Summary was included in the Northern Micro work sheet on page 364 because the account was used to adjust the beginning and ending inventories. These inventory adjustments in the Mitchell & Jenkins work sheet are made using two cost of goods sold accounts that Northern Micro did not maintain. Note also that for Cost of Goods Sold—Golf and Cost of Goods Sold—Tennis two lines were allowed in each case to accommodate the several debits and credits that will be involved. The purpose of the cost of goods sold account is to provide a means of bringing together all the elements that are involved in calculating the amount of this cost: (1) beginning inventory, (2) purchases, (3) purchases returns and allowances, and (4) ending inventory. The account balances were entered in the first pair of columns (trial balance) and these columns were totaled to prove their equality.

Use end-of-year departmental summary accounts for cost of goods sold.

Adjustment of the Merchandise Accounts. Eight entries (a-h), were made in the Adjustments columns of the work sheet to show the calculation of the cost of goods sold for each department and to adjust the merchandise inventory accounts.

Entry (a): The amount of the beginning golf inventory, $221,960, was transferred to Cost of Goods Sold—Golf by a debit to that account and a credit to Merchandise Inventory—Golf.

Entry (b): The amount of the beginning tennis inventory, $95,600, was transferred to Cost of Goods Sold—Tennis by a debit to that account and a credit to Merchandise Inventory—Tennis.

Entry (c): The amount of the purchases of golf equipment for the year, $825,476, was transferred to Cost of Goods Sold—Golf by a debit to that account and a credit to Purchases—Golf.

Entry (d): The amount of the purchases of tennis equipment for the year, $540,025, was transferred to Cost of Goods Sold—Tennis by a debit to that account and a credit to Purchases—Tennis.

Entry (e): The amount of the purchases returns and allowances associated with the sale of golf equipment for the year, $10,894, was transferred to the proper cost of goods sold account by a debit to Purchases Returns and Allowances—Golf, and a credit to Cost of Goods Sold—Golf.

Entry (f): The amount of the purchases returns and allowances associated with the sale of tennis equipment for the year, $8,445, was transferred to the proper cost of goods sold account by a debit to Purchases Returns and Allowances—Tennis, and a credit to Cost of Goods Sold—Tennis.

Entry (g): The cost assigned to the December 31 golf merchandise inventory, $276,411, was debited to that account with an offsetting credit to Cost of Goods Sold—Golf. Mitchell & Jenkins uses the periodic method of accounting for inventory. A physical count of the goods on hand at the year's end had been made. Unit costs for the various items were determined from recent purchase invoices. Each time a physical inventory is taken, the quantities found to be on hand are recorded on detailed physical inventory summary sheets, showing the quantity, unit price, and extension for each type of golfing equipment, as well as the total extensions.

Entry (h): The cost assigned to the December 31 tennis merchandise inventory, $101,528, was debited to that account with an offsetting credit to Cost of Goods Sold—Tennis. The procedure followed in determining the tennis inventory was the same as that described above for golf.

The amount of the cost of goods sold for each department was determined by subtracting the sum of the two credits from the sum of the two debits to each of the cost of goods sold accounts. The amounts, $760,131 for golf and $525,652 for tennis, were extended to the Adjusted Trial Balance Debit column.

Adjustment of the Interest Accounts. On December 31, Mitchell & Jenkins owned $10,000 face value, 12% United States government notes. Interest had been collected on December 16. Since that date, interest of $50 had accrued. In order to have the calculation of the net income for the year reflect the correct amount of interest earned, this type of accrual had to be taken into consideration.

Entry (i): The interest receivable on December 31, $50, was entered on the work sheet by debiting Accrued Interest Receivable and crediting Interest Revenue.

Mitchell & Jenkins
Work
For the Year

#	ACCOUNT TITLE	ACCT. NO.	TRIAL BALANCE DEBIT	TRIAL BALANCE CREDIT	ADJUSTMENTS DEBIT	ADJUSTMENTS CREDIT
1	Cash	111	9 8 6 9 3 00			
2	Petty Cash Fund	112	2 0 0 00			
3	Government Notes	121	1 0 0 0 0 00			
4	Accrued Int. Receivable	122			(i) 5 0 00	
5	Accounts Receivable	131	25 0 0 0 0 00			
6	Allow. for Doubtful Accts.	131.1		7 5 0 00		(q)1 8 7 5 0 00
7	Mdse. Inventory—Golf	141	22 1 9 6 0 00		(g)27 6 4 1 1 00	(a)22 1 9 6 0 00
8	Mdse. Inventory—Tennis	142	9 5 6 0 0 00		(h)10 1 5 2 8 00	(b)9 5 6 0 0 00
9	Store Supplies	151	1 9 7 2 5 00			(n)1 7 9 0 0 00
10	Office Supplies	152	2 0 2 0 0 00			(o)1 8 7 0 0 00
11	Prepaid Insurance	155	4 4 4 5 0 00			(p)3 2 7 0 0 00
12	Store Equipment	181	24 0 0 0 0 00			
13	Accum. Depr.—Store Equip.	181.1		7 0 0 0 0 00		(k)2 0 0 0 0 00
14	Delivery Equipment	185	22 5 0 0 0 00			
15	Accum. Depr.—Delivery Equip.	185.1		4 0 0 0 0 00		(l)2 2 5 0 0 00
16	Office Equipment	191	19 0 0 0 0 00			
17	Accum. Depr.—Office Equip.	191.1		3 0 5 0 0 00		(m)9 5 0 0 00
18	FICA Tax Payable	211		1 6 2 8 00		
19	FUTA Tax Payable	212		3 5 00		
20	State Unemp. Tax Payable	213		1 6 5 00		
21	Employees Income Tax Payable	214		3 1 2 0 00		
22	Notes Payable	216		5 0 4 0 0 00		
23	Accrued Interest Payable	217				(j) 4 2 0 00
24	Vouchers Payable	218		16 2 5 7 5 00		
25	Robert Mitchell, Capital	311		44 6 6 6 3 00		
26	Robert Mitchell, Drawing	312	2 0 0 0 0 00			
27	Jessica Jenkins, Capital	321		37 1 6 4 8 00		
28	Jessica Jenkins, Drawing	322	1 8 0 0 0 00			
29	Sales—Golf	411		142 4 8 0 0 00		
30	Sales Ret. & Allow.—Golf	411.1	4 2 7 4 4 00			
31	Sales—Tennis	421		82 5 2 0 0 00		
32	Sales Ret. & Allow.—Tennis	421.1	1 6 5 0 4 00			
33	Purchases—Golf	511	82 5 4 7 6 00			(c)82 5 4 7 6 00
34	Purchases Ret. & Allow.—Golf	511.1		1 0 8 9 4 00	(e)1 0 8 9 4 00	
35	Purchases—Tennis	521	54 0 0 2 5 00			(d)54 0 0 2 5 00
36	Purchases Ret. & Allow.—Tennis	521.1		8 4 4 5 00	(f)8 4 4 5 00	
37	Cost of Goods Sold—Golf	531			(a)22 1 9 6 0 00	(e)1 0 8 9 4 00
38					(c)82 5 4 7 6 00	(g)27 6 4 1 1 00
39	Cost of Goods Sold—Tennis	532			(b)9 5 6 0 0 00	(f)8 4 4 5 00
40					(d)54 0 0 2 5 00	(h)10 1 5 2 8 00
41	Operating Expenses	540	56 3 7 7 1 00		(k-q)14 0 0 5 0 00	
42	Interest Revenue	431		8 2 5 00		(i) 5 0 00
43	Interest Expense	581	3 8 0 0 00		(j) 4 2 0 00	
44			344 6 8 9 8 00	344 6 8 9 8 00	222 0 8 5 9 00	222 0 8 5 9 00
45	Net Income					
46						

Sporting Goods

Sheet

Ended December 31, 19-F

	ADJUSTED TRIAL BALANCE		INCOME STATEMENT		BALANCE SHEET		
	DEBIT	CREDIT	DEBIT	CREDIT	DEBIT	CREDIT	
	98 693 00				98 693 00		1
	200 00				200 00		2
	10 000 00				10 000 00		3
	50 00				50 00		4
	25 000 00				25 000 00		5
		18 000 00				18 000 00	6
	276 411 00				276 411 00		7
	101 528 00				101 528 00		8
	1 825 00				1 825 00		9
	1 500 00				1 500 00		10
	11 750 00				11 750 00		11
	24 000 00				24 000 00		12
		9 000 00				9 000 00	13
	225 000 00				225 000 00		14
		62 500 00				62 500 00	15
	190 000 00				190 000 00		16
		40 000 00				40 000 00	17
		1 628 00				1 628 00	18
		35 00				35 00	19
		165 00				165 00	20
		3 120 00				3 120 00	21
		50 400 00				50 400 00	22
		420 00				420 00	23
		162 575 00				162 575 00	24
		446 663 00				446 663 00	25
	20 000 00				20 000 00		26
		371 648 00				371 648 00	27
	18 000 00				18 000 00		28
		1 424 800 00		1 424 800 00			29
	42 744 00		42 744 00				30
		825 200 00		825 200 00			31
	16 504 00		16 504 00				32
							33
							34
							35
							36
	760 131 00		760 131 00				37
							38
	525 652 00		525 652 00				39
							40
	703 821 00		703 821 00				41
		875 00		875 00			42
	4 220 00		4 220 00				43
	3 498 029 00	3 498 029 00	2 053 072 00	2 250 875 00	1 444 957 00	1 247 154 00	44
			197 803 00			197 803 00	45
			2 250 875 00	2 250 875 00	1 444 957 00	1 444 957 00	46

Mitchell & Jenkins periodically issues short-term notes payable. Interest paid on these notes through November 30 amounted to $3,800. Since that date $420 of interest had accrued on these notes, but had not yet been paid or entered in the accounting records. In order to have the calculation of the net income for the year reflect the correct amount of interest incurred, this type of accrual had to be taken into consideration.

Entry (j): The accrued interest payable on December 31, $420, was entered on the work sheet by debiting Interest Expense and crediting Accrued Interest Payable.

At this point, work on the summary end-of-year work sheet was suspended temporarily until certain information needed from the supplementary work sheet for operating expenses was determined.

Supplementary Work Sheet for Operating Expenses

Prepare adjustments affecting both the operating expenses work sheet and the summary work sheet.

To provide the desired information, the income statement had to be supplemented by a schedule of operating expenses. The accounting system of Mitchell & Jenkins includes a subsidiary operating expenses ledger which is controlled by the account Operating Expenses (No. 540) in the general ledger. Many of the operating expense accounts required end-of-year debit adjustments. As illustrated in the following paragraphs, the adjustments involved debits to the individual operating expense accounts, a summary debit to the general ledger control account and offsetting credits to various general ledger accounts.

To assemble all the information needed both for the income statement and for the supporting schedule of operating expenses, and to facilitate entering the adjustments in the general ledger and subsidiary ledger accounts (which must be done later), a supplementary operating expenses work sheet was used. As will be seen, it is very closely tied in with the summary work sheet. The Mitchell & Jenkins operating expenses work sheet is reproduced on page 741. An appropriate heading was used that included the period involved. The titles and numbers of all the accounts in the subsidiary operating expenses ledger were placed in the columns provided at the left. (Refer to the chart of accounts given on page 724 for the complete list.) Only three amount columns were needed: (1) to show the account balances when the trial balance was taken, (2) to provide space for certain adjustments, and (3) to show the adjusted amounts. In every case only debits were involved. Observe that many of the accounts had no balance when the trial balance was taken. After the balance of each account was entered in the Trial Balance Debit column, that column was totaled. If the total, $563,771, did not agree with the balance shown on the summary work sheet for Operating Expenses, (the control account), it would have been necessary to discover and correct the discrepancy before the preparation of either work sheet could proceed.

All the adjustments that follow (for depreciation, supplies used, insurance expired, and the doubtful accounts provision) involve both the sum-

Mitchell & Jenkins Sporting Goods

Supplementary Operating Expenses Work Sheet

For the Year Ended December 31, 19-F

ACCOUNT	ACCT. NO.	TRIAL BALANCE DEBIT	ADJUSTMENTS DEBIT	ADJ. TRIAL BALANCE DEBIT
Office Salaries Expense	5401	76 4 5 0 00		76 4 5 0 00
Robert Mitchell, Salary Expense	5402	36 0 0 0 00		36 0 0 0 00
Office Supplies Expense	5403		(o)18 7 0 0 00	18 7 0 0 00
Depreciation Expense—Office Equipment	5404		(m)9 5 0 0 00	9 5 0 0 00
Insurance Expense—Office Equipment	5405		(p)12 0 0 0 00	12 0 0 0 00
Office Rent Expense	5406	13 2 0 0 00		13 2 0 0 00
Payroll Taxes Expense	5407	20 9 2 0 00		20 9 2 0 00
Heat, Light, and Water Expense	5408	21 8 0 0 00		21 8 0 0 00
Telephone Expense	5409	1 4 5 2 00		1 4 5 2 00
Postage Expense	5416	8 4 7 00		8 4 7 00
Uncollectible Accounts Expense	5417		(q)18 7 5 0 00	18 7 5 0 00
Miscellaneous General Expense	5422	8 4 5 0 00		8 4 5 0 00
Store Clerks Salary Expense	5431	88 2 4 5 00		88 2 4 5 00
Truck Drivers Wage Expense	5432	90 4 7 8 00		90 4 7 8 00
Advertising Expense	5433	83 2 3 0 00		83 2 3 0 00
Jessica Jenkins, Salary Expense	5434	48 0 0 0 00		48 0 0 0 00
Depreciation Expense—Delivery Equipment	5435		(l)22 5 0 0 00	22 5 0 0 00
Insurance Expense—Delivery Equipment	5436		(p)9 2 0 0 00	9 2 0 0 00
Depreciation Expense—Store Equipment	5437		(k)20 0 0 0 00	20 0 0 0 00
Insurance Expense—Store Equipment	5438		(p)11 5 0 0 00	11 5 0 0 00
Truck Gas and Oil Expense	5441	34 8 7 6 00		34 8 7 6 00
Truck Repairs and Maintenance Expense	5442	5 2 8 5 00		5 2 8 5 00
Store Rent Expense	5443	26 4 0 0 00		26 4 0 0 00
Store Supplies Expense	5444		(n)17 9 0 0 00	17 9 0 0 00
Miscellaneous Selling Expense	5452	8 1 3 8 00		8 1 3 8 00
		563 7 7 1 00	140 0 5 0 00	703 8 2 1 00

mary work sheet and the supplementary work sheet. One or more operating expense accounts were debited on the operating expenses work sheet, and one or more general ledger accounts were credited on the summary work sheet.

▪ Depreciation Expense. In the general ledger of Mitchell & Jenkins, there are three long-term asset accounts with related accumulated depreciation accounts: Store Equipment, Delivery Equipment, and Office Equipment. In the operating expenses ledger, there are three depreciation expense accounts that correspond to the asset classifications. The firm's policy is that no depreciation is taken on assets owned for less than six months. The schedule shown below was prepared to determine the estimated depreciation expense for the year.

Schedule of Depreciation Expense
For the Year Ended December 31, 19-F

Asset	Cost	Annual (Straight-Line) Rate of Depreciation	Depreciation For the Year
Store Equipment	$200,000*	10%	$20,000
Delivery Equipment	225,000	10	22,500
Office Equipment	190,000	5	9,500

*Note that the balance of the store equipment account shown on the work sheet on page 738 is $240,000. That is because the cost of new store equipment ($40,000) purchased on December 18 is included. Since these assets have been owned for less than six months, no depreciation is taken on them.

Based on the calculations shown on the schedule, the following adjustments were made. The debits were entered on the operating expenses work sheet and the credits on the summary work sheet.

Entry (k): Depreciation Expense—Store Equipment was debited and Accumulated Depreciation—Store Equipment was credited for $20,000.

Entry (l): Depreciation Expense—Delivery Equipment was debited and Accumulated Depreciation—Delivery Equipment was credited for $22,500.

Entry (m): Depreciation Expense—Office Equipment was debited and Accumulated Depreciation—Office Equipment was credited for $9,500.

■ **Supplies Expense.** The general ledger of Mitchell & Jenkins includes two asset accounts for supplies—Store Supplies and Office Supplies. When purchased, the supplies are entered as assets by debiting these accounts. An inventory of unused supplies is taken at the end of the year so that the cost of the supplies used can be calculated and charged to the proper operating expense accounts. The following schedule was prepared to determine the needed adjustments. The amount shown for each type of supplies was determined by a count of the unopened packages and boxes, which were assigned approximate costs of recent purchases.

Schedule of Supplies Used
For the Year Ended December 31, 19-F

Asset	Account Balance December 31, 19-F	Amount on Hand December 31, 19-F	Expense For Year
Store Supplies	$19,725	$1,825	$17,900
Office Supplies	20,200	1,500	18,700

Based upon the calculations, the following adjustments were made on the work sheets:

Entry (n): Store Supplies Expense was debited and Store Supplies was credited for $17,900.

Entry (o): Office Supplies Expense was debited and Office Supplies was credited for $18,700.

Insurance Expense. Prepaid insurance premiums are entered by Mitchell & Jenkins in the same manner as supplies. At the time of payment of a premium, the amount paid is entered as an asset by debiting Prepaid Insurance. At the end of the year, calculations are made to determine the fraction of the total term of each policy that has elapsed during the year. Each amount, thus determined, is classified according to the type of asset insured and is charged to the proper insurance expense account. The operating expenses subsidiary ledger of Mitchell & Jenkins includes insurance expense accounts for the insurance on delivery equipment, store equipment, and office equipment.

The following schedule of insurance expense was prepared from a file of information relating to insurance policies.

Schedule of Insurance Expense
For the Year Ended December 31, 19-F

Type of Property Insured	Expense for Year
Delivery Equipment	$ 9,200
Store Equipment	11,500
Office Equipment	12,000
Total	$32,700

Based upon this schedule, the following adjustment was made on the work sheets:

Entry (p): Insurance Expense—Delivery Equipment was debited for $9,200; Insurance Expense—Store Equipment was debited for $11,500; Insurance Expense—Office Equipment was debited for $12,000; and Prepaid Insurance was credited for $32,700.

Doubtful Accounts. Mitchell & Jenkins uses the allowance method of accounting for doubtful accounts. On the basis of "aging" the accounts receivable, it was estimated that $18,000 of such accounts will not be collected. Since there already is a $750 debit balance in Allowance for Doubtful Accounts, an adjustment for $18,750 is required. The following entry was made on the work sheets:

Entry (q): Uncollectible Accounts Expense was debited and Allowance for Doubtful Accounts was credited for $18,750.

Completing The Operating Expenses Work Sheet

In order to complete this work sheet, the amount for each operating expense account was extended into the Adjusted Trial Balance column. Note that in every case, the extended amount was either the unadjusted amount or the amount of the adjustment. The Adjustments and Adjusted Trial Balance columns were then totaled. Since only debits were involved in this work sheet, the total of the Adjusted Trial Balance column, $703,821, had to be equal to the sum of the totals of the Trial Balance and Adjustments columns ($563,771 + $140,050). A double rule was placed below the three totals.

Completing The Summary Work Sheet

To complete the adjustments on the summary work sheet, the balance of the control account, Operating Expenses, had to be increased to reflect the total of all of the debits to the operating expenses that had been made on the supplementary work sheet. Accordingly, that total, $140,050, was entered on the line for Operating Expenses in the Adjustments Debit column. Note that the debit was identified as "(k-q)," since it was offset by credits to seven general ledger accounts made when adjustments (k) through (q) were entered on the supplementary work sheet to adjust the individual operating expense accounts.

The Adjustments columns were totaled to prove the equality of the debits and credits. The amounts in the Trial Balance columns, adjusted where indicated by amounts in the Adjustments columns, were extended to the Adjusted Trial Balance columns. The latter also were totaled to prove the equality of the debits and credits. Each amount in the Adjusted Trial Balance columns was extended to the proper Income Statement or Balance Sheet column. The last four columns were then totaled.

Note that the Income Statement Credit column exceeded the Debit column by $197,803, and that the Balance Sheet Debit column exceeded the Credit column by the same amount. This means that Mitchell & Jenkins had a profitable year. "Net Income" was written on the next line at the left, and the amount, $197,803, was placed in the Income Statement debit column and Balance Sheet credit column. The Income Statement and Balance Sheet columns were then totaled to prove that each pair was in balance. Double rules were placed below the final totals in all ten columns.

The summary work sheet then can be used to prepare the income statement for the fiscal year (shown on page 772) and the balance sheet as of the last day of that year (shown on page 777). The supplementary work sheet provided the information for the schedule of operating expenses (shown on page 773).

Building Your Accounting Knowledge

1. What three functions does a work sheet perform in the production of year-end (or other period-end) financial reports?
2. What was the first step in the preparation of the Mitchell & Jenkins summary work sheet?
3. Why was the expense and revenue summary account omitted from the Mitchell & Jenkins work sheet when it was included in the Northern Micro work sheet?
4. What is the purpose of each of the cost of goods sold accounts maintained by Mitchell & Jenkins?
5. How many entries were made in the adjustments columns of the Mitchell & Jenkins summary work sheet to show the calculation of the cost of goods sold for each department and to adjust the departmental merchandise inventory accounts? Briefly explain the purpose of each of these adjustments.
6. What was the purpose of the interest adjustments made on the summary work sheet?
7. What is the purpose of the supplementary work sheet for operating expenses? How many columns does it have and what is the purpose of each column?
8. How many entries were made both in the adjustments columns of the Mitchell & Jenkins summary work sheet and in the adjustments column of the supplementary operating expenses work sheet? Briefly explain the purpose of each of these adjustments.

▨▨ Assignment Box

To reinforce your understanding of the preceding text materials, you may complete the following:
Study Guide: Part B
Textbook: Exercises 19A7 through 19A12 or 19B7 through 19B12
Problem 19A2 or 19B2

Expanding Your Business Vocabulary

What is the meaning of each of the following terms:

cash receipts journal (p. 720)
Detail column (p. 722)
operating expense subsidiary ledger
  (p. 724)

sales journal (p. 719)
summary year-end work sheet (p. 735)
supplementary operating expense work
  sheet (p. 740)

Demonstration Problem

Brad Rossa and Deborah Hackett are partners who conduct a whole-sale-retail furniture and appliance business. Furniture and appliances are purchased on account from various manufacturers. Some sales are made on account to retail outlets, but a substantial amount of cash sales are made to retail customers from Rossa & Hackett's own store. Given below is the trial balance of Rossa & Hackett as of December 31, 19--, and a schedule of operating expense accounts and balances as of the same date.

Required:

1. Prepare a summary year-end work sheet for Rossa & Hackett for the year ended December 31, 19--.
2. Prepare a supplementary work sheet for operating expenses for Rossa & Hackett for the year ended December 31, 19--.
   Use the following adjustment data:
   - **(a)** Transfer beginning Inventory—Furniture to Cost of Goods Sold—Furniture.
   - **(b)** Transfer beginning Inventory—Appliances to Cost of Goods Sold—Appliances.
   - **(c)** Transfer balance of Purchases—Furniture to Cost of Goods Sold—Furniture.
   - **(d)** Transfer balance of Purchases—Appliances to Cost of Goods Sold—Appliances.
   - **(e)** Transfer balance of Purchases Returns and Allowances—Furniture to Cost of Goods Sold—Furniture.
   - **(f)** Transfer balance of Purchases Returns and Allowances—Appliances to Cost of Goods Sold—Appliances.
   - **(g)** Enter December 31 furniture inventory, $33,300.
   - **(h)** Enter December 31 appliance inventory, $33,134.
   - **(i)** Enter accrued interest receivable on December 31, $100.
   - **(j)** Enter accrued interest payable on December 31, $180.
   - **(k)** Enter depreciation of store equipment at 10% of cost, $3,448.
   - **(l)** Enter depreciation of delivery equipment at 25% of cost, $33,800.
   - **(m)** Enter depreciation of office equipment at 10% of cost, $4,226.
   - **(n)** Enter store supplies expense on December 31, $15,640.
   - **(o)** Enter office supplies expense on December 31, $14,674.
   - **(p)** Enter insurance expense on December 31 for the following:
        Delivery equipment, $4,560
        Store equipment,   2,300
        Office equipment,   2,440
   - **(q)** Enter uncollectible accounts expense, $480.
3. Complete the ten-column year-end work sheet and determine net income. Insert the net income amount in the appropriate amount columns.

Rossa & Hackett
Trial Balance
December 31, 19--

Account	Acct. No.	Dr. Balance	Cr. Balance
Cash	111	104,980.00	. . .
Petty Cash Fund....................	112	400.00	. . .
Government Notes	121	20,000.00	. . .
Accrued Interest Receivable	122	. . .	. . .
Accounts Receivable	131	6,902.00	. . .
Allowance for Doubtful Accounts	131.1	. . .	144.00
Merchandise Inventory—Furniture	141	33,360.00	. . .
Merchandise Inventory—Appliances	142	33,000.00	. . .
Store Supplies	151	19,020.00	. . .
Office Supplies	152	16,740.00	. . .
Prepaid Insurance...................	155	11,720.00	. . .
Store Equipment	181	34,480.00	. . .
Accum. Depr.—Store Equip.	181.1	. . .	2,660.00
Delivery Equipment	185	135,200.00	. . .
Accum. Depr.—Delivery Equip........	185.1	. . .	99,876.00
Office Equipment	191	42,260.00	. . .
Accum. Depr.—Office Equip..........	191.1	. . .	6,526.00
FICA Tax Payable...................	211	. . .	2,304.00
FUTA Tax Payable	212	. . .	82.40
State Unemployment Tax Payable	213	. . .	431.20
Employees Income Tax Payable	214	. . .	2,000.00
Notes Payable	216	. . .	8,000.00
Accrued Interest Payable..............	217	. . .	. . .
Vouchers Payable	218	. . .	72,088.00
Brad Rossa, Capital	311	. . .	118,444.00
Brad Rossa, Drawing.................	312	21,500.00	. . .
Deborah Hackett, Capital	321	. . .	68,652.00
Deborah Hackett, Drawing............	322	16,600.00	. . .
Sales—Furniture	411	. . .	1,554,250.00
Sales Returns & Allow.—Furniture	411.1	798.00	. . .
Sales—Appliances...................	421	. . .	1,313,698.00
Sales Returns & Allow.—Appliances ...	421.1	718.00	. . .
Interest Revenue....................	431	. . .	1,200.00
Purchases—Furniture	511	1,333,144.00	. . .
Purchases Returns & Allow.—Furniture	511.1	. . .	1,734.00
Purchases—Appliances	521	994,480.00	. . .
Purchases Ret. & Allow.—Appliances ..	521.1	. . .	980.00
Cost of Goods Sold—Furniture	531	. . .	. . .
Cost of Goods Sold—Appliances	532	. . .	. . .
Operating Expenses	540	427,767.60	. . .
Interest Expense	581	. . .	. . .
		3,253,069.60	3,253,069.60

Rossa & Hackett
Schedule of Operating Expense Account Balances
December 31, 19--

Account	Acct. No.	Trial Balance Dr.
Office Salaries Expense	5401	$88,176.00
Brad Rossa, Salary Expense	5402	57,600.00
Office Supplies Expense	5403	
Depreciation Expense—Office Equipment	5404	
Insurance Expense—Office Equipment	5405	
Office Rent Expense	5406	24,000.00
Payroll Taxes Expense	5407	18,765.60
Heat, Light, & Water Expense	5408	11,022.00
Telephone Expense	5409	2,624.00
Postage Expense	5416	1,390.00
Uncollectible Accounts Expense	5417	
Miscellaneous General Expense	5422	1,962.00
Store Clerks Salary Expense	5431	51,764.00
Truck Drivers Wage Expense	5432	55,920.00
Advertising Expense	5433	5,104.00
Deborah Hackett, Salary Expense	5434	57,600.00
Depreciation Expense—Delivery Equipment	5435	
Insurance Expense—Delivery Equipment	5436	
Depreciation Expense—Store Equipment	5437	
Insurance Expense—Store Equipment	5438	
Truck Gas and Oil Expense	5441	13,198.00
Truck Repairs and Maintenance Expense	5442	1,874.00
Store Rent Expense	5443	36,000.00
Store Supplies Expense	5444	
Miscellaneous Selling Expense	5452	768.00
		$427,767.60

Solution

The solution to the Demonstration Problem can be found on pages 749 and 750.

Rossa & Hackett
Work Sheet
For the Year Ended December 31, 19--

Account Title	Acct. No.	Trial Balance Debit	Trial Balance Credit	Adjustments Debit	Adjustments Credit	Adjusted Trial Balance Debit	Adjusted Trial Balance Credit	Income Statement Debit	Income Statement Credit	Balance Sheet Debit	Balance Sheet Credit
Cash	111	104,980.00				104,980.00				104,980.00	
Petty Cash Fund	112	400.00				400.00				400.00	
Government Notes	121	20,000.00				20,000.00				20,000.00	
Accrued Interest Receivable	122			(i) 100.00		100.00				100.00	
Accounts Receivable	131	6,902.00				6,902.00				6,902.00	
Allowance for Doubtful Accounts	131.1		144.00		(q) 480.00		624.00				624.00
Merchandise Inventory—Furniture	141	33,360.00		(g) 33,300.00	(a) 33,360.00	33,300.00				33,300.00	
Merchandise Inventory—Appliances	142	33,000.00		(h) 33,134.00	(b) 33,000.00	33,134.00				33,134.00	
Store Supplies	151	19,020.00			(n) 15,640.00	3,380.00				3,380.00	
Office Supplies	152	16,740.00			(o) 14,674.00	2,066.00				2,066.00	
Prepaid Insurance	155	11,720.00			(p) 9,300.00	2,420.00				2,420.00	
Store Equipment	181	34,480.00				34,480.00				34,480.00	
Accum. Depr.—Store Equip.	181.1		2,660.00		(k) 3,448.00		6,108.00				6,108.00
Delivery Equipment	185	135,200.00				135,200.00				135,200.00	
Accum. Depr.—Delivery Equip.	185.1		99,876.00		(l) 33,800.00		133,676.00				133,676.00
Office Equipment	191	42,260.00				42,260.00				42,260.00	
Accum. Depr.—Office Equip.	191.1		6526.00		(m) 4226.00		10,752.00				10,752.00
FICA Tax Payable	211		2,304.00				2,304.00				2,304.00
FUTA Tax Payable	212		82.40				82.40				82.40
State Unemployment Tax Payable	213		431.20				431.20				431.20
Employees' Income Tax Payable	214		2,000.00				2,000.00				2,000.00
Notes Payable	216		8,000.00				8,000.00				8,000.00
Accrued Interest Payable	217				(j) 180.00		180.00				180.00
Vouchers Payable	218		72,088.00				72,088.00				72,088.00
Brad Rossa, Capital	311		118,444.00				118,444.00				118,444.00
Brad Rossa, Drawing	312	21,500.00				21,500.00				21,500.00	
Deborah Hackett, Capital	321		68,652.00				68,652.00				68,652.00
Deborah Hackett, Drawing	322	16,600.00				16,600.00				16,600.00	
Sales—Furniture	411		1,554,250.00				1,554,250.00		1,554,250.00		
Sales Ret. & Allow.—Furniture	411.1	798.00				798.00		798.00			
Sales—Appliances	421		1,313,698.00				1,313,698.00		1,313,698.00		
Sales Ret. & Allow.—Appliances	421.1	718.00				718.00		718.00			
Interest Revenue	431		1,200.00		(i) 100.00		1,300.00		1,300.00		
Purchases—Furniture	511	1,333,144.00			(c)1,333,144.00						
Purchases Ret. & Allow.—Furniture	511.1		1,734.00	(e) 1,734.00							
Purchases—Appliances	521	994,480.00			(d) 994,480.00						
Purchases Ret. & Allow.—Appliances	521.1		980.00	(f) 980.00							
Cost of Goods Sold—Furniture	531			(a) 33,360.00 (c)1,333,144.00	(e) 1,734.00 (g) 33,300.00	1,331,470.00		1,331,470.00			
Cost of Goods Sold—Appliances	532			(b) 33,000.00 (d) 994,480.00	(f) 980.00 (h) 33,134.00	993,366.00		993,366.00			
Operating Expenses	540	427,767.60		(k-q) 81,568.00		509,335.60		509,335.60			
Interest Expense	581			(j) 180.00		180.00		180.00			
		3,253,069.60	3,253,069.60	2,544,980.00	2,544,980.00	3,292,589.60	3,292,589.60	2,835,867.60	2,869,248.00	456,722.00	423,341.60
Net Income								33,380.40			33,380.40
								2,869,248.00	2,869,248.00	456,722.00	456,722.00

Rossa & Hackett
Supplementary Operating Expense Work Sheet
For the Year Ended December 31, 19--

Account	Acct. No.	Trial Balance Dr.	Adjustments Dr.		Adjusted Trial Balance Dr.
Office Salaries Expense	5401	88,176.00			88,176.00
Brad Rossa, Salary Expense	5402	57,600.00			57,600.00
Office Supplies Expense	5403		(o)	14,674.00	14,674.00
Depreciation Expense—Office Equipment	5404		(m)	4,226.00	4,226.00
Insurance Expense—Office Equipment	5405		(p)	2,440.00	2,440.00
Office Rent Expense	5406	24,000.00			24,000.00
Payroll Taxes Expense	5407	18,765.60			18,765.60
Heat, Light, & Water Expense	5408	11,022.00			11,022.00
Telephone Expense	5409	2,624.00			2,624.00
Postage Expense	5416	1,390.00			1,390.00
Uncollectible Accounts Expense	5417		(q)	480.00	480.00
Miscellaneous General Expense	5422	1,962.00			1,962.00
Store Clerks Salary Expense	5431	51,764.00			51,764.00
Truck Drivers Wage Expense	5432	55,920.00			55,920.00
Advertising Expense	5433	5,104.00			5,104.00
Deborah Hackett, Salary Expense	5434	57,600.00			57,600.00
Depreciation Expense—Delivery Equipment	5435		(l)	33,800.00	33,800.00
Insurance Expense—Delivery Equipment	5436		(p)	4,560.00	4,560.00
Depreciation Expense—Store Equipment	5437		(k)	3,448.00	3,448.00
Insurance Expense—Store Equipment	5438		(p)	2,300.00	2,300.00
Truck Gas and Oil Expense	5441	13,198.00			13,198.00
Truck Repairs and Maintenance Expense	5442	1,874.00			1,874.00
Store Rent Expense	5443	36,000.00			36,000.00
Store Supplies Expense	5444		(n)	15,640.00	15,640.00
Miscellaneous Selling Expense	5452	768.00			768.00
		427,767.60	(k-q)	81,568.00	509,335.60

Note: Now that you have reviewed the Demonstration Problem and Solution you may complete the **Mastery Problem** at the end of the chapter activities.

Applying Accounting Concepts

Series A

Exercise 19A1—Proof of Voucher Register Totals. The following columnar totals were taken from the voucher register of Froemming Florist. What should be the total of the Vouchers Payable column? Identify the total as either a debit or a credit. Then prove the totals.

Column	Debit	Credit
Purchases, Fresh Flowers	$52,540	
Purchases, Silk Flowers	29,052	
Operating Expenses	3,312	
Sundry Accounts	9,088	$1,756
Vouchers Payable	?	?

Exercise 19A2—Proof of Sales Journal Totals. The following totals were taken from the sales journal of Cam Cor Sales & Service. What should be the total of the Accounts Receivable column? Indicate whether the total is a debit or a credit. Then prove the totals.

Column	Debit	Credit
Accounts Receivable	?	?
Sales, Cameras		$17,086
Sales, VCRs		14,150

Exercise 19A3—Proof of Cash Receipts Journal Totals. The following are the columnar totals taken from the cash receipts journal of Cue and Cushion. Determine the total amount of cash sales of Billiard Accessories. Will the total be a debit or a credit? Prove the totals.

Column	Debit	Credit
General Ledger		$ 1,210
Cash	$195,370	
Accounts Receivable		31,526
Sales, Billiard Tables		138,850
Sales, Billiard Accessories	?	?

Exercise 19A4—Proof of Check Register Totals. If the total of the Vouchers Payable column on the check register for Anderson's Antiques is $151,948, what should be the total of the Cash column?

Exercise 19A5—Special Journal Identification. Identify the appropriate journal in which the following transactions would be entered.

1. Issued a voucher.
2. Issued a check in payment of a voucher.
3. Entered cash sales for the day.
4. Entered checks received from customers on account.
5. Made a charge sale.
6. Issued a credit memorandum to a customer.
7. Entered the liability for payroll taxes owed.
8. Issued a voucher for payment of payroll taxes.
9. Deposited interest coupons from government notes held by the bank.
10. Entered payments summarized in the Petty Cash Payments Record.
11. Issued a check to replenish the petty cash fund.

Exercise 19A6—Proving Cash. In completing the end-of-the-week work on April 15, the following amounts were taken from the accounting records of American Home Builders Supply:

Cash balance, April 1	$74,290
Receipts for April 1-15 per Cash Debit column in the cash receipts journal	71,464
Checks issued April 1-15 per Cash Credit column in the check register	46,588

Prove the cash balance as of April 15.

Exercise 19A7—Calculation of Departmental Cost of Goods Sold. The following amounts were taken from the accounts of Sidwell and Skadden, partners of a small retail business. Determine the individual cost of goods sold in the Drugs and Sundries departments for the fiscal year ended September 30, 19-B.

Merchandise Inventory, Drugs, Oct. 1, 19-A	$ 32,260
Merchandise Inventory, Sundries, Oct. 1, 19-A	26,180
Merchandise Inventory, Drugs, Sept. 30, 19-B	31,580
Merchandise Inventory, Sundries, Sept. 30, 19-B	29,980
Purchases, Drugs	1,035,350
Purchases, Sundries	710,200
Purchases Returns and Allowances, Drugs	14,380
Purchases Returns and Allowances, Sundries	7,180

Exercise 19A8—Calculation of Accrued Interest Revenue. On September 30, Sidwell and Skadden owned United States government notes, face value of $10,000, interest rate 12%. Semiannual interest totaling $600 had been collected on August 15.

Determine the amount of interest revenue earned but not yet received that would be entered as an adjustment on the summary work sheet for the year ended September 30, 19-B.

Exercise 19A9—Calculation of Depreciation Expense. Sidwell & Skadden follow the policy of taking depreciation only on assets owned for six months or more. Complete the following schedule to determine the estimated depreciation expense for the year ended Sept. 30, 19-B, rounding to the nearest dollar.

Asset	Cost	Annual Rate of Depreciation	Depreciation for the Year
Store Equipment	$29,730	10%	?
Delivery Equipment	68,200*	12 1/2%	?
Office Equipment	25,000	10%	?

*The balance of the delivery equipment account includes $15,600 for a vehicle purchased on August 15, 19-B.

Exercise 19A10—Calculation of Supplies Expense. Sidwell and Skadden enter payments for supplies as assets when they are purchased. An inventory of unused supplies is taken at the end of the year so that the cost of the supplies used can be calculated and charged to the proper operating expense accounts.

Complete the following schedule to determine the needed adjustments for the fiscal year ended September 30, 19-B.

Asset	Account Balance Sept. 30, 19-B	Amount on Hand Sept. 30, 19-B	Expense For Year
Store Supplies	$13,496	$1,500	?
Office Supplies	11,392	510	?

Exercise 19A11—Calculation of Insurance Expense. At the time of payment of insurance premiums, Sidwell & Skadden enter the amount paid as an asset by debiting Prepaid Insurance. Complete the following schedule to determine the adjustments needed for Insurance Expense for the year ended Sept. 30, 19-B.

Type of Property Insured	Account Balance Sept. 30, 19-B	Unexpired Insurance Premium	Expense For Year
Delivery Equipment	$2,748	$1,832	?
Store Equipment	1,872	936	?
Office Equipment	2,916	1,944	?

Exercise 19A12—Calculation of Uncollectible Accounts Expense. Sidwell & Skadden use the allowance method of accounting for doubtful accounts. On the basis of "aging" the accounts receivable, it was estimated that $2,850 of such accounts would not be collected. For each of the following situations, use a ledger account to show the beginning balance, amount of adjustment, and end-of-the-year balance in Allowance for Doubtful Accounts.

(a) If Allowance for Doubtful Accounts already has a credit balance of $150, what is the amount to be entered as an adjustment to Uncollectible Accounts Expense for the current year?

(b) If Allowance for Doubtful Accounts has an unadjusted debit balance of $110, what is the amount to be entered as an adjustment to Uncollectible Accounts Expense for the current year?

Series B

Exercise 19B1—Proof of Voucher Register Totals. The following columnar totals were taken from the voucher register of Decorator's Greenhouse. What should be the total of the Vouchers Payable column? Identify the total as either a debit or a credit. Then prove the totals.

Column	Debit	Credit
Purchases, Silk Flowers	$39,405	
Purchases, Wreaths..................................	21,789	
Operating Expenses.................................	2,484	
Sundry Accounts	6,816	$1,317
Vouchers Payable	?	?

Exercise 19B2—Proof of Sales Journal Totals. The following totals were taken from the sales journal of Forsyth Computer Sales and Service. What should be the total of the Accounts Receivable column? Indicate whether the total is a debit or credit balance. Then prove the totals.

Column	Debit	Credit
Accounts Receivable....................................	?	?
Sales, Hardware.......................................		$12,814
Sales, Software.......................................		10,612

Exercise 19B3—Proof of Cash Receipts Journal Totals. The following are the columnar totals taken from the cash receipts journal of REK Industries. Determine the total amount of cash sales of Bathroom Equipment. Will the total be a debit or a credit? Prove the totals.

Column	Debit	Credit
General Ledger		$ 9,075
Cash..	$1,390,280	
Accounts Receivable..................................		236,445
Sales, Kitchen Equipment		634,535
Sales, Bathroom Equipment	?	?

Exercise 19B4—Proof of Check Register Totals. If the total of the Vouchers Payable column of the check register for Kiernan's Kandies is $113,963, what should be the total of the Cash column?

Exercise 19B5—Special Journal Identification. Identify the appropriate journal in which the following transactions would be entered.

1. Entered payments summarized in the Petty Cash Payments Record.
2. Issued a check to replenish the petty cash fund.
3. Deposited interest coupons from government notes held by the bank.
4. Issued a voucher for payment of payroll taxes.
5. Entered the liability for payroll taxes owed.
6. Issued a credit memorandum to a customer.
7. Made a charge sale.
8. Entered checks received from customers on account.
9. Entered cash sales for the day.
10. Issued a check in payment of a voucher.
11. Issued a voucher.

Exercise 19B6—Proving Cash. In completing the end-of-the-week work on May 13, the following amounts were taken from the accounting records of Olsen Dairy Supply:

Cash balance, May 1	$55,718
Receipts for May 1-13 per Cash Debit column in the cash receipts journal	53,596
Checks issued May 1-13 per Cash Credit column in the check register...	34,941

Prove the cash balance as of May 13.

Exercise 19B7—Calculation of Departmental Cost of Goods Sold. The following amounts were taken from the accounts of Shearrer and Schloemann, partners of a small wholesale business. Determine the individual cost of goods sold for the Lumber and Sheet Metal departments for the fiscal year ended March 31, 19-D:

Merchandise Inventory, Lumber, April 1, 19-C	$24,195
Merchandise Inventory, Sheet Metal, April 1, 19-C	19,635
Merchandise Inventory, Lumber, March 31, 19-D	23,685
Merchandise Inventory, Sheet Metal, March 31, 19-D	22,485
Purchases, Lumber	776,512
Purchases, Sheet Metal	532,650
Purchases Returns and Allowances, Lumber	3,595
Purchases Returns and Allowances, Sheet Metal	5,385

Exercise 19B8—Calculation of Accrued Interest Revenue. On March 31, Shearrer and Schloemann owned United States government notes, face value of $7,500, interest rate 11%. Semiannual interest totalling $412.50 had been collected on February 15 (not a leap year).

Determine the amount of interest revenue earned but not yet received that would be entered as an adjustment on the summary work sheet for the year ended March 31, 19-D.

Exercise 19B9—Calculation of Depreciation Expense. Shearrer and Schloemann follow the policy of taking depreciation only on assets owned for six months or more. Complete the following schedule to determine the estimated depreciation expense for the year ended March 31, 19-D, rounding to the nearest dollar.

Assets	Cost	Annual Rate of Depreciation	Depreciation for the Year
Store Equipment	$22,299	10%	?
Delivery Equipment	51,150*	12 1/2%	?
Office Equipment	18,750	10%	?

*The balance of the delivery equipment account includes $11,700 for a vehicle purchased on January 15, 19-D.

Exercise 19B10—Calculation of Supplies Expense. Shearrer and Schloemann enter payments for supplies as assets when they are purchased. An inventory of unused supplies is taken at the end of the year so that the cost of the supplies used can be calculated and charged to the proper operating expense accounts.

Complete the following schedule to determine the needed adjustments for the fiscal year ended March 31, 19-D.

Asset	Account Balance March 31, 19-D	Amount on Hand March 31, 19-D	Expense For Year
Store Supplies	$10,122	$1,125	?
Office Supplies	8,544	383	?

Exercise 19B11—Calculation of Insurance Expense. At the time of payment of insurance premiums, Shearrer and Schloemann enter the amount paid as an asset by debiting Prepaid Insurance. Complete the following schedule to determine the adjustments needed for Insurance Expense for the year ended March 31, 19-D.

Type of Property Insured	Account Balance March 31, 19-D	Unexpired Insurance Premium	Expense For Year
Delivery Equipment	$2,061	$1,374	?
Store Equipment	1,404	702	?
Office Equipment	2,187	1,458	?

Exercise 19B12—Calculation of Uncollectible Accounts Expense. Shearrer and Schloemann use the allowance method of accounting for doubtful accounts. On the basis of "aging" the accounts receivable, it was estimated that $2,138 of such accounts would not be collected. For each of the following situations, use a ledger account to show the beginning balance, amount of adjustment, and end-of-the-year balance in Allowance for Doubtful Accounts.

(a) If Allowance for Doubtful Accounts already has a credit balance of $112, what is the amount to be entered as an adjustment to Uncollectible Accounts Expense for the current year?

(b) If Allowance for Doubtful Accounts has an unadjusted debit balance of $83, what is the amount to be entered as an adjustment to Uncollectible Accounts Expense for the current year?

Series A

Problem 19A1   Entries in Special Journals and Proof of Journals

Kevin Lawlor and Gail Martin are partners in a wholesale-retail fishing tackle and apparel business. Tackle and apparel are purchased on account, but sales are both for cash and on account.

The accounts of Lawlor and Martin are kept on the basis of a fiscal year ending December 31. The books of original entry include a voucher register, sales journal, cash receipts journal, check register, and general journal. Following is a narrative of the transactions for the first week in December. Use the following operating expense and sundry accounts where applicable:

5401	Office Salaries Expense
5402	Salary Expense, K. Lawlor
5406	Office Rent Expense
5408	Heat, Light, and Water Expense
5409	Telephone Expense
5431	Store Clerks Salary Expense
5432	Truck Drivers Wage Expense
5433	Advertising Expense
5434	Salary Expense, G. Martin
5443	Store Rent Expense
211	FICA Tax Payable
214	Employees' Income Tax Payable

Monday, December 3

(a) Issued Voucher No. 396 to Mound City Leasing Co. for $3,600, of which $2,400 represents store rent expense and $1,200 represents office rent expense.

(b) Issued Check No. 801 to Graham Paper Co. for $328 in payment of Voucher No. 371 dated November 28, and Check No. 802 in payment of Voucher No. 396. Voucher No. 371 was unpaid from November and has previously been entered in the November Voucher Register (not shown).

(c) Cash sales for the day were $1,650 for Tackle and $725 for Apparel.

Tuesday, December 4

(a) Received checks from customers on account as follows:
All Seasons Bait & Tackle, $2,020, for merchandise sold on November 27.
Paul's Tackle Shop, $570, for merchandise sold on November 27.
Dennis's Hardware, $1,035, for merchandise sold on November 27.

(b) Cash sales for the day were $1,864 for Tackle and $1,459 for Apparel.

(c) Issued Voucher No. 397 to Central States Public Service for November electricity bill, $1,800.

Wednesday, December 5

(a) Issued Check Nos. 803 and 804 in payment of Voucher Nos. 394 and 395. Voucher No. 394 for $2,350 was issued on November 30 payable to Anglin Andy's, and Voucher No. 395 for $2,570 was also issued on November 30 payable to Frontenac Fishing Apparel. Both vouchers were previously entered in the November Voucher Register (not shown).

(b) Issued Voucher No. 398 to The Dispatch for advertising, $525.

(c) Made charge sales as follows:
Shady Valley Tackle, fishing tackle, $4,700, Sale No. 497.
Fenton Fishing Apparel, apparel, $1,455, Sale No. 498.
All Seasons Bait & Tackle, fishing tackle, $1,970, Sale No. 499.

(d) Cash sales for the day were $2,020 for Tackle and $1,160 for Apparel.

Thursday, December 6

(a) Issued Voucher No. 399 to Contel for November telephone service, $135.

(b) Received checks from customers on account as follows:
Old Bridge Tackle Shop, $1,370, for merchandise sold to them on November 30.
Chisholm's Outfitters, $3,420, for merchandise sold to them on November 30.
Della's Sporting Goods, $2,739, for merchandise sold to them on November 30.

(c) Cash sales for the day were $935 for Tackle and $325 for Apparel.

(d) Issued Credit Memorandum No. 9 to Fenton Fishing Apparel, $150, as an allowance for defective fishing boots (part of Sale No. 498).

Friday, December 7

(a) Issued vouchers as follows:
Voucher No. 400 to Bell Brand, Inc., for fishing boots (Apparel), $3,200.
Voucher No. 401 to Omni Sports for fishing attire, $4,250.
Voucher No. 402 to Hargrove Fly Fishing for tackle, $9,275.

(b) Made charge sales as follows:
Della's Sporting Goods, tackle, $1,750; apparel, $785; Sale No. 500.
Bass Pro Shop, tackle, $1,460, Sale No. 501.
Rock Lake Fishing Togs, apparel, $1,472, Sale No. 502.

(c) Cash sales for the day were $1,950 for Tackle and $1,425 for Apparel.

(d) Issued Voucher No. 403 to the Finest National Bank for the payment of the following taxes:

Employees' income tax (withheld during November).....		$5,952
FICA tax imposed:		
On employees (withheld during November)	$3,188	
On the employer.................................	3,188	6,376
Total		$12,328

(e) Issued Voucher No. 404 to Payroll for the weekly wages, $11,119.17, and determined the employer's payroll taxes.

Lawlor & Martin follows the policy of paying employees on Friday of each week. Following is a payroll statement for the week ended December 7, and a statement of the employer's payroll taxes, which should be recorded in the general journal.

Payroll Statement
For the Week Ended December 7

		Deductions		Net
	Total	FICA	Income	Amount
Classification	Earnings	Tax	Tax	Payable
Store clerks wages	$ 3,766.00	$282.45	$ 452.06	$ 3,031.49
Truck drivers wages	3,967.00	297.53	652.76	3,016.71
Office salaries	3,315.00	248.63	495.40	2,570.97
Partners' salaries:				
K. Lawlor	1,000.00	none	none	1,000.00
G. Martin	1,500.00	none	none	1,500.00
	$13,548.00	$828.61	$1,600.22	$11,119.17

Employer's payroll taxes:		
FICA tax (7.5% of $11,048)		$828.60
Unemployment compensation taxes—		
State unemployment compensation tax (3.0% of		
$2,100)	$63.00	
FUTA tax (0.8% of $2,100)	16.80	79.80
		$908.40

(f) Issued Check Nos. 805 and 806 in payment of Voucher Nos. 403 and 404.

Saturday, December 8

(a) Cash sales for the day were $2,640 for Tackle and $1,650 for Apparel.

Required:

1. Enter each of the transactions in the appropriate journal.
2. Foot and prove each of the journals.
3. The cash balance on December 1 was $123,008. Determine the cash balance as of December 8.

Problem 19A2   Summary and Supplementary Work Sheets

Taylor & Dowd are partners in operating a wholesale hardware business. They keep their accounts on the basis of a calendar year ending December 31. Ac-

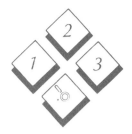

counts with customers and operating expenses are kept in subsidiary ledgers with control accounts in the general ledger. Any needed adjustments in the operating expense accounts are made at the end of each year after a trial balance is taken. A ten-column summary work sheet and a three-column supplementary operating expenses work sheet at the end of each year are prepared as a means of compiling and classifying the information needed in the preparation of an income statement, a balance sheet, and related schedules and statements. The trial balance of the general ledger as of December 31 is given below.

Taylor & Dowd
Trial Balance
December 31, 19--

Account	Acct. No.	Dr. Balance	Cr. Balance
Cash	111	36,336.80	
Petty Cash Fund	112	300.00	
Government Notes	121	30,000.00	
Accrued Interest Receivable	122		
Accounts Receivable	131	46,942.36	
Allowance for Doubtful Accounts	131.1		1,445.26
Merchandise Inventory	141	442,934.48	
Store Supplies	151	2,842.24	
Office Supplies	152	4,642.94	
Postage Stamps	153	1,248.34	
Prepaid Insurance	155	3,845.26	
Store Equipment	181	12,600.00	
Accumulated Depr.—Store Equipment	181.1		2,843.40
Delivery Equipment	185	20,990.00	
Accumulated Depr.—Delivery Equipment	185.1		5,596.00
Office Equipment	191	19,600.00	
Accumulated Depr.—Office Equipment	191.1		5,347.56
FICA Tax Payable	211		1,642.36
Employees' Income Tax Payable	214		845.94
Accounts Payable	218		23,843.22
J. Taylor, Capital	311		208,632.42
J. Taylor, Drawing	312	36,000.00	
R. Dowd, Capital	321		208,632.42
R. Dowd, Drawing	322	36,000.00	
Sales	411		3,924,482.22
Sales Returns and Allowances	411.1	24,422.82	
Purchases	511	3,204,146.20	
Purchases Returns and Allowances	511.1		12,423.66
Cost of Goods Sold	531		
Operating Expenses	540	474,833.02	
Interest Revenue	431		1,950.00
		4,397,684.46	4,397,684.46

Selected operating expense accounts (those requiring adjustment) are also given on the following page.

Taylor & Dowd
Schedule of Operating Expense Accounts
For the Year Ended December 31, 19--

Account	Acct. No.	Trial Balance Dr.
Office Supplies Expense	5403	
Depreciation Expense—Office Equipment	5404	
Postage Expense	5416	1,612.94
Uncollectible Accounts Expense	5417	
Depreciation Expense—Delivery Equipment	5435	
Insurance Expense	5436	
Depreciation Expense—Store Equipment	5437	
Store Supplies Expense	5444	
All other expenses		473,220.08
		474,833.02

Required:

1. Complete a ten-column summary work sheet for the year ended December 31 and a supplementary work sheet for operating expenses (only accounts requiring adjustments are shown). The following data provide the information needed in adjusting the general ledger and operating expense ledger accounts:

   (a-c) Transfer beginning Merchandise Inventory, Purchases, and Purchases Returns and Allowances to Cost of Goods Sold.

   (d) Merchandise inventory, December 31, $458,832.38.

   (e) Allowance for doubtful accounts at end of year should be $2,429.33.

   (f) Store supplies used, $2,243.26.

   (g) Office supplies used, $2,936.42.

   (h) Postage stamps on hand, December 31, $643.70.

   (i) Insurance expense, $2,931.20.

   (j) Depreciation of store equipment, 10% of cost.

   (k) Depreciation of delivery equipment, 25% of cost.

   (l) Depreciation of office equipment, 10% of cost.

   (m) Interest accrued on government notes, December 31, $229.

2. Determine net income for the year ended December 31, 19-- and enter it in the proper amount columns.

Series B

Problem 19B1   Entries in Special Journals and Proof of Journals

Cindy Grad and Kurt Jaeger are partners in a wholesale-retail lawn and garden equipment business. Lawn equipment and garden equipment are purchased on account but sales are both for cash and on account.

The accounts of Grad & Jaeger are kept on the basis of a fiscal year ending June 30. The books of original entry include a voucher register, sales journal, cash receipts journal, check register, and general journal. Following is a narrative of the transactions for the first week in June. Use the following operating expense and sundry accounts where applicable.

5401 Office Salaries Expense
5402 Salary Expense, C. Grad
5406 Office Rent Expense
5408 Heat, Light and Water Expense
5409 Telephone Expense
5431 Store Clerks Salary Expense
5432 Truck Drivers Wage Expense
5433 Advertising Expense
5434 Salary Expense, K. Jaeger
5443 Store Rent Expense
 211 FICA Tax Payable
 214 Employees Income Tax Payable

Monday, June 4

(a) Issued Voucher No. 496 to Truman Leasing Co. for $2,400, of which $1,600 represents store rent expense and $800 represents office rent expense.
(b) Issued Check No. 901 to Paul's Office Supply for $257 in payment of Voucher No. 471 dated May 28. Voucher No. 471 was unpaid from May and had previously been entered in the Voucher Register (not shown).
(c) Issued Check No. 902 in payment of Voucher No. 496.
(d) Cash sales for the day were $1,875 for Lawn and $1,040 for Garden.

Tuesday, June 5

(a) Received checks from customers on account as follows:
Art's Lawn Mower Shop, $2,270, for merchandise sold on May 29.
Atlas Hardware, $895, for merchandise sold on May 29.
Nettie's Garden Center, $1,360, for merchandise sold on May 29.
(b) Cash sales for the day were $2,128 for Lawn and $2,045 for Garden.
(c) Issued Voucher No. 497 to Kansas City Power & Light for May electricity bill, $1,950.

Wednesday, June 6

(a) Issued Check Nos. 903 and 904 in payment of Voucher Nos. 494 and 495. Voucher No. 494 for $2,560 was issued on May 31 payable to AAA Landscape Materials, and Voucher No. 495 for $2,240 was also issued on May 31 payable to Gardeners' Seed Co. Both vouchers were previously entered in the May voucher register (not shown).
(b) Issued Voucher No. 498 to Kansas City Star for advertising, $385.
(c) Made charge sales as follows:
Allen's Garden Shop, garden equipment, $4,575; Sale No. 597.
Hanson Lawn Equipment, lawn equipment, $1,535; Sale No. 598.
Art's Lawn Mower Shop, lawn equipment, $2,055; Sales No. 599.
(d) Cash sales for the day were $2,260 for Lawn and $1,375 for Garden.

Thursday, June 7

(a) Issued Voucher No. 499 to ITT-General for May telephone service, $110.
(b) Received checks from customers on account as follows:
Mangelsdorf Seed Co., $1,625, for merchandise sold to them on May 31.
Lawn Equipment, Inc., $3,670, for merchandise sold to them on May 31.
Suburban Lawn Center, $2,865, for merchandise sold to them on May 31.

(c) Cash sales for the day were $1,245 for Lawn and $675 for Garden.

(d) Issued Credit Memorandum No. 11 to Hanson Lawn Equipment, $200, as an allowance for a defective fertilizer spreader (part of Sale No. 598).

Friday, June 8

(a) Issued vouchers as follows:
Voucher No. 500 to Bayer Garden Shops, Inc., for garden statuary, $2,400.
Voucher No. 501 to Turf Products Co., for lawn fertilizer and turf builder, $2,200.
Voucher No. 502 to Timber Creek Nursery for garden plants & shrubs, $3,580.

(b) Made charge sales as follows:
Suburban Lawn Center, lawn equipment, $1,962; garden equipment, $1,025; Sale No. 600.
Valley Hardware, garden equipment, $1,745; Sale No. 601.
Two Rivers Garden, lawn equipment, $2,895; garden equipment, $1,684; Sale No. 602.

(c) Cash sales for the day were $2,200 for Lawn and $1,625 for Garden.

(d) Issued Voucher No. 503 to the Last National Bank for the payment of the following taxes:

Employees' income tax (withheld during May)		$4,464
FICA tax imposed:		
On employees (withheld during May)	$2,391	
On the employer	2,391	4,782
Total		$9,246

(e) Issued Voucher No. 504 to Payroll for the weekly wages, $5,959.03, and determined the employer's payroll taxes.
Grad & Jaeger follows the policy of paying employees on Friday of each week. Following is a payroll statement for the week ended June 8, and a statement of the employer's payroll taxes, which should be recorded in the general journal.

Payroll Statement
For the Week Ended June 8

		Deductions		Net
Classification	Total Earnings	FICA Tax	Income Tax	Amount Payable
Store clerks wages	$1,838.00	$137.85	$220.56	$1,479.59
Truck drivers wages	1,884.50	141.34	263.83	1,479.33
Office salaries	1,592.50	119.44	222.95	1,250.11
Partners' salaries:				
C. Grad	750.00	none	none	750.00
K. Jaeger	1,000.00	none	none	1,000.00
	$7,065.00	$398.63	$707.34	$5,959.03

Employer's payroll taxes:		
FICA tax (7.5% of $5,315)		$398.63
Unemployment compensation taxes:		
State unemployment compensation tax (4.0% of $1,050)	$42.00	
FUTA tax (0.8% of $1,050)	8.40	50.40
		$449.03

(f)   Issued Check Nos. 905 and 906 in payment of Voucher Nos. 503 and 504.

Saturday, June 9

(a)   Cash sales for the day were $2,870 for Lawn and $1,970 for Garden.

Required:

1.   Enter each of the transactions in the appropriate journal.
2.   Foot and prove each of the journals.
3.   The cash balance on June 1 was $138,002. Determine the cash balance as of June 9.

Problem 19B2   Summary and Supplementary Work Sheets

Chaplin & Mees are partners in operating a wholesale drug business. They keep their accounts on the basis of a calendar year ending December 31. Accounts with customers and operating expenses are kept in subsidiary ledgers with control accounts in the general ledger. Any needed adjustments in the operating expense accounts are made at the end of each year after a trial balance is taken. A ten-column summary work sheet and a three-column supplementary operating expenses work sheet at the end of each year are prepared as a means of compiling and classifying the information needed in the preparation of an income statement, a balance sheet, and related schedules and statements. The trial balance of the general ledger as of December 31 is given on the following page.

Selected operating expense accounts (those requiring adjustment) are also given below.

Chaplin & Mees
Schedule of Operating Expense Accounts
For the Year Ended December 31, 19--

Account	Acct. No.	Trial Balance Dr.
Office Supplies Expense	5403	
Depreciation Expense—Office Equipment	5404	
Postage Expense	5416	1,209.71
Uncollectible Accounts Expense	5417	
Depreciation Expense—Delivery Equipment	5435	
Insurance Expense..	5436	
Depreciation Expense—Store Equipment	5437	
Store Supplies Expense	5444	
All other expenses		354,915.06
		356,124.77

Chaplin & Mees
Trial Balance
December 31, 19--

Account	Acct. No.	Dr. Balance	Cr. Balance
Cash	111	27,252.60	
Petty Cash Fund	112	225.00	
Government Notes	121	22,500.00	
Accrued Interest Receivable	122		
Accounts Receivable	131	35,206.77	
Allowance for Doubtful Accounts	131.1		1,083.95
Merchandise Inventory	141	332,200.86	
Store Supplies	151	2,131.68	
Office Supplies	152	3,482.21	
Postage Stamps	153	936.25	
Prepaid Insurance	155	2,883.95	
Store Equipment	181	9,450.00	
Accumulated Depr.—Store Equipment	181.1		2,132.55
Delivery Equipment	185	15,742.50	
Accumulated Depr.—Delivery Equipment	185.1		4,197.00
Office Equipment	191	14,700.00	
Accumulated Depr.—Office Equipment	191.1		4,010.67
FICA Tax Payable	211		1,231.77
Employees' Income Tax Payable	214		634.45
Accounts Payable	218		17,882.42
K. Chaplin, Capital	311		156,474.32
K. Chaplin, Drawing	312	27,000.00	
A. Mees, Capital	321		156,474.32
A. Mees, Drawing	322	27,000.00	
Sales	411		2,943,361.66
Sales Returns and Allowances	411.1	18,317.11	
Purchases	511	2,403,109.65	
Purchases Returns and Allowances	511.1		9,317.74
Cost of Goods Sold	531		
Operating Expenses	540	356,124.77	
Interest Revenue	431		1,462.50
		3,298,263.35	3,298,263.35

Required:

1. Complete a ten-column summary work sheet for the year ended December 31 and a supplementary work sheet for operating expenses (only accounts requiring adjustment are shown). The following data provide the information needed in adjusting the general ledger and operating expense ledger accounts:

   (a-c) Transfer beginning Merchandise Inventory, Purchases, and Purchases Returns and Allowances to Cost of Goods Sold.

   (d) Merchandise inventory, December 31, $344,124.29.

   (e) Allowance for doubtful accounts at end of year should be $1,822.01.

   (f) Store supplies used, $1,682.45.

   (g) Office supplies used, $2,202.32.

(h) Postage stamps on hand, December 31, $482.78.
(i) Insurance expense, $2,198.40.
(j) Depreciation of store equipment, 10% of cost.
(k) Depreciation of delivery equipment, 25% of cost.
(l) Depreciation of office equipment, 10% of cost.
(m) Interest accrued on government notes, December 31, $171.75.
2. Determine net income for the year ended December 31, 19-- and enter it in the proper amount columns.

Mastery Problem

If the working papers for this textbook are not used, omit the Mastery Problem.

Fred Farmer and Mike Plover are partners in the operation of a wholesale-retail furniture and office supply store. The books of original entry (voucher register, sales journal, cash receipts journal, check register, and general journal) are provided in the working papers. Following is a narrative of representative transactions for the month of June and information concerning the June 30 year-end adjustments. The accounts with customers and operating expenses are kept in subsidiary ledgers with control accounts in the general ledger. A ten-column summary work sheet and a three-column supplementary operating expenses work sheet are used to prepare year-end adjustments and to compile and classify the information needed in the preparation of financial statements. Use the following operating expense and sundry accounts where applicable:

5401 Office Salaries Expense	5409 Telephone Expense	5434 Salary Expense, M. Plover
5402 Salary Expense, F. Farmer	5431 Store Clerks Salary Expense	5443 Store Rent Expense
5406 Office Rent Expense	5432 Truck Drivers Wage Expense	211 FICA Tax Payable
5408 Heat, Light, and Water Expense	5433 Advertising Expense	214 Employees Income Tax Payable

Monday, June 2

(a) Issued Voucher No. 196 to BBB Leasing Co. for $5,200, of which $4,200 represents store rent expense and $1,000 represents office rent expense.
(b) Issued Check No. 101 in payment of Voucher No. 171 and Check No. 102 in payment of Voucher No. 196.
(c) Cash sales for the day were $8,558 for Furniture and $4,200 for Office Supplies.

Tuesday, June 3

(a) Received checks from customers on account as follows:
Stern's Tax Service, $3,620, for merchandise sold on May 29.
Straus Office Supply, $3,399, for merchandise sold on May 29.
Quality Office Supplies, $3,145, for merchandise sold on May 29.
(b) Cash sales for the day were $21,782 for Furniture and $10,675 for Office Supplies.
(c) Issued Voucher No. 197 to Central Power & Light for May electricity bill, $1,450.

Wednesday, June 4

  (a) Issued Check Nos. 103 and 104 in payment of Voucher Nos. 194 and 195.
  (b) Issued Voucher No. 198 to the Pony Express for advertising, $850.
  (c) Made charge sales as follows:
      Wildcat Office Supplies, office supplies, $8,300; Sale No. 197.
      Cardinal Office Center, furniture, $6,450; office supplies, $2,895; Sale No. 198.
      Bowling Green Office Supplies, furniture, $4,267; office supplies, $2,450; Sale No. 199.
  (d) Cash sales for the day were $8,980 for Furniture and $12,200 for Office Supplies.

Thursday, June 5

  (a) Issued Voucher No. 199 to Kentucky Bell for May telephone service, $425.
  (b) Received checks from customers on account as follows:
      Warner Office Supplies, $7,520, for merchandise sold to them on May 30.
      The Old Mill Stream Furniture Store, $5,640, for merchandise sold to them on May 30.
      Clark's Furniture Store, $9,450, for merchandise sold to them on May 30.
  (c) Cash sales for the day were $15,815 for Furniture and $6,845 for Office Supplies.
  (d) Issued Credit Memorandum No. 8 to Billboard Advertising, $50, as an allowance on damaged office supplies.

Friday, June 6

  (a) Issued vouchers as follows:
      Voucher No. 200 to Office Discount Co. for computer furniture, $35,200.
      Voucher No. 201 to Excell Office Supplies for office supplies, $28,400.
      Voucher No. 202 to Hogan's Furniture Inc. for furniture, $28,600.
  (b) Made charge sales as follows:
      Central University, furniture, $8,545; office supplies, $3,258; Sale No. 200.
      Heartland College, office supplies, $3,225; Sale No. 201.
      Wonder Junior College, furniture $4,355; office supplies $2,125; Sale No. 202.
  (c) Cash sales for the day were $4,500 for Furniture and $2,500 for Office Supplies.

Saturday, June 7

  (a) Cash sales for the day were $7,500 for Furniture and $3,250 for Office Supplies.

Monday, June 16

  (a) Issued Voucher No. 213 to the First National Bank for the payment of the following taxes:

Employees' income tax (withheld during May)		$3,855
FICA tax imposed:		
On employees (withheld during May)	$2,122	
On the employer	2,122	4,244
Total		$8,099

(b) Issued Voucher No. 214 to Payroll for the semimonthly wages, $16,102.19, and determined the employee's payroll taxes.

Farmer and Plover follows the policy of paying employees on a semimonthly basis. Following is a payroll statement for the period ended June 16, and a statement of the employer's payroll taxes, which should be recorded in the general journal.

Payroll Statement
Period Beginning June 1 and Ending June 16

Classification	Total Earnings	FICA Tax	Employees' Income Tax	Net Amount Payable
Store clerks wages	$ 5,125.00	$ 384.38	$ 615.00	$4,125.62
Truck drivers wages	5,200.00	390.00	676.00	4,134.00
Office salaries	4,895.00	367.13	685.30	3,842.57
Partners' salaries:				
F. Farmer (5402)	1,500.00	none	none	1,500.00
M. Plover (5434)	2,500.00	none	none	2,500.00
	$19,220.00	$1,141.51	$1,976.30	$16,102.19

Employer's payroll taxes:

FICA tax (7.5% of $15,220)		$1,141.51
Unemployment compensation taxes:		
State unemployment compensation tax (3.0% of $2,300)	$ 69.00	
FUTA tax (0.8% of $2,300)	18.40	87.40
		$1,228.91

(c) Issued Check Nos. 115 and 116 in payment of Voucher Nos. 213 and 214.

(d) Farmer reported that interest coupons amounting to $300 from government notes were deposited in the Credit Union.

(e) Cash sales for the day were $8,250 for Furniture and $3,800 for Office Supplies.

Tuesday June 30

(a) Voucher No. 231 was issued to Petty Cash to replenish the petty cash fund. The following report was submitted by the clerk responsible for the fund.

Statement of Petty Cash Payments for June

Acct. No.	Description	Amount
5409	Telephone Expense	$ 35.00
5422	Miscellaneous General Expense	26.00
5433	Advertising Expense	55.00
5441	Truck Gas & Oil Expense	38.00
5452	Miscellaneous Selling Expense	25.00
Total disbursements		$179.00

(b) Issued Check No. 141 in payment of Voucher No. 231.

Information for year-end adjustments:

(a-d) The cost assigned to the June 30 furniture inventory was $150,000. Farmer and Plover's also makes adjustments to transfer the balances of Purchases and Purchases Returns and Allowances to Cost of Goods Sold.

(e-h)   The cost assigned to the June 30 office supplies inventory was $78,400. Farmer and Plover's also makes adjustments to transfer the balances of Purchases and Purchases Returns and Allowances to Cost of Goods Sold.

(i)   On June 30, Farmer and Plover's Furniture and Office Supplies owned $15,000 face value, 10% United States government notes. Interest had been collected on May 1.

(j)   Farmer and Plover's Furniture and Office Supplies periodically issues short-term notes payable. Interest paid on these notes through May 31 amounted to $1,900. Since that date, $400 of interest has accrued on these notes, but it has not yet been paid or entered in the accounting records.

(k-m)   The firm's policy is that no depreciation is taken on assets owned for less than six months. The following schedule was prepared to determine the estimated depreciation expense for the year.

Schedule of Depreciation Expense
For the Year Ended June 30, 19--

Asset	Cost	Annual (Straight-Line) Rate of Depreciation
Store Equipment	$180,000*	10%
Delivery Equipment	95,000	10
Office Equipment	80,000	5

*Note that the balance of the store equipment account shown on the work sheet is $210,000. That is because the cost of new store equipment ($30,000) purchased on May 23 is included. Since these assets have been owned for less than six months, no depreciation is taken on them.

(n-o)   The general ledger of Farmer and Plover's Furniture and Office Supplies includes two asset accounts for supplies—Store Supplies and Office Supplies. When purchased, the supplies are entered as assets by debiting these accounts. An inventory of unused supplies is taken at the end of the year so that the cost of the supplies used can be calculated and charged to the proper operating expense accounts. The following schedule was prepared to determine the needed adjustments.

Schedule of Supplies Used
For the Year Ended June 30, 19--

Asset	Account Balance June 30 19--	Amount on Hand June 30, 19--
Store Supplies	$22,559	$2,667
Office Supplies	16,128	3,845

(p)   Prepaid insurance premiums are entered by Farmer and Plover's Furniture and Office Supplies in the same manner as supplies. At the time of payment of a premium, the amount paid is entered as an asset by debiting Prepaid Insurance. At the end of the year, calculations are made to determine the fraction of the total term of each policy that elapsed during the year. Each amount thus determined is classified according to the type of asset insured and charged to the proper insurance expense account. The operating expenses subsidiary ledger of Farmer and Plover's Furniture and

Office Supplies includes insurance expense accounts for the insurance on delivery equipment, store equipment, and office equipment. The following schedule of insurance expense was prepared from a file of information relating to insurance policies.

Schedule of Insurance Expense
For the Year Ended June 30, 19--

Type of Property Insured	Expense for Year
Delivery Equipment	$ 6,200
Store Equipment	8,700
Office Equipment	12,000
Total	$26,900

(q)   Farmer and Plover's Furniture and Office Supplies uses the allowance method of accounting for doubtful accounts. Farmer and Plover estimate that 1% of the $825,000 in credit sales will be uncollectible.

Required:

1. Prepare entries for the June transactions in the appropriate journals provided in the working papers.
2. Prepare appropriate adjustments to the summary work sheet and supplementary operating expenses work sheet.
3. Complete the preparation of the summary work sheet and supplementary operating expense work sheet.

CHAPTER 20

The Annual Report and
Year-End Journal Entries

Chapter Objectives

Careful study of this chapter should enable you to:

- Describe and explain the nature of an annual report.

- Prepare a comparative income statement that shows the components and amounts of gross margin on sales by departments and in total, supplemented by schedules of cost of goods sold and of operating expenses.

- Analyze the income statement using comparative analysis and percentage analysis.

- Prepare a comparative statement of owners' equity.

- Prepare a comparative balance sheet supplemented by a schedule of accounts receivable.

- Analyze the balance sheet using ratio analysis and comparative analysis.

- Perform interstatement analysis using the income statement and balance sheet.

- Journalize the adjusting entries in the general journal.

- Post the adjusting entries to the general ledger accounts.

- Journalize the closing entries in the general journal.

- Post the closing entries to the general ledger end-of-period summary accounts.

- Prepare the post-closing trial balance.

- Prepare any reversing entries required in the general journal as of the first day of the new accounting period.

The purpose of this chapter is to complete the illustration of accounting for the operations of the wholesale-retail merchandising business begun in Chapter 19. Once the year-end work sheet has been completed, the next step in the accounting process is the preparation of financial statements. In earlier chapters, financial statements reporting the operating activities for a one-year period were illustrated. Because of the importance of comparing performance over time, most companies prepare comparative financial statements which report the operating results for each of the past two or three years. In this chapter, comparative financial statements for the past two years are illustrated. Various techniques used in analyzing the financial statements are described and illustrated.

This chapter also illustrates the final steps in the year-end accounting process. These steps include the preparation of (1) adjusting and closing entries which prepare the ledger for the new accounting period; (2) a post-closing trial balance which verifies the accuracy of the closing process; and (3) reversing entries which simplify the accounting process in the following accounting period.

The Annual Report

Describe and explain the nature of an annual report.

The term **annual report** as applied to a business usually refers to the financial statements and related schedules of the enterprise for the fiscal year. The report generally includes an income statement, a statement of owners' equity, a balance sheet, and a statement of cash flows. In corporations with thousands of stockholders, the annual report may be a thirty- to sixty-page publication. Often in color, this report might contain numerous pictures of the company's products, production facilities and officers, and it might present various graphs and statistics in addition to the financial statements. Reports of this type usually include a letter addressed to the stockholders which is signed by the president of the corporation and/or by the chairman of the board of directors. The letter is printed in the report booklet and is often described as "highlights" of the year. Such annual reports always include the **auditor's opinion** (sometimes referred to as the **auditor's report**) of the CPA firm that performed the audit of the company's financial statements.

Annual reports of the type described above are not used if the business has few owners. In a partnership, it is probable that only the partners and, possibly, one or two of the officials at their bank will see the reports. The annual report of Mitchell & Jenkins consists of the following statements and schedules:

Income Statement for the Year
Schedule of Cost of Goods Sold
Schedule of Operating Expenses

Statement of Owners' Equity

Balance Sheet as of December 31
Schedule of Accounts Receivable

The Income Statement

Prepare a comparative income statement that shows the components and amounts of gross margin on sales by departments and in total, supplemented by schedules of cost of goods sold and of operating expenses.

A comparative income statement for the year ended December 31, 19-F and 19-E, for Mitchell & Jenkins is shown below. Information for 19-F was taken from the Income Statement columns of the work sheet reproduced on pages 738 and 739. The 19-E income statement is provided for comparison purposes. The income statement is arranged to show the sales, cost of goods sold, and the gross margin on sales for each department as well as in total. A schedule of cost of goods sold for 19-F is also provided to show the components that made up the cost of goods sold for each department and the total.

The schedule of operating expenses reproduced on page 773 was prepared from information provided by the operating expenses work sheet shown on page 741. The schedule provides the detail of what makes up the total amount of operating expenses ($703,821) shown on the income statement. If there were only five or ten accounts for operating expenses, it is probable that (1) there would have been no subsidiary ledger for such expenses and (2) the accounts would have been included in the income statement, in which case no schedule would have been needed. There is wide variation in the form and content of financial statements. Some accountants, for example, may present the components of cost of goods sold in the income statement instead of in the "supporting" schedule as illustrated on page 774.

Mitchell & Jenkins Sporting Goods
Comparative Income Statement
For the Years Ended December 31, 19-F and 19-E

	19-F			19-E		
	Golf	Tennis	Total	Golf	Tennis	Total
Sales	$1,424,800	$825,200	$2,250,000	$1,296,568	$701,420	$1,997,988
Less sales returns and allowances	42,744	16,504	59,248	38,897	14,358	53,255
Net sales	$1,382,056	$808,696	$2,190,752	$1,257,671	$687,062	$1,944,733
Cost of goods sold	760,131	525,652	1,285,783	706,922	452,061	1,158,983
Gross margin on sales	$ 621,925	$283,044	$ 904,969	$ 550,749	$235,001	$ 785,750
Operating expenses			703,821			661,209
Operating income			$ 201,148			$ 124,541
Other revenue and expenses:						
Interest revenue		$ 875				750
Interest expense		(4,220)	(3,345)			
Net income			$ 197,803			$ 125,291

Mitchell & Jenkins Sporting Goods
Schedule of Operating Expenses
For the Year Ended December 31, 19-F

Administrative expenses:

Office salaries expense	$ 76,450	
Robert Mitchell, salary expense	36,000	
Office supplies expense	18,700	
Depreciation expense—office equipment	9,500	
Insurance expense—office equipment	12,000	
Office rent expense	13,200	
Payroll taxes expense	20,920	
Heat, light, and water expense	21,800	
Telephone expense	1,452	
Postage expense	847	
Uncollectible accounts expense	18,750	
Miscellaneous general expense	8,450	
Total administrative expenses		$238,069

Selling expenses:

Store clerks salary expense	$ 88,245	
Truck drivers wage expense	90,478	
Advertising expense	83,230	
Jessica Jenkins, salary expense	48,000	
Depreciation expense—delivery equipment	22,500	
Insurance expense—delivery equipment	9,200	
Depreciation expense—store equipment	20,000	
Insurance expense—store equipment	11,500	
Truck gas and oil expense	34,876	
Truck repairs and maintenance expense	5,285	
Store rent expense	26,400	
Store supplies expense	17,900	
Miscellaneous selling expense	8,138	
Total selling expenses		465,752
Total operating expenses		$703,821

Interpreting the Income Statement

Analyze the income statement using comparative analysis and percentage analysis.

There are numerous ways to analyze an income statement. Two types of analysis will be dealt with in this chapter: (1) comparative analysis, and (2) percentage analysis.

Comparative Analysis. Added meaning is given to the information supplied by an income statement if it is compared with statements for

Mitchell & Jenkins Sporting Goods
Schedule of Cost of Goods Sold
For the Year Ended December 31, 19-F

	Golf	Tennis	Total
Merchandise inventory, January 1, 19-F..	$ 221,960	$ 95,600	$ 317,560
Purchases............................	$ 825,476	$540,025	$1,365,501
Less purchases returns and allowances ..	10,894	8,445	19,339
Net purchases.......................	$ 814,582	$531,580	$1,346,162
Merchandise available for sale..........	$1,036,542	$627,180	$1,663,722
Less merchandise inventory, December 31, 19-F...........................	276,411	101,528	377,939
Cost of goods sold...................	$ 760,131	$525,652	$1,285,783

past periods. By using such comparative analysis, answers will be provided to such vital questions as: Are sales growing or shrinking? How much has net income increased or decreased (both absolutely and relatively)? Has the gross margin percentage become larger or smaller? The first thing each partner probably did after looking at the income statement results for the year just ended was to compare it with the results for the preceding year. For these reasons, income statements and other financial statements generally are prepared in comparative form to aid in their interpretation.

A review of the comparative income statement for Mitchell and Jenkins indicates excellent improvement in profitability over last year's operations. Net sales increased more than 12% [($2,190,752 − $1,944,732)/$1,944,732] while cost of goods sold increased by only 11% [($1,285,783 − $1,158,983)/$1,158,983]. This resulted in a 15% increase in the gross margin on sales [($904,969 − $785,750)/$785,750]. Further, operating expenses only increased by 6% [($703,821 − $661,209)/$661,209]. The combination of these changes resulted in a 58% increase in net income.

▬ Percentage Analysis. In order of importance, the most significant items shown by the annual income statement are the total amounts of (1) net income, (2) sales, (3) cost of goods sold and gross margin (considered together because of the interrelationship), and (4) operating expenses. The dollar amounts of these items take on added meaning if their proportionate relationship to each other is computed and compared. Using Mitchell & Jenkins' income statement as an example, the customary way of studying these relationships is by percentage analysis, illustrated on page 775, using net sales as the base (100%).

This analysis shows that net income grew from 6.4% of net sales to 9.0%, with other revenue and expenses representing relatively minor amounts. In other words, each dollar of net sales resulted in about six

	19-F		19-E	
Net sales	$2,190,752	100.0%	$1,944,733	100.0%
Cost of goods sold	1,285,783	58.7	1,158,983	59.6
Gross margin	$ 904,969	41.3%	$ 785,750	40.4%
Operating expenses	703,821	32.1	661,209	34.0
Operating income	$ 201,148	9.2%	$ 124,541	6.4%
Other revenue & expense	(3,345)	0.2	750	0.0
Net income	$ 197,803	9.0%	$ 125,291	6.4%

and a half cents of net income in 19-E and nine cents of net income in 19-F. Further, it can be seen that cost of goods sold and operating expenses represented a smaller percentage of net sales in 19-F than in 19-E. These are very positive signals of improved performance.

Mitchell & Jenkins may compare these percentages with the same percentages for other similar wholesale/retail sporting goods businesses, or with their own percentages of operating results for prior years, to determine the relative profitability of their operation.

The same type of analysis can be applied to the data for the net sales, cost of goods sold, and gross margin of each department, as shown below.

	Golf		Tennis	
Net sales	$1,382,056	100.0%	$808,696	100.0%
Cost of goods sold	760,131	55.0	525,652	65.0
Gross margin	$ 621,925	45.0%	$283,044	35.0%

Mitchell & Jenkins might find this analysis useful in determining the relative emphasis to place on the sales of each department. Since the gross margin on the sales of golf equipment is 10% higher than tennis, additional efforts might be made to increase sales in this department. These gross margin percentages should also be compared with industry averages to determine whether Mitchell and Jenkins is maintaining reasonable margins. If not, both pricing policies and costs incurred to obtain the golf and tennis merchandise should be reviewed.

The Statement of Owners' Equity

Prepare a comparative statement of owners' equity.

The comparative statement of owners' equity for Mitchell and Jenkins for the years ended December 31, 19-F and 19-E is provided on page 776. The statement for 19-F was prepared from information taken from the Balance Sheet columns of the work sheet. As discussed in Chapter 10, the purpose of this statement is to report changes in the owners' capital accounts. Thus, the statement shows capital balances at the beginning of the year, increases resulting from net income and additional investments during the year, and reductions due to withdrawals during the year. Since neither Mitchell nor Jenkins made additional investments during the year, none is reported. If additional investments had been made, this information would be gathered from the partners' capital accounts in the general ledger and reported as an increase in capital. By adding net income and subtracting withdrawals, the capital balances at the end of the period are determined.

The primary difference between this statement and the one discussed in Chapter 10 for a sole proprietorship is that the information is reported in total and broken down for each partner. Note that the net income is allocated to each partner on a 60 - 40 basis as described in the partnership agreement. In addition, actual withdrawals made by each partner are disclosed. As discussed in the following section, the December 31 balances reported on this statement are also reported under Owners' Equity on the balance sheet.

Mitchell & Jenkins Sporting Goods
Comparative Statement of Owners' Equity
For the Years Ended December 31, 19-F and 19-E

	19-F			19-E		
	R. Mitchell	J. Jenkins	Total	R. Mitchell	J. Jenkins	Total
Capital, January 1	$446,663	$371,648	$ 818,311	$392,488	$338,532	$731,020
Net income for the year	118,682	79,121	197,803	75,175	50,116	125,291
	$565,345	$450,769	$1,016,114	$467,663	$388,648	$856,311
Withdrawals for the year . . .	20,000	18,000	38,000	21,000	17,000	38,000
Capital, December 31	$545,345	$432,769	$ 978,114	$446,663	$371,648	$818,311

The Balance Sheet

Prepare a comparative balance sheet supplemented by a schedule of accounts receivable.

The following comparative balance sheet of Mitchell & Jenkins as of December 31, 19-F and 19-E, is arranged in report form. The statement for 19-F was prepared from information provided by the Balance Sheet columns of the work sheet on pages 738 and 739. Note that the current assets are presented first and listed in their probable order of liquidity. Cash is listed first followed by government notes. These notes are regarded as temporary investments since they can be liquidated with relative ease if a shortage of cash should occur. Accrued interest receivable, accounts receivable (less the allowance for doubtful accounts) and merchandise inventories are shown next, followed by supplies and prepayments. These latter items are included as current assets because their present ownership means that less money will have to be spent for such

Mitchell and Jenkins Sporting Goods
Comparative Balance Sheet
December 31, 19-F and 19-E

Assets	19-F		19-E	
Current assets:				
Cash		$ 98,693		$105,800
Petty cash...................		200		200
Government notes		10,000		10,000
Accrued interest receivable		50		300
Accounts receivable	$250,000		$230,000	
Less allowance for doubtful accounts	18,000	232,000	17,000	213,000
Merchandise inventories:				
Golf	$276,411		$221,960	
Tennis	101,528	377,939	95,600	317,560
Supplies and prepayments:				
Store supplies	$ 1,825		$ 1,648	
Office supplies.............	1,500		1,250	
Prepaid insurance	11,750	15,075	10,780	13,678
Total current assets.........		$ 733,957		$ 660,538
Property, plant and equipment:				
Store equipment	$240,000		$194,000	
Less accum. depr.—store equip.	90,000	$150,000	70,000	$124,000
Delivery equipment	$225,000		$225,000	
Less accum. depr.—deliv. equip.	62,500	162,500	40,000	185,000
Office equipment.............	$190,000		$180,000	
Less accum. depr.—office equip.	40,000	150,000	30,500	149,500
Total property, plant and equipment...............		462,500		458,500
Total assets		$1,196,457		$1,119,038
Liabilities				
Current liabilities:				
Vouchers payable		$162,575		$233,727
Notes payable		50,400		60,000
Accrued and withheld payroll taxes		4,948		6,600
Accrued interest payable		420		400
Total current liabilities		$ 218,343		$ 300,727
Owners' Equity				
Robert Mitchell, capital		$545,345		$446,663
Jessica Jenkins, capital		432,769		371,648
Total owners' equity.........		978,114		818,311
Total liabilities and owners' equity		$1,196,457		$1,119,038

purposes in the near future. It is not expected that these items will be directly converted into cash. Long-term assets of Mitchell & Jenkins are the last assets listed.

All of the liabilities of the firm are current liabilities. The owners' equity section is arranged to show the equity of each partner at year end.

The balance sheet is supported by a schedule of accounts receivable as of December 31, 19-F. This schedule is a list of the subsidiary accounts receivable ledger accounts as of the close of the year. It is not an integral part of the balance sheet.

Mitchell & Jenkins
Schedule of Accounts Receivable
December 31, 19-F

Bradon Tennis Camp	$ 26,987
Courtside	21,136
Crooked Tree Country Club	14,294
Fleetwood Country Club	17,219
Lakeside Country Club	22,445
Pro Tennis and Golf	28,278
The Swing Shop	35,610
The Tennis Racket	12,915
Venturi Pro Shop	38,966
Wimbledon Tennis Club	32,150
	$250,000

Interpreting the Balance Sheet

In interpreting the balance sheet, it is important to remember that the amounts of certain assets as shown on a conventional balance sheet do not necessarily reflect their market values. For example, the inventory is reported at cost, the amount paid by Mitchell & Jenkins. Presumably, this inventory will be sold for much more. Also, the **undepreciated cost** of the long-term assets (the difference between the original cost of these assets and the depreciation so far charged off as expense) does not indicate what these assets would bring if they were to be sold nor does it indicate what it would cost to buy these assets. The difference ($462,500 in total) merely represents the amount, less any expected scrap or salvage value, that is to be charged against future revenues. With these considerations in mind, there are ways to analyze the balance sheet. Two commonly used types of analysis are discussed below: (1) ratio analysis and (2) comparative analysis.

Analyze the balance sheet using ratio analysis and comparative analysis.

■ **Ratio Analysis.** One use of the balance sheet is to aid in judging the **liquidity** of a business, that is, the ability of the enterprise to meet its current debt obligations. In addition to the relative amounts of current assets and current liabilities, the composition of these resources and obligations must also be considered in judging liquidity. Two commonly used measures of liquidity are the **current ratio** and the **quick ratio**. The ratio of the current assets ($733,957) to current liabilities ($218,343) of Mitchell

& Jenkins is 3.36 to 1. This current ratio is adequate, but of equal or greater significance is the quick ratio. The "quick" assets (cash, temporary investments, and current receivables) total $340,943—1.5 times the current liabilities. This indicates that the firm more than passes the acid test (a ratio of quick assets to total current liabilities of at least 1 to 1).

▓▓▓ **Comparative Analysis.** As in the case of income statements, a comparison of current and past balance sheets may be informative. Comparative balance sheets are often presented in annual reports. In some cases, an analysis that involves expressing one amount as a percent of another may be helpful. In other cases, comparisons of ratios may be more meaningful.

This type of analysis can be illustrated by using the comparative balance sheets of Mitchell & Jenkins. Note that the current ratio has improved from 2.19 to 1 ($660,538/$300,727) to 3.36 to 1 ($733,957/$218,343) from the beginning to the end of the year. In addition, current assets amounted to 61% of total assets at the end of the year, compared with only about 59% at the beginning of the year.

These ratios and percentages indicate that Mitchell & Jenkins have strengthened their financial control of the business during the year. The percentages also suggest that Mitchell & Jenkins probably could afford to increase their investment in long-term assets.

Interstatement Analysis

Perform an interstatement analysis using the income statement and balance sheet.

Interstatement analysis involves the use of both income statement and balance sheet data to provide more meaningful measures of the firm's performance. For example, it was noted on page 775 that Mitchell & Jenkins had net income equal to 9.0% of net sales. This is up substantially from 6.4% last year and is a positive sign. However, it is also important to relate net income to the assets and owners' equity required to carry out operations. The relationship between Mitchell & Jenkins' net income and their assets and owners' equity will now be considered.

▓▓▓ **Return on assets.** According to the comparative balance sheet summary on page 777, Mitchell & Jenkins had average total assets for the fiscal year of $1,157,748 [($1,196,457 + $1,119,038)/2]. The ratio of net income to average total assets, which is known as return on assets, was therefore 17.1% (net income of $197,803/average total assets of $1,157,748).

▓▓▓ **Return on equity.** Mitchell & Jenkins' average total owners' equity for the fiscal year was $898,213 [($978,114 + $818,311)/2]. The ratio of net income to average owners' equity, which is known as return on equity, was therefore 22.0% (net income of $197,803/average owners' equity of $898,213).

Both the return on assets and the return on equity of Mitchell & Jenkins appear to be very favorable. In judging these relationships, however, it must be remembered that no income tax has been taken into consideration, since partnerships, as such, do not pay income taxes. In their individual income tax returns, Mitchell & Jenkins must include their shares of the partnership net income along with any "salary" payments or allowances reported as expenses on the partnership income statement. The amount of any cash or other assets received from the firm is not relevant to the calculation of each partner's taxable income. The amount of income tax that each partner must pay depends upon the total amount of each partner's income from various sources, the amount of various deductions and credits that may be taken, and the number of exemptions to which the partner is entitled.

Merchandise Turnover. The data reported in the income statement and balance sheet also make it possible to compute the **merchandise turnover** during the year. For the business as a whole, the average inventory was $347,750 [($317,560 beginning inventory + $377,939 ending inventory)/2]. Since the total cost of goods sold was $1,285,783, the turnover was about 3.7 times ($1,285,783/$347,750). This means that, on the average, goods remained in stock for about 99 days (365/3.7) before being sold. This is typical for this type of business. Using the same calculation for each department reveals that the turnover for tennis equipment is much faster than golf. Tennis equipment turns over every 68 days while golf equipment is held an average of 120 days prior to sale. The turnover ratio can help Mitchell & Jenkins determine whether they are carrying significant amounts of slow moving sporting goods. Based on the departmental turnover ratios, Mitchell & Jenkins might want to examine in detail the turnover of selected products carried in the golf department.

Building Your Accounting Knowledge

1. What four financial statements generally are included in the annual report of a business?
2. What three major items are shown for each department and in total on the Mitchell & Jenkins income statement?
3. What is the source of the information contained in the schedule of operating expenses?
4. What is the customary way of relating cost of goods sold, gross margin, operating expenses, and net income to net sales using percentage analysis? What use is made of such analysis?
5. How is the technique of comparative analysis applied to the information supplied by an income statement? What vital questions does comparative analysis help to answer?
6. In what order are the current assets arrayed on the balance sheet of Mitchell & Jenkins?
7. Why are supplies and prepayments included among the current assets?
8. Give two examples of balance sheet assets that do not necessarily reflect their current values.

9. What are the current ratio and the quick ratio used to judge or measure?
10. What are the percentage of net income to sales, the return on assets, and the return on owner's equity, used to measure?
11. How is the merchandise turnover for the year computed? What use is made of the turnover ratio?

Assignment Box

To reinforce your understanding of the preceding text materials, you may complete the following:

Study Guide: Part A
Textbook: Exercises 20A1 through 20A6 or 20B1 through 20B6
Problems 20A1 through 20A4 or 20B1 through 20B4

Adjusting, Closing, and Reversing Entries

The most important function of the year-end work sheet is to facilitate the preparation of the income statement, statement of owners' equity, and balance sheet as soon as possible after the end of the accounting period. Having completed the preparation of the financial statements, a secondary function of the work sheets is to aid in the process of formally entering adjusting and closing entries in the books.

Journalizing The Adjusting Entries

Journalize the adjusting entries in the general journal.

Adjusting entries as of December 31 were entered in the general journal reproduced on page 782. The form of general journal used by Mitchell & Jenkins provided a special Detail column for charges to the accounts in the operating expenses subsidiary ledger. Journalizing the adjusting entries involved the use of this column as well as the Debit and Credit columns. Several features of these entries should be noted:

1. The general ledger accounts are debited or credited in the conventional form; each subsidiary ledger account and its amount are also entered. However, the account numbers were entered when the journalizing was done, not as a step in the posting process. The check marks were made later as the posting was completed.
2. The entries were made in the same order as shown alphabetically [(a) through (q)] on the work sheets (pages 738-739, and 741). While this order is not essential, the danger of omitting an entry is slightly reduced by using the work sheets as a guide in journalizing the entries.
3. To be sure that the total of the debits equaled the total of the credits, the Debit and Credit columns were footed. The Detail column was footed and found to agree with the total of the Adjustments Debit

column on the operating expenses work sheet. Finally, the totals were entered and the usual rulings were made.

Journal

	DATE	DESCRIPTION	ACCT. NO.	DETAIL	√	DEBIT	√	CREDIT	√	
1	19-F	*Adjusting Entries*								1
2	Dec. 31	Cost of Goods Sold—Golf	531			22 1 9 6 0 00	√			2
3		Merchandise Inventory—Golf	141					22 1 9 6 0 00	√	3
4	31	Cost of Goods Sold—Tennis	532			9 5 6 0 0 00	√			4
5		Merchandise Inventory-Tennis	142					9 5 6 0 0 00	√	5
6	31	Cost of Goods Sold—Golf	531			82 5 4 7 6 00	√			6
7		Purchases—Golf	511					82 5 4 7 6 00	√	7
8	31	Cost of Goods Sold—Tennis	532			54 0 0 2 5 00	√			8
9		Purchases—Tennis	521					54 0 0 2 5 00	√	9
10	31	Purchases Ret.& Allow.—Golf	511.1			1 0 8 9 4 00	√			10
11		Cost of Goods Sold—Golf	531					1 0 8 9 4 00	√	11
12	31	Purchases Ret.& Allow—Tennis	521.1			8 4 4 5 00	√			12
13		Cost of Goods Sold—Tennis	532					8 4 4 5 00	√	13
14	31	Merchandise Inventory—Golf	141			27 6 4 1 1 00	√			14
15		Cost of Goods Sold—Golf	531					27 6 4 1 1 00	√	15
16	31	Merchandise Inventory—Tennis	142			10 1 5 2 8 00	√			16
17		Cost of Goods Sold—Tennis	532					10 1 5 2 8 00	√	17
18	31	Accrued Interest Receivable	122			5 0 00	√			18
19		Interest Revenue	431					5 0 00	√	19
20	31	Interest Expense	581			4 2 0 00	√			20
21		Accrued Interest Payable	217					4 2 0 00	√	21
22	31	Operating Expenses	540			14 0 0 5 0 00	√			22
23		Depr. Exp.—Store Equip.	5437	2 0 0 0 0 00	√					23
24		Accum. Depr.—Store Equip.	181.1					2 0 0 0 0 00	√	24
25		Depr. Exp.—Deliv. Equip.	5435	2 2 5 0 0 00	√				√	25
26		Accum. Depr.—Deliv. Equip.	185.1					2 2 5 0 0 00		26
27		Depr. Exp.—Ofc. Equip.	5404	9 5 0 0 00	√					27
28		Accum. Depr.—Ofc. Equip.	191.1					9 5 0 0 00	√	28
29		Store Supplies Expense	5444	1 7 9 0 0 00	√					29
30		Store Supplies	151					1 7 9 0 0 00	√	30
31		Office Supplies Expense	5403	1 8 7 0 0 00	√					31
32		Office Supplies	152					1 8 7 0 0 00	√	32
33		Ins. Expense—Delivery Equip.	5436	9 2 0 0 00	√					33
34		Ins. Expense—Store Equip.	5438	1 1 5 0 0 00	√					34
35		Ins. Expense—Office Equip.	5405	1 2 0 0 0 00	√					35
36		Prepaid Insurance	155					3 2 7 0 0 00	√	36
37		Uncollectible Accts. Exp.	5417	1 8 7 5 0 00	√					37
38		Allow. for Doubtful Accts.	131.1					1 8 7 5 0 00	√	38
39				14 0 0 5 0 00		222 0 8 5 9 00		222 0 8 5 9 00		39
40				(√)		(√)		(√)		40

Posting The Adjusting Entries

Post the adjusting entries to the general ledger accounts.

As the individual amounts in the Debit and Credit columns were posted to the accounts, a check mark ($\sqrt{}$) was placed to the right of each amount in the column provided. A check mark also was placed in parentheses below the total of each of these two columns to indicate that the amount was not posted to any ledger. In the case of the entries in the Detail column, a check mark was placed to the right of each amount as it was posted. A check mark was also placed in parentheses below the total of that column to indicate that the amount was not posted to any ledger. In both the general ledger and the operating expenses ledger, the page of the general journal (J43) was placed in the Posting Reference column as each posting was made.

Journalizing The Closing Entries

Journalize the closing entries in the general journal.

The page of the general journal showing the **closing entries** as of December 31, 19-F, is reproduced on page 784. Certain features of these entries should be noted:

1. Each closing entry was made in conventional form. As in the case of the adjusting entries, however, the numbers of the accounts were entered at the time of journalizing. The check marks were made later as the posting was completed.
2. The order of the closing entries follows a logical sequence. The revenue accounts are closed first, followed by the expense accounts. The third entry closes the expense and revenue summary account by dividing the income ($197,803) between Mitchell & Jenkins in a 60-40 ratio as their partnership agreement specifies. The last two closing entries transfer the amount of each partner's withdrawals to the related capital account.
3. The amount columns were footed to prove the equality of the debits and credits. The totals were then entered and the usual rulings were made.

Note that, while there was a credit of $703,821 to close Operating Expenses, Account No. 540, the individual credits to close the twenty-five accounts in the operating expenses subsidiary ledger were not shown. One reason is that the form of the journal page does not accommodate credits to the operating expenses accounts, because these accounts rarely are credited (except when they are closed). The occasional transaction that requires a credit to an operating expense account can be handled by noting both the number of the control account (No. 540) and the number of the subsidiary ledger account in the account number column provided just to the left of the Detail column. The amount of the credit will then be posted as a credit to both accounts.

The operating expense accounts in the subsidiary ledger must be closed at the end of the fiscal year. When a general ledger control account is closed, all accounts in a ledger that is subsidiary to that control account also must be closed. The space and time required to list all of the subsidiary ledger accounts, numbers, and balances (twenty-five in the present case) can be saved if all subsidiary ledger expense accounts are closed at the same time that the operating expenses account is closed. The manner of closing an operating expense subsidiary account is illustrated for Advertising Expense, Account No. 5433, on page 785.

Journal   PAGE 44

	DATE	DESCRIPTION	ACCT. NO.	DETAIL	✓	DEBIT	✓	CREDIT	✓	
1	19-F	*Closing Entries*								1
2	Dec. 31	Sales—Golf	411			142 48 00 00	✓			2
3		Sales—Tennis	421			82 52 00 00	✓			3
4		Interest Revenue	431			8 75 00	✓			4
5		Expense and Revenue Summary	331					225 08 75 00		5
6	31	Expense and Revenue Summary	331			205 30 72 00	✓			6
7		Sales Ret. & Allow.—Golf	411.1					4 27 44 00		7
8		Sales Ret. & Allow.—Tennis	421.1					1 65 04 00		8
9		Cost of Goods Sold—Golf	531					76 01 31 00		9
10		Cost of Goods Sold—Tennis	532					52 56 52 00		10
11		Operating Expenses	540					70 38 21 00		11
12		Interest Expense	581					4 22 00 00		12
13	31	Expense and Revenue Summary	331			19 78 03 00	✓			13
14		Robert Mitchell, Capital	311					11 86 82 00	✓	14
15		Jessica Jenkins, Capital	321					7 91 21 00	✓	15
16	31	Robert Mitchell, Capital	311			2 00 00 00	✓			16
17		Robert Mitchell, Drawing	312					2 00 00 00	✓	17
18	31	Jessica Jenkins, Capital	321			1 80 00 00	✓			18
19		Jessica Jenkins, Drawing	322					1 80 00 00	✓	19
20						45 39 75 00 45 39 75 00		45 39 75 00 45 39 75 00		20
21						(✓)		(✓)		21

Posting The Closing Entries

Post the closing entries to the general ledger end-of-period summary accounts.

  The postings were made to the general ledger accounts indicated in the general journal. A check mark was placed in the column provided in the general journal as each posting was made. The page of the general journal (J44) was noted in the Posting Reference column of each account involved as the postings were made. As mentioned in the preceding paragraph, the balance of each account in the subsidiary operating expenses ledger was closed in the manner illustrated in the account for Advertising Expense shown below. (Note that "J44" was entered in the Posting Reference column, since that is the page of the general journal on which the closing entry for the operating expenses control account was made.) The other twenty-four operating expense accounts were closed in a similar fashion.

ACCOUNT *Advertising Expense*   ACCOUNT NO. *5433*

DATE		ITEM	POST. REF.	DEBIT	CREDIT	BALANCE DEBIT	BALANCE CREDIT
19-F Dec	1	Dr. Balance	√			82 722 00	
	4		VR25	4 95 00		83 217 00	
	31		VR25	1 3 00		83 230 00	
	31		J44		83 230 00	- 0 -	- 0 -

The expense and revenue summary account and the two cost of goods sold accounts, after the adjusting and closing entries had been posted, are reproduced below. Note that these accounts are summarizing accounts that are used only at the end of the accounting period. In some accounting systems, cost of goods sold accounts are used throughout the year if such cost is known at the time of sale. This is possible if perpetual inventories are maintained. In the periodic inventory method of Mitchell & Jenkins, the cost of goods sold accounts are used only at the end of the fiscal year.

ACCOUNT *Expense and Revenue Summary*   ACCOUNT NO. *331*

DATE		ITEM	POST. REF.	DEBIT	CREDIT	BALANCE DEBIT	BALANCE CREDIT
19-F Dec.	31		J44		2250 875 00		2250 875 00
	31		J44	2053 072 00			197 803 00
	31		J44	197 803 00		- 0 -	- 0 -

ACCOUNT *Cost of Goods Sold—Golf*   ACCOUNT NO. *531*

DATE		ITEM	POST. REF.	DEBIT	CREDIT	BALANCE DEBIT	BALANCE CREDIT
19-F Dec.	31	Beg. Inventory	J43	221 960 00		221 960 00	
	31	Purchases	J43	825 476 00		1047 436 00	
	31	Purchases R & A	J43		10 894 00	1036 542 00	
	31	End. Inventory	J43		276 411 00	760 131 00	
	31	Exp. & Rev. Summary	J44		760 131 00	- 0 -	- 0 -

ACCOUNT *Cost of Goods Sold—Tennis*   ACCOUNT NO. *532*

DATE		ITEM	POST. REF.	DEBIT	CREDIT	BALANCE DEBIT	BALANCE CREDIT
19-F Dec.	31	Beg. Inventory	J43	95 600 00		95 600 00	
	31	Purchases	J43	540 025 00		635 625 00	
	31	Purchases R & A	J43		8 445 00	627 180 00	
	31	End. Inventory	J43		101 528 00	525 652 00	
	31	Exp. & Rev. Summary	J43		525 652 00	- 0 -	- 0 -

Post-Closing Trial Balance

Prepare the post-closing trial balance.

After the closing entries were posted, a trial balance of the general ledger accounts that remained open was taken to prove the equality of the debit and credit balances. The **post-closing trial balance** of the general ledger of Mitchell & Jenkins is reproduced below.

Mitchell & Jenkins Sporting Goods
Post Closing Trial Balance
December 31, 19-F

Account	Acct. No.	Dr. Balance	Cr. Balance
Cash	111	98,693	
Petty Cash	112	200	
Government Notes	121	10,000	
Accrued Interest Receivable	122	50	
Accounts Receivable	131	250,000	
Allowance for Doubtful Accounts	131.1		18,000
Merchandise Inventory—Golf	141	276,411	
Merchandise Inventory—Tennis	142	101,528	
Store Supplies	151	1,825	
Office Supplies	152	1,500	
Prepaid Insurance	155	11,750	
Store Equipment	181	240,000	
Accumulated Depreciation—Store Equip.	181.1		90,000
Delivery Equipment	185	225,000	
Accumulated Depreciation—Deliv. Equip.	185.1		62,500
Office Equipment	191	190,000	
Accumulated Depreciation—Office Equip.	191.1		40,000
FICA Tax Payable	211		1,628
FUTA Tax Payable	212		35
State Unemployment Tax Payable	213		165
Employees Income Tax Payable	214		3,120
Notes Payable	216		50,400
Accrued Interest Payable	217		420
Vouchers Payable	218		162,575
Robert Mitchell, Capital	311		545,345
Jessica Jenkins, Capital	321		432,769
		1,406,957	1,406,957

Mitchell & Jenkins—Post Closing Trial Balance

Some accountants feel that it is necessary to prepare a post-closing trial balance in the form illustrated and file it with various other records. Others think that it is sufficient merely to use an adding machine tape to list and total (1) the amounts of the debit balances and (2) the amounts of the credit balances to be sure that the totals are the same. In either case, if the ledger was found not to be in balance, the cause of the discrepancy would have to be located and remedied.

Reversing Entries

Prepare any reversing entries required in the general journal as of the first day of the new accounting period.

Adjusting entries for accrued interest receivable and payable (adjustments (i) and (j) on the work sheet) were made on December 31. In order that interest collections and payments may be entered in routine fashion in the new period, Mitchell & Jenkins follows the practice of reversing all accrual adjustments. The first entries for the new period are the reversals of the previous accrual adjustments. The **reversing entries** made on January 1, 19-G, are shown below.

Journal

PAGE *45*

	DATE		DESCRIPTION	ACCT. NO.	DETAIL	√	DEBIT	√	CREDIT	√	
1	19-G		*Reversing Entries*								1
2	*Jan.*	1	*Interest Revenue*	431			5 0 00	√			2
3			*Accrued Interest Receivable*	122					5 0 00	√	3
4		1	*Accrued Interest Payable*	217			4 2 0 00	√			4
5			*Interest Expense*	581					4 2 0 00	√	5

Building Your Accounting Knowledge

1. What is the purpose of the Detail column in Mitchell & Jenkins' general journal?
2. In what two ways are the accounts identified in entering the adjusting entries in the general journal?
3. Why are the Debit and Credit columns of the general journal footed? Why is the Detail column footed?
4. In what two ways are the accounts identified in entering the closing entries in the general journal?
5. What is the purpose of each of the five closing entries made by Mitchell & Jenkins?
6. How is the posting of the individual amounts in the adjusting and closing entries indicated in the general journal? In the general and operating expenses ledgers?
7. What is the purpose of the post-closing trial balance? What do some accountants use as a substitute?
8. Why does the accountant for Mitchell & Jenkins reverse accrual adjustments?

Assignment Box

To reinforce your understanding of the preceding text materials, you may complete the following:

       Study Guide: Part B
       Textbook: Exercises 20A7 through 20A10 or 20B7 through 20B10
              Problem 20A5 or 20B5

Expanding Your Business Vocabulary

What is the meaning of each of the following terms:

acid test (p. 779)	merchandise turnover (p. 780)
adjusting entries (p. 78')	percentage analysis (p. 774)
annual report (p. 771)	post-closing trial balance (p. 786)
auditor's opinion (p. 771)	profitability (p. 775)
auditor's report (p. 771)	quick ratio (p. 778)
closing entries (p. 783)	return on assets (p. 779)
comparative analysis (p. 774)	return on equity (p. 779)
current ratio (p. 778)	reversing entries (p. 787)
interstatement analysis (p. 779)	undepreciated cost (p. 778)
liquidity (p. 778)	

Demonstration Problem

Fox & Palmer are partners in operating a wholesale-retail grocery business. They keep their accounts on the basis of a calendar year ending December 31. Accounts with customers and operating expenses are kept in subsidiary ledgers with control accounts in the general ledger. Any needed adjustments in the operating expense accounts are made at the end of each year after a trial balance is taken. A ten-column summary work sheet and a three-column supplementary operating expenses work sheet at the end of each year are prepared as a means of compiling and classifying the information needed in the preparation of an income statement and a balance sheet. The Income Statement and Balance Sheet columns of their most recent summary work sheet are provided. Fox & Palmer normally prepare comparative statements, but to conserve space only the current year's statements will be prepared in this problem.

Required:

1. Using the income statement columns of the work sheet, prepare a summary income statement.
2. Prepare a schedule of cost of goods sold to support the income statement, using the following additional data:

    Merchandise inventory, Jan. 1 . . . . $ 166,100.46
    Purchases for year 1,201,554.80
    Purchases returns and allowances for year 4,658.87

Fox & Palmer
Work Sheet (partial)
For the Year Ended December 31. 19--

Account	Acct. No.	Income Statement Debit	Income Statement Credit	Balance Sheet Debit	Balance Sheet Credit
Cash	111			13,626.30	
Petty Cash Fund	112			125.00	
Government Notes	121			11,250.00	
Accrued Interest Receivable	122			73.37	
Accounts Receivable	131			37,603.38	
Allowance for Doubtful Accounts	131.1				911.00
Merchandise Inventory	141			172,062.15	
Store Supplies	151			224.61	
Office Supplies	152			639.95	
Postage Stamps	153			241.39	
Prepaid Insurance	155			342.77	
Store Equipment	181			4,725.00	
Accumulated Depr.—Store Equip.	181.1				1,538.78
Delivery Equipment	185			7,871.25	
Accumulated Depr.—Delivery Equip.	185.1				4,066.31
Office Equipment	191			7,350.00	
Accumulated Depr.—Office Equip.	191.1				2,740.34
FICA Taxes Payable	211				615.89
Employees' Income Tax Payable	214				317.22
Accounts Payable	218				8,941.21
J. Fox, Capital	311				98,237.16
J. Fox, Drawing	312			13,500.00	
R. Palmer, Capital	321				98,237.16
R. Palmer, Drawing	322			13,500.00	
Sales	411		1,471,680.83		
Sales Returns and Allowances	411.1	9,158.56			
Cost of Goods Sold	531	1,190,934.24			
Operating Expenses	540	204,875.05			
Interest Revenue	431		817.12		
		1,404,967.85	1,472,497.95	283,135.17	215,605.07
Net Income		67,530.10			67,530.10
		1,472,497.95	1,472,497.95	283,135.17	283,135.17

3. Calculate the following:
   (a) Percentage of cost of goods sold to net sales.
   (b) Percentage of operating expenses to net sales.
   (c) Percentage of operating income to net sales.

(d) Merchandise turnover ratio. (The January 1 inventory was $166,100.43.)

4. Prepare a classified balance sheet in report form, supported by a statement of owners' equity. Assume net income is distributed equally.

5. Calculate the following:
   (a) Ratio of current assets to current liabilities.
   (b) Ratio of quick assets to current liabilities (acid test).
   (c) Percentage of current assets to total assets.
   (d) Return on assets (total assets at the beginning of the year were $195,630.18).
   (e) Return on equity.

Solution

1.

Fox & Palmer
Income Statement
For the Year Ended December 31, 19--

Sales	$1,471,680.83
Less sales returns and allowances	9,158.56
Net sales	$1,462,522.27
Cost of goods sold	1,190,934.24
Gross margin on sales	$ 271,588.03
Operating expenses	204,875.05
Operating income	$ 66,712.98
Other revenue:	
Interest revenue	817.12
Net income	$ 67,530.10

2.

Fox & Palmer
Schedule of Cost of Goods Sold
For the Year Ended December 31, 19--

Merchandise inventory, January 1		$ 166,100.46
Purchases	$1,201,554.80	
Less purchases returns and allowances	4,658.87	
Net purchases		1,196,895.93
Merchandise available for sale		$1,362,996.39
Less merchandise inventory, Dec. 31		172,062.15
Cost of goods sold		$1,190,934.24

3.

(a) Percentage of cost of goods sold to net sales $= \dfrac{\$1,190,934.24}{\$1,462,522.27} = 81.4\%$

(b) Percentage of operating expenses to net sales $= \dfrac{\$\ 204,875.05}{\$1,462,522.27} = 14.0\%$

(c) Percentage of operating income to net sales $= \dfrac{\$\ \ 66,712.98}{\$1,462,522.27} = 4.6\%$

(d) Merchandise turnover ratio $= \dfrac{\text{Cost of Goods Sold for Year}}{\text{Average Inventory for Year}}$

$$= \frac{\$1,190,934.24}{(\text{Beginning Inv. } + \text{ Ending Inv.}) \div 2}$$

$$= \frac{\$1,190,934.24}{(\$166,100.46 + \$172,062.15) \div 2}$$

$$= \frac{\$1,190,934.24}{\$169,081.31} = 7.04$$

---

4.   **Fox & Palmer**
Statement of Owners' Equity
For the Year Ended December 31, 19--

	J. Fox	R. Palmer	Total
Capital, January 1, 19--	$ 98,237.16	$ 98,237.16	$196,474.32
Net income	33,765.05	33,765.05	67,530.10
	$132,002.21	$132,002.21	$264,004.42
Less withdrawals	13,500.00	13,500.00	27,000.00
Capital, December 31, 19--	$118,502.21	$118,502.21	$237,004.42

The balance sheet is on page 792.

5.

(a) Ratio of current assets to current liabilities $= \dfrac{\$235,277.92}{\$9,874.32} = 23.8 \text{ to } 1$

(b) Ratio of quick assets to current liabilities $= \dfrac{\$13,751.30 + \$11,250.00 + \$73.37 + \$36,692.38}{\$9,874.32} = 6.3 \text{ to } 1$

(c) Percentage of current assets to total assets $= \dfrac{\$235,277.92}{\$246,878.74} = 95.3\%$

(d) Return on assets $= \dfrac{\text{Net Income}}{\text{Ave. Total Assets}} = \dfrac{\$67,530.10}{(\$195,630.18 + \$246,878.74) \div 2} = \dfrac{\$67,530.10}{\$221,254.46} = 30.5\%$

(e) Return on equity $= \dfrac{\text{Net Income}}{\text{Ave. Owners' Equity}} = \dfrac{\$67,530.10}{(\$196,474.32 + \$237,004.42) \div 2} = \dfrac{\$67,530.10}{\$216,739.37} = 31.2\%$

Fox & Palmer
Balance Sheet
December 31, 19--

Assets

Current assets:

Cash		$ 13,751.30	
Government notes		11,250.00	
Accrued interest on govt. notes....		73.37	
Accounts receivable	$37,603.38		
Less allow. for doubtful accounts ..	911.00	36,692.38	
Merchandise inventory		172,062.15	
Supplies and prepayments		1,448.72	
Total current assets............			$235,277.92

Plant assets:

Store equipment	$ 4,725.00		
Less accum. depr.—store equip....	1,538.78	$ 3,186.22	
Delivery equipment	$7,871.25		
Less accum. depr.—deliv. equip ...	4,066.31	3,804.94	
Office equipment	$ 7,350.00		
Less accum. depr.—office equip....	2,740.34	4,609.66	
Total plant assets			11,600.82
Total assets			$246,878.74

Liabilities

Current liabilities:

Accrued and withheld payroll taxes	$ 933.11	
Accounts payable	8,941.21	
Total current liabilities		$ 9,874.32

Owners' Equity

J. Fox, Capital.....................	$118,502.21	
R. Palmer, Capital	118,502.21	237,004.42
Total liabilities and owners' equity ...		$246,878.74

Applying Accounting Concepts

Series A

Exercise 20A1—Departmental Schedule of Cost of Goods Sold. The account balances at the top of page 793 were taken from the Income Statement columns of the work sheets of Navajo Sales, a firm owned by Peter White and Alfred Thomas, partners. Navajo's fiscal year ends on December 31.

Prepare a schedule of cost of goods sold for each department and in total for the year ended December 31, 19-D.

	19-D			19-C		
	Carpeting	Wall Covering	Total	Carpeting	Wall Covering	Total
Sales	$1,647,036	$1,039,754	$2,686,790	$1,327,628	$821,803	$2,149,431
Sales Returns and Allowances..............	530	454	984	424	363	787
Merchandise Inventory, Jan. 1	3,806	2,618	6,424	3,045	2,094	5,139
Merchandise Inventory, Dec. 31	3,158	2,998	6,156	3,806	2,618	6,424
Purchases	1,035,348	710,018	1,745,366	828,278	568,014	1,396,292
Purchases Returns and Allowances..............	1,438	718	2,156	1,150	574	1,724
Office Salaries Expense			61,600			61,600
Office Suppies Expense			12,060			9,648
Uncollectible Accounts Expense................			358			286
Miscellaneous General Expense................			1,286			1,029
Sales Salaries Expense			2,982			2,680
Advertising Expense			55,400			44,320
Depreciation Expense—Store Equipment			1,734			1,734
Store Rent Expense			24,000			24,000
Miscellaneous Selling Expense................			486			389

Exercise 20A2—Schedule of Operating Expenses. Using the appropriate account balances from Exercise 20A1, prepare a schedule of operating expenses in total for Navajo Sales for the year ended December 31, 19-D.

Exercise 20A3—Comparative Department Income Statement. Refer to Exercises 20A1 and 20A2. Prepare a comparative summarized income statement for 19-C and 19-D. Show the components and amounts of gross margin on sales by department and in total for Navajo Sales.

Exercise 20A4—Percentage and Ratio Analysis of Operating Performance. Refer to Exercise 20A3. Navajo Sales, using net sales as the base, studies the proportionate relationship between net sales and cost of goods sold, gross margin, operating expenses, and net income by percentage analysis.

1. Calculate these percentages in total for each year. Each dollar of net sales resulted in approximately how many cents of net profit?
2. Calculate these percentages by department for each year for net sales, cost of goods sold, and gross margin. Which department had a higher cost of goods sold percentage? Which department contributed a greater percentage of gross margin to the total?
3. Determine the merchandise turnover for each year. Is the merchandise selling more rapidly or more slowly this year?

Exercise 20A5—Comparative Balance Sheet and Statement of Owners' Equity. The following balances were taken from the Balance Sheet columns of the end-of-year work sheets for the years 19-A and 19-B of Safe Harbor Supplies, a partnership owned by Sarah Bell and Nina Rich. The fiscal year ends on December 31.

	19-B	19-A
Cash	$47,048	$45,296
Government Notes	18,000	18,000
Accrued Interest Receivable	300	300
Accounts Receivable	19,734	17,258
Allowance for Doubtful Accounts	470	410
Merchandise Inventory, Store Supplies	3,158	3,074
Merchandise Inventory, Office Supplies	2,998	2,837
Supplies and Prepayments	3,552	3,021
Store Equipment	37,340	37,340
Accumulated Depreciation—Store Equipment	7,094	6,146
Accounts payable	46,528	31,583
Accrued and withheld payroll taxes	2,958	2,771
Sarah Bell, Capital	55,240	60,951
Nina Rich, Capital	30,976	31,687

Net income for the year 19-B was $40,864; profits were split 50-50; Bell withdrew $28,000 and Rich withdrew $24,000. Net income for the year 19-A was $38,578; profits were split 50-50; Bell withdrew $25,000 and Rich withdrew $20,000.

Prepare a comparative classified balance sheet in report form for Safe Harbor Supplies supported by a comparative statement of owners' equity.

Exercise 20A6—Percentage and Ratio Analysis of Liquidity and Profitability. Refer to Exercise 20A5. For each year, make the following calculations related to the liquidity and profitability of Safe Harbor Supplies: (a) current ratio, (b) quick ratio or acid test, (c) percent of current assets to total assets, (d) return on assets (total assets were $115,240 at the beginning of 19-A), and (e) return on equity for each partner and for the partnership.

Exercise 20A7—Adjusting Entries with Detail Column in General Journal. Prepare adjusting entries for Sidwell & Skadden from the following data, using a general journal with a special Detail column for debits to operating expenses subsidiary ledger accounts. The entries should be dated September 30, 19--. Foot, prove, total, and rule the amount columns of the journal. (Omit account numbers.)

Merchandise inventory, Drugs, Oct. 1	$ 32,260
Merchandise inventory, Sundries, Oct. 1	26,180
Merchandise inventory, Drugs, Sept. 30	31,580
Merchandise inventory, Sundries, Sept. 30	29,980
Purchases, Drugs	1,035,350
Purchases, Sundries	710,200
Purchases returns & allowances, Drugs	14,380
Purchases returns & allowances, Sundries	7,180
Interest receivable on U.S. notes	150

Exercise 20A8—Adjusting Entries with Detail Column in General Journal. Refer to Exercise 20A7. Prepare additional adjusting entries for Sidwell & Skadden in a general journal like that used in the preceding exercise. Foot, prove, total, and rule the Detail, Debit, and Credit columns. (Omit account numbers.) Use the following data:

Asset	Cost	Annual Depr. Rate	Depr. Expense
Store equipment	$29,730	10%	?
Delivery equipment	52,600	12½%	?
Office equipment	25,000	10%	?

Asset	Acct. Balance Sept. 30, 19--	Amount on Hand Sept. 30, 19--	Supplies Expense
Store supplies........................	$13,496	$1,500	?
Office supplies........................	11,392	510	?

Property Insured	Acct. Balance Sept. 30, 19--	Unexpired Insurance Premium	Insurance Expense
Delivery equipment	$2,748	$1,832	?
Store equipment	1,872	936	?
Office equipment	2,916	1,944	?

The Allowance for Doubtful Accounts already has a credit balance of $150. The percentage of receivables method (aging) was used to determine that $2,850 of accounts receivable would not be collected.

Exercise 20A9—Closing Entries with Detail Column in General Journal. The following are account balances taken from the accounting records of Edison Electronic Equipment as of June 30, 19--.

Sales—Personal Computers	$1,247,036
Sales—Video Cassette Recorders	1,039,752
Interest Revenue	468
Sales Returns and Allowances, PC's	530
Sales Returns and Allowances, VCR's	454
Cost of Goods Sold, PC's	1,033,776
Cost of Goods Sold, VCR's...................................	708,900
Operating Expenses...	250,520
Mary Kyle, Drawing...	20,800
Bessie Dixon, Drawing	15,800

1. Using a general journal with a special Detail column for charges to the accounts in the operating expenses subsidiary ledger, enter the necessary closing entries. Divide profits and losses equally. (Omit account numbers.)
2. Foot, prove, total, and rule the amount columns of the journal.
3. Prepare a T account for the expense and revenue summary account. Post the closing entries to this account.

Exercise 20A10—Reversing Entries in General Journal. Refer to Exercises 20A7 and 20A8. Prepare reversing entries in general journal form for any accrual type adjustments so that transactions in the new period may be entered in the usual manner. (Omit account numbers.)

Series B

Exercise 20B1—Departmental Schedule of Cost of Goods Sold. The following account balances were taken from the Income Statement columns of the work sheets of Hopi Sales, a firm owned by George Deer and Warren Lightfoot, partners. Hopi's fiscal year ends on December 31.

	19-D			19-C		
	Footwear	Sportswear	Total	Footwear	Sportswear	Total
Sales	$1,235,277	$779,816	$2,015,093	$ 926,458	$662,844	$1,589,302
Sales Returns and Allowances	398	415	813	318	308	626
Merchandise Inventory, Jan. 1	2,854	1,963	4,817	3,276	2,247	5,523
Merchandise Inventory, Dec. 31	2,368	2,249	4,617	2,854	1,963	4,817
Purchases	676,511	432,514	1,109,025	575,034	324,385	899,419
Purchases Returns and Allowances..	1,078	538	1,616	916	403	1,319
Office Salaries Expense			66,200			66,200
Office Supplies Expense			9,045			7,236
Uncollectible Accounts Expense			268			214
Miscellaneous General Expense			964			771
Sales Salaries Expense			2,237			2,237
Advertising Expense			51,550			41,240
Depreciation Expense—Store						
Equipment			1,300			1,300
Store Rent Expense			18,000			18,000
Miscellaneous Selling Expense......			365			292

Prepare a schedule of cost of goods sold for each department and in total for the year ended December 31, 19-D.

Exercise 20B2—Schedule of Operating Expenses. Using the appropriate account balances from Exercise 20B1, prepare a schedule of operating expenses in total for Hopi Sales for the year ended December 31, 19-D.

Exercise 20B3—Comparative Departmental Income Statement. Refer to Exercises 20B1 and 20B2. Prepare a comparative summarized income statement for 19-C and 19-D. Show the components and amounts of gross margin on sales by department and in total for Hopi Sales.

Exercise 20B4—Percentage and Ratio Analysis of Operating Performance. Refer to Exercise 20B3. Hopi Sales, using net sales as the base, studies the proportionate relationship between net sales and cost of goods sold, gross margin, operating expenses, and net income by percentage analysis.

1. Calculate these percentages in total for each year. Each dollar of net sales resulted in approximately how many cents of net profit?
2. Calculate these percentages by department for each year for net sales, cost of goods sold, and gross margin. Which department had a higher cost of goods sold percentage? Which department contributed a greater percentage of gross margin to the total?
3. Determine the merchandise turnover for each year. Is the merchandise selling more rapidly or more slowly this year?

Exercise 20B5—Comparative Balance Sheet and Statement of Owners' Equity.
The following balances were taken from the Balance Sheet columns of the end-of-year work sheets for the years 19-C and 19-D of Cheerful Cove Supplies, a partnership owned by Kenneth Dodds and Steven Starr. The fiscal year ends on December 31.

	19-D	19-C
Cash	$39,286	$33,875
Government Notes	12,000	12,000
Accrued Interest Receivable	225	225
Accounts Receivable	14,800	12,600
Allowance for Doubtful Accounts	352	307
Merchandise Inventory, Art Supplies	2,368	1,943
Merchandise Inventory, Music Supplies	2,249	1,865
Supplies and Prepayments	2,664	2,382
Store Equipment	28,005	28,005
Accumulated Depreciation—Store Equipment	5,320	4,160
Accounts Payable	34,896	20,221
Accrued and Withheld Payroll Taxes	2,218	2,046
Kenneth Dodds, Capital	41,430	39,962
Steven Starr, Capital	24,731	25,419

Net income for the year 19-D was $32,650; profits were split 60-40; Dodds withdrew $22,000 and Starr withdrew $18,000. Net income for the year 19-C was $35,780; profits were split 60-40; Dodds withdrew $20,000 and Starr withdrew $15,000.

Prepare a comparative classified balance sheet in report form for Cheerful Cove Supplies, supported by a comparative statement of owners' equity.

Exercise 20B6—Percentage and Ratio Analysis of Liquidity and Profitability.
Refer to Exercise 20B5. For each year, make the following calculations related to the liquidity and profitability of Cheerful Cove Supplies: (a) current ratio, (b) quick ratio or acid test, (c) percent of current assets to total assets, (d) return on assets (total assets were $84,670 at the beginning of 19-C), and (e) return on equity for each partner and for the partnership.

Exercise 20B7—Adjusting Entries with Detail Column in General Journal.
Prepare adjusting entries for Shearrer & Schloemann from the following data, using a general journal with a special Detail column for debits to operating expenses subsidiary ledger accounts. The entries should be dated March 31, 19--. Foot, prove, total, and rule the amount columns of the journal. (Omit account numbers.)

Merchandise inventory, Lumber, April 1	$ 24,195
Merchandise inventory, Sheet Metal, April 1	19,635
Merchandise inventory, Lumber, March 31	23,685
Merchandise inventory, Sheet Metal, March 31	22,485
Purchases, Lumber	776,512
Purchases, Sheet Metal	532,650
Purchases returns & allowances, Lumber	10,785
Purchases returns & allowances, Sheet Metal	5,385
Interest receivable on U.S. notes	105

Exercise 20B8—Adjusting Entries with Detail Column in General Journal. Refer to Exercise 20B7. Prepare additional adjusting entries for Shearrer & Schloemann in a general journal like that used in the preceding exercise. Foot, prove, total, and rule the Detail, Debit, and Credit columns. (Omit account numbers.) Use the following data:

Asset	Cost	Annual Depr. Rate	Depr. Expense
Store equipment	$22,290	10%	?
Delivery equipment	39,456	12½%	?
Office equipment	18,750	10%	?

Asset	Acct. Balance Mar. 31, 19--	Amount on Hand Mar. 31, 19--	Supplies Expense
Store supplies	$10,122	$1,125	?
Office supplies	8,544	383	?

Propery Insured	Acct. Balance Mar. 31, 19--	Unexpired Insurance Premium	Insurance Expense
Delivery equipment	$2,061	$1,374	?
Store equipment	1,404	702	?
Office equipment	2,187	1,458	?

The Allowance for Doubtful Accounts already has a credit balance of $112. The percentage of receivables method (aging) was used to determine that $2,138 of accounts receivable would not be collected.

Exercise 20B9—Closing Entries with Detail Column in General Journal. The following are account balances taken from the accounting records of Everhardt TV as of Sept. 30, 19--.

Sales—Video	$935,277
Sales—Stereo	779,814
Interest Revenue	351
Sales Returns and Allowances, Video	398
Sales Returns and Allowances, Stereo	340
Cost of Goods Sold, Video	775,332
Cost of Goods Sold, Stereo	531,675
Operating Expenses	187,890
Gerry Everhardt, Drawing	15,600
Russell Everhardt, Drawing	11,850

1. Using a general journal with a special Detail column for charges to the accounts in the operating expenses subsidiary ledger, enter the necessary closing entries. Divide profits and losses equally. (Omit account numbers.)
2. Foot, prove, total, and rule the amount columns of the journal.
3. Prepare a T account for the expense and revenue summary account. Post the closing entries to this account.

Exercise 20B10—Reversing Entries in General Journal. Refer to Exercises 20B7 and 20B8. Prepare reversing entries in general journal form for any accrual type adjustments so that transactions in the new period may be entered in the usual manner. (Omit account numbers.)

Series A

Problem 20A1   Comparative Summary Income Statement and Schedule of Cost of Goods Sold.

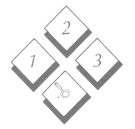

This problem relates to the wholesale-retail merchandise firm of Morris & Vogel for the years ended December 31, 19-B and 19-A. Provided are the Income Statement columns of the year-end summary work sheets. They differ slightly in form from the work sheet illustrated in the textbook. The various amounts entered in Cost of Goods Sold for each department are shown (rather than the net amount). In each case, the debits to Cost of Goods Sold represent, in order, (a) beginning merchandise inventory and (b) purchases. The credits to Cost of Goods Sold represent, in order, (a) purchases returns and allowances and (b) the ending merchandise inventory.

The accounting records used by Morris & Vogel include a subsidiary operating expense ledger, but it is not involved in this problem.

	19-B		19-A	
Sales—Washing Machines		826,418.00		721,134.00
Sales Returns and Allowances—Washing Machines ..	12,486.00		9,989.00	
Sales—Dryers..................................		144,386.00		85,509.00
Sales Returns and Allowances—Dryers	2,052.00		1,642.00	
Cost of Goods Sold—Washing Machines	202,830.00	4,288.00	192,824.00	6,430.00
	717,242.00	228,414.00	593,794.00	202,830.00
Cost of Goods Sold—Dryers	21,974.00	400.00	19,638.00	320.00
	66,590.00	26,232.00	43,272.00	21,974.00
Operating Expenses	122,588.00		128,070.00	
Interest Revenue		514.00		411.00
Interest Expense	722.00		578.00	
Charitable Contributions Expense	994.00		795.00	
	1,147,478.00	1,230,652.00	990,602.00	1,038,608.00
Net Income	83,174.00		48,006.00	
	1,230,652.00	1,230,652.00	1,038,608.00	1,038,608.00

Required:

1. Prepare a comparative summary income statement for 19-B and 19-A.
2. Prepare a schedule of cost of goods sold to support the income statement for 19-B.

Problem 20A2   Percentage and Ratio Analysis of Operating Performance

Based on the partial summary work sheets and the comparative income statement for Morris & Vogel in Problem 20A1, calculate the following for the year 19-A and the year 19-B. (Carry the percentages to one decimal place.)

(a) Percentage of cost of goods sold to net sales for the (1) Washing Machines department, (2) the Dryers department and (3) both departments combined.

(b) Percentage of operating expenses to net sales.

(c) Percentage of operating income to net sales.

(d) Merchandise turnover for (1) the Washing Machines department and (2) the Dryers department.

Problem 20A3   Comparative Balance Sheet and Statement of Owners' Equity

Given on page 801 are the Balance Sheet columns of the summary year-end work sheets of the firm of Morris & Vogel for the years ended December 31, 19-B and 19-A. Prepare a comparative classified balance sheet in the form illustrated in the textbook. Supplies and prepayments may be entered together as one item. Support the balance sheet with a comparative statement of owners' equity. Assume net income is distributed 60% to Morris and 40% to Vogel.

(The accounting records of Morris & Vogel include subsidiary ledgers for accounts receivable and accounts payable, but these are not involved in this problem.)

Problem 20A4   Percentage and Ratio Analysis of Liquidity and Profitability

Based on the partial summary work sheet and the balance sheet for Morris & Vogel in Problem 20A3, calculate the following for the years 19-B and 19-A. (Carry the ratios and percentages to one decimal place.)

(a) Ratio of current assets to current liabilities.

(b) Ratio of quick assets to current liabilities (acid test).

(c) Percentage of current assets to total assets.

(d) Return on assets (Total assets as of the beginning of the year 19-A were $301,282).

(e) Return on equity.

	19-B		19-A	
Cash.........................	7,934.00		11,696.00	
Petty Cash Fund	300.00		300.00	
Government Notes	10,000.00		10,000.00	
Accrued Interest on Gov't. Notes	194.00		194.00	
Accounts Receivable............	32,604.00		36,083.00	
Allowance for Doubtful Accounts		1,406.00		1,125.00
Merchandise Inventory—Washing Machines....................	228,414.00		202,830.00	
Merchandise Inventory—Dryers ...	26,232.00		21,974.00	
Store Supplies	400.00		320.00	
Advertising Supplies	920.00		736.00	
Office Supplies	278.00		222.00	
Postage Stamps	172.00		138.00	
Prepaid Insurance	842.00		674.00	
Store Equipment	10,422.00		10,422.00	
Accumulated Depr.—Store Equip.		1,894.00		1,486.00
Delivery Equipment	15,396.00		15,396.00	
Accumulated Depr.—Delivery Equip.		2,842.00		2,064.00
Office Equipment	8,422.00		8,422.00	
Accumulated Depr.—Office Equip.		3,248.00		2,878.00
FICA Tax Payable		852.00		682.00
FUTA Tax Payable		132.00		106.00
State Unemployment Tax Payable		272.00		218.00
Employees' Income Tax Payable ..		968.00		774.00
Notes Payable		20,334.00		20,000.00
Accrued Interest Payable		88.00		70.00
Accounts Payable		16,582.00		13,266.00
G.A. Morris, Capital		167,110.00		163,306.00
G.A. Morris, Drawing	36,000.00		25,000.00	
J.L. Vogel, Capital..............		109,628.00		105,426.00
J.L. Vogel, Drawing	30,000.00		15,000.00	
	408,530.00	325,356.00	359,407.00	311,401.00
Net Income		83,174.00		48,006.00
	408,530.00	408,530.00	359,407.00	359,407.00

Problem 20A5   Adjusting, Closing, and Reversing Entries with Detail Column in General Journal

Selected information from the work sheets of Rhodes and Morse for the year ended December 31, 19-- is provided below. The net income (balance of the expense and revenue summary account) is distributed equally between the two partners, and each partner's drawing account has a year-end balance of $42,000.

Account Title	Acct. No.	Adjustments Debit	Adjustments Credit	Income Statement Debit	Income Statement Credit
Cash	111				
Petty Cash Fund	112				
Government Notes	121				
Accrued Interest Receivable	122				
Accounts Receivable	131				
Allowance for Doubtful Accounts..........	131.1		(j)1,924.88		
Merchandise Inventory	141	(b)625,242.64	(a)443,395.16		
Store Supplies	151		(f)3,178.34		
Office Supplies	152		(g)3,562.70		
Postage Stamps	153		(h)2,955.92		
Prepaid Insurance......................	155		(i)2,086.36		
Store Equipment	181				
Accumulated Depr.—Store Equip...........	181.1		(c)1,251.20		
Delivery Equipment	185				
Accumulated Depr.—Delivery Equip........	185.1		(d)4,900.00		
Office Equipment	191				
Accumulated Depr.—Office Equip..........	191.1		(e)2,283.70		
FICA Tax Payable.......................	211				
Employees' Income Tax Payable...........	214				
Notes Payable..........................	216				
Accrued Interest Payable	217		(k)228.00		
Vouchers Payable.......................	218				
C. Rhodes, Capital	311				
C. Rhodes, Drawing	312				
S. Morse, Capital	321				
S. Morse, Drawing......................	322				
Sales	411				1,032,642.30
Sales Returns and Allow.	411.1			6,244.32	
Purchases	511		(l)802,447.64		
Purchases Returns and Allow..............	511.1	(m)8,429.62			
Cost of Goods Sold	531	(a)443,395.16	(b)625,242.64		
		(l)802,447.64	(m)8,429.62	612,170.54	
Operating Expenses	540	(c-j)22,143.10		180,373.56	
Interest Expense	581	(k)228.00		1,071.20	
		1,901,886.16	1,901,886.16	799,859.62	1,032,642.30
Net Income				232,782.68	
				1,032,642.30	1,032,642.30

Account	Acct. No.	Adjustments Debits
Office Supplies Expense	5403	(g)3,562.70
Depreciation Expense—Office Equipment	5404	(e)2,283.70
Postage Expense	5416	(h)2,955.92
Uncollectible Accts. Expense	5417	(j)1,924.88
Depreciation Expense—Delivery Equipment	5435	(d)4,900.00
Insurance Expense.......................................	5436	(i)2,086.36
Depreciation Expense—Store Equipment	5437	(c)1,251.20
Store Supplies Expense	5444	(f)3,178.34
		22,143.10

Required:

1. Prepare the entries necessary to adjust the general ledger accounts and the operating expense ledger accounts as of December 31, 19--.
2. Prepare the entries required to close the following types of accounts in the general ledger:

   Revenue accounts

   Expense accounts

   Expense and revenue summary account (No. 331)

   Partners' drawing accounts

   Distribute the balance of the expense and revenue summary account equally between the two partners.
3. Assuming that the individual posting to the general ledger accounts and the operating expense ledger accounts has been completed, insert the necessary check marks in the general journal. Foot, prove, and enter the totals of the amount columns on each page and rule each page of the general journal.
4. Prepare the necessary entries to reverse the accrual adjustments as of January 1, 19--.

Series B

Problem 20B1 — Comparative Summary Income Statement and Schedule of Cost of Goods Sold

This problem relates to the wholesale-retail merchandise firm of Hauser & Perry for the years ended December 31, 19-D and 19-C. Provided on the next page are the Income Statement columns of the year-end summary work sheets. They differ slightly in form from the work sheet illustrated in the textbook. The various amounts entered in Cost of Goods Sold for each department are shown (rather than the net amount). In each case, the debits to Cost of Goods Sold represent, in order, (a) beginning merchandise inventory and (b) purchases. The credits to Cost of Goods Sold represent, in order (a) purchases returns and allowances and (b) the ending merchandise inventory.

The accounting records used by Hauser & Perry include a subsidiary operating expense ledger, but it is not involved in this problem.

Required:

1. Prepare a comparative summary income statement for 19-D and 19-C.
2. Prepare a schedule of cost of goods sold to support the income statement for 19-D.

	19-D		19-C	
Sales—Doors		619,814.00		515,851.00
Sales Returns and				
Allowances—Doors	9,365.00		7,492.00	
Sales—Windows		108,290.00		96,632.00
Sales Returns and				
Allowances—Windows	1,539.00		1,231.00	
Cost of Goods Sold—Doors ..	152,123.00	3,216.00	121,698.00	2,573.00
	547,932.00	171,311.00	438,346.00	152,123.00
Cost of Goods Sold—Windows	16,480.00	300.00	15,739.00	240.00
	59,942.00	19,674.00	47,954.00	16,480.00
Operating Expenses..........	81,941.00		95,553.00	
Interest Revenue		385.00		308.00
Interest Expense	542.00		434.00	
Charitable Contributions				
Expense	745.00		596.00	
	870,609.00	922,990.00	729,043.00	784,207.00
Net Income	52,381.00		55,164.00	
	922,990.00	922,990.00	784,207.00	784,207.00

Problem 20B2 Percentage and Ratio Analysis of Operating Performance

Based on the partial summary work sheets and the comparative income statement for Hauser & Perry in Problem 20B1, calculate the following for the year
19-C and the year 19-D. (Carry the percentages to one decimal place.)

(a) Percentage of cost of goods sold to net sales for the (1) Doors department,
the (2) Windows department and (3) both departments combined.
(b) Percentage of operating expenses to net sales.
(c) Percentage of operating income to net sales.
(d) Merchandise turnover for the (1) Doors department and (2) Windows department.

Problem 20B3 Comparative Balance Sheet and Statement of Owners' Equity

Given below are the Balance Sheet columns of the summary year-end work
sheets of the firm of Hauser & Perry for the years ended December 31, 19-D and
19-C. Prepare a comparative classified balance sheet in the form illustrated in the

textbook. Supplies and prepayments may be entered together as one item. Support the balance sheet with a comparative statement of owners' equity. Assume net income is distributed 60% to Hauser and 40% to Perry.

(The accounting records of Hauser & Perry include subsidiary ledgers for accounts receivable and accounts payable, but these are not involved in this problem.)

	19-D		19-C	
Cash	5,950.00		15,626.00	
Petty Cash Fund	225.00		225.00	
Government Notes	7,500.00		7,500.00	
Accrued Interest on Gov't. Notes	146.00		146.00	
Accounts Receivable	26,453.00		31,162.00	
Allowance for Doubtful Accounts		1,055.00		844.00
Merchandise Inventory—Doors	171,311.00		152,123.00	
Merchandise Inventory—Windows	19,674.00		16,480.00	
Store Supplies	300.00		240.00	
Advertising Supplies	690.00		552.00	
Office Supplies	208.00		166.00	
Postage Stamps	129.00		103.00	
Prepaid Insurance	632.00		506.00	
Store Equipment	7,816.00		7,816.00	
Accumulated Depr.—Store Equip.		1,420.00		1,136.00
Delivery Equipment	11,547.00		11,547.00	
Accumulated Depr.—Delivery Equip.		2,131.00		1,015.00
Office Equipment	6,316.00		6,316.00	
Accumulated Depr.—Office Equip.		2,436.00		1,624.00
FICA Tax Payable		639.00		511.00
FUTA Tax Payable		99.00		79.00
State Unemployment Tax Payable		204.00		163.00
Employees' Income Tax Payable		726.00		581.00
Notes Payable		15,250.00		15,000.00
Accrued Interest Payable		66.00		52.00
Accounts Payable		12,437.00		9,950.00
A.J. Hauser, Capital		131,732.00		128,634.00
A.J. Hauser, Drawing	27,000.00		30,000.00	
S.N. Perry, Capital		87,821.00		85,755.00
S.N. Perry, Drawing	22,500.00		20,000.00	
	308,397.00	256,016.00	300,508.00	245,344.00
Net Income		52,381.00		55,164.00
	308,397.00	308,397.00	300,508.00	300,508.00

Problem 20B4 Percentage and Ratio Analysis of Liquidity and Profitability

Based on the partial summary work sheet and the balance sheet for Hauser & Perry in Problem 20B3, calculate the following for the years 19-D and 19-C. (Carry the ratios and percentages to one decimal place.)

(a) Ratio of current assets to current liabilities.
(b) Ratio of quick assets to current liabilities (acid test).
(c) Percentage of current assets to total assets.
(d) Return on assets (total assets as of the beginning of the year 19C were $225,962).
(e) Return on equity.

Problem 20B5   Adjusting, Closing, and Reversing Entries with Detail Column in General Journal

Selected information from the work sheets of Buer and Lowe for the year ended December 31, 19-- is provided below and on the next page. The net income (balance of the expense and revenue summary account) is distributed equally between the two partners, and each partner's drawing account has a year-end balance of $31,500.

Account	Acct. No.	Adjustments Debits
Office Supplies Expense	5403	(g)2,672.02
Depreciation Expense—Office Equipment	5404	(e)1,712.78
Postage Expense	5416	(h)2,216.94
Uncollectible Accts. Expense	5417	(j)1,443.66
Depreciation Expense—Delivery Equipment	5435	(d)3,675.00
Insurance Expense	5436	(i)1,564.77
Depreciation Expense—Store Equipment	5437	(c)938.40
Store Supplies Expense	5444	(f)2,383.76
		16,607.33

Required:

1. Prepare the entries necessary to adjust the general ledger accounts and the operating expense ledger accounts as of December 31, 19--.
2. Prepare the entries required to close the following types of accounts in the general ledger:

   Revenue accounts
   Expense accounts
   Expense and revenue summary account (No. 331)
   Partners' drawing accounts

   Distribute the balance of the expense and revenue summary account equally between the two partners.
3. Assuming that the individual posting to the general ledger accounts and the operating expense ledger accounts has been completed, insert the necessary check marks in the general journal. Foot, prove, and enter the totals of the amount columns on each page and rule each page of the general journal.
4. Prepare the necessary entries to reverse the accrual adjustments as of January 1, 19--.

Account Title	Acct. No.	Adjustments Debit	Adjustments Credit	Income Statement Debit	Income Statement Credit
Cash	111				
Petty Cash Fund	112				
Government Notes	121				
Accrued Interest Receivable	122				
Accounts Receivable	131				
Allowance for Doubtful Accounts	131.1		(j)1,443.66		
Merchandise Inventory	141	(b)468,931.98	(a)332,546.37		
Store Supplies	151		(f)2,383.76		
Office Supplies	152		(g)2,672.02		
Postage Stamps	153		(h)2,216.94		
Prepaid Insurance	155		(i)1,564.77		
Store Equipment	181				
Accumulated Depr.—Store Equip.	181.1		(c)938.40		
Delivery Equipment	185				
Accumulated Depr.—Delivery Equip.	185.1		(d)3,675.00		
Office Equipment	191				
Accumulated Depr.—Office Equip.	191.1		(e)1,712.78		
FICA Tax Payable	211				
Employees' Income Tax Payable	214				
Notes Payable	216				
Accrued Interest Payable	217		(k)171.00		
Vouchers Payable	218				
O. Buer, Capital	311				
O. Buer, Drawing	312				
C. Lowe, Capital	321				
C. Lowe, Drawing	322				
Sales	411				774,481.73
Sales Returns and Allowances	411.1			4,683.24	
Purchases	511		(l)601,835.73		
Purchases Returns and Allowances	511.1	(m)6,322.21			
Cost of Goods Sold	531	(a)332,546.37 (l)601,835.73	(b)468,931.98 (m)6,322.21	459,127.91	
Operating Expenses	540	(c-j)16,607.33		135,280.17	
Interest Expense	581	(k)171.00		803.40	
		1,426,414.62	1,426,414.62	599,894.72	774,481.73
Net Income				174,587.01	
				774,481.73	774,481.73

Mastery Problem

Dick and Nancy Steeves own and operate Steeves' Surf and Turf Market. For the past several years they have sold fresh fish, sea food, and meat on a wholesale and retail basis throughout the New England area sharing profits on a 40-60 basis. Provided on the following pages are a summary work sheet and a supplementary operating expense work sheet for December 31, 19-F, and a partial work sheet showing the Income Statement and Balance Sheet columns for December 31, 19-E.

Steeves' Surf and Turf Market
Supplementary Operating Expenses Work Sheet
for the Year Ended December 31, 19-F

Account	Acct. No.	Trial Balance Debit	Adjustments Debit	Adjusted Trial Balance Debit
Office Salaries Expense	5401	96,500		96,500
Dick Steeves, Salary Expense	5402	44,000		44,000
Office Supplies Expense	5403	0	(o)22,038	22,038
Depreciation Expense—Office Equipment	5404	0	(m)4,560	4,560
Insurance Expense—Office Equipment	5405	0	(p)12,500	12,500
Office Rent Expense	5406	15,500		15,500
Payroll Taxes Expense	5407	18,800		18,800
Heat, Light, and Water Expense	5408	18,450		18,450
Telephone Expense	5409	1,545		1,545
Postage Expense	5416	525		525
Uncollectible Accounts Expense	5417	0	(q)11,800	11,800
Miscellaneous General Expense	5422	15,500		15,500
Store Clerks Salary Expense	5431	175,397		175,397
Truck Drivers Wage Expense	5432	88,572		88,572
Advertising Expense	5433	78,400		78,400
Nancy Steeves, Salary Expense	5434	49,000		49,000
Depreciation Expense—Delivery Equipment	5435	0	(l)10,800	10,800
Insurance Expense—Delivery Equipment	5436	0	(p)8,400	8,400
Depreciation Expense—Store Equipment	5437	0	(k)30,000	30,000
Insurance Expense—Store Equipment	5438	0	(p)11,500	11,500
Truck, Gas and Oil Expense	5441	32,450		32,450
Truck Repairs and Maintenance Expense	5442	14,300		14,300
Store Rent Expense	5443	32,400		32,400
Store Supplies Expense	5444	0	(n)31,290	31,290
Miscellaneous Selling Expense	5452	9,424		9,424
		690,763	142,888	833,651

Steeves' Surf and Turf Market
Work Sheet
For the Year Ended December 31, 19-F

Account Title	Acct. No.	Trial Balance Debit	Trial Balance Credit	Adjustments Debit	Adjustments Credit	Adjusted Trial Balance Debit	Adjusted Trial Balance Credit	Income Statement Debit	Income Statement Credit	Balance Sheet Debit	Balance Sheet Credit
Cash	111	82,440				82,440				82,440	
Petty Cash Fund	112	240				240				240	
Government Notes	121	30,000				30,000				30,000	
Accrued Interest Rec.	122			(i) 900		900				900	
Accounts Receivable	131	295,800				295,800				295,800	
Allowance for Doubtful Accounts	131.1		400		(q) 11,800		11,400				11,400
Mdse. Inv.—Fish	141	6,480		(a) 5,280	(b) 6,480	5,280				5,280	
Mdse. Inv.—Meat	142	3,900		(e) 2,760	(f) 3,900	2,760				2,760	
Store Supplies	151	33,120			(n) 31,290	1,830				1,830	
Office Supplies	152	24,150			(o) 22,038	2,112				2,112	
Prepaid Insurance	155	43,920			(p) 32,400	11,520				11,520	
Store Equipment	181	300,000				300,000				300,000	
Accum. Depr.—Store Equipment	181.1		114,000		(k) 30,000		144,000				144,000
Delivery Equipment	185	108,000				108,000				108,000	
Accum. Depr.—Delivery Equipment	185.1		61,200		(l) 10,800		72,000				72,000
Office Equipment	191	93,600				93,600				93,600	
Accum. Depr.—Office Equipment	191.1		31,680		(m) 4,560		36,240				36,240
FICA Tax Payable	211		2,208				2,208				2,208
FUTA Tax Payable	212		60				60				60
State Unemp. Tax Pay.	213		252				252				252
Employees Inc. Tax Pay.	214		4,182				4,182				4,182
Notes Payable	216		24,000				24,000				24,000
Accrued Interest Pay.	217				(j) 240		240				240
Vouchers Payable	218		163,616				163,616				163,616
Dick Steeves, Capital	311		204,210				204,210				204,210
Dick Steeves, Drawing	312	38,400				38,400				38,400	
Nancy Steeves, Capital	321		278,577				278,577				278,577
Nancy Steeves, Drawing	322	37,200				37,200				37,200	
Sales—Fish	411		1,629,773				1,629,773		1,629,773		
Sales Returns & Allow.—Fish	411.1	41,520				41,520		41,520			
Sales—Meat	421		778,200				778,200		778,200		
Sales Returns & Allow.—Meat	421.1	34,200				34,200		34,200			
Purchases—Fish	511	982,085			(c) 982,085						
Purchases Returns & Allow.—Fish	511.1		12,120	(d) 12,120							
Purchases-Meat	521	463,840			(g) 463,840						
Purchases Returns & Allow.—Meat	521.1		6,700	(h) 6,700							
Cost of Goods Sold—Fish	531			(b) 6,480 (c) 982,085	(a) 5,280 (d) 12,120	971,165		971,165			
Cost of Goods Sold—Meat	532			(f) 3,900 (g) 463,840	(e) 2,760 (h) 6,700	458,280		458,280			
Operating Expenses	540	690,763		(k-q) 142,888		833,651		833,651			
Interest Revenue	431		1,440		(i) 900		2,340		2,340		
Interest Expense	581	2,160		(j) 240		2,400		2,400			
		3,312,218	3,312,218	1,627,193	1,627,193	3,351,298	3,351,298	2,341,216	2,410,313	1,010,082	940,985
Net Income								69,097			69,097
								2,410,313	2,410,313	1,010,082	1,010,082

Partial Work Sheet
Steeves' Surf and Turf Market
December 31, 19-E

Account Title	Acct. No.	Income Statement Debit	Income Statement Credit	Balance Sheet Debit	Balance Sheet Credit
Cash........................	111			69,840	
Petty Cash Fund	112			240	
Government Notes	121			30,000	
Accrued Interest Receivable	122			840	
Accounts Receivable...........	131			286,436	
Allowance for Doubtful Accts...	131.1				11,040
Merchandise Inventory—Fish ...	141			6,480	
Merchandise Inventory—Meat ..	142			3,900	
Store Supplies	151			2,136	
Office Supplies	152			2,310	
Prepaid Insurance	155			10,147	
Store Equipment	181			300,000	
Accum. Depr.-Store Equipment	181.1				114,000
Delivery Equipment	185			108,000	
Accum. Depr.-Delivery Equip. ...	185.1				61,200
Office Equipment	191			93,600	
Accum. Depr.-Office Equipment	191.1				31,680
FICA Tax Payable	211				2,129
FUTA Tax Payable	212				58
State Unemp. Tax Payable	213				246
Employees Income Tax Payable	214				4,026
Notes Payable	216				24,000
Accrued Interest Payable	217				215
Vouchers Payable	218				182,548
Dick Steeves, Capital	311				210,538
Dick Steeves, Drawing.........	312			36,000	
Nancy Steeves, Capital	321				267,669
Nancy Steeves, Drawing	322			33,600	
Sales—Fish	411		1,497,000		
Sales Returns & Allow.—Fish ...	411.1	38,933			
Sales-Meat...................	421		753,720		
Sales Returns & Allow.—Meat ..	421.1	30,720			
Purchases-Fish	511				
Purchases Ret. & Allow.—Fish ..	511.1				
Purchases—Meat	521				
Purchases Ret. & Allow.—Meat	521.1				
Cost of Goods Sold—Fish	531	943,131			
Cost of Goods Sold—Meat	532	403,585			
Operating Expenses............	540	758,845			
Interest Revenue	431		2,214		
Interest Expense	581	3,540			
		2,178,754	2,252,934	983,529	909,349
Net Income		74,180			74,180
		2,252,934	2,252,934	983,529	983,529

Required:

Based on this information, prepare the following:

1. Comparative summary income statement reporting gross margin by department and in total, operating expenses, operating income, other revenue and expenses, and net income for the firm.
2. Schedule of cost of good sold for 19-F.
3. Schedule of operating expenses for 19-F.
4. Comparative statement of owners' equity reporting capital for each partner and in total. (Round net income to the nearest dollar.)
5. Comparative, classified balance sheet.
6. Compute the following ratios for each year:
   (a) current ratio
   (b) quick ratio
   (c) current assets to total assets
   What is the general trend?
7. Perform interstatement analysis by computing the following for each year:
   (a) return on assets (Total Assets on 1/1/19-E were $685,400.)
   (b) return on equity (Owners' Equity on 1/1/19-E was $475,100.)
   (c) merchandise turnover (Merchandise Inventory on 1/1/19-E was $9,480.)
8. Prepare the required adjusting, closing, and reversing entries.

INDEX